13th Conference of the Association for Machine Translation in the Americas (AMTA 2018)

Volume 1: MT Researchers' Track

Boston, Massachusetts, USA
17 –21 March 2018

Editors:

Colin Cherry
Graham Neubig

ISBN: 978-1-5108-6726-0

The 13th Conference of
The Association for Machine Translation
in the Americas

www.conference.amtaweb.org

PROCEEDINGS

Vol. 1: MT Researchers' Track

Editors: Colin Cherry & Graham Neubig

Introduction

This year's research track proceedings reflect AMTA's long-standing tradition of bringing together machine translation researchers, practitioners and users. We invited ten long papers and four short papers for oral presentation, with the authors coming from around the world, and the papers spanning a diverse range of topics. These include improvements to the now-dominant neural machine translation paradigm, which address its lexical accuracy, its handling of morphology and its use of wider context. Meanwhile, we see papers that re-examine machine translation under specific lenses, studying its ability to maintain sentiment, to resist noisy inputs, and to retain user trust.

We have also introduced a new category to the research track proceedings: the Open Source Showcase, with the intent of bringing together the machine translation open source software community, and to highlight their amazing work to the rest of the AMTA community. This year, we are excited to present six open source system descriptions.

It has been a pleasure working with Olga Beregovaya and the rest of the AMTA 2018 organizing committee. We would like to especially thank steering committee members George Foster and Alon Lavie for their advice and support, as well as all the authors and reviewers, whose hard work made this conference possible. Please enjoy this year's AMTA research track.

Sincerely,

Colin Cherry
Graham Neubig

Research Program Committee

Tim Anderson	Air Force Research Laboratory
Amittai Axelrod	Amazon
Marine Carpuat	University of Maryland
Daniel Cer	Google
Boxing Chen	Alibaba
David Chiang	University of Notre Dame
Nadir Durrani	QCRI
Minwei Feng	IBM Watson Group
George Foster	Google
Yvette Graham	Dublin City University
Yifan He	Bosch Research and Technology Center
Ulf Hermjakob	USC Information Sciences Institute
Matthias Huck	LMU Munich
Marcin Junczys-Dowmunt	Microsoft Research
Philipp Koehn	Johns Hopkins University
Roland Kuhn	National Research Council of Canada
Gregor Leusch	eBay
Lemao Liu	Tencent AI Lab
Qun Liu	Dublin City University
Saab Mansour	Apple
Daniel Marcu	USC Information Sciences Institute
Haitao Mi	Alipay US
Rico Sennrich	University of Edinburgh
Michel Simard	National Research Council of Canada
Raymond Slyh	Air Force Research Laboratory
Jörg Tiedemann	University of Helsinki
Christoph Tillmann	IBM Research
Taro Watanabe	Google
Philip Williams	University of Edinburgh
François Yvon	LIMSI/CNRS
Bing Zhao	SRI International

Contents

1   Document-Level Information as Side Constraints for Improved Neural Patent Translation

Laura Jehl and Stefan Riezler

13   Fluency Over Adequacy: A Pilot Study in Measuring User Trust in Imperfect MT

Marianna J. Martindale and Marine Carpuat

26   Combining Quality Estimation and Automatic Post-editing to Enhance Machine Translation output

Rajen Chatterjee, Matteo Negri, Marco Turchi, Frédéric Blain and Lucia Specia

39   Neural Morphological Tagging of Lemma Sequences for Machine Translation

Costanza Conforti, Matthias Huck and Alexander Fraser

54   Context Models for OOV Word Translation in Low-Resource Languages

Angli Liu and Katrin Kirchhoff

68   How Robust Are Character-Based Word Embeddings in Tagging and MT Against Wrod Scramlbing or Randdm Nouse?

Georg Heigold, Stalin Varanasi, Günter Neumann and Josef van Genabith

81   Balancing Translation Quality and Sentiment Preservation (Non-archival Extended Abstract)

Pintu Lohar, Haithem Afli and Andy Way

89   Register-sensitive Translation: a Case Study of Mandarin and Cantonese (Non-archival Extended Abstract)

Tak-sum Wong and John Lee

97   An Evaluation of Two Vocabulary Reduction Methods for Neural Machine Translation

Duygu Ataman and Marcello Federico

111   A Smorgasbord of Features to Combine Phrase-Based and Neural Machine Translation

Benjamin Marie and Atsushi Fujita

125   Exploring Word Sense Disambiguation Abilities of Neural Machine Translation Systems (Non-archival Extended Abstract)

Rebecca Marvin and Philipp Koehn

132   Improving Low Resource Machine Translation using Morphological Glosses (Non-archival Extended Abstract)

Steven Shearing, Christo Kirov, Huda Khayrallah and David Yarowsky

140   A Dataset and Reranking Method for Multimodal MT of User-Generated Image Captions

Shigehiko Schamoni, Julian Hitschler and Stefan Riezler

154   Simultaneous Translation using Optimized Segmentation

Maryam Siahbani, Hassan S. Shavarani, Ashkan Alinejad and Anoop Sarkar

Open Source Showcase

168   Neural Monkey: The Current State and Beyond

       Jindřich Helcl, Jindřich Libovický, Tom Kocmi, Tomáš Musil, Ondřej Cífka, Dusan Varis and Ondřej Bojar

177   OpenNMT: Neural Machine Translation Toolkit

       Guillaume Klein, Yoon Kim, Yuntian Deng, Vincent Nguyen, Jean Senellart and Alexander Rush

185   XNMT: The eXtensible Neural Machine Translation Toolkit

       Graham Neubig, Matthias Sperber, Xinyi Wang, Matthieu Felix, Austin Matthews, Sarguna Padmanabhan, Ye Qi, Devendra Singh Sachan, Philip Arthur, Pierre Godard, John Hewitt, Rachid Riad and Liming Wang

193   Tensor2Tensor for Neural Machine Translation

       Ashish Vaswani, Samy Bengio, Eugene Brevdo, Francois Chollet, Aidan N. Gomez, Stephan Gouws, Llion Jones, Łukasz Kaiser, Nal Kalchbrenner, Niki Parmar, Ryan Sepassi, Noam Shazeer and Jakob Uszkoreit

200   The Sockeye Neural Machine Translation Toolkit at AMTA 2018

       Felix Hieber, Tobias Domhan, Michael Denkowski, David Vilar, Artem Sokolov, Ann Clifton and Matt Post

208   Why not be Versatile? Applications of the SGNMT Decoder for Machine Translation

       Felix Stahlberg, Danielle Saunders, Gonzalo Iglesias and Bill Byrne

Document Information as Side Constraints for Improved Neural Patent Translation

Laura Jehl   jehl@cl.uni-heidelberg.de
Computational Linguistics, Heidelberg University, Germany

Stefan Riezler   riezler@cl.uni-heidelberg.de
Computational Linguistics & IWR, Heidelberg University, Germany

Abstract

We investigate the usefulness of document information as side constraints for machine translation. We adapt two approaches to encoding this information as features for neural patent translation: As special tokens which are attached to the source sentence, and as tags which are attached to the source words. We found that sentence-attached features produced the same or better results as word-attached features. Both approaches produced significant gains of over 1% BLEU over the baseline on a German-English translation task, while sentence-attached features also produced significant gains of 0.7% BLEU on a Japanese-English task. We also describe a method to encode document information as additional phrase features for phrase-based translation, but did not find any improvements.

1   Introduction

Document information beyond the text is readily available in many data sets, but is rarely used when building translation systems. Such information could comprise the document's origin (time, place, author), its topic, or its connections to other documents. It exists, for example, in patents, textual content on the web, or e-commerce data. We aim to investigate the usefulness of document information as *side constraints* for translation. We use the term *side constraints* as it is used in Sennrich et al. (2016a) to mean information that is not present in a source string, but can influence translation choice in the target string.[1] For example, patents are assigned to a hierarchical classification system indicating their topic(s) in various degrees of granularity. Depending on the topic, different translation choices may be required. The correct choice will not always be apparent from the sentence context. By providing the classification information to the translation model, we enable the model to select the correct translation, given the constraints.

In this paper, we focus on patent translation. Patent translation lends itself particularly well to our endeavor since patent documents are annotated with different types of information, from hierarchical categorization to information about individual inventors. We are interested in seeing whether patent translation can be improved by this information and if so, which kind of information and which model integration is most useful.

Since 2014, neural machine translation (NMT) has become the state of the art in machine translation (Luong and Manning, 2015; Jean et al., 2015). We hypothesize that NMT is well-suited to the integration of document information. Since the model works on sentence representations, it can decide whether or not to pay attention to this information for each particular

---

[1] Sennrich et al. (2016a) explore politeness as a side constraint for translation.

translation in context. What is more, annotations could be highly correlated. For example, a patent document's subclass label contains its class label. Deep models are capable of learning these correlations.

Based on work by Kobus et al. (2016), this paper explores two ways of integrating patent document annotations as features into a neural machine translation system: (1) by attaching the annotations as special tokens to the source sentence, and (2) by attaching annotations as tags to each source word. Unlike our predecessors, we consider a setting where we have multiple annotation categories, and where each category can have more than one value at the same time. To our knowledge, our work is also the first to apply these methods to patent translation. We show that these features can positively influence translation choice of ambiguous words or phrases in a neural patent translation system. We also describe a method of integrating patent annotations into phrase-based machine translation (PBMT) as additional phrase features, but found that these features were unable to improve the model.

Related work is reviewed in Section 2. Section 3 describes the details of our approach. Using the experimental setup described in Section 4, we found that the simple approach of attaching annotations as additional tokens to the source sentence produced significant improvements – 0.7% BLEU for Japanese-English translation and 1% BLEU for German-English translation – in the right configuration. For German-English, similar improvements were gained by attaching the same information as tags to the source words. Detailed results are discussed in Section 5.

2 Related Work

2.1 Side Constraints

Our work is inspired by the work of Kobus et al. (2016) on multi-domain adaptation. This work uses the domain label as a side constraint for translation in a multi-domain setup: A combined NMT model is trained on subcorpora from different domains, and each training sentence is marked with its subcorpus information. Test data come from one of the known domains and are marked in the same way. We take the idea of using sentence-attached and word-attached source side features to represent side constraints from this paper and modify it to fit our scenario of multi-category, multi-valued patent annotations. Kobus et al. (2016) observed no improvements for sentence-attached features, but saw an improvement of 0.8% BLEU when testing on all but the largest subdomain.

Incorporating side constraints via *sentence-attached* features has also been applied in other work. Originally, this method was proposed by Sennrich et al. (2016a) to model politeness as a side constraint. Johnson et al. (2016) have used it to indicate the desired target language for multilingual NMT. Chu et al. (2017) apply it to neural domain adaptation in combination with fine tuning methods (Luong and Manning, 2015). Passing additional information to a neural network via *word-attached* features was first introduced by Collobert et al. (2011) as a way to add linguistic annotation for various NLP tasks using feed-forward and convolutional networks. Sennrich and Haddow (2016) transferred this idea to neural translation models. The word-attached features used by Kobus et al. (2016) were first presented by Crego et al. (2016), where they were used to encode case information.

The idea of leveraging document information as a side constraint for translation was recently investigated by Chen et al. (2016). They focus on integrating product category information for translation of product descriptions in e-commerce, and also apply their method to online lecture translation (Cettolo et al., 2012), where the lectures are annotated with topic keywords. They also experimented with attaching document information as an artificial token to the source sentence, but found no gains for this method. They then propose to integrate topic information on the target side by including it as an additional read-out layer in the decoder before the softmax layer. This method improved e-commerce data translation by 1.4% BLEU, lecture translation by 0.3% BLEU. For e-commerce translation, only product titles are used, for which it is likely that there is less context information available than would be for product descriptions.

We do not know of any prior work on using document information as side constraints for phrase-based machine translation. Niehues and Waibel (2010) and Bisazza et al. (2011) both modify the phrase table to include corpus (or in-domain/out-of-domain) identifiers, which they find beneficial for domain adaptation. However, they do not use more fine-grained information. For phrase-based patent translation, Wäschle and Riezler (2012b) use patent section labels to partition training data for multi-task learning, but do not look into the more fine-grained classification information.

2.2 Relation to Domain Adaptation

This work is related to the problem of domain adaptation in machine translation, which has been researched extensively for phrase-based translation, among others by Foster and Kuhn (2007); Axelrod et al. (2011); Matsoukas et al. (2009); Chen et al. (2013); Eidelman et al. (2012); Hewavitharana et al. (2013); Hasler et al. (2014), and is currently also being explored for neural machine translation (see Freitag and Al-Onaizan (2016); Zhang et al. (2016); Chen and Huang (2016); Chu et al. (2017); Wang et al. (2017); Chen et al. (2017) inter alia). There are two main scenarios for domain adaptation in the literature: In the first scenario, a translation model is adapted to a known, fixed target domain. A sample from the target domain is usually available. The aim of adaptation in this scenario is to make use of the in-domain sample to shift the model parameters to better match the target distribution. In a second scenario, called dynamic adaptation, the target domain is unknown and possibly shifting. No in-domain sample is available. Data from the target domain are only provided at test time, and their domain may change with each document. In this scenario, unsupervised methods have been used to infer a soft domain or topic attribution of the test context (document or sentence).

Our scenario is similar to dynamic adaptation, as we do not restrict our test data to one subdomain, but allow test data from any patent section or class. This setup precludes us from using the methods proposed for the first scenario, because they would require us to re-train the model for each document. However, unlike dynamic adaptation, in our case document information is provided as side constraints. As we are specifically interested in ways to utilize this information, we do not consider the unsupervised approaches to dynamic adaptation in this work. In future work, it could be informative to compare using human-assigned document information to inferred topic distributions, or to combine both sources of information.

3 Side Constraints for Patent Translation

We extract five types of side constraints from patent document annotations. The first three constraints reflect a patent's classification according to the hierarchical international patent classification system (IPC).[2] Patents are classified by their subject matter as belonging to one or more of 8 different sections (A-H). The sections are divided into 130 classes and 639 subclasses. The hierarchy branches out further, but we only use the top three hierarchy levels, which we call *IPC1* to *IPC3*. We also treat the name of the filing company (*COMP*) and the names of the inventors (*INV*) as side constraints. In this section, we describe how we integrate these side constraints into PBMT and NMT as phrase-, sentence-, and word-attached features. Since each patent can be assigned to more than one section, class and subclass, and be filed by more than one company or inventor, we are dealing with multiple feature categories which can have multiple values for each document.

---

[2]see www.wipo.int/classifications/ipc/en/

3.1 Phrase-based Machine Translation

In PBMT, side constraints can influence phrase selection. Given an annotated input document, it is our intuition that the model should prefer translations that have been extracted from documents with the same annotations. For example, the German-English phrase table contained both *impact plates* and *deflector plates* as translation candidates for the word *Prallplatten* (see Table 5, EXAMPLE 2, for the context). The German input document had been assigned to IPC section A. Of the two translation candidates, only *impact plates* had been seen in a document from IPC section A. This points to *impact plates* being the more suitable translation. We capture the degree of overlapping annotations between training and test document via additional phrase table features. At training time, the annotations of all documents containing a phrase pair are extracted. At test time, the intersection between the phrase pair annotations and the test document annotations is computed for each phrase. The actual features are computed by counting the overlapping annotations for each feature category (IPC section, class, and subclass; filing company and inventor). In total, five count-based features for the five patent specific feature categories were added to the standard PBMT model features.

3.2 Neural Machine Translation

Sentence-attached features Despite poor performance in previous work on domain adaptation, our first approach takes up the idea of integrating side constraints by attaching them as special tokens to the source sentence. On the one hand, this approach is simple and efficient, as it does not increase the number of model parameters. On the other hand, it allows the model to learn to pay attention to the beginning or end of sentence as needed. Since we are dealing with multiple values per category, we append each value to the sentence in alphabetical order. For example, if a patent document has been assigned to IPC sections B and C, the marked up input will look as follows:

<IPC1:B> <IPC1:C> *in die Matrix sind Verstärkungsfasern (5 , 6 , 7) eingebettet .*

Previous work has differed on where to attach the tag(s), leading us to run experiments for attaching at the front, back, or both front and back of a sentence.

Word-attached features Our second approach attaches side constraints as features to each input word, e.g.:

in|IPC1:B *die*|IPC1:B *Matrix*|IPC1:B ...

Note that in our case, the same annotations will be attached to every word in one source document. In the sequence-to-sequence model without word-attached side constraints, the hidden encoder state $h^{(t)}$ at time t is computed recursively as:

$$h^{(t)} = tanh(W(E_0 x_0^{(t)}) + U h^{(t-1)})$$

where E_0 is the word embedding matrix, and $x_0^{(t)}$ is the t-th source word, represented as a one-hot vector. The model with word-attached features computes $h^{(t)}$ from a concatenation of the source word embedding and a vector representation r_f of each word-attached feature f as follows:

$$h^{(t)} = tanh(W([E_0 x_0^{(t)}, r_1, \ldots, r_F]) + U h^{(t-1)})$$

where $[\ ]$ signifies vector concatenation and $r_1, \ldots, r_F$ are representations of each word-attached feature f.

There are different ways of computing r_f: In Kobus et al. (2016), the representation r_f of feature f for input $x_f^{(t)}$ at time t is constructed as follows:

$$r_f^{(t)}[i] = \begin{cases} \frac{1}{|f|} & \text{if } x_f^{(t)} \text{ has the } i\text{-th value of } f \\ 0 & \text{otherwise} \end{cases}$$

where $|f|$ is the number of possible values of f and $r_f \in \mathbb{R}^{|f|}$. Hence, they use a normalized sparse vector representation. This is unproblematic if f only takes few values, but would become unwieldy for large $|f|$.

As we want to be able to handle features with many possible values, we would like to use a dense representation r_f. Following Sennrich and Haddow (2016)'s approach for adding linguistic features to the NMT input, we want to construct feature representations using separate embedding matrices for each feature. The matrices are learned during training and feature representations are computed via a lookup layer. The hidden state $h^{(t)}$ of the encoder RNN at time t is then computed as:

$$h^{(t)} = tanh(W([E_0 x_0^{(t)}, E_1 x_1^{(t)}, \dots, E_F x_F^{(t)}]) + U h^{(t-1)})$$

where $[\ ]$ signifies vector concatenation, $E_0 x_0^{(t)}$ computes the source word embedding, and $E_1 \dots E_F$ are separate embedding matrices for each feature type, with $x_1 \dots x_F$ encoding each feature's value as a one-hot vector.

This approach assumes that each feature only takes one value and representations can be computed efficiently by embedding lookup. Since patent documents can have more than one value for the same annotation category, our setup does not meet this assumption. We solve the problem by looking up the embeddings for all values of the same feature f in the same embedding matrix E_f, and then summing over embeddings belonging to the same feature. The representation r_f for feature f is then computed as:

$$r_f = \sum_{i=1}^{K_f} E_f x_{f,i}^{(t)}$$

where $x_{f,i}^{(t)}$ is a one-hot vector encoding the i-th value of feature f at source position t, and K_f is a hyperparameter to be set by the user, which determines the maximum number of values each feature can take. We pick this value by looking at the distribution of the number of values for each feature in the training documents, and select a cutoff value if less than 5% of training documents have more values for the same feature. For documents with more than K_f annotations, a subset of the annotations is sampled. For documents with fewer than K_f annotations for feature f, empty values are marked by an extra token.

We select this approach for comparison with the sentence-attached features, because it also operates on the source-side and does not necessarily require increasing the model parameters. See our system description in Section 4 for details. The advantage of word-attached features is that this method makes combining multiple side constraints easier, as we cannot attach very long sequences of special tokens to the beginning and end of the sentence. The concatenated embeddings will also allow the model to learn correlations between annotations.

4 Experiment Setup

4.1 Data

We ran experiments on Japanese-English and German-English patent translation. We trained Japanese-English models on the NTCIR-7 Patent Translation training set (Utiyama and Isahara,

DATA SET	ORIGIN	# SENTENCE PAIRS	# DOCUMENTS
train	NTCIR-7 train	1,798,571	51,040
dev	NTCIR-8 pat-dev-2006-2007	2,000	115
devtest	NTCIR-8 Test Intrinsic	1,251	114
test	NTCIR-9 Test Intrinsic	2,001	417

Table 1: Data sets used in Japanese-English translation

DATA SET	ORIGIN	# SENTENCE PAIRS	# DOCUMENTS
train	PatTR abstracts before 2008	694,609	280,009
dev	PatTR abstracts since 2008	2,000	899
devtest	PatTR abstracts since 2008	2,001	864
test (filtered)	PatTR abstracts since 2008	1,716	724

Table 2: Data sets used in German-English translation

2007). We used the NTCIR-8 development and test sets for development, and the NTCIR-9 intrinsic evaluation set for testing. For German-English, we used the abstracts section of the PatTR corpus (Wäschle and Riezler, 2012a). Patents published before 2008 were used for training. Development, devtest and test data of about 2,000 sentences each were randomly selected from the remaining patents. Sentences from the same document were always assigned to the same set. We applied a length-ratio based filter to the test set prior to evaluation to filter out noise from automatic sentence alignment. Tables 1 and 2 contain information about the data sets. Japanese data was segmented using MeCab[3]. All English data was tokenized and true-cased using the Moses toolkit[4]. German data was tokenized, lowercased, and compounds were split, also using Moses tools.

4.2 Translation Systems

We used the `Nematus` NMT system[5] (Sennrich et al., 2017) to train an attentional encoder-decoder network (Bahdanau et al., 2015). The model parameters were optimized with ADADELTA (Zeiler, 2012), using a maximum sentence length of 80 and a minibatch size of 80. We trained a subword model using BPE (Sennrich et al., 2016b) with 29,500 merge operations. We used 500-dimensional word embeddings and set hidden layer size to 1024. For the sentence-attached features, we experiment with IPC section (*IPC1*) and class (*IPC2*) labels, appending them at the front, back, or front and back of the source sentence. For the word-attached features we used IPC section and class labels (*IPC1/IPC2*) together. The maximum number of values per feature for *IPC1* and *IPC2* were set to 2 and 3, the embedding sizes were set to 5 and 20. In order to avoid improvements from merely increasing the number of parameters, we used 475-dimensional source word embeddings when adding word-attached features. The concatenated embedding vectors then have the same length (500) as the original word embedding vectors. We trained all NMT models using early stopping based on training cost on heldout data with a patience of 10. Results are reported on the final model.

For the PBMT experiments, we trained and tested a hierarchical PBMT model using `cdec` (Dyer et al., 2010). The baseline used 21 built-in dense features. A 5-gram target-side language

---

[3] `taku910.github.io/mecab/`

[4] `github.com/moses-smt/mosesdecoder`

[5] `github.com/EdinburghNLP/nematus`

	BLEU↑	TER↓
PBMT Baseline	27.2	57.8
5 phrase features	27.2	58.3
NMT Baseline	36.9	49.3
sentence, IPC1, front	37.4	49.1
sentence, IPC1, back	37.5*	48.5*
sentence, IPC1, front/back	37.6*	48.3*
sentence, IPC2, front	37.2	49
sentence, COMP, front	37	48.9
word, IPC1/IPC2	37.2	49.2

Table 3: Japanese-English translation results.

	BLEU↑	TER↓
PBMT Baseline	41.7	45
5 phrase features	41.7	45.2
NMT Baseline	42.5	47.2
sentence, IPC1, front	43.5*	45.6*
sentence, IPC1, back	43.2*	46.3*
sentence, IPC1, front/back	42.7	46.9
sentence, IPC2, front/back	43.9*	45.3*
word, IPC1/IPC2	43.5*	46.3*

Table 4: German-English translation results.

model was built with `lmplz` (Heafield et al., 2013). Feature weights were trained with `dtrain` (Simianer et al., 2012) for 15 epochs. Results are reported on the final epoch. All five annotations categories (IPC section, class, and subclass, company, inventor) are used to compute 5 phrase level features.

We report BLEU (Papineni et al., 2002) and TER (Snover et al., 2006) on tokenized output, as computed by `multeval` (Clark et al., 2011).

5 Results

Table 3 shows results for Japanese-English patent translation, German-English results are shown in Table 4. For both language pairs, adding side constraints to PBMT did not improve the baseline. Results which improve significantly over the NMT baseline at $p \leq 0.05$ are marked with an asterisk*.

For Japanese-English, switching to NMT improved scores strikingly (+9.7% BLEU, -8.4% TER), probably due to NMT's superiority at handling word order differences in long patent sentences. Attaching IPC section labels (*IPC1*) as special tokens at the *front and back* of the sentence produced a small, significant, improvement over the NMT baseline (+0.7% BLEU, -1% TER), as did attaching them at the *back* of the sentence. Attaching IPC section labels (*IPC1*), class labels (*IPC2*) or company names (*COMP*) at the *front* of the source sentence did not significantly improve the baseline, nor did the word-attached features.

For German-English, the performance gap between PBMT and NMT was much narrower at 0.9% BLEU, probably due to more similar word order. We even see a reversed ranking for

TER (+2.2%). Unlike Japanese-English, attaching IPC section labels (*IPC1*) as special tokens at the *front* of the sentence improved significantly over the NMT baseline (+1% BLEU, -1.6% TER), while attaching them at the *front and back* did not produce a significant improvement. Interestingly, attaching IPC class labels (*IPC2*) at the *front and back* also produced a significant improvement (+1.4% BLEU, -1.9% TER). Word-attached features also produced a significant improvement (+1% BLEU, -0.9% TER), but did not outperform sentence-level features. These results differ from previous work, where sentence-attached domain or topic labels produced no gains. We also tried to combine word-attached and sentence-attached features, but did not see additional gains.

Due to time constraints we were only able to evaluate all sentence-attachment variations for both language pairs for the *IPC1* feature. For Japanese-English, attaching features at the *back* and *front/back* was more successful than attaching them at the *front* of the sentence. For German-English, attachment at the *front* produced better BLEU and TER scores then attachment at the *back*, and *front/back* was worst. This observation invites speculation that there could be a connection between the more beneficial attachment location and the word order of the source language leading the model to pay more attention to the front or back of the sentence, but further experiments would be necessary to confirm or dismiss this speculation. For now, we can conclude from our experiments that there is no general recommendation on which attachment location is best.

Table 5 shows example sentences from the German-English test set and their translations by different models. In EXAMPLE 1, the NMT model with side constraints correctly translated the German word "Kupplung" as *clutch*, which was incorrectly translated as *coupling* by the PBMT and NMT baseline. The correct phrase translation for "elektrischen Maschine", *electric machine*, was also only selected by the model with side constraints. In EXAMPLE 2, the correct translation *impact plates* for German "Prallplatten" was produced by all NMT models. However, the word "Wasserschleiers" was only translated correctly as *water curtain* by the model with side constraints. It was passed through the decoder in PBMT and omitted entirely by the NMT baseline. The NMT model with side constraints also selected the correct translation *steam cabin* for German "Dampfkabine", where PBMT produced *cubicle* and the NMT baseline produced *steam booth*.

6 Conclusion

In this paper, we have investigated methods for using document information as side constraints for phrase-based and neural translation models for patent translation. Document information was incorporated into the model as phrase-, word-, or sentence-attached features. Contrary to previous work, we have looked at incorporating multiple annotation categories with multiple values. For phrase-based machine translation, our features based on annotation overlap between test documents and phrase context were not helpful. For neural machine translation, attaching patent annotations as special tokens to the source sentence – a method which was unsuccessful in previous work – improved German-English translation by over 1% BLEU, and Japanese-English translation by 0.7% BLEU. Word-attached features also produced improvements of 1% BLEU for German-English patent translation, but did not improve Japanese-English translation significantly. Overall, the results indicate that document information can improve patent translation and that neural machine translation is well-suited to integrating this kind of information. However, choosing the right configuration requires some experimentation.

Acknowledgements

This work was supported by DFG Research Grant RI 2221/1-2 "Weakly Supervised Learning of Cross-Lingual Systems". We thank the anonymous reviewers for their insightful comments.

EXAMPLE 1

Source
(...) mit einer **Kupplung** (8) , die den Verbrennungsmotor (2) auswählbar vollständig mit der **elektrischen Maschine** (10) selektiv verbindet (...)

PBMT baseline
(...) with a <u>coupling</u> (8) , the internal combustion engine (2) can be completely selectively connects with the <u>electrical machine</u> (10) (...)

NMT baseline
(...) comprising a <u>coupling</u> (8) which can be selectively connected to the <u>electric motor</u> (10) (...)

+IPC1 front
(...) comprising a **clutch** (8) which selectively connects the internal combustion engine (2) to the **electric machine** (10) (...)

Reference
(...) having a **clutch** (8) which selectively connects the internal combustion engine (2) completely to the **electric machine** (10) (...)

EXAMPLE 2

Source
Sie weist (...) **Prallplatten** (531) auf zur Erzeugung eines flächigen **Wasserschleiers** (25) zumindest im oberen Bereich der **Dampfkabine** (...)

PBMT baseline
it has (...) <u>deflector plates</u> (531) for generating a flat <u>wasserschleiers</u> (25) at least in the upper region of the <u>cubicle</u> (...)

NMT baseline
(...) **impact plates** (531) , at least in the upper region of the <u>steam booth</u> (...)

+IPC1 front
(...) it has (...) **impact plates** (531) for producing a flat **water curtain** (25) at least in the upper region of the **steam cabin** (...)

Reference
(...) said steam cabin comprises (...) **impact plates** (531) for producing a flat **water curtain** (25) at least in the upper area of the **steam cabin** . (...)

Table 5: Examples for German-English translation: We compare output from PBMT and NMT baselines to the NMT model with sentence-attached IPC section features (+IPC1 front). **Boldfaced** portions highlight correct translations. Incorrect translations are <u>underlined</u>.

References

Axelrod, A., He, X., and Gao, J. (2011). Domain adaptation via pseudo in-domain data selection. In *Proceedings of the Conference on Empirical Methods in Natural Language Processing (EMNLP)*, pages 355–362, Edinburgh, United Kingdom.

Bahdanau, D., Cho, K., and Bengio, Y. (2015). Neural Machine Translation by Jointly Learning to Align and Translate. In *Proceedings of the International Conference on Learning Representations* , San Diego, CA, USA.

Bisazza, A., Ruiz, N., and Federico, M. (2011). Fill-up versus interpolation methods for phrase-based smt adaptation. In *Proceedings of the International Workshop on Spoken Language Translation*, San Francisco, CA, USA.

Cettolo, M., Girardi, C., and Federico, M. (2012). WIT^3: Web Inventory of Transcribed and Translated Talks. In *Proceedings of the 16th Conference of the European Association for Machine Translation*, pages 261–268, Trento, Italy.

Chen, B., Cherry, C., Foster, G., and Larkin, S. (2017). Cost weighting for neural machine translation domain adaptation. In *Proceedings of the First Workshop on Neural Machine Translation*, pages 40–46, Vancouver, Canada.

Chen, B. and Huang, F. (2016). Semi-supervised convolutional networks for translation adaptation with tiny amount of in-domain data. In *Proceedings of The 20th SIGNLL Conference on Computational Natural Language Learning*, pages 314–323, Berlin, Germany.

Chen, B., Kuhn, R., and Foster, G. F. (2013). Vector Space Model for Adaptation in Statistical Machine Translation. In *Proceedings of the 51st Annual Meeting of the Association for Computational Linguistics*, pages 1285–1293, Sofia, Bulgaria.

Chen, W., Matusov, E., Khadivi, S., and Peter, J. (2016). Guided Alignment Training for Topic-Aware Neural Machine Translation. *arXiv preprint arXiv:1607.01628*.

Chu, C., Dabre, R., and Kurohashi, S. (2017). An empirical comparison of simple domain adaptation methods for neural machine translation. *arXiv preprint arXiv:1701.03214*.

Clark, J. H., Dyer, C., Lavie, A., and Smith, N. A. (2011). Better hypothesis testing for statistical machine translation: controlling for optimizer instability. In *Proceedings of the 49th Annual Meeting of the Association for Computational Linguistics*, pages 176–181, Portland, Oregon.

Collobert, R., Weston, J., Bottou, L., Karlen, M., Kavukcuoglu, K., and Kuksa, P. (2011). Natural language processing (almost) from scratch. *Journal of Machine Learning Research*, 12(Aug):2493–2537.

Crego, J., Kim, J., Klein, G., Rebollo, A., Yang, K., Senellart, J., Akhanov, E., Brunelle, P., Coquard, A., Deng, Y., et al. (2016). SYSTRAN's Pure Neural Machine Translation Systems. *arXiv preprint arXiv:1610.05540*.

Dyer, C., Lopez, A., Ganitkevitch, J., Weese, J., Ture, F., Blunsom, P., Setiawan, H., Eidelman, V., and Resnik, P. (2010). cdec: A Decoder, Alignment, and Learning Framework for Finite-State and Context-Free Translation Models. In *Proceedings of the ACL 2010 System Demonstrations*, pages 7–12, Uppsala, Sweden.

Eidelman, V., Boyd-Graber, J., and Resnik, P. (2012). Topic models for dynamic translation model adaptation. In *Proceedings of the 50th Annual Meeting of the Association for Computational Linguistics*, pages 115–119, Jeju Island, Korea.

Foster, G. and Kuhn, R. (2007). Mixture-model adaptation for smt. In *Proceedings of the Second Workshop on Statistical Machine Translation (WMT)*, Prague, Czech Republic.

Freitag, M. and Al-Onaizan, Y. (2016). Fast domain adaptation for neural machine translation. *arXiv preprint arXiv:1612.06897*.

Hasler, E., Haddow, B., and Koehn, P. (2014). Dynamic Topic Adaptation for SMT using Distributional Profiles. In *Proceedings of the Ninth Workshop on Statistical Machine Translation*, pages 445–456, Baltimore, Maryland, USA.

Heafield, K., Pouzyrevsky, I., Clark, J. H., and Koehn, P. (2013). Scalable Modified Kneser-Ney Language Model Estimation. In *Proceedings of the 51st Annual Meeting of the Association for Computational Linguistics*, pages 690–696, Sofia, Bulgaria.

Hewavitharana, S., Mehay, D., Ananthakrishnan, S., and Natarajan, P. (2013). Incremental topic-based translation model adaptation for conversational spoken language translation. In *Proceedings of the 51st Annual Meeting of the Association for Computational Linguistics*, pages 697–701, Sofia, Bulgaria.

Jean, S., Firat, O., Cho, K., Memisevic, R., and Bengio, Y. (2015). Montreal Neural Machine Translation Systems for WMT'15. In *Proceedings of the Tenth Workshop on Statistical Machine Translation*, pages 134–140, Lisbon, Portugal.

Johnson, M., Schuster, M., Le, Q. V., Krikun, M., Wu, Y., Chen, Z., Thorat, N., Viégas, F., Wattenberg, M., Corrado, G., et al. (2016). Google's multilingual neural machine translation system: enabling zero-shot translation. *arXiv preprint arXiv:1611.04558*.

Kobus, C., Crego, J., and Senellart, J. (2016). Domain Control for Neural Machine Translation. *arXiv preprint arXiv:1612.06140*.

Luong, M.-T. and Manning, C. D. (2015). Stanford neural machine translation systems for spoken language domains. In *Proceedings of the International Workshop on Spoken Language Translation*, Da Nang, Vietnam.

Matsoukas, S., Rosti, A.-V. I., and Zhang, B. (2009). Discriminative corpus weight estimation for machine translation. In *Proceedings of the 2009 Conference on Empirical Methods in Natural Language Processing*, pages 708–717, Singapore.

Niehues, J. and Waibel, A. (2010). Domain adaptation in statistical machine translation using factored translation models. In *Proceedings of the Annual Conference of the European Association or Machine Translation*, Saint-Rapha"el, France.

Papineni, K., Roukos, S., Ward, T., and Zhu, W.-J. (2002). Bleu: a method for automatic evaluation of machine translation. In *Proceedings of the 40th Annual Meeting of the Association for Computational Linguistics*, pages 311–318, Philadelphia, PA, United States.

Sennrich, R., Firat, O., Cho, K., Birch, A., Haddow, B., Hitschler, J., Junczys-Dowmunt, M., Läubli, S., Miceli Barone, A. V., Mokry, J., and Nadejde, M. (2017). Nematus: a Toolkit for Neural Machine Translation. In *Proceedings of the Software Demonstrations of the 15th Conference of the European Chapter of the Association for Computational Linguistics*, pages 65–68, Valencia, Spain.

Sennrich, R. and Haddow, B. (2016). Linguistic Input Features Improve Neural Machine Translation. In *Proceedings of the First Conference on Machine Translation*, pages 83–91, Berlin, Germany.

Sennrich, R., Haddow, B., and Birch, A. (2016a). Controlling Politeness in Neural Machine Translation via Side Constraints. In *Proceedings of the 2016 Conference of the North American Chapter of the Association for Computational Linguistics: Human Language Technologies*, pages 35–40, San Diego, CA, USA.

Sennrich, R., Haddow, B., and Birch, A. (2016b). Neural Machine Translation of Rare Words with Subword Units. In *Proceedings of the 54th Annual Meeting of the Association for Computational Linguistics*, pages 1715–1725, Berlin, Germany.

Simianer, P., Riezler, S., and Dyer, C. (2012). Joint Feature Selection in Distributed Stochastic Learning for Large-scale Discriminative Training in SMT. In *Proceedings of the 50th Annual Meeting of the Association for Computational Linguistics*, Jeju Island, Korea.

Snover, M., Dorr, B., Schwartz, R., Micciulla, L., and Makhoul, J. (2006). A study of translation edit rate with targeted human annotation. In *Proceedings of the Association for Machine Translation in the Americas*, pages 223–231, Cambridge, MA, United States.

Utiyama, M. and Isahara, H. (2007). A Japanese-English patent parallel corpus. *Proceedings of the MT summit XI*, pages 475–482.

Wang, R., Utiyama, M., Liu, L., Chen, K., and Sumita, E. (2017). Instance weighting for neural machine translation domain adaptation. In *Proceedings of the 2017 Conference on Empirical Methods in Natural Language Processing*, pages 1482–1488, Copenhagen, Denmark.

Wäschle, K. and Riezler, S. (2012a). Analyzing Parallelism and Domain Similarities in the MAREC Patent Corpus. *Multidisciplinary Information Retrieval*, pages 12–27.

Wäschle, K. and Riezler, S. (2012b). Structural and topical dimensions in multi-task patent translation. In *Proceedings of the 13th Conference of the European Chapter of the Association for Computational Linguistics*, pages 818–828, Avignon, France.

Zeiler, M. D. (2012). ADADELTA: an adaptive learning rate method. *arXiv preprint arXiv:1212.5701*.

Zhang, J., Li, L., Way, A., and Liu, Q. (2016). Topic-informed neural machine translation. In *Proceedings of the 26th International Conference on Computational Linguistics*, pages 1807–1817, Osaka, Japan.

Fluency Over Adequacy: A Pilot Study in Measuring User Trust in Imperfect MT

Marianna J. Martindale   mmartind@umd.edu
iSchool, University of Maryland, College Park, 20740, USA

Marine Carpuat   marine@cs.umd.edu
Dept. of Computer Science, University of Maryland, College Park, 20740, USA

Abstract

Although measuring intrinsic quality has been a key factor in the advancement of Machine Translation (MT), successfully deploying MT requires considering not just intrinsic quality but also the user experience, including aspects such as trust. This work introduces a method of studying how users modulate their trust in an MT system after seeing errorful (disfluent or inadequate) output amidst good (fluent and adequate) output. We conduct a survey to determine how users respond to good translations compared to translations that are either adequate but not fluent, or fluent but not adequate. In this pilot study, users responded strongly to disfluent translations, but were, surprisingly, much less concerned with adequacy.

1 Introduction

Machine translation has reached a level of quality such that it can now provide fast, cheap, "good enough" translations for a wide variety of information sources in an increasingly diverse set of languages and dialects. These systems are becoming available for real users who have no other way to understand content in languages in which they are not proficient. While the overall quality of MT output is important, in practice the utility of MT also depends on the willingness of users to accept the technology.

Trust is an important factor in that willingness regardless of use case. In the case of MT for communication, users may choose not to communicate if they do not trust the MT available to them. If translators do not trust the MT in their computer-assisted translation environment, they may be less efficient. When there is a need for MT for understanding, insufficient trust in MT may lead the user to simply avoid content in languages they do not understand. However lack of trust is not the only issue. Implicit trust in incorrect MT can be at least as problematic. Users may misunderstand inaccurately translated information, an automatically translated website could reflect badly on the company, and inaccurate translations used in communication could be embarrassing. However, there could be more serious repercussions if the MT is used in critical tasks. This is not merely theoretical: In October 2017, a Palestinian man was mistakenly arrested by Israeli police based on an inaccurate Facebook translation (Berger, 2017).

Because trust is so important, we need to understand how users modulate their trust in MT. However trust has been a neglected element of MT evaluation to date. To be most effective, trust evaluation must be taken into consideration not only at deployment time, but also during research and development. Understanding what factors affect user trust can help identify the most problematic error types, informing research directions. In this paper, we introduce a method of studying user trust in MT in a lab setting, based on previous work on trust in other forms of automation. We apply this approach in a pilot study comparing the effects of fluency and adequacy errors on user trust, and find that fluency appears to have a much greater effect than adequacy.

2 Related Work

To the best of our knowledge, there has been no prior work focused on evaluating user trust in MT. Automatically generated confidence scores have been referred to as "trust" (Soricut and Echihabi, 2010), but user trust has not been evaluated. There has, however, been extensive work in human evaluation of MT quality and in user trust of other types of automation.

2.1 Human Evaluation of Machine Translation

Automated quality metrics such as BLEU (Papineni et al., 2002) and METEOR (Banerjee and Lavie, 2005) have been invaluable for improving and training MT systems, and have been shown to correlate with human rankings at the system level (Papineni et al., 2002), but human judgments remain the gold standard for competitions like the Workshop (now Conference) on Machine Translation (WMT) (Callison-Burch et al., 2007, 2008, 2009, 2010, 2011, 2012; Bojar et al., 2013, 2014, 2015, 2016, 2017). However, these human judgments have focused almost entirely on intrinsic quality rather than the user experience and particularly trust.

Common approaches to human evaluation of MT include ranking and direct assessment. Ranking was the official metric for WMT 2008 - 2016 (Callison-Burch et al., 2008, 2009, 2010, 2011, 2012; Bojar et al., 2013, 2014, 2015, 2016). In each evaluation, participants ranked five translations of individual segments (usually sentences) from different MT systems against each other based on a reference translation. While rankings indicate user preference, they do not explicitly address user trust in the system and do not directly provide insight into aspects of quality that affect user judgments of the translation. The setting is also very different from a typical user experience, in which they would see only one translation of a whole document with no reference translation rather than multiple translations of individual segments and a human translation to compare against. This difference makes it difficult to draw conclusions about the user experience.

Direct assessment of adequacy and fluency is slightly more like the typical user experience in that they only see one translation. WMT initially adopted a direct assessment approach for the 2006 and 2007 workshops (Koehn and Monz, 2006; Callison-Burch et al., 2007), but the inter-annotator agreement was low that the metric was abandoned until WMT16 (Bojar et al., 2016). The change came as a result of a pilot direct assessment, conducted in parallel to the official rankings, that tested the technique from Graham et al. (2013) on a larger scale. Graham et al. had found that they could improve inter-annotator agreement by accounting for the personal preferences of the judges: They used a near-continuous scale (100 points instead of only five) and standardized each judge's score to a z-score based on the mean and standard deviation of that judge's scores. The results in the WMT16 pilot correlated so well that WMT17 used direct assessment of adequacy as the official metric (Bojar et al., 2017). However, the measure is still focused on intrinsic quality and the judges still only see one segment at a time rather than a whole document.

Although there is much less research on evaluating the user experience with MT than there is on evaluating MT quality, there have been a few user studies of MT. User studies have looked directly at how MT is used in assimilation, dissemination, and communication contexts, but have not focused on trust. For example, Yang and Lange (1998) looked at user reactions to the first free online MT system, AltaVista's Babelfish (powered by SYSTRAN). They analyzed feedback sent to the company during the first five months the system was available. They found the use was largely assimilation, but there were also examples of using the system for dissemination (e.g., websites using the service to provide translations of their own site), and communication (e.g., interacting with relatives or employees who don't speak English). In addition to providing insights into the applications of the system, the feedback provides positive or negative reactions. The study does not address trust or acceptance of the system, and it would be difficult to determine from this feedback since those who chose to contact the company may not be a representative sample of the pool of potential users.

Hara and Iqbal (2015) conducted a user study of MT for communication. They used spoken language translation, which adds speech-to-text and text-to-speech technology to the MT. Participants were not asked to directly rate fluency and adequacy of the MT, but in the feedback some mentioned grammatical and word order errors as well as problems with idiomatic expressions. While they discussed the effects these errors had on their ability to communicate, they did not address trust in the system.

To the best of our knowledge, the only published research specifically mentioning user trust in MT is Karamanis et al. (2011), who conducted a qualitative study of translation practices at a language service provider, including the use of MT. They observed that translators trusted translations from team members more than translations from remote freelancers and that they trusted MT and information gleaned from web searches even less. This study was focused on the actual work practices of the translators and the high-level interactions with MT and other translators, so it does not investigate why they distrust MT or whether they would trust one MT system over another. This dissemination setting is also different from an online MT for assimilation setting not only in the purpose but in the nature of the users. While translators may use MT to translate more efficiently, for the most part they are able to translate with their own knowledge and other resources. Those who do not know the source language are dependent on the MT to understand the text. These differences may affect their trust in the system.

2.2 User Trust in Automation

Although trust has been largely neglected in the context of MT, it has been studied in the context of other types of automation. It has been measured in a number of ways from simply asking the user (Yang et al., 2016) to measuring the user's expectations of system performance and actions taken (de Vries et al., 2003).

In de Vries et al. (2003), they used a route-planning scenario to see what effect errors would have on users' trust of the system. They define trust as a user's expectations of how a system will perform in a situation of uncertainty with some risk associated. Participants were asked to perform 26 route-planning tasks. For each task, they were asked to stake a bet on how good the route would be and they were told that the credits they earned across the whole task would affect their compensation. Ten of these trials were manual, ten automated, and in the final six the participant was allowed to choose manual or automatic. Trust was measured based on the user's stated trust in the system on a five-point scale, the number of times they chose the automated system in the last six trials, and the amount they wagered on each trial. They found that all things being equal, users preferred manual mode, but when the automated system made more errors, they trusted the automated system even less according to all measures.

Scenarios based on perception have also been used to explore user trust in automated systems, e.g. Dzindolet et al. (2003) and Yang et al. (2016). The latter is particularly relevant to this work. They looked at how negative experiences can affect trust in automation for a face recognition task. Participants were shown a set of photos of target faces to remember. They were later shown a target photo and a distractor and were asked to identify the target photo. They were evaluated based on their performance on the task. They were also provided with a suggested answer which they could choose to accept or reject. Users self-reported their trust in the system using a six-point scale. If trust were a purely statistical process, an incorrect suggestion by the system should have the same effect on trust whether or not the user chose to accept the system's suggestion. However, they observed that when the participant accepted the system's suggestion and then learned that the answer was wrong, their trust in the system dropped much more than when they rejected the system's incorrect suggestion.

3 Assessing Trust in MT

Like the examples in Section 2.2, MT is a kind of automation. It performs a typically human task (translation) and the results can be good or bad in terms of both fluency and adequacy. User reactions to an MT system may change over time as the user is exposed to more translations and the resulting change in trust of those interactions may not correspond with a simple statistical measure like intrinsic quality. In the assimilation setting, users will not typically know the adequacy of a translation but can readily judge its fluency. This means fluency may have an immediate effect on trust while adequacy will only have an effect if the user subsequently learns that the translation was wrong.

We can think of a user's trust in a specific machine translation like the wagers in de Vries et al. (2003) or the choice to agree or disagree with the system prediction in Yang et al. (2016). As users see translations that are disfluent or inadequate, we expect that their trust in the system will decrease. A situation where the user trusts a translation based on fluency but then subsequently learns that it was not adequate could be compared to the case in Yang et al. (2016) where users accept the system prediction and then learn that it was incorrect. If the findings in Yang et al. also apply to the machine translation scenario, we would expect that user trust in the MT system will go down further when they see this type of bad translation compared to translations that are merely disfluent.

Because these fluent-but-not-adequate translations may lead the user to an incorrect conclusion, we will refer to them as *misleading*. Although misleading translations are rare–only 434 out of 43,911 segments (0.99%) in system output submissions for WMT16 (Bojar et al., 2016), the potential for mistakes in understanding and degradation of user trust makes the translations particularly problematic when they occur. This is especially important as the MT community moves to neural machine translation (NMT), as NMT has been shown to consistently provide more fluent translations than previous MT paradigms (Bentivogli et al., 2016; Toral and Sánchez-Cartagena, 2017; Koehn and Knowles, 2017), but is also prone to producing output that is fluent but unrelated to the input when there is out of domain or insufficient training data (Koehn and Knowles, 2017).

We propose a survey-based approach to see how users react to misleading translations as compared to their reactions to disfluent translations. Our pilot study seeks to evaluate the following hypotheses:

H1: Exposure to good translations will maintain or increase user trust in the system

H2: Exposure to bad MT output of either type will decrease user trust in the system

H3: Misleading translations will have a bigger effect on trust than disfluent translations

For the purposes of this study, we focus on an assimilation use case, reading foreign language news. Assimilation tasks are the most practical to implement as they do not require specialized skills or interaction between participants. We chose the news domain because it is an established domain for MT research and output from state-of-the art systems is available through WMT.

4   Survey Methodology

The task of *studying trust in MT* differs from the task of *evaluating MT quality* in several important ways. MT quality evaluations are focused on a specific system or a comparison between systems. This requires many segments each evaluated by several judges. In effect, the segments of MT output are a sample from the population of all segments that could be translated by the system. Trust could potentially be used as an additional dimension in such an evaluation. However, it is valuable to study the phenomenon of user trust in MT in order to know how to help users have an appropriate level of trust in MT output. Studying the phenomenon of trust in MT is focused in the opposite direction of system evaluations: the users are the population that is randomly sampled and the segments cannot be randomly selected but must be carefully chosen to demonstrate the specific properties being compared while mediating confounding variables.

Survey Overview   For this study, we obtained Institutional Review Board approval for and conducted a survey in which participants were shown outputs from a hypothetical MT system constructed from actual MT output. In order to establish a baseline trust level and to account for biases, the participants were first asked their familiarity with machine and human translation as well as their overall opinion of machine translation. After these initial questions, they were shown a series of five machine translation outputs and asked to rate their level of trust. Presenting a series of outputs makes it possible to study change in trust over consecutive translation examples. For each translation, they first saw only the MT output and were asked their level of trust in that specific translation and their trust in the overall system based on all of the translations they had seen so far. They were then shown a human translation of the text and asked whether their judgment of the MT output had changed as well as their overall trust of the system.

Three Conditions   All participants saw the same three good (fluent and adequate) translations in the same order to establish a baseline trust level. To test the impact of misleading translations as opposed to good translations or obviously bad translations, the participants were split into three groups for the fourth translation: a control group which saw another good translation; a disfluent group which saw a disfluent but adequate translation; and a misleading group which saw the misleading translation. These alternate translations were translations of the same passage by different MT systems to ensure that fluency and adequacy were the only difference and not topic or complexity of the source. Finally, all participants were shown the same good translation as their fifth translation to see if changes in trust would carry over to the next translation. The flow of the survey is illustrated in Figure 1.

Comprehension Questions for Quality Control   To ensure participants were paying attention and understood the translation examples, they were also asked to answer a simple comprehension question for each translation before seeing the human translation. This consisted of a choice between two gists of the translation with opposite meanings. For the misleading translation, the correct answer was what the machine translation said rather than what it should have said. This not only ensured that participants were being misled but also primed them with the misleading meaning to increase the chance that they would feel misled when they saw the human translation. An example question is shown in Figure 2.

4.1   Participants

To represent typical, non-specialist MT users, participants were recruited via Qualtrics from their pool of participants over 18 and located in the U.S. Participants were not asked their age, gender, or native language, as age and gender are unlikely to be relevant in understanding

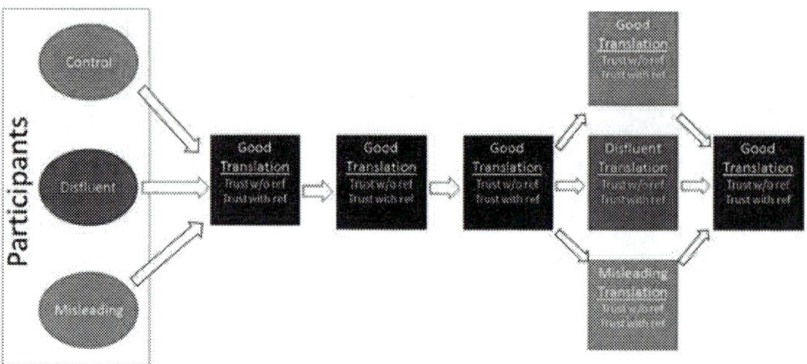

Figure 1: Diagram illustrating the flow of the survey for all three groups.

machine translation output and the comprehension questions would serve to judge participants' English language ability. Any responses that appeared to be invalid (e.g., giving the same value for every question) were excluded. Of the remaining responses, only responses that correctly answered all of comprehension questions for the four good translations were included in the final analysis. From the control and misleading groups, those who incorrectly answered the comprehension question for the fourth translation were also excluded. For the disfluent group, the fourth comprehension question was ignored because the lack of fluency made the translation so difficult to understand that half of the participants who answered all other comprehension questions correctly responded incorrectly to the question.

Figure 2: Example survey question

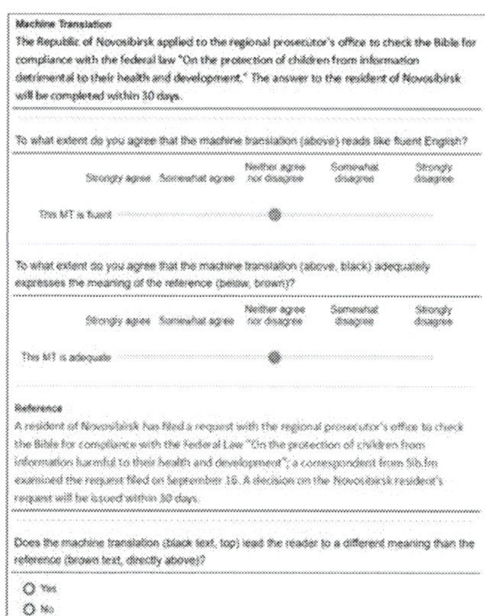

Figure 3: Example translation annotation task question

There were a total of 89 qualifying responses, of which 32 saw the disfluent translation, 29 saw the good translation, and 28 saw the misleading translation. The background information

Group	No Familiarity	Some Familiarity	Very Familiar
Control	60.1%	20.7%	17.2%
Disfluent	40.6%	34.4%	25.0%
Misleading	57.1%	17.9%	25.0%
All	52.8%	24.7%	22.5%

Table 1: Participant familiarity with machine translation

Group	No Familiarity	Some Familiarity	Very Familiar
Control	65.5%	31.0%	3.5%
Disfluent	78.1%	15.6%	6.3%
Misleading	78.5%	17.9%	3.6%
All	74.2%	21.3%	4.5%

Table 2: Participant familiarity with human translation

Group	Negative	Neutral	Positive
Control	13.8%	51.7%	34.5%
Disfluent	3.1%	65.6%	31.3%
Misleading	7.1%	35.7%	57.1%
All	7.9%	51.7%	40.4%

Table 3: Participant overall perception of MT

about the participants is summarized in Tables 1-3. In all three groups, the majority of participants were unfamiliar with human translation and a plurality of participants were unfamiliar with machine translation. This unfamiliarity with both human translation and machine translation fits our expectations for typical users of MT for assimilation. Initial perceptions of MT were primarily neutral or positive.

All of the translation examples were taken from the system outputs for the news translation task at WMT16, the 2016 Conference on Machine Translation (Bojar et al., 2016). The evaluation included a ranking evaluation by MT researchers as well as a direct assessment of fluency and adequacy by crowd-workers on Amazon Mechanical Turk. Based on the direct assessment, we selected segments in three categories: "good" segments (high fluency, high adequacy), low fluency segments, and potentially misleading (high fluency, low adequacy) segments.

To create a more realistic setting, one or two segments from the text surrounding each of the chosen segments in the machine translation were added. This context could provide information that clarifies (or contradicts) a single segment translation, so an annotation task was launched to verify that these longer translations matched the original labels of good, disfluent, or misleading. Figure 3 shows an example of one of these annotation questions. Based on those annotations, we selected translations that were rated high fluency and high adequacy by all annotators as good examples. The disfluent example used in the survey was chosen based on low fluency ratings. It also had fairly low adequacy as low fluency translations were generally also rated as low adequacy, but the adequacy score was higher than fluency. The misleading example was moderately high fluency, low adequacy, and marked by all annotators as leading the reader to a different meaning than the human reference translation.

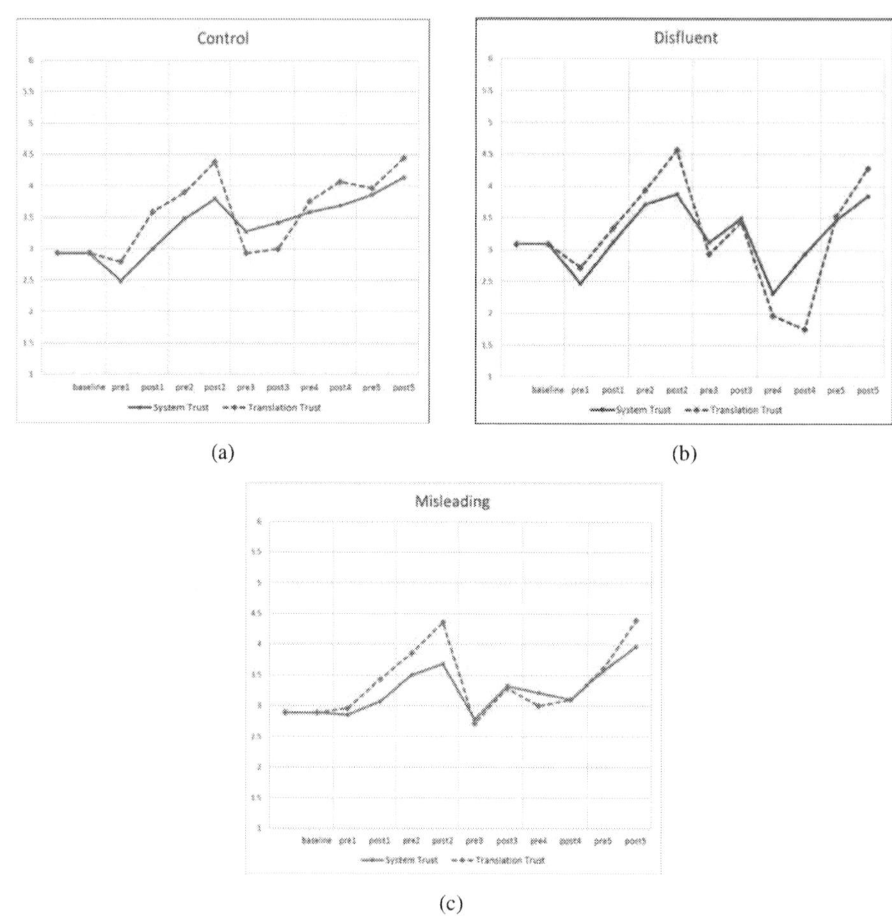

(a)

(b)

(c)

Figure 4: System and translation trust for the control group (a), disfluent group (b), and misleading group (c)

5   Results

The results from the three conditions, control, disfluent, and misleading, are shown in Figure 4 (a), (b), and (c), respectively. For each translation, the system trust score is the average of the trust scores across all responses for that setting. The pre score is before seeing the human translation and the post score is after. The pre translation score is the value reported by the user and the post is that score adjusted based on the reported change in trust.

Figure 4a shows the average translation and system trust scores for the control group. The translation trust is, not surprisingly, more volatile than the system trust. In all three conditions it basically tracks the system trust but with higher peaks and lower valleys. There are no instances where the difference between the translation trust before and after seeing the reference translation was significant ($p > 0.1$). This is somewhat surprising in the case of the misleading translation which would have been expected to yield lower trust if the users understood the reference translation. Instead, the users' opinion of the misleading translation ($M = 3.00, SD = 1.76$) appears to have increased slightly when the reference translation was revealed ($M = 3.11, SD = 2.51$), however, this difference is likely statistical error as the change is not a significant increase; $t(54) = -0.18, p = 0.85$.

Turning to system trust, with the exception of translation 3, H1 appears to hold: the trust in the system increases as the user sees more translations that are both fluent and adequate. Although translation 3 was judged as both fluent and adequate in the validation task, it appears that participants may have had difficulty understanding the translation. This confusion was not unique to those in the control group but also appeared in the other two conditions. If we set aside translation 3, the consistent increases in trust lead us to accept H1.

Figure 4b shows the results for the disfluent group. There was a significant negative change between the trust in the system after the third translation ($M = 3.50, SD = 1.27$) and after the disfluent translation ($M = 2.31, SD = 1.47$); $t(62) = 3.46, p < 0.001$, so we can reject the null hypothesis and accept H2 for the case of fluency errors. It is interesting to note that when the final translation (fluent and adequate) was displayed the trust quickly bounced back to as high as it had been before. Figure 4c, the misleading group, also has the drop in trust on the third translation, but the misleading translation had surprisingly little effect on the users' trust.

The change in system trust for the misleading translation ($M = -0.21, SD = 1.50$) did not have a significant effect on user trust compared with the control; $t(55) = 1.36, p = 0.18$, so we cannot confirm H3: misleading translations do not appear to have a stronger effect than fluency errors. This indicates that either fluency more strongly affects user trust than adequacy does or users have a more difficult time judging adequacy than fluency. Previous research (Callison-Burch et al., 2007; Graham et al., 2017) has shown that fluency and adequacy scores are highly correlated, leading to only adequacy being measured in WMT17 (Bojar et al., 2017). The correlation was taken to mean that adequacy was sufficient to judge translation quality. The results of this experiment suggest that it may in fact be the case that fluency has an out-sized effect that overshadows adequacy. The single score for adequacy should perhaps be treated as an overall quality score rather than a true adequacy score.

6 Limitations and Future Work

This study shows that user surveys can reveal impact of different MT errors on trust. However, it is a small scale pilot study, and further work will be needed to refine the survey design, and further compare the impact of fluency and adequacy on user trust. We highlight limitations identified in this study and how they could be addressed in future work.

Additional Examples   A five translation sequence may not be enough to get a good sense of how trust changes over time. For instance, based on the control group, it appears that the trust levels off after a few good translations, but without more translations it is hard to know for sure. In addition, participants were exposed to a single translation example for each error category. In future experiments, having more than one series of translations would make it possible to observe whether participant reactions are consistent across distinct representative examples.

Double-Checking Comprehension   Asking comprehension questions before displaying the reference ensured that participants understood the translation, but there was no measure of whether they understood the reference translation. This means that those who were misled by the misleading example might not have realized that they were misled. As suggested above, having more than one possible misleading example would help, but it would also be useful to repeat the comprehension question after the reference is displayed to see whether their answers changed.

Include Obvious Errors   In addition to the kind of misleading example that was tested in this study, another type of error that could provide insight into how users perceive adequacy would be translations that are fluent but not adequate, but the inadequacy is obvious without even seeing the reference. Perhaps if they recognize the error in meaning immediately it will have a stronger effect on trust than if they need to read the human translation to determine adequacy.

Users' Involvement in Outcome   One key difference between this study and previous work on trust in automation is that this study did not provide an external motivation such as a monetary incentive (as in de Vries et al. (2003)) or an evaluation of the user (as in Yang et al. (2016)). It would be beneficial to conduct any future studies in an environment where the participants felt more of an investment, such as through a rewards system. The users would be more intrinsically motivated if the test were conducted in a scenario closer to the real-world experience of the participants. One example would be setting up conversations as in Hara and Iqbal (2015). A social media scenario could be an alternative to two-way communication: participants could be given a message to promote and asked whether they would be willing to use the output of MT to post in their name in another language. Another option could be recruiting actual MT users and mimicking their work environment. This scenario would have highly motivated and informed participants but would be more difficult to create.

7   Conclusion

We have argued that trust is an important metric for machine translation and proposed a survey to determine how fluency and adequacy errors affect user trust in machine translation. Because it is impossible for MT researchers and developers to educate every possible user about the strengths and weaknesses of MT, it is incumbent on the MT community to understand how users modulate their trust and use that information to develop systems that encourage an appropriate level of trust in the output.

In our study, users reacted more strongly to fluency errors than adequacy errors. If this finding holds in large-scale studies with improvements to the experimental design as outlined in section 6, it would have implications for the development of MT systems. Although misleading translations are rare, the implicit trust users place in fluent translations obligates MT system developers to pay particular attention to adequacy. Care should be taken to reduce the frequency of misleading translations and/or to flag them as suspect and notify the user.

Acknowledgments

We thank Jen Golbeck and Hernisa Kacorri for their feedback on this work. This work was partially supported by the Clare Boothe Luce Program.

References

Satanjeev Banerjee and Alon Lavie. 2005. METEOR: An automatic metric for MT evaluation with improved correlation with human judgments. In *Proceedings of the acl workshop on intrinsic and extrinsic evaluation measures for machine translation and/or summarization.* volume 29, pages 65–72.

Luisa Bentivogli, Arianna Bisazza, Mauro Cettolo, and Marcello Federico. 2016. Neural versus phrase-based machine translation quality: a case study. In *Proceedings of the 2016 Conference on Empirical Methods in Natural Language Processing.* Association for Computational Linguistics, Austin, Texas, pages 257–267.

Yotam Berger. 2017. Israel Arrests Palestinian Because Facebook Translated 'Good Morning' to 'Attack Them'. *Haaretz* [Online; accessed 6-Dec-2017].

Ondřej Bojar, Christian Buck, Chris Callison-Burch, Christian Federmann, Barry Haddow, Philipp Koehn, Christof Monz, Matt Post, Radu Soricut, and Lucia Specia. 2013. Findings of the 2013 Workshop on Statistical Machine Translation. In *Proceedings of the Eighth Workshop on Statistical Machine Translation*. Association for Computational Linguistics, Sofia, Bulgaria, pages 1–44.

Ondřej Bojar, Christian Buck, Christian Federmann, Barry Haddow, Philipp Koehn, Johannes Leveling, Christof Monz, Pavel Pecina, Matt Post, Herve Saint-Amand, Radu Soricut, Lucia Specia, and Aleš Tamchyna. 2014. Findings of the 2014 Workshop on Statistical Machine Translation. In *Proceedings of the Ninth Workshop on Statistical Machine Translation*. Association for Computational Linguistics, Baltimore, Maryland, USA, pages 12–58.

Ondřej Bojar, Rajen Chatterjee, Christian Federmann, Yvette Graham, Barry Haddow, Shujian Huang, Matthias Huck, Philipp Koehn, Qun Liu, Varvara Logacheva, Christof Monz, Matteo Negri, Matt Post, Raphael Rubino, Lucia Specia, and Marco Turchi. 2017. Findings of the 2017 Conference on Machine Translation (WMT17). In *Proceedings of the Second Conference on Machine Translation, Volume 2: Shared Task Papers*. Association for Computational Linguistics, Copenhagen, Denmark, pages 169–214.

Ondřej Bojar, Rajen Chatterjee, Christian Federmann, Yvette Graham, Barry Haddow, Matthias Huck, Antonio Jimeno Yepes, Philipp Koehn, Varvara Logacheva, Christof Monz, Matteo Negri, Aurelie Neveol, Mariana Neves, Martin Popel, Matt Post, Raphael Rubino, Carolina Scarton, Lucia Specia, Marco Turchi, Karin Verspoor, and Marcos Zampieri. 2016. Findings of the 2016 Conference on Machine Translation. In *Proceedings of the First Conference on Machine Translation*. Association for Computational Linguistics, Berlin, Germany, pages 131–198.

Ondřej Bojar, Rajen Chatterjee, Christian Federmann, Barry Haddow, Matthias Huck, Chris Hokamp, Philipp Koehn, Varvara Logacheva, Christof Monz, Matteo Negri, Matt Post, Carolina Scarton, Lucia Specia, and Marco Turchi. 2015. Findings of the 2015 Workshop on Statistical Machine Translation. In *Proceedings of the Tenth Workshop on Statistical Machine Translation*. Association for Computational Linguistics, Lisbon, Portugal, pages 1–46.

Chris Callison-Burch, Cameron Fordyce, Philipp Koehn, Christof Monz, and Josh Schroeder. 2007. (Meta-) Evaluation of Machine Translation. In *Proceedings of the Second Workshop on Statistical Machine Translation*. Association for Computational Linguistics, Prague, Czech Republic, pages 136–158.

Chris Callison-Burch, Cameron Fordyce, Philipp Koehn, Christof Monz, and Josh Schroeder. 2008. Further Meta-Evaluation of Machine Translation. In *Proceedings of the Third Workshop on Statistical Machine Translation*. Association for Computational Linguistics, Columbus, Ohio, pages 70–106.

Chris Callison-Burch, Philipp Koehn, Christof Monz, Kay Peterson, Mark Przybocki, and Omar Zaidan. 2010. Findings of the 2010 Joint Workshop on Statistical Machine Translation and Metrics for Machine Translation. In *Proceedings of the Joint Fifth Workshop on Statistical Machine Translation and MetricsMATR*. Association for Computational Linguistics, Uppsala, Sweden, pages 17–53.

Chris Callison-Burch, Philipp Koehn, Christof Monz, Matt Post, Radu Soricut, and Lucia Specia. 2012. Findings of the 2012 Workshop on Statistical Machine Translation. In *Proceedings of the Seventh Workshop on Statistical Machine Translation*. Association for Computational Linguistics, Montréal, Canada, pages 10–51.

Chris Callison-Burch, Philipp Koehn, Christof Monz, and Josh Schroeder. 2009. Findings of the 2009 Workshop on Statistical Machine Translation. In *Proceedings of the Fourth Workshop on Statistical Machine Translation*. Association for Computational Linguistics, Athens, Greece, pages 1–28.

Chris Callison-Burch, Philipp Koehn, Christof Monz, and Omar Zaidan. 2011. Findings of the 2011 Workshop on Statistical Machine Translation. In *Proceedings of the Sixth Workshop on Statistical Machine Translation*. Association for Computational Linguistics, Edinburgh, Scotland, pages 22–64.

Peter de Vries, Cees Midden, and Don Bouwhuis. 2003. The effects of errors on system trust, self-confidence, and the allocation of control in route planning. *International Journal of Human-Computer Studies* 58(6):719–735.

Mary T Dzindolet, Scott A Peterson, Regina A Pomranky, Linda G Pierce, and Hall P Beck. 2003. The role of trust in automation reliance. *International Journal of Human-Computer Studies* 58(6):697–718.

Yvette Graham, Timothy Baldwin, Alistair Moffat, and Justin Zobel. 2013. Continuous measurement scales in human evaluation of machine translation. In *Proceedings of the 7th Linguistic Annotation Workshop & Interoperability with Discourse*. pages 33–41.

Yvette Graham, Timothy Baldwin, Alistair Moffat, and Justin Zobel. 2017. Can machine translation systems be evaluated by the crowd alone. *Natural Language Engineering* 23(1):3–30.

Kotaro Hara and Shamsi T. Iqbal. 2015. Effect of Machine Translation in Interlingual Conversation: Lessons from a Formative Study. In *Proceedings of the 33rd Annual ACM Conference on Human Factors in Computing Systems*. ACM, Seoul, Republic of Korea, pages 3473–3482.

Nikiforos Karamanis, Saturnino Luz, and Gavin Doherty. 2011. Translation practice in the workplace: contextual analysis and implications for machine translation. *Machine Translation* 25(1):35–52.

Philipp Koehn and Rebecca Knowles. 2017. Six Challenges for Neural Machine Translation. In *Workshop on Neural Machine Translation*. Vancouver, BC. ArXiv: 1706.03872.

Philipp Koehn and Christof Monz. 2006. Manual and Automatic Evaluation of Machine Translation between European Languages. In *Proceedings on the Workshop on Statistical Machine Translation*. Association for Computational Linguistics, New York City, pages 102–121.

Kishore Papineni, Salim Roukos, Todd Ward, and Wei-Jing Zhu. 2002. BLEU: a method for automatic evaluation of machine translation. In *Proceedings of the 40th annual meeting on association for computational linguistics*. Association for Computational Linguistics, pages 311–318.

Radu Soricut and Abdessamad Echihabi. 2010. Trustrank: Inducing trust in automatic translations via ranking. In *Proceedings of the 48th Annual Meeting of the Association for Computational Linguistics*. Association for Computational Linguistics, Stroudsburg, PA, USA, ACL '10, pages 612–621.

Antonio Toral and Víctor M. Sánchez-Cartagena. 2017. A Multifaceted Evaluation of Neural versus Phrase-Based Machine Translation for 9 Language Directions. In *Proceedings of the 15th Conference of the European Chapter of the Association for Computational Linguistics*. Association for Computational Linguistics, Valencia, Spain, volume 1, pages 1063–1073.

Jin Yang and Elke D Lange. 1998. SYSTRAN on AltaVista a user study on real-time machine translation on the Internet. In *Conference of the Association for Machine Translation in the Americas*. Springer, pages 275–285.

X Jessie Yang, Christopher D Wickens, and Katja Hölttä-Otto. 2016. How users adjust trust in automation: Contrast effect and hindsight bias. In *Proceedings of the Human Factors and Ergonomics Society Annual Meeting*. SAGE Publications Sage CA: Los Angeles, CA, volume 60, pages 196–200.

Combining Quality Estimation
and Automatic Post-editing
to Enhance Machine Translation Output

Rajen Chatterjee   chatterjee@fbk.eu
Matteo Negri   negri@fbk.eu
Marco Turchi   turchi@fbk.eu
Fondazione Bruno Kessler, Trento, Italy

Frédéric Blain   f.blain@sheffield.ac.uk
Lucia Specia   l.specia@sheffield.ac.uk
University of Sheffield, Sheffield, UK

Abstract

We investigate different strategies for combining quality estimation (QE) and automatic post-editing (APE) to improve the output of machine translation (MT) systems. The joint contribution of the two technologies is analyzed in different settings, in which QE serves as either: *i)* an *activator* of APE corrections, or *ii)* a *guidance* to APE corrections, or *iii)* a *selector* of the final output to be returned to the user. In the first case (QE as activator), sentence-level predictions on the raw MT output quality are used to trigger its automatic correction when the estimated (TER) scores are below a certain threshold. In the second case (QE as guidance), word-level binary quality predictions ("good"/"bad") are used to inform APE about problematic words in the MT output that should be corrected. In the last case (QE as selector), both sentence- and word-level quality predictions are used to identify the most accurate translation between the original MT output and its post-edited version. For the sake of comparison, the underlying APE technologies explored in our evaluation are both phrase-based and neural. Experiments are carried out on the English-German data used for the QE/APE shared tasks organized within the First Conference on Machine Translation (WMT 2016). Our evaluation shows positive but mixed results, with higher performance observed when word-level QE is used as a selector for neural APE applied to the output of a phrase-based MT system. Overall, our findings motivate further investigation on QE technologies. By reducing the gap between the performance of current solutions and "oracle" results, QE could significantly add to competitive APE technologies.

1 Introduction

In recent years, the steady progress of machine translation (MT) technology motivated research on a number of ancillary tasks. MT's wide adoption, especially in the translation industry, has in fact raised new challenges, which are not only related to model training, optimization, adaptation and evaluation, but also to aspects that are external to the core translation approach. Among them, quality estimation (QE) and automatic post-editing (APE) deal respectively with the possibility of *predicting* the quality of MT output and *correcting* it via downstream post-processing. QE (Specia et al., 2010) is motivated by the need for estimating output quality at run-time, that is when reference-based evaluation is unfeasible (the typical scenario when MT is deployed in production). APE (Simard et al., 2007) is motivated by the need of improving MT systems' output in black-box conditions, in which the translation models are not accessible for internal modification, retraining or adaptation (a typical situation for companies that rely on third-party MT systems).

Both QE and APE have been successfully explored as standalone tasks in previous work, in particular within the well-established framework of the Conference on Machine Translation (WMT[1]). In six editions of the WMT QE shared task (2012-2017), the MT quality prediction problem has been formulated in different ways (*e.g.* ranking, scoring) and attacked at different levels of granularity (sentence/phrase/word-level). Constant state-of-the-art advancements are making QE a more appealing technology, for instance to enhance the productivity of human translators operating with computer-assisted translation tools (Bentivogli et al., 2016). Three rounds of the APE shared task at WMT (2015-2017) followed a similar trend, with improvements that reflect a steady progress of the underlying technology developed by participants.

Despite the growing interest in the two tasks and the fact that the proposed evaluation exercises shared the same training/test data, previous research on both topics has mainly followed independent paths. As a consequence, the potential usefulness of leveraging the two technologies to achieve better MT has been scarcely explored and no systematic analysis of the possible combination strategies has been reported. Along this direction, this paper investigates how QE and APE can be jointly deployed to boost the overall quality of the output produced by an MT system, without any intervention on the actual MT technology. By experimenting with the same data, we explore different ways to approach the problem. The main difference between the proposed strategies lies in the degree of integration between the two technologies. A light integration is pursued when QE is used either to trigger the automatic correction of machine-translated text (QE as *activator*, see Section 3.1) or to validate an automatic correction by comparing it with the original MT output (QE as *selector*, see Section 3.3). A tighter integration is pursued when QE is used to inform the automatic correction process by identifying problematic passages in the machine-translated text (QE as *guidance*, see Section 3.2). Depending on the applied strategy, QE predictions can be done at different levels of granularity. In this first exploration we focus on the two most studied levels, namely sentence and word levels, leaving for future work the exploitation of phrase level estimates (Logacheva and Specia, 2015; Bojar et al., 2016).

Overall, this paper presents the following main contributions:

- The first systematic analysis of different strategies for the integration of QE and APE towards better MT quality;

- Experimental results, computed on the same public test set, indicating that state-of-the-art QE methods can improve APE and that, in turn, their joint contribution can boost MT output quality;

- A verification of our findings, based on "oracle" quality scores, indicating a large room for improvement conditioned to the reliability of QE predictions. This motivates further research on the task.

2 Background

This section introduces the two MT ancillary tasks relevant to this paper (QE and APE), and summarizes related research. It also gives an overview of the few initiatives in which the interaction between the QE and APE technologies has been previously explored.

---

[1] http://www.statmt.org/wmt17/

2.1 Quality Estimation

Machine translation quality estimation is the task of predicting the quality of machine-translated text at run-time, without relying on hand-crafted reference translations (Specia et al., 2010). Its possible uses include: *i)* deciding whether a given translation (or portions of it) is good enough for publishing as-is or needs post-editing by professional translators (*e.g.* in a computer-assisted translation environment), *ii)* informing readers of the target language about the reliability of a translation, *iii)* selecting the best translation among options from multiple MT and/or translation memory systems.

QE is usually cast as a supervised learning task, in which systems trained on (*input, output, quality_label*) triplets have to predict a quality label for unseen (*input, output*) test instances. In previous works, this problem has been attacked from different perspectives that, in recent years, reflected the formulation of various sub-tasks proposed within the WMT shared evaluation framework.[2] Major differences concern the granularity and type of the predictions, as well as the underlying learning paradigm. The granularity of QE predictions can range from the document to the sentence, phrase or word level. Relevant to this paper are the sentence and word levels, the former being also the most widely studied type of QE.

In sentence-level QE, the required predictions can be post-editing effort estimates (*e.g.* the expected number of editing operations required to correct the MT output), post-editing time estimates (*e.g.* the time required to make an automatic translation acceptable), ranking of multiple translation options, binary ("good"/"bad") scores or Likert-scale scores (*e.g.* 1-to-5 scores indicating overall translation quality as perceived by a human). Depending on the type of prediction required, the proposed supervised learning approaches span from classification to regression and ranking. Together with the batch learning solutions that characterize the majority of the proposed approaches, recent work also explored the application of online and multitask learning methods (Turchi et al., 2014; C. de Souza et al., 2015) targeting flexibility and robustness to domain differences between training and test data.

In word-level QE, the required predictions can be either binary "good"/"bad" labels for each MT output token, or more fine-grained multi-class labels indicating the type of error occurring in a specific word. The problem, initially approached as a sequence labelling task (Luong et al., 2013), has then been successfully tackled with neural solutions that now represent the state-of-the-art (C. de Souza et al., 2014; Kreutzer et al., 2015; Martins et al., 2016; Kim et al., 2017).

For the experiments discussed in this paper (see Section 4.2) sentence-level and word-level quality estimates are obtained with the winning systems at the WMT 2016 QE shared task, described respectively in (Kozlova et al., 2016) and (Martins et al., 2016). For a comprehensive overview of the evolution of the QE task and the proposed approaches, we refer the reader to the rich WMT literature (Callison-Burch et al., 2012; Bojar et al., 2013, 2014, 2015, 2016, 2017).

2.2 Automatic Post-editing

Automatic post-editing is the task of correcting errors produced by a machine translation system, typically by exploiting knowledge acquired from human post-edits. APE research dates back to the work of (Knight and Chander, 1994; Simard et al., 2007), in which the problem is approached as a "monolingual translation" task. Similar to MT, in which systems are trained on bilingual data consisting of parallel (*source, MT*) pairs, APE systems are built by learning from monolingual data consisting of "parallel" (*source, MT, post_edited MT*) triplets, in which a source sentence and its raw MT output are associated with a human-corrected version of the translation. Under this general formulation, previous work concentrated on several aspects, with outcomes that indicate a steady evolution of the approaches.

---

[2]http://www.statmt.org/wmt17/quality-estimation-task.html

In terms of methods, early works rely on a statistical phrase-based approach (Simard et al., 2007), possibly integrating source information to reduce systems' tendency to over-correct and enhance their precision (Béchara et al., 2011; Chatterjee et al., 2015). More recently, large performance gains comparable to those achieved in MT by the adoption of neural approaches have also been observed in APE (Junczys-Dowmunt and Grundkiewicz, 2016), especially with multi-source neural systems (Chatterjee et al., 2017a) enhancing decoding with source language information.

In order to evaluate the effects of combining QE with different APE technologies, the experiments discussed in Section 4.3 are performed with both phrase-based (Chatterjee et al., 2016) and neural-based (Junczys-Dowmunt and Grundkiewicz, 2016) architectures. The latter is the winning system at the WMT 2016 APE shared task.[3] For a comprehensive overview of the evolution of the APE task and the proposed approaches, we refer the reader to the aforementioned WMT literature.

2.3 Combination of QE and APE

So far, the interaction and the possible joint contribution of QE and APE technology has been scarcely explored. This is particularly surprising if we consider that both the tasks can rely on the type of same training data consisting of (*source, MT, post_edited MT*) parallel triplets, which in principle allow for knowledge transfer and model sharing.

Building on this consideration, (Martins et al., 2017) exploited the synergies between the two related tasks by using the output of an APE system as an extra feature to boost the performance of a neural QE architecture. The intuition is that word-level quality labels can be automatically obtained through TER (Snover et al., 2006) alignments between the translated and the post-edited sentence (used as "pseudo human post-edit"). The resulting APE-based QE system achieves state-of-the-art performance at the word and sentence-level QE tasks on the WMT 2015 and WMT 2016 data sets.

Another line of research that is closer to our work has focused on improving APE performance by leveraging word-level QE predictions. In (Hokamp, 2017), this is done by incorporating word-level features as factors in the input (*i.e.* a concatenation of different word embedding representations) to a neural APE system. By taking a different approach, Chatterjee et al. (2017b) explore a "guided-decoding" mechanism to guide a neural APE system with word-level binary QE judgments. The idea of constraining the decoding process (*i.e.* forcing the system to keep "good" tokens in the APE output) is the basis for the integration approach described in Section 3.2: "QE as APE guidance".

A third solution for the integration of QE and APE is explored in (Chatterjee et al., 2016), in which sentence-level quality predictions are used to select the best translation between the raw output or the correction produced by a factored phrase-based APE model. This integration strategy is the basis for the integration approach described in Section 3.3: "QE as MT/APE selector".

3 QE and APE Integration Strategies

QE and APE can be combined in different ways to enhance MT quality. In the following sections we identify and evaluate the following three alternative strategies:

1. QE as APE *activator*: QE predictions are used to trigger APE decoding when the estimated quality of the MT segment is below a certain threshold;

2. QE as *guidance* for the APE decoder: QE labels are used to inform the APE decoding process by discriminating which tokens in the MT output should be kept or changed;

---

[3] http://www.statmt.org/wmt16/ape-task.html

3. QE as *selector*: QE predictions are used to identify the best alternative between the raw MT and its automatically corrected version. This decision can be performed either at the level of entire sentences or for portions of the two alternative outputs.

3.1 QE as APE activator

In this first scenario, QE is used to take a decision on whether activating APE or not. This is done by running a sentence-level QE on the MT segment to predict its TER score, and then setting a threshold on this prediction. If the predicted TER is below the threshold,[4] the translation will be considered as good enough and the application of an automatic post-editing step unnecessary. Instead, if the predicted TER is above the threshold, the APE decoder is run, and its output is shown to the end user.

3.2 QE as APE guidance

In the "QE as APE activator" strategy, the APE decoder is not directly aided by the QE information to improve its performance, because QE is applied before running the correction process. This prevents QE from supporting APE in addressing specific problems such as over-correction, a well known issue of APE systems: they tend to "re-translate" the raw MT output, even when it is already good. Indeed, as evidenced by the last editions of the APE shared task at WMT (Bojar et al., 2016), the submitted systems performed unnecessary corrections that could either be penalized by automatic evaluation against references consisting of minimal human corrections (*i.e.* only those that are strictly necessary) or, in the worst case, even worsen the MT segment.

To overcome this limitation, an alternative strategy is a QE+APE pipeline in which fine-grained word-level QE judgments for each MT token are passed as additional information to the APE decoder, with the aim of guiding it to change only the words marked as "bad" (or, in other terms, to keep the correct MT tokens in the APE output). While implementing this "QE as guidance" strategy under the phrase-based framework is straightforward, its application to neural APE decoding requires some adaptation work.

In the case of phrase-based APE decoding, the XML markup technique can be easily applied. With this approach, word-level QE labels are directly passed to the APE decoder by specifying a fixed translation for a specific span of the source sentence. If the predicted label is "good", the suggested span contains the original MT words (*i.e.* the decoder is forced to preserve them in the final output). If the label is "bad", instead, the corresponding MT word is not marked, thus giving the decoder the freedom to modify it. Among the different strategies to combine the suggested translation options and those proposed by the APE model, in Section 5 we experiment with the *inclusive* setting, in which the proposed options compete against the other translation candidates in the phrase table.

When the APE system is based on a neural decoder, the XML markup strategy is implemented following the guided decoding mechanism proposed in (Chatterjee et al., 2017b). Differently from a standard neural decoder that predicts one word at a time by leveraging the previously predicted word, the context and the previous hidden states, the guided decoder is enhanced by *i)* a method to prioritize the suggested word in the beam search, *ii)* a look-ahead mechanism to avoid duplicates of the suggested words, and *iii)* a strategy to generate continuous and discontinuous target phrases. More details about the algorithm are available in (Chatterjee et al., 2017b). Similarly to the XML markup, the "good" labels are transformed in suggested spans containing the MT words, thus pushing the decoder towards using them. For "bad" word-level predictions, in contrast, the decoder does not receive any constraint and is free to produce the most probable output.

---

[4] Recall that TER is an error metric, so lower scores indicate better translations.

3.3 QE as MT/APE selector

A third possible strategy is to exploit QE predictions at a downstream level, after APE processing. After the APE decoder has generated its output, QE can be used to determine the best output option between the original MT and the post-edited segments. In our experiments, this is done in two ways, namely: *i)* by annotating only the MT segment with word-level QE labels, or *ii)* by annotating both the MT and the APE outputs at sentence or word-level.

In the first scenario, the MT and APE segments are first word aligned. Then, by using the MT output as a backbone, words are retained or modified based on their QE predicted labels. MT words labelled as "good" will be retained, while those marked as "bad" will be replaced by the corresponding alignments from the APE output.

In the second scenario, both the MT and APE sentences are labelled with sentence-level QE predictions (TER scores), and the one with the lower predicted TER score is selected as final output. To make the decision process more robust, a threshold τ can be set on the difference in TER between the two segments. For instance, if the goal is to take a conservative approach favouring the MT system, such threshold can be set such that APE outputs are selected only if their predicted TER is much lower than the MT ($TER_{MT} - TER_{APE} > \tau$).

When both the MT and APE sentences are annotated with word-level binary labels, the tokens marked as "good" are selected from one of the two segments. In detail, the MT and APE segments are first word aligned, then the MT is taken as backbone. For each MT word, the QE labels are compared. If the MT label is "good" and the APE is "bad", the MT word is taken. If the MT label is "bad" and the APE is "good", the APE word is selected. In case the annotations are both either "bad" or "good", the MT word is chosen. In the case where either MT or APE word is aligned to NULL with a "good" label, the word is added to the final output. Although this technique is rather simple, as shown in Section 5, it results in competitive performance.

4 Experimental Settings

4.1 Data

The experiments in this paper are performed using the English-German (En-De) datasets released for the APE and QE shared tasks at WMT 2016 (Bojar et al., 2016), wich are a subset of a larger collection presented in (Specia et al., 2017). Each item consists of a triplet (*source*, *MT*, *post_edited MT*) obtained by first translating the source sentence with a phrase-based statistical MT (PBSMT) system, and then by post-editing the translated segment. The data belongs to the Information Technology domain and the post-edits are created by professional translators. The training set contains 12,000 triplets, the development set, 1,000 and the test set 2,000 items. For the word-level QE task, the three sets have 21.4%, 19.54% and 19.31% "bad" labels, showing an unbalanced distribution towards the "good" quality tokens.

4.2 QE systems

For generating the sentence-level predictions, the best system submitted at the 2016 QE shared task is used (Kozlova et al., 2016). It consists in a pipeline of two regressors, where the first one, given a set of features, predicts the BLEU score (Papineni et al., 2002) and the second one, given the predicted BLEU value, predicts the TER score. Several features are combined, including features extracted from the parse trees of the sentences, pseudo-references, back-translation, web-scale language model, and word alignments.

At word-level, the best performing system at the 2016 QE shared is used (Martins et al., 2016). It is a stacked architecture that combines three neural models: one feed-forward and two recurrent ones. The predictions of these three models are added as features in a feature-based linear sequential model. Syntactic dependency-based features are combined with the baseline features released by the task organizers.

In our experiments we test different QE-APE integration strategies using either the predicted QE annotations produced by the aforementioned systems or the gold (ORACLE) labels released by the task organizers. The main idea behind the use of oracle labels is to evaluate the improvements in MT quality that would be possible given a perfect QE predictor.[5]

4.3 APE systems

The outputs of two APE systems are used in the "QE as APE activator" and "QE as MT/APE selector" experiments. These systems are the best PBSMT APE system (Chatterjee et al., 2016), and the best neural APE approach (Junczys-Dowmunt and Grundkiewicz, 2016) at the second edition of the APE shared task.

The fist method relies on a factored PBSMT decoder that combines the classic monolingual approach ($MT \rightarrow pe$ translation) with the context-aware method ($MT\#src \rightarrow pe$) that improves the decoding process with information from the source sentence. This system is enhanced with the addition of several language models including part-of-speech-tag, neural class-based and statistical word-based. In addition to these components, the *primary* submitted run includes a quality estimator as MT/APE selector, which did not result in better performance compared to a system without it. To avoid any bias in our evaluation, we use the submission that does not include the QE component (*i.e.* the submitted *contrastive* run). It relies on the Moses platform (Koehn et al., 2007), a 5-gram word-based statistical language model, and 8-gram POS-tag and class-based language models. obtained with statistical and neural language model toolkits.

The neural system is an attentional encoder-decoder model trained with sub-word units. The primary submission is an ensemble of monolingual ($MT \rightarrow pe$) and cross-lingual (*source* $\rightarrow pe$) systems combined in a log-linear model. A task-specific feature based on string matching is added to the log-linear combination to control the faithfulness of the APE results with regards to the input. Differently from the PBSMT system, the neural model requires a large quantity of training data. This data is obtained by a "round-trip translation" process that generates source and MT segments starting from the reference sentences. In total, $\sim$4 million artificial triplets are used to train a generic neural APE system that is then fine-tuned on the task-specific (APE) data.

In the "QE as APE activator" and "QE as MT/APE selector" strategies, the interaction between the QE and the APE systems is performed before and after decoding. For this reason, we directly take the submissions of the two systems to the APE shared task. In the tighter integration explored in the "QE as APE guidance" experiments, the test set needs to be post-edited using the QE labels. For this purpose, the PBSMT APE system, that is an instance of the Moses toolkit with standard parameters, is trained only on the task-specific data. This is different from the best PBSMT APE system at WMT 2016, because we only use a statistical word-level language model. For the guided decoder, the implementation and settings from Chatterjee et al. (2017b) are used. This means that the neural APE model has been trained by the authors of the winning system at the WMT 2016 APE shared task (Junczys-Dowmunt and Grundkiewicz, 2016) using the large "round-trip translation" dataset, and then adapted to task-specific data. The network parameters are: word embedding dimensionality of 600, hidden unit size of 1,024, maximum sentence length of 50, batch size of 80, and vocabulary size of 40K. The network parameters are optimized with Adadelta (Zeiler, 2012).

For the guided decoder, the best value step of the look-ahead mechanism is defined on the development set. The data is segmented using the Byte-Pair Encoding (BPE) technique (Sennrich et al., 2016). Each QE word-level annotation is projected to all the subword units. We only use a single $MT \rightarrow pe$ model instead of an ensemble of models.

---

[5]It is important to note that there are several perfectly valid translations of the same input text, so the gold QE predictions that we use are a subset of possible oracle labels generated based on the available reference sentence.

It is important to note that both the APE systems are strong. In fact, they significantly improve over the MT output (respectively +2.64 and +5.54 BLEU points for the phrase-based and the neural-based system) and, compared to the best system at WMT 2017 that uses twice the size of the task-specific data and leverages the multi-source neural architecture, the performance gap is limited to 2 BLEU score points.

5   Results and Discussion

In this section, the light and tight integration of QE and APE are evaluated to identify conditions where translation quality can be enhanced. In all the experiments, the combined QE and APE systems are compared against *i)* the original MT baseline and *ii)* the APE system without QE (official WMT submissions when possible, our implementations in the results reported in Table 2). Both PBSMT and neural APE are considered. In the APE shared task at WMT 2016, both systems outperform significantly the MT baseline. The performance of all the systems is evaluated in terms of BLEU score against the reference translation.

QE as APE activator.   In this set of experiments we investigate if the light integration of QE, as a way to trigger the automatic correction of machine translated texts, is able to improve translation quality. For this purpose, both sentence-level QE predictions and ORACLE values are computed for each MT sentence. If these values are larger than a threshold, then the APE decoder is run to improve the translation. Different TER thresholds on the QE scores are tested on the development set (*i.e.* ranging from 0 to 100 with step 5) and the best performing value is applied to the test set. The performances of the MT, APE (WMT systems), APE+QE predictions and APE+QE$_{ORACLE}$ are reported in Table 1.

	APE System	
	PBSMT	Neural
MT	62.11	62.11
APE (WMT systems)	64.75	67.65
APE + QE	64.47	67.19
APE + QE$_{ORACLE}$	64.58	67.56

Table 1: QE as APE activator (BLEU scores). These results are obtained using a threshold of 10 TER points.

As it can be seen in Table 1, for the two APE+QE configurations, a marginal drop in performance indicates that using sentence-level QE does not help this task. The use of the ORACLE labels (last row in table) is marginally better than the use of predicted QE scores, but it is still worse than using the top performing APE systems without QE. This is true for both the PBSMT and neural APE systems. Our intuition is that sentence-level QE scores provide information that is too coarse-grained, which does not give any hint to the APE system about what is wrong in the MT output and how difficult it is to correct it. For instance, not running the APE decoder when the TER (either oracle or predicted) is small does not mean that APE could not correct the (few) errors present in the MT segment.

"QE as APE guidance".   To better support APE, a tighter integration of the two technologies is obtained by injecting word-level QE annotations directly into the decoder. This is done by using the XML markup in the case of the PBSMT model and by means of guided decoding for the neural model. Results are reported in Table 2.[6]

---

[6]The APE results are different compared to the ones reported in Table 1 because our PBSMT APE only uses the word-level language model, and our neural APE is a single *MT* → *pe* system instead of an ensemble.

	APE System	
	PBSMT	Neural
MT	62.11	62.11
APE (our implementation)	63.47	65.25
APE + QE	63.57	65.50
APE + QE$_{ORACLE}$	63.78	67.03

Table 2: QE as APE guidance (BLEU scores).

Differently from the sentence-level QE predictions, the word-level predictions are effective and their use results in a small but significant gain in performance over the APE system alone. This improvement also exists with the neural decoder, which is already a stronger APE module on its own. When using the ORACLE labels, there are further improvements in BLEU score. This is more evident for the neural system (+1.53 BLEU), bringing it closer to the ensemble APE system (67.75 BLEU) shown in Table 1. A possible explanation of this larger gain compared to the PBSMT APE is that the higher generalization capability of the neural approach, which forces the APE system to perform a large number of changes, can be kept under control using information from QE. Moreover, the guided decoder proposes a tighter integration of the QE annotations than the XML markup, which is not able to decode phrases spanning across the suggested words and those for which a modification is required.

It is worth noticing that the observed relative improvements are obtained on top of simpler implementations of PBSMT and neural APE systems. For this reason, they are not directly comparable with the APE results reported in Tables 1, 3, 4 and 5, which are obtained from participants' official submissions at WMT 2016. However, while lower than those achieved by the top WMT 2016 systems, these positive results suggest that it would be worth testing the QE-guided APE approach on more competitive state-of-the-art APE solutions.

"QE as MT/APE selector". In the last round of experiments we use QE information after the APE decoding. For this configuration, two solutions are explored. In the first one (see Table 3), only the MT segment is labelled with word-level QE annotations (predicted and ORACLE). In the second one, both the MT and APE sentences are annotated with sentence or word-level QE information (Tables 4 and 5 respectively). The results in Table 3 show that both predicted and ORACLE sentence level annotations of the MT output can enhance the quality obtained by the standard APE (WMT systems). Similarly to the "QE as APE guidance" approach, the neural APE is more sensitive to QE information, achieving a significant +0.2 (predictions) and +1.56 (ORACLE) BLEU scores over the standard APE. We hypothesize that these results stem from the tendency of neural APE systems to perform a large number of modifications on the MT output which are not always correct. QE information on the MT thus limits unnecessary changes made by the APE module.

	APE System	
	PBSMT	Neural
MT	62.11	62.11
APE (WMT systems)	64.75	67.65
APE + QE	64.87	67.86
APE + QE$_{ORACLE}$	65.13	69.21

Table 3: QE as MT/APE selector (BLEU scores). Word-level QE annotations are produced only for the MT segment.

When both the MT and the APE segments are annotated with the sentence-level QE scores, a threshold is set to decide whether to show the MT or the APE translation to the end user. The best results, reported in Table 4, are obtained with τ equal to 5 and 1, respectively for the predicted and ORACLE TER values. These experiments confirm that the use of the predicted sentence information is not useful: both the PBSMT and neural APE+QE systems produce outputs that are worse than the standard APE (WMT systems). when using the ORACLE annotations, the BLEU scores achieved are better than those for the APE system on its own, and in line with the performance obtained by ORACLE word-level QE information on the MT segments (last row in Table 3). This indicates that better QE scores would be helpul in this setting.

	APE System	
	PBSMT	Neural
MT	62.11	62.11
APE (WMT systems)	64.75	67.65
APE + QE	64.49	66.49
APE + QE$_{ORACLE}$	65.26	69.50

Table 4: QE as MT/APE selector (BLEU scores). Sentence-level QE annotations both on the MT and APE segments.

The final experiment consists in annotating both the MT and the APE segments with word-level QE information and defining a simple strategy to merge the two outputs (see Section 3.3). Table 5 shows that both PBSMT and neural APE systems take advantage of the QE labels, slightly improving over the APE systems on their own. Unsurprisingly, larger gains with both techniques are obtained using the ORACLE annotations: a performance boost of +0.68 and +3.34 BLEU scores respectively. Again, the neural APE achieves the best performance and largest potential improvement, confirming that the large variability of the applied changes is indeed an advantage, and that it can be kept under control using information from QE.

	APE System	
	PBSMT	Neural
MT	62.11	62.11
APE (WMT systems)	64.75	67.65
APE + QE	64.83	67.79
APE + QE$_{ORACLE}$	65.51	71.13

Table 5: QE as MT/APE selector (BLEU scores). Word-level QE annotations both on the MT and APE segments.

Overall, by taking into consideration all the experiments we report in this paper, our main findings can be summarized as follows:

- Integration strategies exploiting word-level QE seem to be more promising than those based on sentence-level QE. Our results show that sentence-level QE information is too coarse to support APE decoding, while having the QE annotations on each MT and/or APE token can help to enhance overall translation quality.

- At word-level, predicted QE labels yield limited but constant gains, up to $\sim$0.2 BLEU points over standard APE systems. These values are small, but support the intuition that QE and APE integration has some potential.

- ORACLE results indicate that there is large scope for improvement if better QE systems can be designed. Although it is not guaranteed that a QE model could achieve the ORACLE performance, it is interesting to notice that increasing the quality of the QE annotations results in significant translation quality improvements.

6 Conclusion

We proposed a systematic analysis of different techniques to combine QE and APE to achieve better MT quality. These strategies range from light integration, where QE is used either to trigger automatic post-editing or to compare the APE with the original MT segment, to tighter integration, in which QE annotations are directly used to guide the inner workings of the APE decoder. Our experiments show that QE can help APE to produce better MT outputs. Among the proposed strategies, "QE as guidance" and "QE as selector" lead to improvements in MT quality. The use of neural APE and word-level QE, on both MT and APE, results in the largest gains over the top WMT 2016 APE system (+0.2 BLEU score with the predicted QE annotations, and +3.34 BLEU score with the ORACLE labels).

These findings motivate further research in this area, which can be explored with different directions. First, all the proposed strategies have been applied to the output of a PBSMT MT system, but the recent advancements in neural MT call for testing our integrated approaches also on the output of a NMT model. Second, the progress of deep learning methods in APE and QE suggests that the development of a single end-to-end model that would simultaneously leverage both technologies could be beneficial (*e.g.* pointer network (Vinyals et al., 2015) for neural APE).

References

Béchara, H., Ma, Y., and van Genabith, J. (2011). Statistical Post-Editing for a Statistical MT System. In *Proceedings of the 13th Machine Translation Summit*, pages 308–315, Xiamen, China.

Bentivogli, L., Bertoldi, N., Cettolo, M., Federico, M., Negri, M., and Turchi, M. (2016). On the evaluation of adaptive machine translation for human post-editing. *IEEE/ACM Transactions on Audio, Speech, and Language Processing*, 24(2):388–399.

Bojar, O. et al. (2013). Findings of the 2013 Workshop on Statistical Machine Translation. In *Proceedings of the 8th Workshop on Statistical Machine Translation*, pages 1–44, Sofia, Bulgaria.

Bojar, O. et al. (2014). Findings of the 2014 Workshop on Statistical Machine Translation. In *Proceedings of the 9th Workshop on Statistical Machine Translation*, pages 12–58, Baltimore, Maryland, USA.

Bojar, O. et al. (2015). Findings of the 2015 Workshop on Statistical Machine Translation. In *Proceedings of the 10th Workshop on Statistical Machine Translation*, pages 1–46, Lisbon, Portugal.

Bojar, O. et al. (2016). Findings of the 2016 Conference on Machine Translation. In *Proceedings of the 1st Conference on Machine Translation*, pages 131–198, Berlin, Germany.

Bojar, O. et al. (2017). Findings of the 2017 Conference on Machine Translation (WMT17). In *Proceedings of the 2nd Conference on Machine Translation*, pages 169–214, Copenhagen, Denmark.

C. de Souza, J. G., González-Rubio, J., Buck, C., Turchi, M., and Negri, M. (2014). FBK-UPV-UEdin Participation in the WMT14 Quality Estimation shared-task. In *Proceedings of the 9th Workshop on Statistical Machine Translation*, Baltimore, MD, USA.

C. de Souza, J. G., Negri, M., Ricci, E., and Turchi, M. (2015). Online Multitask Learning for Machine Translation Quality Estimation. In *Proceedings of the 53rd Annual Meeting of the Association for Computational Linguistics and the 7th International Joint Conference on Natural Language Processing (Volume 1: Long Papers)*, pages 219–228, Beijing, China.

Callison-Burch, C. et al. (2012). Findings of the 2012 Workshop on Statistical Machine Translation. In *Proceedings of the 7th Workshop on Statistical Machine Translation*, pages 10–51, Montréal, Canada.

Chatterjee, R., C. de Souza, J. G., Negri, M., and Turchi, M. (2016). The FBK Participation in the WMT 2016 Automatic Post-editing Shared Task. In *Proceedings of the 1st Conference on Machine Translation*, pages 745–750, Berlin, Germany.

Chatterjee, R., Farajian, M. A., Negri, M., Turchi, M., Srivastava, A., and Pal, S. (2017a). Multi-source Neural Automatic Post-Editing: FBK's Participation in the WMT 2017 APE Shared Task. In *Proceedings of the 2nd Conference on Machine Translation*, pages 630–638, Copenhagen, Denmark.

Chatterjee, R., Negri, M., Turchi, M., Federico, M., Specia, L., and Blain, F. (2017b). Guiding Neural Machine Translation Decoding with External Knowledge. In *Proceedings of the 2nd Conference on Machine Translation*, pages 157–168, Copenhagen, Denmark.

Chatterjee, R., Weller, M., Negri, M., and Turchi, M. (2015). Exploring the Planet of the APEs: a Comparative Study of State-of-the-art Methods for MT Automatic Post-Editing. In *Proceedings of ACL '15*, pages 156–161, Beijing, China.

Hokamp, C. (2017). Ensembling factored neural machine translation models for automatic post-editing and quality estimation.

Junczys-Dowmunt, M. and Grundkiewicz, R. (2016). Log-linear Combinations of Monolingual and Bilingual Neural Machine Translation Models for Automatic Post-Editing. In *Proceedings of the 1st Conference on Machine Translation*, Berlin, Germany.

Kim, H., Lee, J.-H., and Na, S.-H. (2017). Predictor-estimator using multilevel task learning with stack propagation for neural quality estimation. In *Proceedings of the 2nd Conference on Machine Translation*, pages 562–568, Copenhagen, Denmark.

Knight, K. and Chander, I. (1994). Automated postediting of documents. In *Proceedings of the 12th National Conference on Artificial Intelligence*, pages 779–784, Seattle, WA.

Koehn, P. et al. (2007). Moses: Open Source Toolkit for Statistical Machine Translation. In *Proceedings ACL '07*, Stroudsburg, PA, USA.

Kozlova, A., Shmatova, M., and Frolov, A. (2016). Ysda participation in the wmt'16 quality estimation shared task. In *Proceedings of the 1st Conference on Machine Translation*, pages 793–799, Berlin, Germany.

Kreutzer, J., Schamoni, S., and Riezler, S. (2015). Quality estimation from scratch (quetch): Deep learning for word-level translation quality estimation. In *Proceedings of the 10th Workshop on Statistical Machine Translation*, pages 316–322, Lisbon, Portugal.

Logacheva, V. and Specia, L. (2015). Phrase-level quality estimation for machine translation. In *Proceedings of the 12th International Workshop on Spoken Language Translation, Da Nang, Vietnam*.

Luong, N. Q., Lecouteux, B., and Besacier, L. (2013). LIG System for WMT13 QE Task: Investigating the Usefulness of Features in Word Confidence Estimation for MT. In *Proceedings of the 8th Workshop on Statistical Machine Translation*, pages 386–391, Sofia, Bulgaria.

Martins, A., Astudillo, R., Hokamp, C., and Kepler, F. (2016). Unbabel's participation in the wmt16 word-level translation quality estimation shared task. In *Proceedings of the 1st Conference on Machine Translation*, pages 806–811, Berlin, Germany.

Martins, A., Junczys-Dowmunt, M., Kepler, F., Astudillo, R., Hokamp, C., and Grundkiewicz, R. (2017). Pushing the limits of translation quality estimation. *Transactions of the Association for Computational Linguistics*, 5:205–218.

Papineni, K., Roukos, S., Ward, T., and Zhu, W.-J. (2002). Bleu: a Method for Automatic Evaluation of Machine Translation. In *Proceedings of ACL '02*, pages 311–318, Philadelphia, Pennsylvania, USA.

Sennrich, R., Haddow, B., and Birch, A. (2016). Neural Machine Translation of Rare Words with Subword Units. In *Proceedings of ACL '16*, pages 1715–1725, Berlin, Germany.

Simard, M., Goutte, C., and Isabelle, P. (2007). Statistical Phrase-Based Post-Editing. In *Proceedings of NAACL HLT '07*, pages 508–515, Rochester, New York.

Snover, M., Dorr, B., Schwartz, R., Micciulla, L., and Makhoul, J. (2006). A Study of Translation Edit Rate with Targeted Human Annotation. In *Proceedings of AMTA 2006*, pages 223–231, Cambridge, Massachusetts, USA.

Specia, L., Harris, K., Blain, F., Burchardt, A., Macketanz, V., Negri, M., and Turchi, M. (2017). Translation quality and productivity: A study on rich morphology languages. In *Proceedings of the 16th Machine Translation Summit*, Nagoya, Japan.

Specia, L., Raj, D., and Turchi, M. (2010). Machine Translation Evaluation versus Quality Estimation. *Machine translation*, 24(1):39–50.

Turchi, M., Anastasopoulos, A., C. de Souza, J. G., and Negri, M. (2014). Adaptive Quality Estimation for Machine Translation. In *Proceedings of ACL '14*, pages 710–720, Baltimore, Maryland.

Vinyals, O., Fortunato, M., and Jaitly, N. (2015). Pointer networks. In *Advances in Neural Information Processing Systems 28*, pages 2692–2700.

Zeiler, M. D. (2012). ADADELTA: An Adaptive Learning Rate Method. *CoRR*, abs/1212.5701.

Neural Morphological Tagging
of Lemma Sequences for Machine Translation

Costanza Conforti   cc918@cam.ac.uk
Matthias Huck   mhuck@cis.lmu.de
Alexander Fraser   fraser@cis.lmu.de
Center for Information and Language Processing, LMU Munich, Munich, Germany

Abstract

Translation to morphologically rich languages is a difficult task because of sparsity caused by
morphological richness. In this work we perform a pilot study on predicting the morphologically rich POS tags of sequences of lemmas. Similar studies have been conducted in the context
of phrase-based statistical machine translation. We implement a state-of-the-art tagger taking
lemmas as input and show that we can successfully predict the morphologically rich POS tags,
with accuracies of up to 91%.

1   Introduction

Modeling sequences of tokens in morphologically rich languages (MRLs) is a difficult task of
great importance in many applications of NLP. For instance, translation from a morphologically
poor language (such as English) to an MRL (such as German or Czech) is known to be difficult.
An effective approach for modeling MRLs is to break the sequence into a factorized representation, such as lemmas paired with their morphologically rich POS representations (e.g., for a
German noun, the rich representation includes the noun POS tag, and the three grammatical
features gender, number, and case).

In this paper, we assume that we have a good system for generating lemmas and study
whether we can automatically recover the morphologically rich POS representation. This is
more difficult than morphologically rich POS tagging, which takes a sequence of surface forms
and recovers the most likely morphologically rich POS representation, because lemma input
is underspecified. This task was previously studied by Minkov et al. (2007). We differ in
two ways: (1.) we implement a state-of-the-art neural tagger, rather than a Maximum Entropy
Markov model, and (2.) we predict rich morphological POS, rather than surface forms.

Studying the prediction of morphologically rich POS given lemmas is an interesting problem in its own right. It has implications for NLP applications involving the generation of MRL
sentences including machine translation. A concrete application is to apply it in an end-to-end
MT system. Similar morphological prediction systems have been applied by Toutanova et al.
(2008), Bojar and Kos (2010) and Fraser et al. (2012) in phrase-based SMT. A pipeline of such
a system is depicted in Figure 1.

Given the promising results in this initial study, we plan to combine our tagger with a
standard neural machine translation model, resulting in a multi-task system which produces
pairs of lemmas and morphologically rich POS tags. An important benefit of such a system
over previous approaches which produce such pairs directly using a standard NMT model (e.g.,
Tamchyna et al. (2017)) is that we will be able to train it in a multi-task fashion, where some

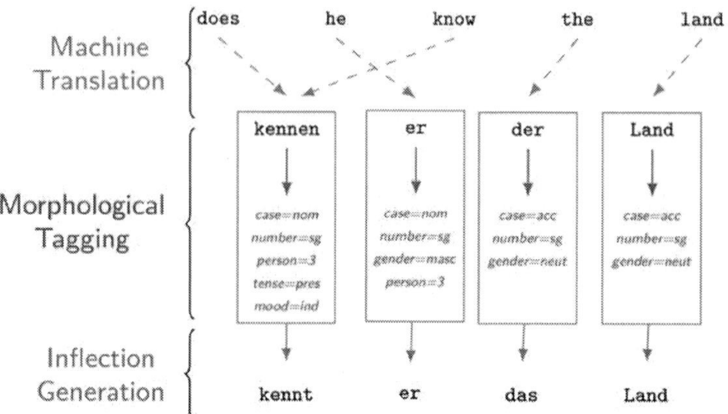

Figure 1: Example of a machine translation system using our morphology tagger (in red) as an intermediate step in the translation process into a target MRL.

training examples contain source language text (from parallel data), while others do not (from monolingual data).

In this paper, we present our language-independent neural tagging system implemented and trained for this task. German, an MRL belonging to the Indo-European family, has been chosen for a case study. This choice is motivated by the fact that, within MRLs, German has been widely studied in recent years, and many resources are publicly available.

2 Motivation

2.1 Rich Morphology in Machine Translation: Still Challenging

MRLs are difficult to deal with in natural language processing applications. Naive technological approaches without any proper analysis and modeling of morphological phenomena tend to result in underperforming systems for MRLs. Computational morphology research is therefore a long-standing subdiscipline of NLP, with an impact on almost any use case that involves an MRL. Information retrieval systems have traditionally benefited from stemmers or lemmatizers, which reduce inflected surface forms to a word stem or a canonical form. In MT, translating *from* source-side English *into* an MRL is notoriously more difficult than the other way around (Bojar et al., 2017). The English→MRL direction requires the system to decide amongst many possible inflected forms on the output side. The source-side lexical counterpart is morphologically underspecified, which complicates both statistical modeling and search. Data-driven approaches over MRLs furthermore suffer eminently from data sparsity issues under medium- to low-resource conditions. Many inflected forms are observed rarely.

Source-side MRL. Rich morphology on the source side can to some extent be tackled via preprocessing. Syntactic and morphological analyzers can be employed, based on which a source sentence representation can be constructed which is more appropriate as the input to a translation system (Popović and Ney, 2004; Popović et al., 2005; Goldwater and McClosky, 2005). E.g., certain morphological features of the source words may be dismissed beforehand. Non-reversible modifications are uncritical on the source side and can potentially alleviate the modeling problem and counteract data sparsity. Arabic is a prominent example of a language that typically undergoes heavy morphosyntactic analysis and preprocessing on the source side (Lee, 2004; Habash and Sadat, 2006; Hasan et al., 2011).

Target-side MRL.   The more challenging question of how to tackle rich morphology on the target side has undergone quite some research. Factored phrase-based models (Koehn and Hoang, 2007) can be used to produce inflected output via a separate decoding path and a generation step (Bojar, 2007). The blow-up of the search space can make such models impractical. Backoff techniques (Koehn and Haddow, 2012) or flat factored models with supplementary features over lemmas and linguistic annotation (Stymne et al., 2008; Huck and Birch, 2015) are more tractable alternatives.

Phrase-based translation models, accompanied with n-gram language models, have a relatively limited local view. Some morphological phenomena go beyond local context and require agreement across long distances. In syntax-based systems with a chart-based decoding procedure, engineering adequate agreement constraints is more viable (Williams and Koehn, 2011, 2014). Pursuing a different idea, Avramidis and Koehn (2008) and Daiber and Sima'an (2015) have attempted to annotate input sentences beforehand with morphological features that are exhibited by the target-side MRL, thus taking the burden of the inflection selection away from the phrase-based decoder. Chahuneau et al. (2013) and Huck et al. (2017c), on the other hand, have specifically looked into how to produce unseen morphological variants without resorting to a factored generation step. To that end, they augment their phrase tables with synthetic entries.

Other researchers have proposed two-step approaches to MT into MRLs, where the output of the first step (the actual translation) lacks certain morphological features of the MRL, which in turn have to be predicted by a separate module in a second step in order to end up with inflected target language sentences (Toutanova et al., 2008; Fraser et al., 2012). Slightly less supervision might be required by another technique for tackling rich morphology on the target side: word segmentation, and subsequent modeling on a subword level. Inflected target words in the training data can e.g. be segmented into stems and morphological affixes (Fishel and Kirik, 2010; Clifton and Sarkar, 2011; Passban et al., 2017). The segmentation of output hypotheses of the MT system needs to be reverted in postprocessing.

In modern neural machine translation engines, word segmentation by means of a Byte Pair Encoding (BPE) style algorithm is a common trick to shrink the vocabulary size (Sennrich et al., 2016). Recent research has shown that NMT of MRLs benefits from word segmentation techniques that are linguistically more informed than plain BPE (Ataman et al., 2017; Pinnis et al., 2017; Huck et al., 2017b,a). Not all prior research on MRLs in traditional phrase-based MT can be readily transferred to NMT. One of the most promising attemps to date is following the theme of two-step MT. A second-step module generates inflections from lemmas and morphological tags. The first-step NMT module outputs interleaved sequences of such lemmas and their respective tags (Burlot et al., 2016, 2017; Tamchyna et al., 2017). Research on how to best model morphology with neural networks is ongoing, in MT and in other areas of NLP (Botha and Blunsom, 2014; Ebert et al., 2016; Vania and Lopez, 2017; Belinkov et al., 2017; García-Martínez et al., 2016; García-Martínez et al., 2017; Burlot and Yvon, 2017).

2.2   Morphological Tagging of Lemmas: Utility and Limitations

Morphological tagging is the task of marking up each token in an input sequence with the corresponding morphological features which describe its inflectional properties. In the case of morphologically poor languages, a word can usually be described sufficiently using information about its POS tag (Mueller et al., 2013). MRLs require a more detailed analysis. The term MRL refers to a language where word shapes encode a consistent number of syntactic and semantic features. This behavior is particularly productive in fusional and agglutinating languages, where it can involve both verbal conjugation and nominal declination. In these situations, a more accurate morphological label is usually attached to the POS tag. For this reason, morphological tagging has been also defined as fine-grained POS tagging (Labeau et al., 2015).

A divide-and-conquer approach is often adopted to deal with data sparsity in MRLs. First, the MRL inflectional structure is simplified, thus reducing the number of word types and consequently data sparsity. Then, the NLP task is carried out over the simplified MRL data. Finally, the complete MRL's inflection is reconstructed as a separate post-processing step. In this way, a complex problem is decoupled into approachable subtasks. Previous authors have pursued this approach in MT, e.g. from English or Chinese into simplified representations of MRLs like Czech (Bojar, 2007), German (Fraser et al., 2012), Spanish (Costa-Jussà and Escolano, 2016). A disadvantage of these previous attempts is that they require a careful, linguistically-motivated analysis in order to optimize the choice of morphological features which can be removed from the MRL, thus decreasing data sparsity, without increasing the difficulty of the final morphology generation step too much (as in Costa-Jussà and Escolano (2016)). In this work, by contrast, we investigate the possibility of generating morphological annotations from *completely underspecified* input sequences. We implement and train a neural morphological tagger which deals with lemma sequences. The lemmas are uninflected canonical base forms with no morphological features at all. Given a morphologically fully underspecified lemma sequence, the task considered in this work consists of annotating each input symbol with the complete set of morphological features needed to generate the inflected word forms.

However, in our approach, not all morphological features can in each and every case accurately be recovered from target-side lemma sequences only, without ever taking the source sentence into account. Consider the English sentence *"the flowers are blossoming"* and its German translation *"die Blumen blühen"*. The German lemma sequence is *"der Blume blühen"*. Rather than annotating the article lemma *"der"*, the noun lemma *"Blume"*, and the verb lemma *"blühen"* as plural each, a morphological tagger could just as well predict singular here, resulting in the grammatically correct sentence *"die Blume blüht"* (English: *"the flower is blossoming"*). Under many circumstances, however, our morphological tagger is able to correctly disambiguate most features. E.g., for the English sentences (1.) *"a flower is blossoming"* and (2.) *"many flowers are blossoming"* with their respective German lemma correspondences (1.) *"ein Blume blühen"* and (2.) *"viel Blume blühen"*, the number feature can be unambiguously established from the first lemma in each of the two German lemma sequences, the indefinite article *"ein"* and the adverb *"viel"*. Given their context, noun and verb should also be annotated correctly as singular in the first example and plural in the second. In ambiguous cases, the morphological tagger will benefit from such contextual clues, as well as from the semantics of the lemmas, their syntactic order, and co-occurrence frequencies in the training data. Our neural morphological tagger performs very well on the very difficult task of predicting rich POS from this very underspecified representation.

3 A Neural Architecture for Morphological Tagging of Lemmas

We consider a tagging task in which, given a lemmatized input sequence $\mathbf{x} = \{x_1, x_2, ..., x_N\}$, each input symbol is assigned one out of a set $\mathcal{T}$ of predefined fine-grained tags, resulting in the output sequence $\mathbf{y} = \{y_1, y_2, ..., y_N\}$, where $\mathbf{x}$ and $\mathbf{y}$ have the same length N. Our architecture leverages information coming from multiple input channels. For each token, three features are considered, none of which requires any language-specific tool to be extracted:

- **Lemma.** The input token itself, which is a canonical word form.
- **Capitalization.** Following Collobert et al. (2011) and Santos and Zadrozny (2014), a capitalization feature has been implemented, which indicates whether a given lemma is completely uppercased, completely lowercased, capitalized, contains at least one uppercase character in a position other than the first, or none of these cases. Encoding information about the capitalization of a token can be useful, in particular for unknown input symbols.

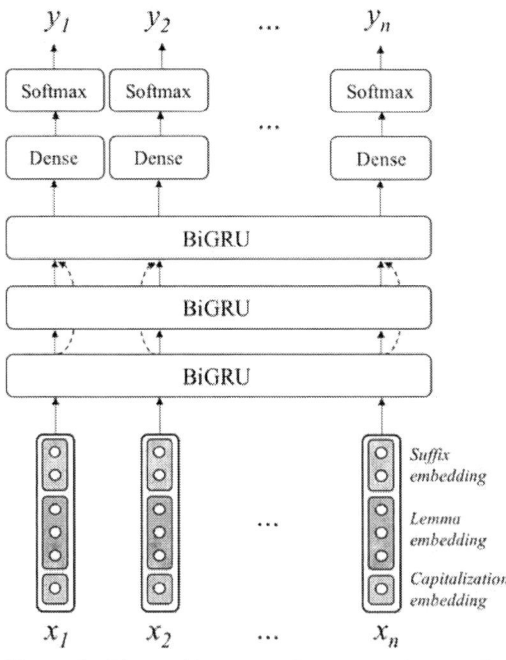

Figure 2: The architecture of our neural network model for morphological tagging.

Tagset	Tagset size	Avg. # labels/stem	Max. # labels/stem
morph	255	3.96	96
POS+morph	678	4.00	128

Table 1: Tagset statistics.

Feature	Values
Gender	`Masc, Fem, Neut, *`
Case	`Nom, Gen, Dat, Acc, *`
Number	`Sg, Pl, *`
Person	`1, 2, 3`
Degree	`Pos, Comp, Sup`
Tense	`Pres, Past`
Mood	`Ind, Subj, Imp`

Table 2: Morphological features.

Parameter	Value
batch size	32
optimizer	adadelta
dropout	0.3
lemma embedding size	128
suffix embedding size	40
capitalization embedding size	10
recurrent layer size	256

Table 3: Hyperparameters of the network.

- **Suffix.** For our purposes, a suffix is defined as the last n characters of a token. Suffixes can be indicative of a lemma's syntactic category, or POS. As the inflection pattern largely depends on the POS, suffixes can also help predict the morphological features of lemmas.

3.1 Neural Network Components

The proposed architecture is composed of a series of modules, or layers (Figure 2). Given an input sequence of length N, in the first layer each input symbol is mapped to three one-hot vector representations, corresponding to the three features described above. The one-hot vector representations are then projected into real-valued dense vector representations (embeddings). The lemma, the capitalization, and the suffix embeddings are then concatenated in order to obtain a single vector representation for each input symbol.

The central body of the architecture are three stacked bidirectional recurrent layers, using GRUs as recurrent cells. The choice of bidirectional recurrent layers over traditional feedforward layer was motivated by the promising results obtained in other labeling tasks, such as named entity recognition (Lample et al., 2016). The use of GRUs was preferred over LSTMs because their simpler internal structure allows for faster training, showing comparable results in preliminary experiments. Inspired by Heigold et al. (2016), we add *skip connections* between the first and the third bidirectional recurrent layer to allow for direct propagation of information between layers at different levels of depth. At the top of the architecture, a time-distributed densely-connected layer produces one $|\mathcal{T}|$-dimensional vector per time step, where $|\mathcal{T}|$ is the tagset size. Finally, the output label at each time step is given by a softmax operation over the tagset. The weights of the network (θ) are jointly estimated using the conditional log-likelihood $F(\theta) = -\sum_{n=1}^{N} \log p_\theta(y_n|x_1, ..., x_N)$.

3.2 Training

In order to train our neural model, a high amount of lemmatized data, tagged with morphological annotations, is required. In a multi-component end-to-end NLP system that involves our tagger, one would typically strive for a good match between the training data of the tagger and the training data of the other components, so as to achieve ideal interaction between them. But corpora that are manually annotated with lemma and fine-grained POS will rarely ever be at hand for most tasks. Common practice in most practical scenarios would be to synthetically annotate the task-specific training corpus. We follow this real-world rationale and work with synthetic annotation in our study.

Data and preprocessing. We train on the Europarl v7 corpus (Koehn, 2005). The conventional Europarl test sets (*test2006*, *test2007*, *test2008*) that had been released for the WMT shared task are used for development and testing.[1] Our main tagging evaluation results will be reported on *test2007*, which we abbreviate as *test* in most tables, while *test2006* serves as our *dev* set. The corpora are tokenized and frequent-cased using scripts from the Moses toolkit.[2] They are then annotated with lemmas, POS tags, and morphological tags with the pretrained tagging model for German provided by the MARMOT toolkit.[3] MARMOT is a CRF-based tagger with a reported accuracy of 97.94 for POS tagging and of 91.65 for morphological annotations on the TIGER test set (Mueller et al., 2013). The toolkit produces lemmas using LEMMING (Müller et al., 2015), a language-independent token-based lemmatizer which is reaching state-of-the-art accuracy of 98.10 for the German language. Our training corpus contains 1.9M sentences, the dev and test set 2,000 sentences each.

Tagsets. As in (Mueller et al., 2013), two tagsets are considered in our work. The first tagset (morph) is composed of morphological annotations, while the second (POS+morph) is obtained by concatenating the POS tag and the morphological annotation of each input lemma. For example, the lemma "Parlament" in the context "im Parlament" (in the parliament) would receive the POS+morph label `NN+case=dat|number=sg|gender=neut`, where `NN` is the POS tag and the segment `case=dat|number=sg|gender=neut` corresponds to the morph label, specifying the values taken by the morphological features case, number, and gender. As shown in Table 1, considering POS+morph labels increases both tagset size and classification ambiguity. Morphological labels show a compositional property (Cotterell and Schütze, 2015). In fact, each label is represented by a concatenation operation over a set of `feature : value` pairs. Table 2 reports the morphological features used for annotation. Some features are specific to certain word classes, such as mood for finite verbs. Other features can occur in more contexts, such as gender and case (articles, pronouns, adjectives, and nouns).

Vocabularies. In order to increase training speed, we reduce the lemma vocabulary to the 40K most frequent entries. This allows for an OOV rate of 0.016 over the training and of 0.019 on the test sets. After some preliminary experiments, we commited to suffixes of size $n = 4$. No vocabulary reduction is performed on the suffix vocabulary.

Model setup. Neural models are trained to predict labels from the two tagsets, morph and POS+morph, respectively. The same hyperparameters of the network architecture are configured for both models (Table 3). During training, the input sequences are padded or cut up to the length of 70 tokens for the morph tagset and of 60 for the POS+morph tagset. At test time, the sentences are padded up to the length of the longest sequence in the dataset. Our implementation takes around one week to train 15 epochs on a Nvidia GeForce GTX 750 GPU.

---

[1] `http://www.matrix.statmt.org/test_sets/list/`
[2] `https://github.com/moses-smt/mosesdecoder/`
[3] `https://github.com/muelletm/cistern/tree/master/marmot`

Tagset	Max. Freq.		Freq. Lookup		CRF		Our Neural Tagger	
	dev	test	dev	test	dev	test	dev	test
morph	39.15	38.92	59.97	60.32	87.77	87.91	**91.22**	**91.34**
POS+morph	7.65	7.47	56.52	56.78	86.96	86.78	**90.61**	**90.92**

Table 4: Accuracy obtained on morphological tagging of lemmas considering morph and POS+morph tagsets.

4 Empirical Evaluation

Three non-neural baselines have been built to provide lower bounds, two dummy classifiers and a CRF-based model:

- **Maximum frequency.** The first baseline (Max. Freq.) always predicts the most frequent label in the tagset.
- **Frequency lookup.** The second baseline (Freq. Lookup) uses a lookup table to return, for each lemma, the label it is most frequently annotated with in the training corpus.
- **CRF.** A CRF model was trained on the lemmatized Europarl corpus, using the MARMOT toolkit with its default parameters.

4.1 Intrinsic Evaluation: Tagging

Table 4 reports on the results of tagging on the development and test set. Our neural tagger clearly beats all the baselines taken as lower bound, considering both tagsets.

Quantitative analysis. In order to understand the performance of our models at predicting each single feature, the morphological labels were split into their components and performance is measured according to the following metrics:

- **F1-score A.** Performance is measured only across word classes which present the given feature in the gold. For example, degree is measured only in adjectives.
- **F1-score B.** Performance is measured across all word classes. If a given feature is not predicted for a label, or it is not present in the gold annotation, its value is set to an artificial NNN class. In this way, features which are correctly *not* predicted by the system, such as gender for verbs, count as true positives.

Results of this evaluation are reported in Table 5. The overall feature performance is satisfactory in line with both evaluation criteria. The performance scores for all features are slightly improved using the model predicting POS+morph labels. In fact, as POS tags are indicators of word classes, jointly predicting them with the morphological labels could help the system learn which features should be predicted and which should not be produced.

Considering evaluation of type A, the best results are obtained for the gender feature. Contrary to what happens for the other features, gender constitutes a lexical attribute of nouns, and an inflectional feature for other nominal constituents. This could have had the effect of simplifying the classification problem for nouns, thus also strengthening performance on dependent tokens, such as determiners and adjectives. Moving to evaluation of type B, an overall enhancement in performance can be observed for all features, suggesting that the systems are successfully able to learn when a certain morphological feature should be predicted or not.

In general, the performance of tagging with respect to single morphological features seems to highly depend on the distributional characteristics of the corpus, as well as on the relative balance within a single feature's values. Highest performance is obtained on the morphological features which present the highest support in the training set. Figure 3 reports the confusion

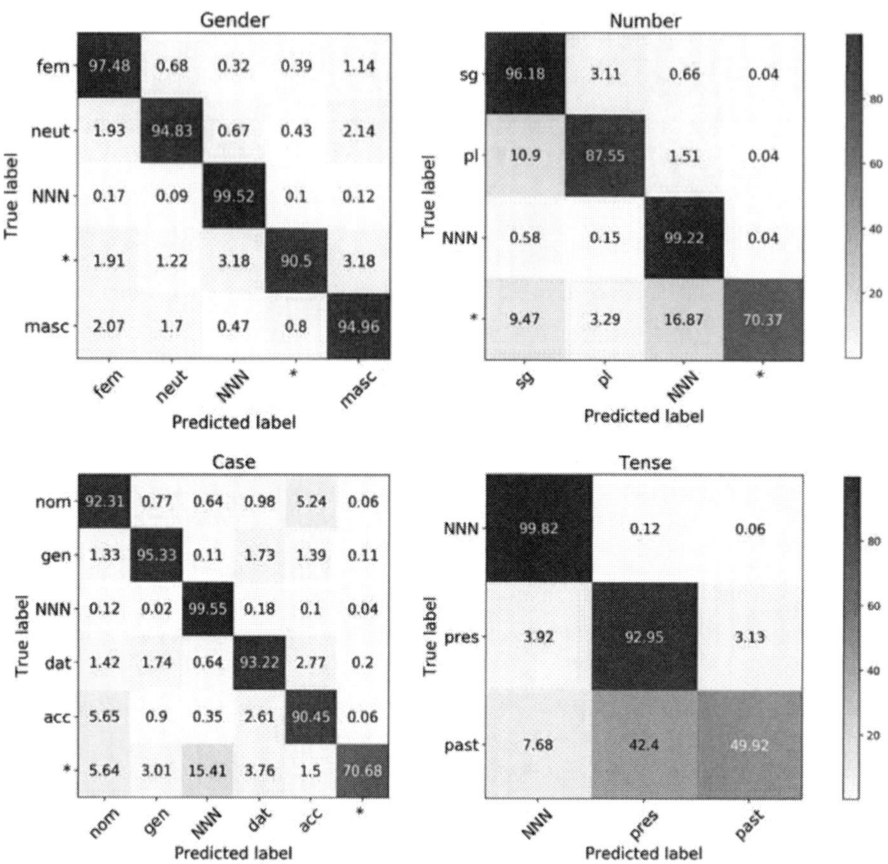

Figure 3: Normalized confusion matrices considering the morphological features gender, number, case, and tense. The value NNN refers to morphological labels where the given feature is *not* present in gold or predicted by the system, while ⋆ indicates that the given feature is present or predicted, but undefined.

Morph Feature	Support (% in train set)	Number of values	morph labels		POS+morph labels	
			F1-score A	F1-score B	F1-score A	F1-score B
POS	100.00	48	-	-	98.45	98.45
Case	50.41	5	93.69	96.41	93.87	96.52
Gender	49.86	4	96.57	97.93	96.61	97.94
Number	58.05	3	95.12	96.63	94.99	96.57
Person	12.00	3	94.69	99.52	94.70	99.56
Degree	8.42	3	82.36	99.63	82.21	99.63
Mood	7.65	2	90.14	99.27	90.01	99.29
Tense	7.64	2	85.06	98.86	85.44	98.90

Table 5: Performance of tagging considering single morphological features. Support is defined as the number of labels where a given feature is defined, divided by the total number of labels in the training set.

matrices of case and gender, two highly frequent morphological features which distinguish between the highest number of possible values. Considering case, the tagger was able to learn to discriminate relatively well between the four cases, due to their distributionally different characteristics. The highest number of misclassifications occurs between Nom and Acc, which present some similar distributional patterns in the German language. Excluding the $\star$ value, which occurs with a support lower than 1%, the lowest performance is obtained on Gen, which is also the less frequent value for this morphological feature. Moving to gender, the best performance is achieved with Fem. This is not only the most frequent value, but also the gender which contains most of the substantives obtained through derivational morphology (Matthews, 1991), thus presenting a pattern which can be easily spotted by the suffix feature. In contrast, misclassifications are more common in case of morphological features which present a high class imbalance, especially when the classes tend to appear in similar context. This is exemplified by the features number and tense, whose confusion matrices are reported in Figure 3. In the case of number, the morphological feature with the highest support, our tagger tends to misclassify Plur occurrences in favour of the most frequent value Sing, which occurs roughly twice as often. The same pattern can be observed also in the confusion matrix of tense, a feature with a considerably lower support in the training corpus (as it occurs only for verbs). Here, the extreme feature imbalance induces the system to wrongly label almost half of the Past occurrences as Pres, which accounts alone for almost 85% of the training samples.

Qualitative analysis. These observations are supported by a qualitative analysis of the systems' output on the test set[4]. In particular, our tagger is able to learn to produce verbs in the correct tense when an explicit temporal mention is present in the sentence, as in the example below, which contains both a past and a present adverbs (in italics):

> Wie ich bereits *gestern Abend* sagte, und ich tue dies *heute* erneut, [...]
> *As I said last night - I will say it again today, [...]*

Number can be disambiguated when a clue such as *viel* (En.: *many*) is found:

> [...], enthält der diesjährige Haushaltsentwurf viele politische Botschaften [...]
> *[...], there are many political announcements coming out of this year's Budget [...]*

Moreover, our system can also learn complex distributional patterns, being also able to cope with long-distance dependencies. In the following example, the combination of the two modal verbs *hätten ... müssen* (separated by 16 tokens) can only accept the Subj mood. The tagger correctly predicts:

> Dann *hätten* sich die französischen Behörden [...] an uns *wenden müssen*.
> *The French authorities ought to have consulted us [...]*

However, when no explicit clue is present in the sentence, and the distributional characteristics of a morphological feature's values are similar, the tagger chooses the value which was most frequently associated with the given lemma in the training corpus, such as the Plur Number considering the substantive in the Nominative case *Nachbarland* (English: *neighbouring country*):

> Unsere Nachbarländer haben (*correct*: Unser Nachbarland hat) sich [...] während der letzten zehn Jahre [...] bemüht.
> *Our neighbouring countries have (correct: Our neighbouring country has) struggled [...] over the last decade [...]*

---

[4]For the sake of clarity, in this section we report the re-inflected samples obtained using the predicted morphological labels, instead of showing the labels themselves (which could be difficult to interpret).

Our Tagger					LAMB	
Suffix Embeddings			Lemma Embeddings			
-ISCH	-RUNG	-EREN	SOLIDARISCH	KOOPERATION	SOLIDARISCH	KOOPERATION
-lich	-lung	-rken	generell	Kommunikation	Solidarität	Zusammenarbeit
-ativ	-hung	-ösen	uneingeschränkt	Kohäsion	Elitenförderung	Kooperationsprojekt
-rell	-tung	-üben	systematisch	Steuerung	Selbstverantwortung	Gemeinschaftsprojekt
-iell	-gung	-üfen	schrittweise	Produktion	Lebensrecht	Kooperationsvertrag

Table 6: 4-nearest neighbors of the embeddings encoding of three suffixes (columns 1-3) and two lemmas (columns 4-5) from the training set, computed using cosine similarity on the vectors jointly learned by our POS+morph neural tagger after 15 epochs. The 4-nearest neighbors of the corresponding purely semantic LAMB lemma embeddings (Ebert et al., 2016) are reported for comparison purposes (columns 6-7).

In fact, where the sentence offers no clue to disambiguate a particular morphological feature, it is in principle impossible to recover the correct feature's value from the lemmatized sequence. The system can rely only on the statistical characteristics of the corpus to infer it. It should be observed, however, that even when the system predicts a wrong morphological feature, the complete sequence of labels is nevertheless usually grammatical and coherent, as shown in the example above (where the singular subject *unser Nachbarland* agrees in number with the principal verb *hat*).

An analysis of the embedding matrices jointly learned during training shows that our model is able to learn complex relations of *morphological similarity*, leveraging information coming from both lemmas and suffixes. As reported in Table 6, our learned suffix embeddings tend to cluster together with suffixes denoting the same word class (adjectives for *-isch*, feminine nouns for *-rung*, and verbs for *-eren*). This holds true also for lemma embeddings, which cluster with input symbols belonging to the same morphological class, and with which they share almost no semantic content. This is particularly evident when comparing our learned lemma embeddings with the purely semantic LAMB embeddings (Ebert et al., 2016). The nearest neighbor of the lemmatized adjective *solidarisch* (En.: *solidary*) in our model is the adjective *generell* (En.: *general*), while the corresponding LAMB nearest neighbor is the noun *Solidarität* (En.: *solidarity*), as reported in Table 6. For *Kooperation* (feminine noun, En.: *cooperation*), the nearest neighbors in our space are all feminine nouns, while the nearest LAMB vectors are semantically related nouns with different genders.

4.2 Extrinsic Evaluation: Inflection Generation

Inflection generation, also called *morphology generation*, is the NLP task of generating an inflected word from its lemma paired with its morphological tag. This task offers a nice opportunity for an extrinsic evaluation of our tagger's predictions. We implemented an inexpensive lookup-based inflection generation system. At each position i, the inflected word w_i corresponding to the lemma l_i is produced according to the following chain of backoff operations:

1. POS+morph bigram$_{+1}$: $\max_{w_i}(count(\{(l_i, t_i, t_{i+1}) \to w_i\}))$
2. POS+morph unigram: $\max_{w_i}(count(\{(l_i, t_i) \to w_i\}))$
3. Lemma bigram$_{+1}$: $\max_{w_i}(count(\{(l_i, l_{i+1}) \to w_i\}))$
4. Lemma unigram: $\max_{w_i}(count(\{(l_i) \to w_i\}))$
5. Unseen lemma: $l_i \to l_i$

where t_i corresponds to the POS+morph label predicted by our tagger. Lookup tables are calculated over the training corpus.

MT System	Lemma-BLEU	
	test2007	test2008
Baseline	28.9	28.7
Lemma NMT	29.3	29.2

Table 7: Quality of lemma translation. Baseline hypothesis translations and references have been lemmatized with LEMMING.

MT System	BLEU	
	test2007	test2008
Baseline	25.8	25.7
Pipelined	24.8	24.5

Table 8: Machine translation quality. We report case-sensitive BLEU of fully inflected, postprocessed translations.

Reinflection accuracy over the test set reaches **99.22** using gold labels, and **95.54** using our predicted labels. We believe that adopting state-of-the-art neural inflection generation systems such as the one by Kann and Schütze (2016), or using language-specific tools, as done in previous works on German (Fraser et al., 2012) and Spanish (Costa-Jussà and Escolano, 2016), could further enhance this performance. The purpose of this extrinsic evaluation, however, was not to propose a new competitive Inflection Generation system, but rather to prove that our labels constitute a good input to such a system and that, even with the limitations discussed in the previous section, it is possible to obtain satisfactory results in reconstructing the inflection of lemmatized input.

4.3 Machine Translation Evaluation

We build neural machine translation engines to evaluate the pipelined MT approach as illustrated in Figure 1. For comparison, a baseline NMT system translates directly from English to fully inflected German word surface forms. The pipelined architecture from Figure 1 is evaluated against this baseline. For the pipelined architecture, we train an NMT engine on a parallel corpus with lemmatized German target side. At test time, the latter engine performs the first step (MT from English words to German lemmas) in the pipeline. The second step is conducted by our tagger, which annotates the lemma hypothesis translation with morphological tags. Finally, the lookup-based inflection generator from Section 4.2 is employed to map the paired lemmas and predicted morphological tags to inflected German words.

We use the Nematus toolkit's implementation of encoder-decoder NMT with attention and GRUs (Sennrich et al., 2017). We train and test on the English–German Europarl data. In the NMT systems' training corpus, words are tokenized and frequent-cased, then segmented via byte-pair-encoding (BPE) (Sennrich et al., 2016) with 50K merge operations; likewise for lemmas, but with BPE operations extracted from the lemmatized data. We configure dimensions of 500 for the embeddings and 1024 for the hidden layer. We train with the Adam optimizer, a learning rate of 0.0001, batch size of 50, and dropout with probability 0.2 applied to the hidden layer. Translation quality is measured case-sensitive with BLEU (Papineni et al., 2002).

In Table 7, we use BLEU computed on lemmas (Lemma-BLEU), to show that we get a small gain in lexical choice (of the lemma) in the pipelined approach, where the NMT engine is trained to produce lemmas. However, the BLEU scores over fully inflected words in Table 8 suggest that a simple pipelined approach is not sufficient for end-to-end MT. We looked at the MT output and saw that it was mostly coherent, but there was confusion on features like number, tense, and mood. The slightly improved lexical choice of the lemma does not compensate for the loss that derives from the inherent limitations of completely decoupling lemma prediction and morphology prediction, as was discussed intuitively in Section 2.2 and later highlighted in detail empirically (Section 4.1, Figure 3, Table 5). The neural architecture yields surprisingly strong accuracy at morphological tagging of lemma sequences, but the pipelined approach from Figure 1 with completely underspecified lemma sequences and strict decoupling of the different components is too limiting for MT.

5   Relation to Previous Work on Morphological Tagging

Morphological tagging of inflected sequences.   Fine-grained tagging of completely under-specified lemma sequences has not been studied much before, possibly because earlier non-neural models were deemed not powerful enough to tackle the task. Morphological tagging of inflected words, however, has been intensely investigated. The best performance for German (92% accuracy on TIGER) was achieved by Heigold et al. (2016) with a neural system which combines word and character embeddings. As observed by Santos and Zadrozny (2014) for POS tagging, character embeddings are particularly useful for processing MRLs, since they can help spot inflectional regularities. However, when dealing with completely uninflected input, this property is less useful. It is true that lemmas sometimes retain some kind of morphological information, like in derivation; however, this can be easily captured with suffix embeddings. In fact, a character-based model did not outperform our architecture in preliminary experiments.

Morphological tagging of (partially) underspecified sequences.   Recently, Costa-Jussà and Escolano (2016) proposed a three-staged approach to Chinese–Spanish MT. First, a statistical MT system translates from Chinese into a morphologically impoverished version of Spanish which does not present two features: number and gender. Then, two neural classifiers separately annotate the simplified Spanish tokens with the missing features. As a last step, full forms are generated.In this way, the authors claim to beat the previous state-of-the-art performance for this specific language pair, reaching a classification accuracy higher than 90% on both features. No direct comparison can be drawn with our system, since their separate neural classifiers are trained on *partially uninflected* input (all other morphological features are still present). In our work, on the contrary, *all* features are considered. In particular, instead of *separately* training a different network for each feature, our single architecture makes one *joint* decision at each time step. In this way, our system, which is trained for a more complex task, can reach good results on all features. Furthermore, our choice of a joint prediction strategy allows for a *completely language-independent* approach. The carefully selected morphological simplification proposed by Costa-Jussà and Escolano (2016) would not generalize to other language pairs.

6   Conclusion

This work introduces a system for morphological tagging over lemmatized (that is, completely unspecified) input sequences. A detailed intrinsic and extrinsic evaluation showed that our language independent tagger reaches a very high performance by jointly predicting up to 8 morphological features, leading up to 678 possible combinations (considering POS+morph labels).

As a next step we will explore the implementation of a a multi-task system which produces pairs of lemmas and morphological labels. Niehues and Cho (2017) explored a multi-task NMT system producing coarse POS labels for the source language as well as words in the target language. We will instead produce lemmas in the target language, and at the same time use our tagger component to produce rich target POS. By giving our tagger access to the source sentences, we will overcome the limitations in our currently semantically underspecified representation, where, e.g., plural is not marked. Importantly, we will be able to train this system in a multi-task fashion, where some training examples contain source language text (from parallel data), while others do not. These examples will be taken from target monolingual data, allowing us to learn from large monolingual corpora how to inflect lemmas, as we did in this paper.

Acknowledgments

This work has received funding from the European Research Council (ERC) under grant agreement № 640550. We thank the anonymous reviewers of this paper for their efforts and for the constructive comments and suggestions.

References

Ataman, D., Negri, M., Turchi, M., and Federico, M. (2017). Linguistically Motivated Vocabulary Reduction for Neural Machine Translation from Turkish to English. *PBML*, 108:331–342.

Avramidis, E. and Koehn, P. (2008). Enriching Morphologically Poor Languages for Statistical Machine Translation. In *Proc. of ACL*, pages 763–770, Columbus, OH, USA.

Belinkov, Y., Durrani, N., Dalvi, F., Sajjad, H., and Glass, J. (2017). What do Neural Machine Translation Models Learn about Morphology? In *Proc. of ACL*, pages 861–872, Vancouver, Canada.

Bojar, O. (2007). English-to-Czech Factored Machine Translation. In *Proc. of WMT*, pages 232–239, Prague, Czech Republic.

Bojar, O. et al. (2017). Findings of the 2017 Conference on Machine Translation (WMT17). In *Proc. of WMT*, pages 169–214, Copenhagen, Denmark.

Bojar, O. and Kos, K. (2010). 2010 Failures in English-Czech Phrase-Based MT. In *Proc. of WMT*, pages 60–66, Uppsala, Sweden.

Botha, J. A. and Blunsom, P. (2014). Compositional Morphology for Word Representations and Language Modelling. In *Proc. of ICML*, Beijing, China.

Burlot, F., García-Martínez, M., Barrault, L., Bougares, F., and Yvon, F. (2017). Word Representations in Factored Neural Machine Translation. In *Proc. of WMT*, pages 20–31, Copenhagen, Denmark.

Burlot, F., Knyazeva, E., Lavergne, T., and Yvon, F. (2016). Two-Step MT: Predicting Target Morphology. In *Proc. of IWSLT*, Seattle, WA, USA.

Burlot, F. and Yvon, F. (2017). Evaluating the morphological competence of Machine Translation Systems. In *Proc. of WMT*, pages 43–55, Copenhagen, Denmark.

Chahuneau, V., Schlinger, E., Smith, N. A., and Dyer, C. (2013). Translating into Morphologically Rich Languages with Synthetic Phrases. In *Proc. of EMNLP*, pages 1677–1687, Seattle, WA, USA.

Clifton, A. and Sarkar, A. (2011). Combining Morpheme-based Machine Translation with Post-processing Morpheme Prediction. In *Proc. of ACL*, pages 32–42, Portland, OR, USA.

Collobert, R., Weston, J., Bottou, L., Karlen, M., Kavukcuoglu, K., and Kuksa, P. (2011). Natural language processing (almost) from scratch. *Journal of Machine Learning Research*, 12(Aug):2493–2537.

Costa-Jussà, M. R. and Escolano, C. (2016). Morphology generation for statistical machine translation using deep learning techniques. *arXiv preprint arXiv:1610.02209*.

Cotterell, R. and Schütze, H. (2015). Morphological Word-Embeddings. In *Proc. of NAACL*, pages 1287–1292, Denver, CO, USA.

Daiber, J. and Sima'an, K. (2015). Machine Translation with Source-Predicted Target Morphology. In *Proc. of MT Summit*, pages 283–296, Miami, FL, USA.

Ebert, S., Müller, T., and Schütze, H. (2016). LAMB: A Good Shepherd of Morphologically Rich Languages. In *Proc. of EMNLP*, pages 742–752, Austin, TX, USA.

Fishel, M. and Kirik, H. (2010). Linguistically Motivated Unsupervised Segmentation for Machine Translation. In *Proc. of LREC*, Valletta, Malta.

Fraser, A., Weller, M., Cahill, A., and Cap, F. (2012). Modeling Inflection and Word-Formation in SMT. In *Proc. of EACL*, pages 664–674, Avignon, France.

García-Martínez, M., Barrault, L., and Bougares, F. (2016). Factored Neural Machine Translation. In *Proc. of IWSLT*, Seattle, WA, USA.

García-Martínez, M., Barrault, L., and Bougares, F. (2017). *Neural Machine Translation by Generating Multiple Linguistic Factors*, pages 21–31. Springer International Publishing, Cham.

Goldwater, S. and McClosky, D. (2005). Improving Statistical MT through Morphological Analysis. In *Proc. of EMNLP*, pages 676–683, Vancouver, BC, Canada.

Habash, N. and Sadat, F. (2006). Arabic Preprocessing Schemes for Statistical Machine Translation. In *Proc. of NAACL*, pages 49–52, New York City, USA.

Hasan, S., Mansour, S., and Ney, H. (2011). A comparison of segmentation methods and extended lexicon models for Arabic statistical machine translation. *Machine Translation*, pages 1–19.

Heigold, G., Neumann, G., and van Genabith, J. (2016). Neural morphological tagging from characters for morphologically rich languages. *arXiv preprint arXiv:1606.06640*.

Huck, M. and Birch, A. (2015). The Edinburgh Machine Translation Systems for IWSLT 2015. In *Proc. of IWSLT*, pages 31–38, Da Nang, Vietnam.

Huck, M., Braune, F., and Fraser, A. (2017a). LMU Munich's Neural Machine Translation Systems for News Articles and Health Information Texts. In *Proc. of WMT*, pages 315–322, Copenhagen, Denmark.

Huck, M., Riess, S., and Fraser, A. (2017b). Target-side Word Segmentation Strategies for Neural Machine Translation. In *Proc. of WMT*, pages 56–67, Copenhagen, Denmark.

Huck, M., Tamchyna, A., Bojar, O., and Fraser, A. (2017c). Producing Unseen Morphological Variants in Statistical Machine Translation. In *Proc. of EACL*, pages 369–375, Valencia, Spain.

Kann, K. and Schütze, H. (2016). MED: The LMU System for the SIGMORPHON 2016 Shared Task on Morphological Reinflection. In *Proc. of SIGMORPHON*, pages 62–70, Berlin, Germany.

Koehn, P. (2005). Europarl. A Parallel Corpus for Statistical Machine Translation. In *Proc. of MT Summit*, Phuket, Thailand.

Koehn, P. and Haddow, B. (2012). Interpolated Backoff for Factored Translation Models. In *Proc. of AMTA*, San Diego, CA, USA.

Koehn, P. and Hoang, H. (2007). Factored Translation Models. In *Proc. of EMNLP-CoNLL*, pages 868–876, Prague, Czech Republic.

Labeau, M., Löser, K., and Allauzen, A. (2015). Non-lexical neural architecture for fine-grained POS Tagging. In *Proc. of EMNLP*, pages 232–237, Lisbon, Portugal.

Lample, G., Ballesteros, M., Subramanian, S., Kawakami, K., and Dyer, C. (2016). Neural Architectures for Named Entity Recognition. In *Proc. of NAACL*, pages 260–270, San Diego, CA, USA.

Lee, Y.-S. (2004). Morphological Analysis for Statistical Machine Translation. In *Proc. of NAACL*, pages 57–60, Boston, MA, USA.

Matthews, P. H. (1991). Morphology (Cambridge Textbooks in Linguistics). *Cambridge University*.

Minkov, E., Toutanova, K., and Suzuki, H. (2007). Generating Complex Morphology for Machine Translation. In *Proc. of ACL*, pages 128–135, Prague, Czech Republic.

Mueller, T., Schmid, H., and Schütze, H. (2013). Efficient Higher-Order CRFs for Morphological Tagging. In *Proc. of EMNLP*, pages 322–332, Seattle, WA, USA.

Müller, T., Cotterell, R., Fraser, A., and Schütze, H. (2015). Joint Lemmatization and Morphological Tagging with Lemming. In *Proc. of EMNLP*, pages 2268–2274, Lisbon, Portugal.

Niehues, J. and Cho, E. (2017). Exploiting Linguistic Resources for Neural Machine Translation Using Multi-task Learning. In *Proc. of WMT*, pages 80–89, Copenhagen, Denmark.

Papineni, K., Roukos, S., Ward, T., and Zhu, W.-J. (2002). Bleu: a Method for Automatic Evaluation of Machine Translation. In *Proc. of ACL*, pages 311–318, Philadelphia, PA, USA.

Passban, P., Liu, Q., and Way, A. (2017). Providing Morphological Information for SMT Using Neural Networks. *PBML*, 108:271–282.

Pinnis, M., Krišlauks, R., Deksne, D., and Miks, T. (2017). *Neural Machine Translation for Morphologically Rich Languages with Improved Sub-word Units and Synthetic Data*, pages 237–245. Springer.

Popović, M. and Ney, H. (2004). Towards the Use of Word Stems and Suffixes for Statistical Machine Translation. In *Proc. of LREC*, pages 1585–1588, Lisbon, Portugal.

Popović, M., Vilar, D., Ney, H., Jovičić, S., and Šarić, Z. (2005). Augmenting a Small Parallel Text with Morpho-Syntactic Language Resources for Serbian-English Statistical Machine Translation. In *Proc. of the ACL Workshop on Building and Using Parallel Texts*, pages 41–48, Ann Arbor, MI, USA.

Santos, C. D. and Zadrozny, B. (2014). Learning Character-level Representations for Part-of-Speech Tagging. In *Proc. of ICML*, pages 1818–1826, Bejing, China.

Sennrich, R. et al. (2017). Nematus: a Toolkit for Neural Machine Translation. In *Proc. of EACL*, pages 65–68, Valencia, Spain.

Sennrich, R., Haddow, B., and Birch, A. (2016). Neural Machine Translation of Rare Words with Subword Units. In *Proc. of ACL*, pages 1715–1725, Berlin, Germany.

Stymne, S., Holmqvist, M., and Ahrenberg, L. (2008). Effects of Morphological Analysis in Translation between German and English. In *Proc. of WMT*, pages 135–138, Columbus, OH, USA.

Tamchyna, A., Weller-Di Marco, M., and Fraser, A. (2017). Modeling Target-Side Inflection in Neural Machine Translation. In *Proc. of WMT*, pages 32–42, Copenhagen, Denmark.

Toutanova, K., Suzuki, H., and Ruopp, A. (2008). Applying Morphology Generation Models to Machine Translation. In *Proc. of ACL*, pages 514–522, Columbus, OH, USA.

Vania, C. and Lopez, A. (2017). From Characters to Words to in Between: Do We Capture Morphology? In *Proc. of ACL*, pages 2016–2027, Vancouver, Canada.

Williams, P. and Koehn, P. (2011). Agreement Constraints for Statistical Machine Translation into German. In *Proc. of WMT*, pages 217–226, Edinburgh, Scotland.

Williams, P. and Koehn, P. (2014). Using Feature Structures to Improve Verb Translation in English-to-German Statistical MT. In *Proc. of HyTra*, pages 21–29, Gothenburg, Sweden.

Context Models for OOV Word Translation in Low-Resource Languages

Angli Liu anglil@cs.washington.edu
Department of Computer Science, University of Washington, Seattle, WA, 98195

Katrin Kirchhoff kk2@u.washington.edu
Department of Electrical Engineering, University of Washington, Seattle, WA, 98195

Abstract

Out-of-vocabulary word translation is a major problem for the translation of low-resource languages that suffer from a lack of parallel training data. This paper evaluates the contributions of target-language context models towards the translation of OOV words, specifically in those cases where OOV translations are derived from external knowledge sources, such as dictionaries. We develop both neural and non-neural context models and evaluate them within both phrase-based and self-attention based neural machine translation systems. Our results show that neural language models that integrate additional context beyond the current sentence are the most effective in disambiguating possible OOV word translations. We present an efficient second-pass lattice-rescoring method for wide-context neural language models and demonstrate performance improvements over state-of-the-art self-attention based neural MT systems in five out of six low-resource language pairs.

1 Introduction

Translation of out-of-vocabulary (OOV) words (words occurring in the test data but not in the training data) is of major importance in statistical machine translation (MT). It is a particularly difficult problem in low-resource languages, i.e., languages for which parallel training data is extremely sparse, requiring recourse to techniques that are complementary to standard statistical machine translation approaches. The approaches described in this paper were developed for scenarios where the training data comprises at most 100k sentences pairs. Most previous studies in this area have focused on how to generate translation candidates for OOV words, either by segmentation into subword units, projection from other languages, or by leveraging external knowledge sources like dictionaries. Often, however, these methods generate multiple candidates for each OOV word, and the MT system is insufficiently trained to choose the appropriate translation according to the context.

In this paper we address this problem by utilizing more sophisticated context models based on target-language information. In particular, we develop wide-context models that incorporate information from context beyond current sentence boundaries to resolve translation ambiguity.

We compare these against models incorporating information from the current sentence only, and evaluate neural models vs. count-based sentence completion and graph reranking models. All are evaluated within both phrase-based and attention-based neural machine translation models for 6 low-resource language pairs. Our paper makes several contributions:

- We evaluate recently proposed neural machine translation (NMT) architectures (purely attention-based neural MT) on low-resource languages and show that, contrary to previous results obtained with sequence-to-sequence models, neural MT performs similarly to phrase-based machine translation (PBMT) in these scenarios, without modifications to the basic model.

- We develop and compare several wide-context target-language based models for translation disambiguation and find that document-level neural language models are the most effective at resolving translation ambiguities.

- We present an efficient lattice rescoring algorithm for wide-context neural language models.

- We compare our approach against directly adding external translation resources to the training data and show that our approach provides small but consistent improvements on five out of six language pairs.

The rest of the paper is organized as follows. Section 2 discusses prior work on OOV translation. Section 3 describes our general approach and presents various context models for translation disambiguation. Section 4 describes the datasets and baseline systems. Section 5 provides experimental results followed by a final conclusion in Section 6.

2 Prior Work

Several techniques for OOV word translation have been developed in the past. The simplest of these involves copying OOV words from the source sentence to the MT output. This is a reasonable procedure if most OOV words can be assumed to be numbers or named entities that do not require transliteration. In traditional PBMT systems, the unknown words can simply be passed through to the output. NMT models typically map all OOVs (as well as rare words) to a single unknown word token. Luong et al. (2014) trained an NMT system using external word alignment information, which allowed the system to output positional information about OOVs, which were then translated using a dictionary trained from parallel data. Working within the context of neural sequence-to-sequence models with attention, Bahdanau et al. (2014) and Jean et al. (2014) pursued the same strategy, with the exception that alignment information was derived from the attention layer in the neural model rather than an external knowledge source. In Gulcehre et al. (2016) a pointer model was used that can perform both copying and dictionary lookup. None of these studies address the problem of translation ambiguities resulting from added external knowledge sources. In truly low-resource languages, a dictionary obtained from the parallel training data will not have sufficient information to translate OOVs in the test data, as most of these will never have occurred in the training data. External dictionaries could be used in this case, which however requires a principled method of choosing between different translations.

An alternative strategy to address the rare and unknown word problem is to use subword units, i.e., the original text is segmented into chunks of characters, individual characters, or byte sequences. In Chung et al. (2016), a pure character-level decoder is used while Luong and Manning (2016) use a mixed model where the word-level decoder can fall back on the character-level decoder. The byte-pair encoding (BPE) approach of Sennrich et al. (2015) segments the input text into subword units based on an iterative merging of frequent character n-grams and a fixed upper size of the subword inventory. The main motivation given for the subword unit approach is that often a transparent relationship exists between OOVs and other known words: compound words and morphological variants can benefit from substantial overlap with other words in the same language, and cognates and named entities benefit from cross-lingual overlap. However, in resource-poor settings a substantial percentage of OOVs has no overt relationship with other words; instead, genuinely novel translations must be produced for words that were never seen and that are unrelated to other words.

A third class of approaches tries to leverage cognates and lexical borrowing. Tsvetkov and Dyer (2015) show that OOV words in low-resource languages that are loan words from a high-resource language can be translated via the high-resource language. However, the translation of OOV words in that work uses a fixed lexicon, not taking possibly multiple candidates into consideration. Finally, other studies have tried to exploit additional monolingual data in the source and/or target language. In Irvine and Callison-Burch (2013) new translation pairs were induced from monolingual corpora based on predictive features such as document timestamps, topic features, word frequency, and orthographic features. Saluja et al. (2014) and Zhao et al. (2015) explored the possibility of extracting features from extra monolingual corpora to help cover untranslated phrases. Specifically, Saluja et al. (2014) induced new translation rules from monolingual data with a semi-supervised algorithm. Zhao et al. (2015) obtained translation rules for OOV words based on phrases with similar continuous representations for which a translation is known.

Most of the studies described above have focused on neural MT for language pairs with sufficient training data. Recent work on OOV translation for low-resource languages includes Gujral et al. (2016), where a combination of approaches (surface and word-embedding based word similarity, transliteration) is used to generate multiple translation candidates for each OOV to improve phrase-based MT. The choice of a particular translation is then made either by a target-side language model or by the translation model itself through a secondary phrase table enriched with OOV-specific features.

3   OOV Disambiguation With Context Models

Our goal is to facilitate the integration of externally generated translation candidates, such as translation dictionaries, by utilizing a larger amount of target-side context information. We adopt a second-pass lattice rescoring approach that is compatible with both phrase-based and neural MT systems (or their combination) and that can accommodate extra monolingual information without increasing the number of parameters of the MT system itself. OOVs in the MT system's output are expanded to all translation options of that word found in our external knowledge sources. Target-language context models, possibly including context from beyond the current sentence boundaries, are then used to assign a score to each possible path in the extended lattice representing a particular combination of OOV translation hypotheses (see Figure 1).

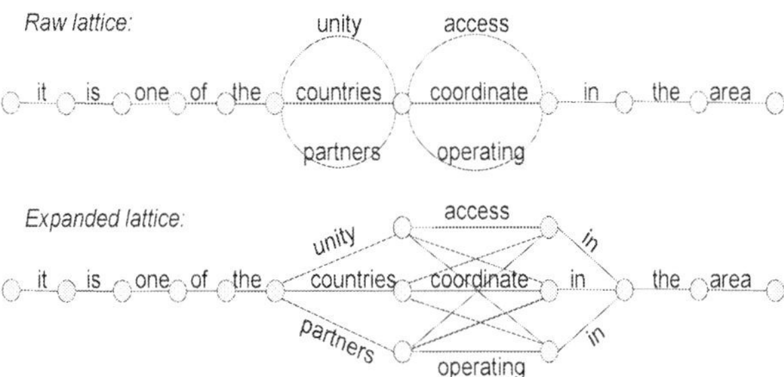

Figure 1: Compressed and expanded lattice representations of an MT hypothesis enriched with candidate translations of OOV words.

3.1 Count-Based Models

We compare several different models for rescoring, the simplest of which is a *sentence completion* model. OOV word translation can be formulated as sentence completion problem, where contextual information informs the filling of blanks in a sentence. Gubbins and Vlachos (2013) proposed to use a language model over a dependency tree for this task, whereas Woods (2016) and Röder et al. (2015) measure the degree of association between candidate words and other parts of the sentence using mutual information. In the same spirit our model chooses one out of several possible translation options for each OOV slot in the lattice based its average point-wise mutual information (PMI) with surrounding content words in the sentence (stopwords are ignored). PMI between words x and y is computed as:

$$PMI(x, y) = log \frac{P(x, y)}{P(x)P(y)} \tag{1}$$

The algorithm chooses one word at a time, proceeding from left to right. The chosen translation becomes part of the context used for computing PMI for the next set of OOV words. Therefore, the entire space of possible combinations of OOV translations is never fully explored but only searched greedily from left to right. Moreover, this method only focuses on content words and ignores word order in the PMI computation.

The second model is a graph-based reranking model (Mihalcea (2005); Yang and Kirchhoff (2012)), where an undirected graph is built over all OOV translation options and content words in a sentence. Graph edges are weighted with the same PMI values as in the sentence completion approach. PageRank (Page et al. (1999)) is then used to score each option based on 'votes' from connected words, and for each OOV slot, the options with the highest score is chosen. The PageRank score is computed as

$$R(v_i) = (1 - d) + d \cdot \sum_{j \in IN(v_i)} \frac{R(v_j)}{|OUT(v_j)|} \tag{2}$$

where v is a vertex in the graph, d is a damping factor, and $IN()$ and $OUT()$ are in-degree and out-degree of the vertex, respectively. The difference to the sentence completion approach is that the entire space of translation combinations is explored globally rather than greedily. The reason we use the two above methods as baselines is that they can be trained cheaply and readily allow the integration of a larger document context by simply extending the list of content words with words from the previous or following sentences.

3.2 Neural Models

We next turn to neural models. At the sentence-level we utilize a recurrent neural language model, specifically a two-layer long-short term memory (LSTM) model. In order to extend the sentence-level LSTM to include information from previous sentences we follow the approach in Ji et al. (2015), which proposed several variants of document-context language models (DCLMs). Here, we use an attentional DCLM, which enriches a standard recurrent neural network with a context vector aggregating the hidden vectors in the previous sentence. A standard RNN computes the probability over output classes as

$$\mathbf{y}_{s,n} = softmax(\mathbf{W}_o \mathbf{h}_{s,n} + \mathbf{b}) \tag{3}$$

where s is the current sentence, n is the current time step in the sentence, $\mathbf{h}$ is a hidden vector, $\mathbf{b}$ is a bias vector, and $\mathbf{W}$ is a weight matrix. The hidden vector $\mathbf{h}_{s,n}$ is computed as

$$\mathbf{h}_{s,n} = g(\mathbf{h}_{s,n-1}, \mathbf{x}_{s,n}) \tag{4}$$

where g is a non-linear function (in this case, representing a two-layer LSTM) and x is an input vector (current word embedding). The attentional DCLM adds a context vector $c_{s,n}$ to both the hidden and the output layer as follows:

$$\mathbf{h}_{s,n} = g(\mathbf{h}_{s,n-1}, [\mathbf{x}_{s,n}^T, \mathbf{c}_{s-1,n}^T]^T) \tag{5}$$

$$\mathbf{y}_{s,n} = softmax(\mathbf{W}_o tanh(\mathbf{W}_h \mathbf{h}_{s,n} + \mathbf{W}_c \mathbf{c}_{s-1,n} + \mathbf{b})) \tag{6}$$

The context vector c is a position-dependent weighted linear combination of all hidden states $1, ..., M$ in the previous sentence.

$$\mathbf{c}_{s-1,n} = \sum_{m=1}^{M} \alpha_{m,n} \mathbf{h}_{s-1,m} \tag{7}$$

The attention weights are computed as

$$a_{n,m} = w_a^T tanh(\mathbf{W}_{a1} \mathbf{h}_{s,n} + \mathbf{W}_{a2} \mathbf{h}_{s-1,m}) \tag{8}$$

$$\alpha_n = softmax(a_n) \tag{9}$$

The attention weights $a_{n,m}$ encode the importance of each word in the previous sentence for the current word. DCLMs were shown to obtain reductions in perplexity compared to standard and hierarchical recurrent language models (Ji et al. (2015)); however, they were also observed to have a tendency towards overfitting when training data is sparse (Kirchhoff and Turner (2016)).

A different issue in applying neural language models to lattice rescoring is that each path in the lattice defines a different context; however, it is computationally infeasible to exhaustively rescore all paths. The number of OOV words per sentence is typically 3-5 in our tasks, and the number of translation candidates per word may go up to 30. In standard back-off n-gram models, lattice paths are merged based on identical truncated word histories, but this options is not available to us in neural language models where each hidden state encodes the cumulative untruncated history. Inspired by sentence-level lattice rescoring techniques explored in speech recognition (Liu et al. (2016)), we utilize a document-level lattice rescoring procedure that merges lattice paths based on the similarity of hidden state vectors in the model. The main steps are:

1. Start depth-first lattice traversal from the initial node $< s >$.

2. Use the context matrix c_{s-1} from the previous sentence initialize the hidden representation of the first word $< s >$.

3. At each lattice node, compute the hidden representation and the posterior probability of the word on the incoming arc according to a DCLM.

4. If there is another lattice path that shares the last word with the current lattice path, and in addition, if the hidden representations of these words fall below some distance threshold γ, then merge the two paths and update the probability and the hidden representation of the frontier word in the merged lattice path.

A detailed description of the algorithm is provided below in Algorithm 1. As a distance measure

---

Algorithm 1 Document-level lattice rescoring

1: **for** each sentence S in document D **do**
2:      $L \leftarrow len(S)$
3:      **for** each node n_i in the lattice **do**
4:          initialize its expanded node list $N_i = []$
5:          initialize its expanded outgoing arc list $A_i = []$
6:      $N_0 \leftarrow [n_0'^0]$
7:      $A_0 \leftarrow [a_{01}'^0, a_{01}'^1, ...]$
8:      **for** each expanded node $n_i'^j \in N_i$ **do**
9:          create outgoing arcs $a_{i,i+1}'^0, a_{i,i+1}'^1, ...$ according to translation candidates at node n_{i+1}
10:          **for** each outgoing arc $a_{i,i+1}'^k \in A_i$ **do**
11:              create expanded node $n_{i+1}'^k$
12:              $h_{i,i+1}^k \leftarrow$ hidden representation of the DCLM at $a_{i,i+1}'^k$
13:              $Pr(a_{i,i+1}'^k | a_{i-1,i}'^k, ...) \leftarrow$ posterior probability of the lattice path at $a_{i,i+1}'^k$
14:              **if** $\exists a_{i-1,i}'^l \in A_{i-1}$ **and** $a_{i-1,i}'^k = a_{i-1,i}'^l$ **and** $d(h_{i,i+1}^k, h_{i,i+1}^l) < \gamma$ **then**
15:                  **if** $Pr(a_{i,i+1}'^k | a_{i-1,i}'^k, ...) > Pr(a_{i,i+1}'^l | a_{i-1,i}'^l, ...)$ **then**
16:                      delete $n_{i+1}'^l$
17:                      prune the lattice branch that leads to $n_{i+1}'^l$
18:                  **else**
19:                      delete $n_{i+1}'^k$
20:                      prune the lattice branch that leads to $n_{i+1}'^k$
21:      Backtrack from the expanded node $n_L'^j \in N_L$ lattice path that has the highest probability to obtain the decoded sentence.

---

we use Euclidean distance between the hidden state vectors. The merging step is illustrated in

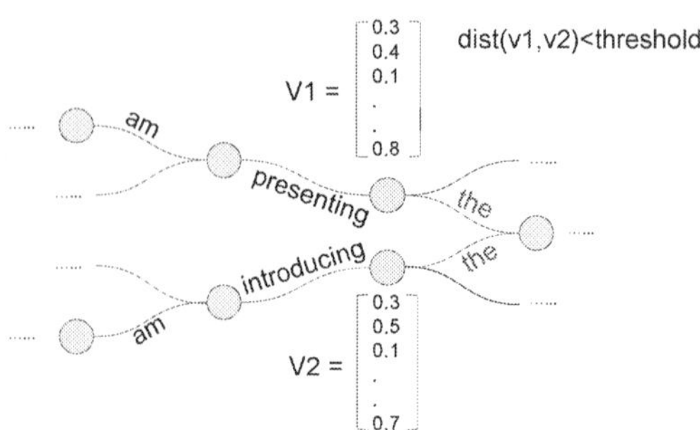

Figure 2: **Lattice path merging.** Paths ending in states whose associated hidden vectors are within a threshold distance of each other are merged.

Figure. 2. In practice, the procedure can be made computationally efficient by using a cache that maps each explored word to its (possibly multiple) hidden representations and posterior probabilities. In order to find the best path at the end of the traversal, the algorithm looks at all the remaining paths in the cache, finds the one that has the highest log-probability according to the context model, and traces back to the beginning of the path for the entire translation of this sentence. Also, the context matrix for this best path is propagated from the cache to the next sentence in the document for rescoring.

4 Data and Systems

4.1 MT Training Data

Our experiments are conducted on corpora for six different source languages (Amharic (amh), Uighur (uig), Somali (som), Yoruba (yor), Vietnamese (vie) and Hausa (hau)), with English as the target language. The corpora were provided as part of the DARPA LORELEI project on low-resource human language technology. Details of the training, development and test set sizes are provided in Table 1. Vocabulary sizes and OOV rates are shown in Table 3.

4.2 Context Model Training Data

The training data for the PMI-based context models consists of 4,264,684 Wikipedia articles[1]. PMI was computed based on the method and implementation described in Röder et al. (2015)[2]. The training data for each DCLM was selected from the Wiki-103 data set (Merity et al. (2016)), a collection of 28,475 Wikipedia articles (103M tokens) specifically curated for document-level language modeling. Data was selected separately for each language pair. For each article, a measure of overlap (Jaccard index) was computed between the article's vocabulary and the combined vocabulary extracted from the dev set target references and the one-best MT hypotheses on the test set. All articles with an index higher than 0.1 were included in the language model

---

[1] Wikipedia dump of 07/30/2014

[2] https://github.com/dice-group/Palmetto

	amh	uig	som	yor	hau	vie
train	63,181 / 5,941 / 1,237,172	99,005 / 18 / 2,587,335	52,288 / 8,872 / 1,097,616	41,525 / 7,538 / 933,932	43,370 / 3,554 / 423,935	28,686 / 439 / 423,069
dev	992 / 158 / 23,085	686 / 3 / 5,156	1,054 / 252 / 23,113	1,060 / 228 / 23,080	957 / 135 / 25,782	1,802 / 24 / 25,730
test	511 / 90 / 11,484	347 / 3 / 2,570	552 / 135 / 11,504	594 / 139 / 11,560	443 / 80 / 4,263	196 / 7 / 4,227

Table 1: Number of sentence pairs/documents/target language words in the training, development and test sets for each language.

training data. The same data was used for training the sentence-level LSTMs, to be able to directly compare the effect of document-level vs. sentence-level context on OOV disambiguation.

4.3 Baseline MT Systems

Baseline MT systems were developed for these tasks using phrase-based MT and attention-based neural MT (the Transformer model of Vaswani et al. (2017))[3]. The PBMT system was trained using Moses (Koehn et al. (2007)) and uses a flat phrase-based model with a maximum phrase length of 7, a backoff 4-gram language model trained on the target side of the parallel training data, and a bidirectional reordering model. The log-linear weights were trained using minimum error rate training on the dev set. The Transformer model was trained using a shared byte-pair encoding, resulting in a subword vocabulary of 8,000 word pieces. The hyperparameters of the Transformer models were tuned on the development sets with respect to the number of layers, layer dimensionality, learning rate, and regularization (dropout). The best parameters turned out to be: dropout rate of 0.1 at all layers, a learning rate of 0.2, 2 layers in the encoder and 2 layers in the decoder, and a hidden layer dimensionality of 512. The beam size during decoding is 4. Baseline results are shown in Table 2. Scoring was done in a case-insensitive fashion against a single reference translation.

Previous studies of neural sequence-to-sequence models for resource-poor scenarios (e.g., Koehn and Knowles (2017)) have found that PBMT models performed significantly better on low-resource languages unless the NMT models were enriched with additional components, such as a lexical memory (Nguyen and Chiang (2017)). By contrast, we find that self-attention based neural MT model performs comparably to PBMT, without any modifications to the basic model. A major contributor to the performance of the NMT models is the segmentation induced by byte-pair encoding, which results in system that outperform PBMT systems in 4 out of 6 language pairs. With a word-based vocabulary, NMT underperforms PBMT in most cases. Not surprisingly, languages with rich concatenative morphology (Amharic, Uighur) seem to benefit most from the subword approach.[4]

---

[3]We used the implementation provided at `https://github.com/tensorflow/tensor2tensor`

[4]PBMT models trained on the segmented text yielded worse scores than either word-based PBMT or Transformer

Language	PBMT	Transformer	Transformer w/ BPE
amh	16.93/49.6	13.15/46.0	**17.41/51.3**
uig	7.27/37.8	11.33/41.9	**17.22/46.7**
som	23.22/57.9	20.56/54.9	**25.36/59.9**
yor	18.22/50.8	15.68/49.1	**19.22/51.4**
hau	**21.86/57.8**	18.61/54.7	21.06/56.4
vie	**25.17/55.6**	22.83/53.1	23.00/54.2

Table 2: BLEU/unigram precision on test sets for phrase-based MT (PBMT), Transformer model, and Transformer model with byte-pair encoding (BPE).

	amh	uig	som	yor	hau	vie
Vocab	149,797	25,875	102,539	54,072	44,834	17,267
OOV rate	18.4%/	32.4%/	14.5%/	13.4%/	8.5%/	10.5%/
(type)/(token)	8.8%	17.2%	4.2%	3.1%	1.7%	6.9%
Coverage	99.8%	47.6%	85.0%	83.7%	80.1%	86.4%
(type)/(token)	91.2%	82.8%	95.8%	96.9%	98.3%	90.3%
Accuracy	5.6%	10.5%	15.9%	8.3%	8.8%	22.7%
# Candidates	8.0	22.0	15.4	18.4	20.6	28.6

Table 3: Vocabulary sizes, OOV rates, coverage, accuracy of external translation sources, and average number of translation candidates per OOV word.

4.4 Translation Candidate Generation

We obtain translation candidates for OOV words from (a) a large collection of web-crawled bilingual lexicons (Rolston and Kirchhoff (2016)) and (b) translations projected from related languages through Levenshtein distance based retrieval of words similar in their orthographic form. While the former is a reliable source, the latter method may introduce noise. Table 3 shows the number of OOVs, the coverage obtained by our external sources, accuracy (i.e., percentage of OOVs that have a translation matching the reference translation), and the average number of translation candidates per OOV. For all language pairs except for Uighur (which is morphologically highly complex), at least 80% of all OOV words receive a translation; however, the accuracy is at most 26% (note, however, that only a single reference translation was available; thus, synonyms are not counted).

5 Experimental Results

As an additional baseline we integrate the externally derived translations by simply adding them to the parallel training data, i.e., each translation pair is treated as an additional 'sentence'. Results are shown in Table 4. In this scenario, each of the new translation pairs is seen only once and without context; the final translation choice is still made by the MT system that has

---

models, even when using a larger maximum phrase length.

	PBMT	Transformer
amh	17.01 / 50.9	17.32 / 50.5
uig	7.84 / 42.2	**20.66 / 51.4**
som	23.91 / 58.6	**25.45 / 59.6**
yor	18.35/ 50.6	**19.87 / 51.9**
hau	**21.94 / 57.8**	21.55 / 56.7
vie	25.15 / 55.4	22.54 / 52.4

Table 4: Results (BLEU/unigram precision) of adding external translations to parallel training data. Boldface numbers are improvements over the best baseline system from Table 2.

Model	amh	uig	som	yor	hau	vie
LSTM	115.0	111.7	110.4	122.5	116.4	103.4
DCLM	101.7	103.1	100.3	98.6	97.3	95.4

Table 5: Perplexities obtained by LSTM vs. DCLM on dev sets.

been trained on the parallel data only. Compared to the baseline results in Table 2, we observe only mild improvements, except for Uighur, where the improvement is more pronounced.

We next conduct a diagnostic experiment designed to evaluate the different context models. To this end we enrich the list of translation candidates for each OOV word with the reference translation, in order to determine to what extent the different models are able to recover the correct translation if it is present in the candidate list. For simplicity we run these experiments on the output of the PBMT system, which, unlike the NMT output, contains the location of OOV words. Translation lattices were constructed from the one-best MT hypothesis and OOV translation candidates. The PMI and Pagerank systems were trained as described in Section 3. For PageRank, both sentence-level and document-level versions were trained, where the document context was defined to include the previous 4 sentences. We compare these against a sentence-level LSTM and the attentional DCLM described in Section 3. The sentence-level LSTM is a unidirectional model with two hidden layers of dimensionality 48. The DCLMs have a hidden layer size of 48 and also utilize a context size of 4 sentences. Word embedding vectors in both types of language models are initialized randomly. Both LSTMs and DCLMs were trained with DyNet (Neubig et al. (2017)).[5] The vocabulary for the language models consists of the OOV translation candidates and the words from the one-best MT hypotheses. A comparison between sentence-level and document-level model perplexities on the dev sets for each language pair is shown in Table 5.

The lattice rescoring results from the diagnostic experiment (Table 6) show that the attentional DCLM generally works best. The remaining experiments therefore use this model only.

We next apply the DCLM based rescoring method to our best baseline system, i.e., the Transformer system with BPE. Since this system decomposes all words into word pieces, it is not obvious which part of the output corresponds to an original OOV. We therefore align the PBMT and Transformer outputs, retain only the Transformer output and the aligned OOV slots, and replace OOV slots with their external translation options. We used fastAlign (Dyer et al.

---

[5]https://github.com/clab/dynet/tree/v1.1

	amh	uig	som	yor	hau	vie
PMI sent	16.68 / 49.3	7.82 / 37.8	22.56 / 57.4	17.91 / 49.6	20.89 / 57.3	25.87 / 55.8
PageRank sent	17.00 / 50.7	7.81 / 38.2	23.11 / 58.5	18.14 / 50.2	21.55 / 57.9	25.93 / 55.8
PageRank doc	16.97 / 50.8	8.04 / 38.9	**23.13** / 58.6	18.17 / 50.2	21.55 / 57.9	25.95 55.9
LSTM	17.01 / 50.7	9.91 / 49.0	22.98 / 59.1	17.87 / 50.2	21.21 / 57.7	25.97 / 56.0
DCLM	**17.39** / **52.9**	**9.96** / **50.4**	23.03 / **59.4**	**18.60** / **50.8**	**22.21** **57.9**	**26.19** / **56.9**

Table 6: BLEU/unigram precision for lattice rescoring of PBMT output with reference translation included (diagnostic experiment).

(2013)) for this procedure, treating the Transformer output as source and the PBMT output as target for amh, uig, som, and yor. For vie and hau, we use the PBMT system's output as source since it outperforms the Transformer model. The results are shown in Row 3 in Table 7.

With the exception of Uighur, we find that our method slightly but consistently outperforms systems that utilize the external translations as additional training data (Row 2), indicating that contextual information is useful. For further calibration of the results we also provide topline results from an oracle experiment where the correct reference translation was substituted for every OOV slot (Row 4) – these numbers indicate the maximum possible improvement in BLEU/unigram precision that can be obtained from OOV translation on these tasks. For completeness we also provide the original baseline system scores (Row 1) and results obtained from full system combination (e.g., both the PBMT and the NMT's outputs are represented in the rescoring lattice, in addition to OOV translation options). Not surprisingly, system combination adds further improvements (except for Uighur), in some cases bringing the overall performance close to the topline. An example of the different system outputs is shown below:

	Method	amh	uig	som	yor	hau	vie
1	No OOV rescoring	17.41/ 51.3	17.22/ 46.7	25.36/ 59.9	19.22/ 51.4	21.86/ 57.8	25.17/ 55.6
2	Add'l train data	17.32/ 50.5	20.66/ 51.4	25.45/ 59.6	19.87/ 51.9	21.94/ 57.8	25.15/ 55.4
3	OOV rescoring	17.76 / 53.8	17.33 / 47.1	25.50 / 60.2	19.97 / 52.8	22.42 / 59.9	27.25 / 57.7
4	OOV topline	18.62 / 58.4	21.48 / 60.5	27.57 / 64.4	21.40 / 56.8	22.77 / 61.5	28.61 / 59.4
5	sys. comb.	18.24 / **56.1**	18.10 / 50.9	**27.00** / **63.0**	**20.82** / **55.5**	**22.65** / **60.7**	**28.19** / **58.5**

Table 7: BLEU/unigram precision of (1) baseline system without OOV handling; (2) systems trained with external translations as additional training data; (3) lattice rescoring with context models; (4) oracle; (5) full system combination of PBMT and Transformer outputs plus OOV translation.

Source sentence (with OOVs in italics):
saraakiisha ayaa sheegaya in qaraxu ka dhacay meel u dhow *albaadka* aqalka baarlamaanka ,
kaddib markii ilaaladu ay rasaas ku furtay *baabuurkaasi*
No oov rescoring:
officials said that the explosion took place near the parliament albaadka, after they opened fire
on baabuurkaasi
Transformer output:
officials say that the explosion occurred near the house of the parliament after the guards opened
fire on that vehicle
After rescoring with context model (our method):
officials said that the explosion took place near the parliament entrance, after they opened fire
on kondoo
System combination:
officials said that the explosion occurred near the entrance of the parliament after the guards
opened fire on that vehicle
Reference:
officials said the explosion took place near the entrance of the parliament building when guards
opened fire on the vehicle

The best baseline system (Transformer with BPE) was able to correctly handle *baabuurkaasi*
(vehicle) but not *albaddka* (entrance), which the rescoring procedure corrected. While this procedure also introduces an incorrect word (*kondoo*), rescoring of the lattice representing both the
PBMT and Transformer output (system combination) in addition to OOV translations results in
the correct output.

6   Conclusion

We have presented an approach towards the resolution of ambiguous translations of OOV words
that arise when adding word translation pairs from external knowledge sources to an MT system. Of the different context models proposed, document-context language models with a context including previous sentences were shown to be most effective at identifying the correct
translations. Our method showed substantial gains over baseline systems without special OOV
handling and small but consistent gains over adding external translations directly to the training
data, in five out of six language pairs. Future work will be concerned with integrating external
resources and contextual information directly into neural MT architectures.

Acknowledgements
This paper was funded by DARPA under cooperative agreement no. HR0011-15-2-0043. The
content of the information does not necessarily reflect the position or the policy of the Government, and no official endorsement should be inferred.

References

Bahdanau, D., Cho, K., and Bengio, Y. (2014). Neural machine translation by jointly learning to align and translate. *arXiv preprint arXiv:1409.0473*.

Chung, J., Cho, K., and Bengio, Y. (2016). A character-level decoder without explicit segmentation for neural machine translation. *arXiv preprint arXiv:1603.06147*.

Dyer, C., Chahuneau, V., and Smith, N. A. (2013). A simple, fast, and effective reparameterization of ibm model 2. Association for Computational Linguistics.

Gubbins, J. and Vlachos, A. (2013). Dependency language models for sentence completion. In *EMNLP*, volume 13, pages 1405–1410. Citeseer.

Gujral, B., Khayralla, H., and Koehn, P. (2016). Translation of unknown words in low-resource languages. In *Proceedings of AMTA*.

Gulcehre, C., Ahn, S., Nallapati, R., Zhou, B., and Bengio, Y. (2016). Pointing the unknown words. *arXiv preprint arXiv:1603.08148*.

Irvine, A. and Callison-Burch, C. (2013). Supervised bilingual lexicon induction with multiple monolingual signals. In *Proceedings of HLT-NAACL*, page 518–523.

Jean, S., Cho, K., Memisevic, R., and Bengio, Y. (2014). On using very large target vocabulary for neural machine translation. *arXiv preprint arXiv:1412.2007*.

Ji, Y., Cohn, T., Kong, L., Dyer, C., and Eisenstein, J. (2015). Document context language models. *arXiv preprint arXiv:1511.03962*.

Kirchhoff, K. and Turner, A. M. (2016). Unsupervised resolution of acronyms and abbreviations in nursing notes using document-level context models. *EMNLP 2016*, page 52.

Koehn, P., Hoang, H., Birch, A., Callison-Burch, C., Federico, M., Bertoldi, N., Cowan, B., Shen, W., Moran, C., Zens, R., et al. (2007). Moses: Open source toolkit for statistical machine translation. In *Proceedings of the 45th annual meeting of the ACL on interactive poster and demonstration sessions*, pages 177–180. Association for Computational Linguistics.

Koehn, P. and Knowles, R. (2017). Six challenges for neural machine translation. In *Proceedings of the First Workshop on Neural Machine Translation*, pages 28–39, Vancouver. Association for Computational Linguistics.

Liu, X., Chen, X., Wang, Y., Gales, M., and Woodland, P. (2016). Two efficient lattice rescoring methods using recurrent neural network language models. volume 24(8).

Luong, M.-T. and Manning, C. D. (2016). Achieving open vocabulary neural machine translation with hybrid word-character models. *arXiv preprint arXiv:1604.00788*.

Luong, M.-T., Sutskever, I., Le, Q. V., Vinyals, O., and Zaremba, W. (2014). Addressing the rare word problem in neural machine translation. *arXiv preprint arXiv:1410.8206*.

Merity, S., Xiong, C., Bradbury, J., and Socher, R. (2016). Pointer sentinel mixture models. *arXiv preprint arXiv:1609.07843*.

Mihalcea, R. (2005). Unsupervised large-vocabulary word sense disambiguation with graph-based algorithms for sequence data labeling. In *Proceedings of EMNLP*.

Neubig, G., Dyer, C., Goldberg, Y., Matthews, A., Ammar, W., Anastasopoulos, A., Ballesteros, M., Chiang, D., Clothiaux, D., Cohn, T., Duh, K., Faruqui, M., Gan, C., Garrette, D., Ji, Y., Kong, L., Kuncoro, A., Kumar, G., Malaviya, C., Michel, P., Oda, Y., Richardson, M., Saphra, N., Swayamdipta, S., and Yin, P. (2017). Dynet: The dynamic neural network toolkit. *arXiv preprint arXiv:1701.03980*.

Nguyen, T. Q. and Chiang, D. (2017). Improving lexical choice in neural machine translation. *arXiv preprint arXiv:1710.01329*.

Page, L., Brin, S., Motwani, R., and Winograd, T. (1999). The pagerank citation ranking: Bringing order to the web. Technical Report 1999-66, Stanford InfoLab.

Röder, M., Both, A., and Hinneburg, A. (2015). Exploring the space of topic coherence measures. In *Proceedings of the eighth ACM international conference on Web search and data mining*, pages 399–408. ACM.

Rolston, L. and Kirchhoff, K. (2016). Collection of bilingual data for lexicon transfer learning. Technical Report UW-EE-2016-0001.

Saluja, A., Hassan, H., Toutanova, K., and Quirk, C. (2014). Graph-based semi-supervised learning of translation models from monolingual data. In *ACL (1)*, pages 676–686.

Sennrich, R., Haddow, B., and Birch, A. (2015). Neural machine translation of rare words with subword units. *arXiv preprint arXiv:1508.07909*.

Tsvetkov, Y. and Dyer, C. (2015). Lexicon stratification for translating out-of-vocabulary words. In *ACL (2)*, pages 125–131.

Vaswani, A., Shazeer, N., Parmar, N., Uszkoreit, J., Jones, L., Gomez, A., Kaiser, L., and Polosukhin, I. (2017). Attention is all you need. arXiv:1706.03762.

Woods, A. M. (2016). Exploiting linguistic features for sentence completion. In *The 54th Annual Meeting of the Association for Computational Linguistics*, page 438.

Yang, M. and Kirchhoff, K. (2012). Unsupervised translation disambiguation for cross-domain statistical machine translation. In *Proceedings of association for machine translation in the Americas*.

Zhao, K., Hassan, H., and Auli, M. (2015). Learning translation models from monolingual continuous representations. In *HLT-NAACL*, pages 1527–1536.

How Robust Are Character-Based Word Embeddings in Tagging and MT Against Wrod Scramlbing or Randdm Nouse?

Georg Heigold   georg.heigold@dfki.de
Stalin Varanasi   Stalin.Varanasi@dfki.de
Günter Neumann   Guenter.Neumann@dfki.de
Josef van Genabith   Josef.Van_Genabith@dfki.de
DFKI, Saarbrücken, Germany

Abstract

This paper investigates the robustness of NLP against perturbed word forms. While neural approaches can achieve (almost) human-like accuracy for certain tasks and conditions, they often are sensitive to small changes in the input such as non-canonical input (e.g., typos). Yet both stability and robustness are desired properties in applications involving user-generated content, and all the more so as humans easily cope with such noisy or adversary conditions. In this paper, we study the impact of noisy input. We consider different noise distributions (different density and different types) and mismatched noise distributions for training and testing. Moreover, we empirically evaluate the robustness of different models (convolutional neural networks, recurrent neural networks, non-neural models), different basic units (characters, byte pair encoding units, and words), and different NLP tasks (morphological tagging, machine translation). Our experiments confirm that (i) noisy input substantially degrades the output of models trained on clean data, that (ii) training on noisy data can help models achieve performance on noisy data similar to that of models trained on clean data tested on clean data, that (iii) models trained noisy data can achieve good results on noisy data almost without performance loss on clean data, that (iv) error type mismatches between training and test data can have a greater impact than error density mismatches, that (v) character based approaches are almost always better than byte pair encoding (BPE) approaches with noisy data, that (vi) the choice of neural models (recurrent, convolutional) is not significant, and that (vii) for morphological tagging, under the same data conditions, the neural models outperform a conditional random field (CRF) based model.

1   Introduction

In this paper, we study the effect of non-normalized text on natural language processing (NLP). Non-normalized text includes non-canonical word forms, noisy word forms, and word forms with "small" perturbations, such as informal spellings, typos, scrambled words. Compared to normalized text, the variability of non-normalized text is much greater and aggravates the problem of data sparsity.

Non-normalized text dominates in many real world applications. Similar to humans, ideally NLP should perform reliably and robustly also under suboptimal or even adversarial conditions, without a significant degradation in performance. Web-based content and social media are a rich source for noisy and informal text. Noise can also be introduced in a downstream NLP application where errors are propagated from one module to the next. For example, speech translation where the machine translation (MT) module needs to be robust against errors introduced by the automatic speech recognition (ASR) module. Moreover, NLP should not be vulnerable to adversarial input examples. While all these examples do not pose a real challenge to an experienced human reader, even "small" perturbations from the canonical form can make a state-of-the-art NLP system fail.

To illustrate the typical behavior of state-of-the-art NLP on normalized and non-normalized text, we discuss an example in the context of neural MT (NMT). Different research groups have shown that NMT can generate natural and fluent translations (Bentivogli et al., 2016), achieving human-like performance in certain settings (Wu et al., 2016). The state-of-the-art NMT engine *Google Translate*[1], for example, perfectly translates the English sentence

I used my card to purchase a meal on the menu and the total on my receipt was $ 8.95 but when I went on line to check my transaction it shows $ 10.74 .

into the German sentence

Ich benutzte meine Karte , um eine Mahlzeit auf der Speisekarte zu kaufen und die Gesamtsumme auf meiner Quittung war $ 8,95 , aber als ich online ging , um meine Transaktion zu überprüfen , zeigt es $ 10,74 .

Adding some noise to the source sentence by swapping a few neighboring characters, e.g.,

I used my card ot purchase a meal no the mneu and the total no my receipt was $ 8.95 but whne I went on line to check ym transaction it show $ 1.074 .

confuses the same NMT engine considerably:

Ich benutzte meine Karte ot Kauf eine Mahlzeit nicht die Mneu und die insgesamt nicht meine Quittung war $ 8,95 aber whne ging ich auf Linie zu überprüfen ym Transaktion es $ 1.074 .

By contrast, an experienced human reader can still understand and correctly translate the noisy sentence and compensate for some information loss (including real word errors such as "no" vs. "on", but rather not "10.74" vs. "1.074"), with little additional effort and often not even noticing "small" perturbations.

One might argue that a good translation should in fact translate corrupted language into corrupted language. Here, we rather adopt the position that the objective is to preserve the intended content and meaning of a sentence regardless of noise.

It should be noted that neural networks with sufficient capacity, in particular recurrent neural networks, are universal function approximators (Schäfer and Zimmermann, 2006). Hence, the performance degradation on non-normalized text is not so much a question whether the model can capture the variability but rather how to train a robust model. In particular, it can be expected that training on noisy data will make NLP more robust, as it was successfully demonstrated for other application domains including vision (Cui et al., 2015) and speech recognition (Doulaty et al., 2016).

In this paper, we empirically evaluate the robustness of different models (convolutional neural networks, recurrent neural networks, non-neural models), different basic units (characters, byte pair encoding units), and different NLP tasks (morphological tagging, NMT). Due to easy availability and to have more control on the experimental setup with respect to error type and error density, we use synthetic data generated from existing clean corpora by perturbing the word forms. The perturbations include character flips and swaps of neighboring characters to imitate typos, and word scrambling.

The contributions of this paper are the following. Our experiments confirm that (i) noisy input substantially degrades the output of models trained on clean data. The experiments show that (ii) training on noisy data can help models achieve performance on noisy data similar to that of models trained on clean data tested on clean data, that (iii) models trained noisy data

---

[1] https://translate.google.com/, February 2017

can achieve good results on noisy data almost without performance loss on clean data, that
(iv) *error type* mismatches between training and test data can have a greater impact than *error
density* mismatches, that (v) character based approaches are almost always better than byte pair
encoding (BPE) approaches with noisy data, that (vi) the choice of neural models (recurrent,
convolutional) is not as significant, and that (vii) for morphological tagging, under the same
data conditions, the neural models outperform a conditional random field (CRF) based model.

The remainder of the paper is organized as follows. Section 2 discusses related work.
Section 3 describes the noise types and Section 4 briefly summarizes the modeling approaches
used in this paper. Experimental results are shown and discussed in Section 5. The paper is
concluded in Section 6.

2   Related Work

A large body of work on regularization techniques to learn robust representations and models exists. Examples include ℓ_2-regularization, dropout (Hinton et al., 2012), Jacobian-based
sensitivity penalty (Rifai et al., 2011; Li et al., 2016), and data noising. Compared to other
application domains such as vision (LeCun et al., 1998; Goodfellow et al., 2014) and speech
(Lippmann et al., 1987; Tüske et al., 2014; Cui et al., 2015; Doulaty et al., 2016), work on noisy
data (Gimpel et al., 2011; Derczynski et al., 2013; Plank, 2016) and in particular data noising
(Yitong et al., 2017), do not have a long and extensive history in NLP.

While invariance transformations such as rotation, translation in vision or vocal tract
length, reverberation, and noise in speech have all been harnessed, we do not have a good
intuition on useful perturbations for written language yet. Label dropout and flip (cf. typos)
have been proposed both on the byte-level (Gillick et al., 2015) and the word-level (Xie et al.,
2017). Syntactic and semantic noise for semantic analysis was studied in Yitong et al. (2017).
From a human perception perspective, word scrambling may be of interest (Rawlinson, 1976;
Rayner et al., 2006).

The arbitrary relationship between the orthography of a word and its meaning in general
is a well known assumption in linguistics (de Saussure, 1916). However, the word form often
carries additional important information. This is, for example, the case in morphologically rich
languages or in non-normalized text where small perturbations result in similar word forms.
Recently, sub-word units have attracted some attention in NLP to handle rarely and unseen
words and to reduce the computational complexity in neural network approaches (Ling et al.,
2015; Gillick et al., 2015; Sennrich et al., 2015; Chung et al., 2016; Heigold et al., 2017).
Examples for sub-word units include BPE based units Sennrich et al. (2015), characters (Ling
et al., 2015; Chung et al., 2016; Heigold et al., 2017) or even bytes (Gillick et al., 2015). A
comparison of BPE and characters for machine translation regarding grammaticality can be
found in Sennrich (2016). Similarly Sajjad et al. (2017) showed that BPE worked better for MT
and char-based models worked better for part-of-speech (POS) tagging.

3   Noise Types

In this work, we experiment with three different noise types: character swaps, character flips,
and word scrambling. Character flips and swaps are rough approximations to typos. Word
scrambling is motivated from psycholinguistic studies (Rawlinson, 1976). This choice of noise
types allows us to automatically generate noisy text with different type and density distributions
from existing properly edited "clean" corpora. Using synthetic data is clearly suboptimal, but
we use synthetic data because of their easy availability and because it gives us better control on
the experimental setup.

Character swaps This type of perturbation randomly swaps two neighboring characters in a word. The words are processed from left to right. A swap is performed at each position with a pre-defined probability. Hence, movements from the left to the right beyond neighboring characters are possible. A character-swapped version (10% swapping probability) of the clean example sentence in the introduction may look like this:

I used my card ot purchase a meal no the mneu and the total no my receipt was $ 8.95 but whne I went on line to check ym transaction it show $ 1.074 .

Word scrambling Humans appear to be good at reading scrambled text[2]. In a word scramble, the characters can be in an arbitrary order. The only constraint is that the first and last character be at the right place. In particular, all word scrambles are assumed to be equally likely. A scrambled version of the clean example sentence in the introduction may look like this:

I uesd my card to pchasure a mael on the mneu and the ttaol on my repciet was $ 89.5 but wehn I went on line to chcek my tanrsactoin it sohw $ 1.074 .

Clearly, some word scrambles are easier than others. Word scrambling approximately includes character swaps.

Character flips This type of perturbation randomly replaces a character with another character at a pre-specified rate. Characters are drawn uniformly, but special symbols (e.g., end of stream) are excluded. We do not assume any correlation across characters. A character-flipped version (10% flipping probability) of the clean example sentence in the introduction may look like this:

I used my car¿ to purch.s' a meal on the menu and the total on my receipv tas $ 8.95 but whe3 = wen+ on lin4 to chece my tran&awtion it shzw $ 10.74 .

Character flips preserve the order of characters but replace some information with random information, whereas character swaps and word scrambling relax the order of characters but do not add random information. Other simple perturbations include randomly removing or adding (in particular, repeating) characters.

In the experimental section, we will consider different noise distributions (as regards density and types of noise) and mismatched noise distributions for training and testing.

A word of length n with at most one character flip can have up to nC different word forms, where C denotes the number of characters in the vocabulary. Word scrambling multiplies the number of word forms by a factor of $(n - 2)!$. In general, perturbing word forms introduces a great deal of variability and data becomes much more sparse, implying that efficient handling of rare and unseen words will be crucial.

4 Modeling

This section briefly summarizes the modeling approaches used in this work. First, we address the choice of unit. As illustrated in Table 1 on an example from the UD English corpus[3], a word-based unit does not seem to be an appropriate unit in the presence of perturbations. Any change of the word form implies a different, independent word index. Even worse, most perturbed word forms do not represent valid words and are mapped to the <unk>-token and no word-specific information is preserved. This suggests the use of sub-word units. Here, we use BPE units (Sennrich et al., 2015) and characters as the basic units.

BPE is based on character co-occurrence frequency distributions and has the effect of representing frequent words as whole words and splitting rare words into sub-word units (e.g.,

---

[2] http://www.mrc-cbu.cam.ac.uk/people/matt-davis/cmabridge/, note the word scramble in the URL!

[3] http://universaldependencies.org/

"used" as "used", "purchase" as "purcha@@se"). BPE provides a good tradeoff between modeling efficiency (i.e., the model does not need to learn for the frequent words how to assemble them) and handling unknown words. However, BPE may not be efficient at representing noisy word forms as small perturbations can lead to a different representation using different BPE units (e.g., "used" vs. "u@@es@@d", "purcha@@se" vs. "p@@cha@@sure"). As the example illustrates (Table 1), perturbations tend to break longer units into smaller units, which makes the use of whole word units less useful.

Finally, characters as the basic units have similar representations for similar word forms, but result in longer sequences, which makes the modeling of long-range dependencies harder and increases the computational complexity. It should be noted that the lower the BPE size is, the closer BPE is to character based encoding and the higher the BPE size is, the closer it is to word-based approaches.

Table 1: Clean (left) vs. scrambled (right) example sentence using a word-based (top), a BPE-based (middle), and a character-based (bottom) representation

I used my card to purchase a meal on the menu and the total on my receipt was $ 8.95 but when i went on line to check my transaction it show $ 10.74 .	I <unk> my card to <unk> a <unk> on the <unk> and the <unk> on my <unk> was $ 89.5 but <unk> i went on line to <unk> my <unk> it <unk> $ 1.074 .
I used my c@@ ard to purcha@@ se a me@@ al on the men@@ u and the to@@ tal on my recei@@ pt was $ 8@@ .@@ 9@@ 5 but when I went on line to check my trans@@ action it show $ 10@@ .@@ 7@@ 4 .	I u@@ es@@ d my c@@ ard to p@@ cha@@ sure a ma@@ el on the m@@ ne@@ u and the t@@ ta@@ ol on my rep@@ ci@@ et was $ 8@@ 9@@ .@@ 5 but we@@ h@@ n I went on line to ch@@ c@@e@@ k my t@@ on@@ tri@@ as@@ ac@@ n it so@@ h@@ w $ 1@@ .@@ 0@@ 7@@ 4 .

```
I used my card to purchase a meal        I uesd my card to pchasure a mael
on the menu and the total on my          on the mneu and the ttaol on my
receipt was $ 8.95 but when i            repciet was $ 89.5 but wehn I
went on line to check my                 went on line to chcek my
transaction it show $ 10.74 .            tanrsactoin it sohw $ 1.074 .
```

Noise modeling for a word-level system is straightforward as perturbed word forms are mapped to <unk>, i.e., noise modeling reduces to word-level label dropout (and rarely word-level label flips) (Xie et al., 2017). This is not true for sub-word level representations, for which more detailed noise modeling will be important.

We use model architectures based on recurrent and convolutional neural networks in this work. Assuming that a word segmentation is given, we first map the sub-word units of a word to a word vector and then continue as for word-based approaches. Deep neural networks are universal function approximators (Schäfer and Zimmermann, 2006). Hence, a neural network with sufficient capacity is expected to learn the variability induced by perturbations. We compare the neural networks with a conditional random field (Lafferty et al., 2001).

5 Experiments

In this section, we empirically evaluate the robustness against perturbed word forms (Section 3) for the two common NLP tasks morphological tagging and machine translation.

5.1 Morphological Tagging

We used the model configurations and setups from Heigold et al. (2017) for the morphological tagging experiments in this paper. Training and testing was performed on the UD English data set[4]. Figure 1 summarizes the results. We explored the three main dimensions of noise type and

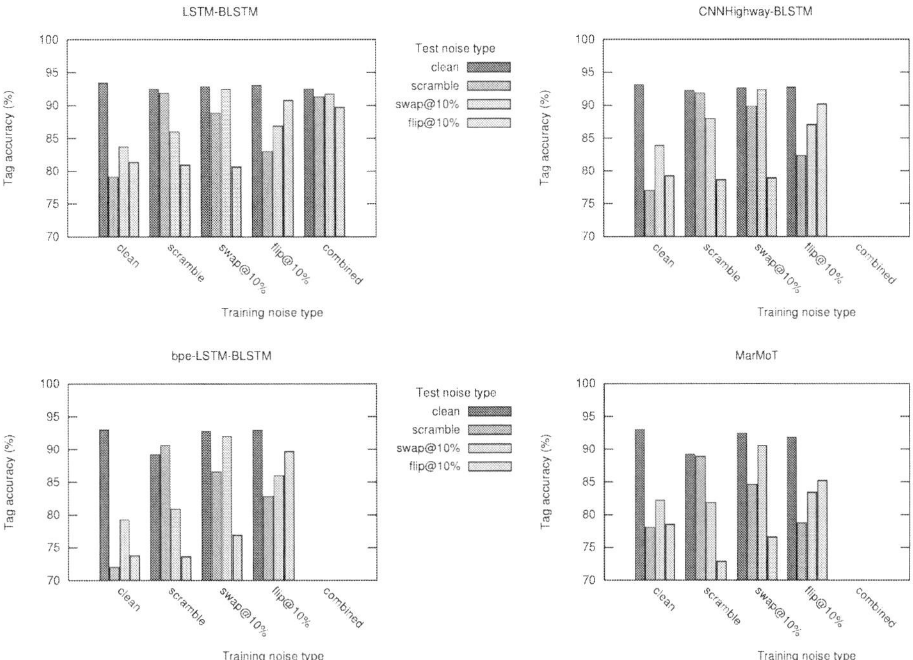

Figure 1: Noise behavior for morphological tagging for different models and units on UD English test data. Upper left: character-based LSTM-BLSTM. Upper right: character-based CNNHighway-BLSTM. Lower left: BPE-based LSTM-BLSTM. Lower right: MarMoT (CRF).

distribution, choice of unit, and type of model. Noise-adaptive training means standard training on noisy input sentences (but with correct labels: rich morphological tags or target language translation). We distinguish the noise type and distribution used for training ("training noise type") and testing ("test noise type").

We start our discussion with the upper left histogram in Figure 1 for the character-based LSTM-BLSTM architecture. It shows a clear performance degradation from around 95% to around 80% tag accuracy across all noise types compared to when trained on clean data ("clean"). Here, we consider the noise types word scrambling ("scramble", note that all words are scrambled), character swaps with probability 10% ("swap@10%), and character flips with probability 10% ("flip@10%"). Bar groups 2, 3 and 4 in the upper left histogram in Figure 1 show that noise-adaptive training helps in all cases, bringing the tag accuracy back to above 90% and without substantially affecting the accuracy on clean data. As expected, the accuracy under matched training and test conditions is highest in all cases. The transferability from a noise type to another depends on the noise types. For example, noise-adaptive training for "swap@10%" improves the accuracy on the "scramble" test condition by approximately 10%. On the other hand, the "flip@10%" test condition gets slightly worse. This outcome may be expected because characters swaps are more closely related with word scrambling than character flips. The transferability does not need to be symmetric. An example is "flip@10%"-adaptive

---

[4]http://universaldependencies.org/

training which improves on the "swap@10%" and "scramble" test conditions, whereas we observe slight degradation in the opposite direction.

Finally, can we train a model that performs well across all these noise types as well as on clean data? For this, we mixed different noise types at the sentence level for training ("combined"), i.e., a clean sentence, followed by a sentence with scrambling inside words, followed by a sentence with swapped characters inside words, followed by a sentence with flipped characters inside words, and so forth in the training data. The test data, by contrast, was pure clean ("clean"), scrambled ("scramble"), swapped ("swap@10%"), or flipped ("flip@10%") data. According to the results summarized in the final group of bars in the upper left histogram in Figure1, this is approximately possible. This result again suggests that noise strongly impacts on models trained on clean data, and that injecting noise at training time is critical but the exact noise distribution is not so important in this case.

The upper left and lower left histograms in Figure 1 differ in the choice of unit on the input text side, "char-LSTM-BLSTM" uses characters and "bpe-LSTM-BLSTM" 2,000 BPE units[5]. The overall behavior is similar, but characters seem to degrade more gracefully than BPE units for mismatched noise conditions (compare bar columns 2, 3 and 4 between the upper left and lower left histograms in Figure 1).

Finally, we explore how different models behave on noisy input (compare bar columns 2, 3 and 4 between the upper left, upper right and lower right histograms in Figure 1). For this, we compare a char-LSTM-BLSTM, a char-CNNHighway-BLSTM (same as char-LSTM-BLSTM but uses a convolutional neural network to compute the word vectors) (Heigold et al., 2017), and a conditional random field (Müller and Schütze, 2015) including word-based features and prefix/suffix features up to length 10 for rare words (we used MarMoT[6] for the experiments). The upper left, upper right and lower right histograms in Figure1 show that the qualitative behavior of the three models is very similar. char-LSTM-BLSTM and char-CNNHighway-BLSTM achieve similar performance. One might speculate if char-LSTM-BLSTM is slightly better at flip@10% and char-CNNHighway-BLSTM at swap@10% and word scrambling, but the differences are most likely not significant. MarMoT's tag accuracies for all noise conditions is worse by 5-10%.

As indicated above, Figure 1 shows results on English morphological tagging. In a suite of experiments (not shown here in full detail for reasons of space) we have confirmed similar overall results for morphologically-richer languages such as German. Morphological tagging for German is much harder than for English: while the English UD training data exhibit 119 distinct types of sequences of POS tags followed by morphological feature descriptions, the TIGER training data for German exhibit 681 distinct types of such sequences.

To give one result from our German experiments, Figure 2 shows the dependency of the test accuracy on the amount of character flips in the test data, for various amounts of character flips in training. Assuming an average word length of 6 characters, 10% character flips correspond with one typo in every second word, 20% character flips with one typo per word, and 30% character flips with two typos per word. This result suggests that injecting noise at training time is critical, whereas the test accuracy does not depend so much on the exact amount of training noise (curves for 10%, 20% and 30% character flips) and that models trained on noise injected data are still able to tag clean data with almost no loss in performance compared to a model trained on clean data only.

Morphological tagging is a sequence-to-sequence labelling task, where (to a first approxi-

---

[5]In neural MT, BPE size is usually around 50,000. For morphological tagging we adjust the number of BPE units according to the amount of data: the UD English training data roughly includes 2,000 unique words with at least 10 occurrences. For our NMT based experiments in Section 5.2, we use the customary BPE setting in NMT.

[6]`http://cistern.cis.lmu.de/marmot/`

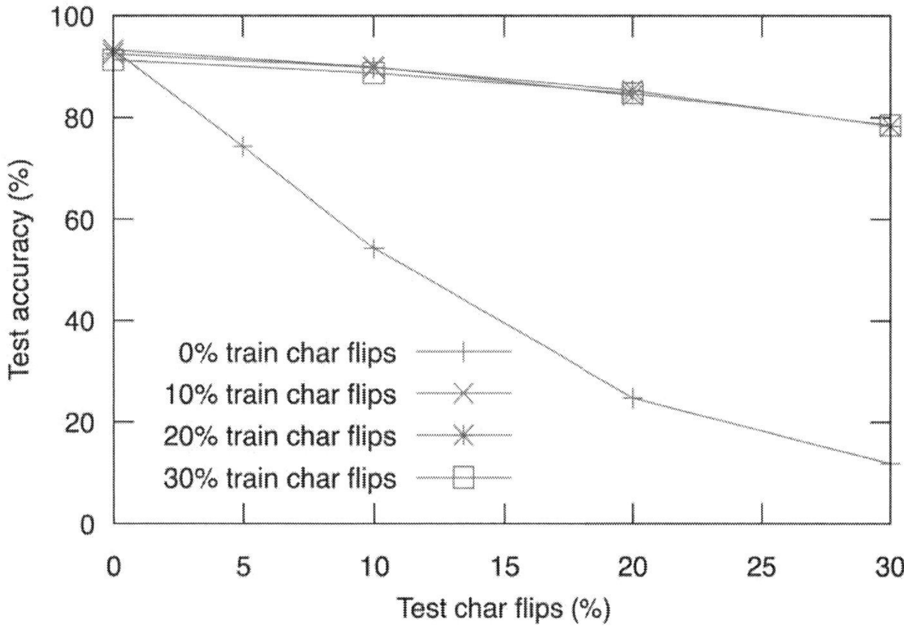

Figure 2: Noise density (mis-) matches-effect of amount of character flips in training and testing for morphological tagging on German TIGER test data

mation) the number and order of elements in the two sequences is the same (each word/token is paired with a POS tag plus morphological description). Translation is arguably a much harder task as it often relates sequences of different lengths with possibly substantial changes in the order of corresponding words/tokens between source and target and, compared to morphological tagging, much larger sizes of output vocabularies. In a second set of experiments, we explore the impact and handling of noise in the input to machine translation.

5.2 Machine Translation

Our NMT setup is based on the setup in Heigold and van Genabith (2016). We use BPE units or characters as the basic units at the source side and always BPE units at the target side (following common practice in our experiments we use a BPE size of 50,000), resulting in the two model configurations "BPE-BPE" and "char-BPE". For the character-based encoder, we assume the word segmentation and map the word string consisting of characters or BPE units to a word vector by a two-layer unidirectional LSTM. The baseline model ("clean") is trained on the German-English (DE-EN) parallel corpora provided by WMT'16[7]. Results for the newstest2016-deen data set are shown in Table 2. For noise-adaptive training, we perform transfer learning on the perturbed source sentence-target sentence pairs ("noise-adapted"). For training, we choose the following sentence-level noise distribution: 50% clean sentences, 20% sentences with character swaps (5% swap probability), 10% sentences with word scrambles, and 20% sentences with character flips (5% flip probability). We refer to this noise distribution as "noisy." Beside this "noisy" noise distribution, we also use mismatched noise conditions at test time, consisting of a single noise type only, referred to as "clean", "swap@5%", "scramble", and "flip@5%".

---

[7]http://www.statmt.org/wmt16/translation-task.html

Table 2: BLEU on newstest2016-deen for clean and noisy NMT and different test noise types

| Test | BPE-BPE | | char-BPE | |
| noise | | noise- | | noise- |
type	clean	adapted	clean	adapted
clean	31.6	30.4	30.7	30.6
swap@5%	19.8	25.0	25.0	29.2
scramble	3.6	9.4	5.4	20.0
flip@5%	16.1	22.5	21.7	27.1
noisy	21.9	25.6	21.1	28.5

The baseline's performance drop for noisy test data is drastic and clearly depends on the noise type. Word scrambling seems to be the hardest noise type, for which BLEU goes down from around 30 to around 5 for BPE-BPE and char-BPE. Overall, however, the results suggest that the char-BPE baseline degrades much more gracefully than the BPE-BPE baseline.

The results in Table 2 show that noise-adaptive training can considerably improve the performance on noisy data and the gap between clean and noisy conditions can be almost closed for the "easy" noise conditions. Similar to the baseline, char-BPE tends to be less sensitive to mismatched noise conditions. This may be best seen from the fact that char-BPE performs better or no worse than BPE-BPE for all noise conditions. Moreover, noise-adaptive training does not affect BLEU for char-BPE (30.7 vs. 30.6) but there is a small performance penalty for BPE-BPE (31.6 vs. 30.4). Furthermore, the "noisy" BLEU is the highest among the noisy conditions for BPE-BPE while the "swap@5%" BLEU is the best for char-BPE.

We show an example for the different noise types and source representations in Table 3. The example reflects the general findings based on BLEU scores (Table 2). The example also highlights the potential difficulty of correctly translating proper names in noisy conditions.

6   Conclusion

In this paper, we presented an empirical study on morphological tagging and machine translation for noisy input. Mostly as expected from other application domains such as vision and speech, we found that state-of-the-art NLP systems are very sensitive to slightly perturbed word forms that do not pose a challenge to humans and that injecting noise at training time can improve the robustness of such systems considerably. The best results were observed for matched training and test noise conditions but generalization across certain noise type and noise distributions is possible. Character-based approaches seem to degrade more gracefully compared with BPE-based approaches. We observe similar overall trends across tasks (morphological tagging and machine translation) and languages (English and German for morphological tagging). The results in this paper are promising but should be taken with a grain of salt as we used synthetic data based on a limited number of idealized perturbation types. Future work will aim at a better comprehension of relevant and hard or even adversarial perturbations and noise types (including noisy sentence structure) in language and testing on real noisy user input. Moreover, the observation that the lower the BPE size is, the closer BPE is to character based encoding and the higher the BPE size is, the closer BPE is to word based approaches, will allow us to tune the system for the optimal granularity, providing a good tradeoff between quality, efficiency and robustness. A reasonable assumption is that the error correction is task-independent and could be trained independently of the actual NLP task, or shared across NLP tasks and jointly optimized.

Acknowledgments This work was partially funded by the BMBF through the projects ALL SIDES (01IW14002) and DEEPLEE (01IW17001) and the European Unions Horizon 2020 grant agreement No. 645452 (QT21).

References

Bentivogli, L., Bisazza, A., Cettolo, M., and Federico, M. (2016). Neural versus phrase-based machine translation quality: a case study. *CoRR*, abs/1608.04631.

Chung, J., Cho, K., and Bengio, Y. (2016). A character-level decoder without explicit segmentation for neural machine translation. *CoRR*, abs/1603.06147.

Cui, X., Goel, V., and Kingsbury, B. (2015). Data augmentation for deep neural network acoustic modeling. *IEEE/ACM Trans. Audio, Speech & Language Processing*, 23(9):1469–1477.

de Saussure, F. (1916). Course in general linguistics.

Derczynski, L., Ritter, A., Clark, S., and Bontcheva, K. (2013). Twitter part-of-speech tagging for all: Overcoming sparse and noisy data. In *Proceedings of the International Conference on Recent Advances in Natural Language Processing*. Association for Computational Linguistics.

Doulaty, M., Rose, R., and Siohan, O. (2016). Automatic optimization of data perturbation distributions for multi-style training in speech recognition. In *Proceedings of the IEEE 2016 Workshop on Spoken Language Technology (SLT2016)*.

Gillick, D., Brunk, C., Vinyals, O., and Subramanya, A. (2015). Multilingual language processing from bytes. *CoRR*, abs/1512.00103.

Gimpel, K., Schneider, N., O'Connor, B., Das, D., Mills, D., Eisenstein, J., Heilman, M., Yogatama, D., Flanigan, J., and Smith, N. A. (2011). Part-of-speech tagging for twitter: Annotation, features, and experiments. In *Proceedings of the 49th Annual Meeting of the Association for Computational Linguistics: Human Language Technologies: Short Papers - Volume 2*, HLT '11, pages 42–47, Stroudsburg, PA, USA. Association for Computational Linguistics.

Goodfellow, I. J., Shlens, J., and Szegedy, C. (2014). Explaining and harnessing adversarial examples. *CoRR*, abs/1412.6572.

Heigold, G., Neumann, G., and van Genabith, J. (2017). An extensive empirical evaluation of character-based morphological tagging for 14 languages. In *EACL*.

Heigold, G. and van Genabith, J. (2016). Character-based neural machine translation. Technical report, DFKI GmbH.

Hinton, G. E., Srivastava, N., Krizhevsky, A., Sutskever, I., and Salakhutdinov, R. (2012). Improving neural networks by preventing co-adaptation of feature detectors. *CoRR*, abs/1207.0580.

Lafferty, J. D., McCallum, A., and Pereira, F. C. N. (2001). Conditional random fields: Probabilistic models for segmenting and labeling sequence data. In *Proceedings of the Eighteenth International Conference on Machine Learning*, ICML '01, pages 282–289, San Francisco, CA, USA. Morgan Kaufmann Publishers Inc.

LeCun, Y., Bottou, L., Bengio, Y., and Haffner, P. (1998). Gradient-based learning applied to document recognition. *Proceedings of the IEEE*, 86(11):2278–2324.

Li, Y., Cohn, T., and Baldwin, T. (2016). Learning robust representations of text. *CoRR*, abs/1609.06082.

Ling, W., Dyer, C., Black, A. W., Trancoso, I., Fermandez, R., Amir, S., Marujo, L., and Luis, T. (2015). Finding function in form: Compositional character models for open vocabulary word representation. In *Proceedings of the 2015 Conference on Empirical Methods in Natural Language Processing*, pages 1520–1530, Lisbon, Portugal. Association for Computational Linguistics.

Lippmann, R., Martin, E., and Paul, D. (1987). Multi-style training for robust isolated-word speech recognition. In *ICASSP*, volume 12, pages 705–708.

Müller, T. and Schütze, H. (2015). Robust morphological tagging with word representations. In *Proceedings of the 2015 Conference of the North American Chapter of the Association for Computational Linguistics: Human Language Technologies*, pages 526–536, Denver, Colorado. Association for Computational Linguistics.

Plank, B. (2016). What to do about non-standard (or non-canonical) language in NLP. *CoRR*, abs/1608.07836.

Rawlinson, G. (1976). *The significance of letter position in word recognition*. PhD thesis, Psychology Department, University of Nottingham, Nottingham UK. Unpublished Ph.D. Thesis.

Rayner, K., White, S., Johnson, R., and Liversedge, S. (2006). Raeding wrods with jubmled lettres there is a cost. *Psychological Science*, 17(3):192–193.

Rifai, S., Dauphin, Y., Vincent, P., Bengio, Y., and Muller, X. (2011). The manifold tangent classifier. In *NIPS'2011*. Student paper award.

Sajjad, H., Dalvi, F., Durrani, N., Abdelali, A., Belinkov, Y., and Vogel, S. (2017). Challenging language-dependent segmentation for arabic: An application to machine translation and part-of-speech tagging. In *Proceedings of the 55th Annual Meeting of the Association for Computational Linguistics, ACL 2017, Vancouver, Canada, July 30 - August 4, Volume 2: Short Papers*, pages 601–607.

Schäfer, A. M. and Zimmermann, H. G. (2006). Recurrent neural networks are universal approximators. In *Proceedings of the 16th International Conference on Artificial Neural Networks - Volume Part I*, ICANN'06, pages 632–640, Berlin, Heidelberg. Springer-Verlag.

Sennrich, R. (2016). How grammatical is character-level neural machine translation? Assessing MT quality with contrastive translation pairs. *CoRR*, abs/1612.04629.

Sennrich, R., Haddow, B., and Birch, A. (2015). Neural machine translation of rare words with subword units. *CoRR*, abs/1508.07909.

Tüske, Z., Golik, P., Nolden, D., Schlüter, R., and Ney, H. (2014). Data augmentation, feature combination, and multilingual neural networks to improve asr and kws performance for low-resource languages. In *INTERSPEECH*, pages 1420–1424.

Wu, Y., Schuster, M., Chen, Z., Le, Q. V., Norouzi, M., Macherey, W., Krikun, M., Cao, Y., Gao, Q., Macherey, K., Klingner, J., Shah, A., Johnson, M., Liu, X., Kaiser, L., Gouws, S., Kato, Y., Kudo, T., Kazawa, H., Stevens, K., Kurian, G., Patil, N., Wang, W., Young, C., Smith, J., Riesa, J., Rudnick, A., Vinyals, O., Corrado, G., Hughes, M., and Dean, J. (2016). Google's neural machine translation system: Bridging the gap between human and machine translation. *CoRR*, abs/1609.08144.

Xie, Z., Wang, S. I., Li, J., Lévy, D., Nie, A., Jurafsky, D., and Ng, A. Y. (2017). Data Noising as Smoothing in Neural Network Language Models. arXiv:1703.02573v1.

Yitong, L., Cohn, T., and Baldwin, T. (2017). Robust training under linguistic adversity. In *Proceedings of the 15th Conference of the European Chapter of the Association for Computational Linguistics (EACL 2017)*, pages 21–27, Valencia, Spain.

Table 3: Example sentence for different noise types (clean, character swaps, word scrambling, character flips) and NMT configurations (BPE/characters and standard training/noise-adaptive training)

source (clean)	Herr Modi befindet sich auf einer fünftägigen Reise nach Japan , um die wirtschaftlichen Beziehungen mit der drittgrößten Wirtschaftsnation der Welt zu festigen .
unadapted (BPE-BPE)	Mr Modi is on a five-day trip to Japan to consolidate economic relations with the world 's third largest economies .
noise-adapted (BPE-BPE)	Mr Modi is on a five-day trip to Japan to consolidate economic relations with the third largest economic nation in the world .
unadapted (char-BPE)	Mr Modi is on a five-day trip to Japan to consolidate economic relations with the world 's third largest economy .
noise-adapted (char-BPE)	Mr Prodi is on a five-day trip to Japan in order to consolidate economic relations with the world 's third largest economy.
source (swap@5%)	Herr Modi befindet sich auf einer fünftägigen Reise nach Japan, um die wirtschaftlichen Beziehungen mit der rdtitgrößten Wirtschaftsnation der Welt zu festiegn.
unadapted	Mr Modi is on a five-day trip to Japan to entrench economic relations with the world 's most basic economic nation .
noise-adapted (BPE-BPE)	Mr Modi is on a five-day trip to Japan to establish economic relations with the world 's largest economic nation .
unadapted	Mr Modi is on a five-day trip to Japan to establish economic relations with the world's largest economy.
noise-adapted (char-BPE)	Mr Prodi is on a five-day trip to Japan in order to consolidate economic relations with the world's third largest economy.
source (scramble)	Hrer Modi bfdneeit scih auf eienr fggnefüiätn Reise ncah Jpaan , um die wctathhilsfecirn Buzegehnein mit der drtiößettrgn Wsfactohtairsntin der Welt zu fgteesin .
unadapted	Hrer modes Bfdneeit scih on eienr fggnefün journey ncah Jpaan to get the wctathsusfecirn Buzehno with the drone Wsfactohtairsntin in the world .
noise-adapted (BPE-BPE)	Mr Modi is looking forward to a successful trip to Jpaan in order to find the scientific evidence with the world 's largest economy in the world .
unadapted	Hear Is a member of the United States of America and the United States of America .
noise-adapted (char-BPE)	Mr Prodi is working on a fictitious journey to Japan in order to address economic relations with the world 's third largest economy .
source (flip@5%)	Herr Modi befindet sicC 0uf einer fünftägigen Reise nach Japan , u" die wirtsch_ätlichen Beziehungen mi4 dLr drittgrößten Wirtschaftsn,tion der Welt zu f?stigen .
unadapted	Mr. Modi is located at sicC 0uf a five-day trip to Japan , u" the wiring relations mi4 dLr third-largest economy of the world .
noise-adapted (BPE-BPE)	Mr Modi is on a five-day trip to Japan to promote economic relations with the world 's third largest economy .
unadapted	Mr Modi is going to Japan on a five-day trip to Japan to fudge economic relations with the world's third largest economy .
noise-adapted (char-BPE)	Mr Prodi is on a five-day trip to Japan to consolidate economic relations with the world 's third largest economy .

Balancing Translation Quality and Sentiment Preservation

Pintu Lohar[1]
Haithem Afli[1-2]
Andy Way[1]
[1]ADAPT Centre, School of Computing, Dublin City University
[2]Cork Institute of Technology

pintu.lohar@adaptcentre.ie
haithem.afli@cit.ie
andy.way@adaptcentre.ie

Abstract

Social media platforms such as Twitter and Facebook are hugely popular websites through which Internet users can communicate and spread information worldwide. On Twitter, messages (tweets) are generated by users from all over the world in many different languages. Tweets about different events almost always encode some degree of sentiment. As is often the case in the field of language processing, sentiment analysis tools exist primarily in English, so if we want to understand the sentiment of the original tweets, we are forced to translate them from the source language into English and pushing the English translations through a sentiment analysis tool.

However, Lohar et al. (2017) demonstrated that using freely available translation tools often caused the sentiment encoded in the original tweet to be altered. As a consequence, they built a series of sentiment-specific translation engines and pushed tweets containing either positive, neutral or negative sentiment through the appropriate engine to improve sentiment preservation in the target language. For certain tasks, maintaining sentiment polarity in the target language during the translation process is arguably more important than the absolute translation quality obtained. In the work of Lohar et al. (2017), a small drop off in translation quality *per se* was deemed tolerable. In this work, we focus on maintaining the level of sentiment preservation while trying to improve translation quality still further. We propose a nearest sentiment class-combination method to extend the existing sentiment-specific translation systems by adding training data from the nearest-sentiment class. Our experimental results on German-to-English reveal that our approach is capable of achieving a proper balance between translation quality and sentiment preservation.

1   Introduction

The rapid development of internet technologies has given rise to a significant growth in generating and sharing of user-generated content (UGC). Internet users from all over the world stay connected via widely used social networking websites such as Twitter and Facebook by sharing information in different languages. On Twitter, tweets on different events related to sports, festivals, conferences and political events almost always encode some degree of sentiment. Accordingly, the task of sentiment analysis is important on datasets such as these. However, given the lack of such tools for most languages, this can only be achieved via an MT-based sentiment analysis approach, where the tweets are first translated from the original language to English and then sentiment analysis is performed on th English translations (Araujo et al. (2016)).

However, the 140-character limitation – recently expanded to 280 – in Twitter encourages users to use short forms at word and phrase levels. Moreover, tweets often contain (deliberate) spelling errors, hashtags, user names and URLs which pose challenges in the translation process. In order to build corpus-based MT systems, a parallel corpus is a prerequisite, but parallel UGC data is in very short supply. In recent work based on sentiment translation system, Lohar et al. (2017) collected a parallel data comprising $4,000$ English–German tweet pairs[1] in the football domain (extracted from the FIFA World Cup 2014 Twitter feed) and built sentiment translation engines using a sentiment classification approach. In that work, the sentiment translation models were built using the (i) negative, (ii) neutral, and (iii) positive tweet pairs, respectively. Their experimental results showed that the sentiment classification approach is very useful for preserving the sentiment in the target language during translation. However, the MT quality deteriorated a little due to dividing the small corpus of $4,000$ parallel tweets into even smaller ones with different sentiment classes for training sentiment-specific MT engines.

In this work, we try to retain the degree of sentiment while at the same time minimizing any loss in translation quality. We propose to extend the sentiment-specific translation models by incorporating neighbouring sentiment data. We perform the following steps to build our extended sentiment translation system: (i) building a single baseline translation model by using the whole Twitter data regardless of the sentiment classes, (ii) building separate negative, neutral and positive sentiment translation models using the negative, neutral and positive tweet pairs, respectively, (iii) combining the negative and neutral tweet pairs to build a translation system conveying both of these sentiments, and (iv) combining the positive and neutral tweet pairs to build a translation system conveying both of these sentiments. Steps (iii) and (iv) are the main contributions in this work that extend the previously mentioned sentiment translation system of Lohar et al. (2017). The reason behind such combinations of sentiment classes is that the neutral class is relatively closer to both the negative and positive classes, compared to the distance between the negative and positive classes in terms of sentiment score. This is motivated by the fact that in their work, Lohar et al. (2017) demonstrated that while MT can alter the original sentiment, it typically transfers to the immediately neighbouring class (i.e. from negative to neutral (or vice-versa) or from positive to neutral (or vice-versa)), but rarely from positive to negative (or vice-versa).

The remainder of this paper is organised as follows. We briefly describe some relevant related work in Section 2. In Section 3, we provide an architectural overview of our sentiment classification MT system. The experimental set ups are discussed in Section 4, followed by a detailed discussion of the results in Section 5. Finally, Section 6 concludes together with some avenues for future work.

2 Related work

Translating UGC creates new challenges in the area of MT. Jiang et al. (2012) describe how to handle shortforms, acronyms, typos, punctuation errors, non-dictionary slang, wordplay, censor avoidance and emoticons, phenomena which are characteristic of UGC but not of 'normal' written forms in language. The combination of statistical machine translation (SMT) and a preprocessor was also applied to remove a significant amount of noise from tweets in order to convert them into a more readable format (Kaufmann and Kalita (2010)). Gotti et al. (2013) use an SMT system to translate Twitter feeds published by agencies and organisations. They create tuning and training sets by mining parallel web pages linked from the URLs contained in English–French pairs of tweets.

There exists quite a lot of research in the area of sentiment analysis of UGC. For example,

---

[1]Recently released in Lohar et al. (2018) and available at: `https://github.com/HAfli/FooTweets_Corpus`

Fang and Zhan (2015) analyse the sentiment polarity of online product reviews extracted from *Amazon.com* using both sentence-level and review-level categorization techniques. Gräbner et al. (2012) classify customer reviews of hotels by extracting a domain-specific lexicon of semantically relevant words based on a given corpus (Scharl et al. (2003); Pak and Paroubek (2010)). Broß (2013) focus on the following two main subtasks of aspect-oriented review mining: (i) identification of the relevant product aspects, and (ii) determining and classifying the expressions of the sentiment.

Some existing work applies MT for the task of sentiment analysis. For example, Mohammad et al. (2016) show that the sentiment analysis of English translations of Arabic text produces competitive results compared to Arabic sentiment analysis *per se*. In a similar vein, Araujo et al. (2016) reveal that simply translating the non-English input text into English and using the English sentiment analysis tool can be better than the existing language-specific efforts evaluated. In contrast, Afli et al. (2017) demonstrate that building a sentiment analysis tool for a low-resource language, namely Irish, can outperform strategies including translation as an integral sub-task. Their approach includes the following strategies: (i) using the existing English sentiment analysis resources to both manually and automatically translated tweets, and (ii) manually creating an Irish-language sentiment lexicon – Senti-Foclóir – to build the first Irish sentiment analysis system – SentiFocalTweet – which produces superior results to the first method.

Importantly, although MT can be useful for the sentiment analysis task, it can alter the sentiment of the source-language text in the target language during the translation process (Mohammad et al. (2016)). For example, a text in the source language (say Arabic) with positive sentiment may not retain its positivity when translated into the target language (say English). To address such problems, Lohar et al. (2017) propose a sentiment classification approach to build sentiment-specific translation models that aim at maintaining the sentiment polarity of the source-language text during the translation process. The results revealed that it is possible to increase the sentiment preservation score by using the sentiment translation systems. In the present paper, we extend that work by incorporating the nearest neighbour sentiment classes in order to build extended sentiment translation engines that incorporate the sentiment of the neighbouring sentiment class. To the best of our knowledge, no existing work has attempted such an approach to addressing the problems of maintaining translation quality and sentiment preservation in parallel.

3   Architecture of the sentiment translation system

Figure 1 shows the architecture of our proposed sentiment translation system using the nearest neighbour sentiment classes. The complete workflow of the whole system can be described in following steps:

(i) sentiment classification is performed on the whole corpus,

(ii) the negative and the neutral tweet pairs are grouped together as the nearest neighbour sentiment classes,

(iii) apart from being used for combination, the neutral tweet pairs are also kept for separate usage,

(iv) the positive and the neutral tweet pairs are grouped together as the nearest neighbour sentiment classes,

(v) from the above three corpus sets, three different translation systems are built: negative_neutral, neutral and positive_neutral models, respectively,

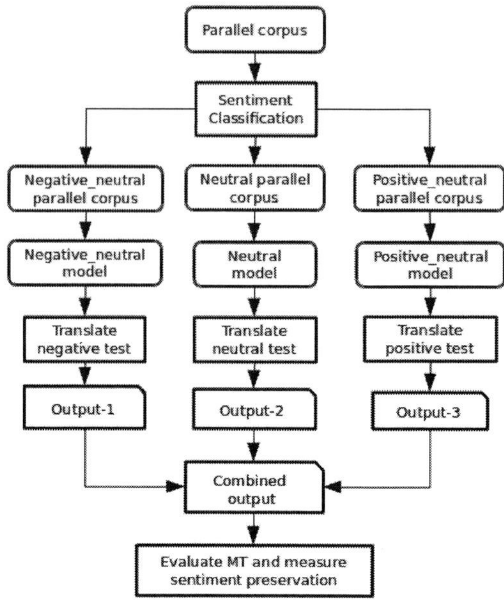

Figure 1: Sentiment translation using nearest neighbour sentiment classes

(vi) the test data is divided into negative, neutral and positive sentiment classes,

(vii) the negative, neutral and the positive test data are translated by the negative_neutral, neutral and the positive_neutral translation models, respectively,

(viii) the outputs produced by these three translation models are combined, and

(ix) the combined output is used to measure the MT and sentiment-preservation quality.

4 Experiments

4.1 Data statistics

Lohar et al. (2017) held out a small subset of only 50 tweet pairs per sentiment class (negative, neutral and positive, so 150 sentence pairs in total) for testing purposes in order to maintain as large an amount as possible for training the sentiment translation systems. However, it has to be acknowledged that it is difficult to judge the system's performance with only 150 test pairs. We therefore maintain two different distributions of the whole data set and use each of them separately in the two different experimental set-ups (*Exp1* and *Exp2*). We hope that by slightly increasing the size of the development and test sets, our analysis of the performance of the proposed system with these two different set-ups will be somewhat more informative.

Exp. setup	Train	Development			Test		
		#neg.	#neu.	#pos.	#neg.	#neu.	#pos.
Exp1	3, 700	50	50	50	50	50	50
Exp2	3, 400	100	100	100	100	100	100

Table 1: Data statistics

4.2 Resources and tools

All the translation models are built by using the widely used open source Moses SMT toolkit
(Koehn et al. (2007)). The word and phrase alignments are obtained by using the Giza++
tool (Och and Ney (2003)). Once the translation models are built, we tune all the sentiment
translation systems for both experimental set-ups (*Exp1* and *Exp2*) via minimum error rate
training (Och (2003)).

4.3 Evaluation process

We use the automatic MT evaluation metrics BLEU (Papineni et al. (2002)), METEOR
(Denkowski and Lavie (2014)) and TER (Snover et al. (2006)) to evaluate the absolute translation quality obtained. We measure the sentiment preservation score by calculating what percentage of the tweets belongs to the same sentiment class before and after translation.

5 Results

Table 2 shows the results obtained from the first experimental setup (*Exp1*) which is comparable
with the previous results obtained in the work of Lohar et al. (2017) because the data distribution
is the same (i.e. 150 tweet pairs for each of the development and test data sets).

System (Exp1)	BLEU	METEOR	TER	Sent_Pres.
Twitter_Baseline	50.3	60.9	31.9	66.66%
Twitter_SentClass	48.2	59.4	34.2	72.66%
Twitter_NearSent	49.0	60.1	34.0	66.66%

Table 2: Experiment 1: performance comparison on small test sets

The 2nd and the 3rd rows in Table 2 show the comparison between the two different sys-
tems (i.e., Twitter_Baseline and Twitter_SentClass) that were reported in Lohar et al. (2017).
Twitter_Baseline is the translation system where sentiment classification is not used, whereas
Twitter_SentClass is the system where it is switched on.

In contrast, "Twitter_NearSent" is our proposed system (including nearest sentiment class-
combination) with the same amount of training, development and test data. As can be seen
in this table, Twitter_SentClass obtains the highest sentiment preservation score of 72.66% but
the BLEU, METEOR and TER scores are worse than the Baseline. Lohar et al. (2017) state
that as expected, as the sentiment-classification approach divides the whole corpus into smaller
parts with specific sentiment classes, the translation models built from each data set are much
smaller than the baseline model and so the performance decreases accordingly. However, the
sentiment preservation score is significantly *increased* (from 66.66% to 72.66%) which was the
main objective of that work. In this work, our objective is to reduce this gap. More precisely,
we are interested in obtaining better MT scores than the Twitter_SentClass system but at the
same achieving the better sentiment preservation than the Baseline, which we hope to achieve
using the Twitter_NearSent system. Although the sentiment preservation score is not increased
at all, we do indeed manage to increase the MT scores: BLEU and METEOR increase by 0.8
(1.7% relative) and 0.7 (1.2% relative) points, respectively, while TER decreases by 0.2 points
(1.5% relative improvement).

These results demonstrate that using such a small amount of test data set (i.e. only 150
tweet pairs) is insufficient to confirm the utility of our approach. We therefore decided to rerun
the whole set of experiments on the new distribution (*Exp2*, see the 3rd row of Table 1) of the
training, development and test data (i.e. 100 sentence-pairs per sentiment for both the development and test data sets, respectively). Table 3 shows the results produced during our second

stage of experiments using the "Exp2" setup. As this data distribution is different from "Exp1", the results obtained are different and so are not directly comparable with the results shown in Table 2.

System (Exp2)	BLEU	METEOR	TER	Sent_Pres.
Twitter_Baseline	51.3	62.5	31.0	52.33%
Twitter_SentClass	47.3	59.1	35.2	60.33%
Twitter_NearSent	48.3	59.6	34.4	60.0%

Table 3: Experiment 2: performance comparison on larger test sets

It can be observed from this table that the "Twitter_SentClass" system produces the highest sentiment-preservation score of 60.33% – 8% (or 15.3% relative) better than the Baseline – but the MT scores are much lower than the Baseline. For example, the BLEU score is reduced by exactly 4 points (from 51.3 down to 47.3, an almost 8% relative reduction in translation quality), with the other automatic metrics corroborating this deterioration in performance. In contrast, our proposed system (Twitter_NearSent) raises the BLEU score by exactly 1 point (from 47.3 to 48.3, a 2.1% relative improvement) while at the same time the sentiment-preservation score is reduced by only 0.33%. In parallel, METEOR score is also increased from 59.1 to 59.6 (a 0.85% relative improvement) and the TER score is also improved (drops from 35.2 to 34.4, a 2.3% relative improvement). These results suggest that using a comparatively larger test set gives us a clearer picture of the performance of the various engines than the smaller one with "Exp1" set-up (see Table 2).

The above observations are important in terms of the balance between translation quality and sentiment preservation. Our new system is still able to significantly improve the sentiment-preservation score (from 52.33% to 60.0%) over the Baseline which is very close to the maximum value obtained (60.33%), yet at the same time manages to increase the MT score compared to the original engines built in Lohar et al. (2017).

6   Conclusion and Future Work

The current paper presented a novel extension to building sentiment-translation engines based on the combination of the nearest sentiment-class parallel data. Our new translation models are built by: (i) combining the negative and the neutral tweet pairs in order to build our first nearest neighbour sentiment translation model (*Negative_neutral model*), and (ii) combining the positive and the neutral tweet pairs to build the second nearest neighbour sentiment translation model (*Positive_neutral model*). We performed experiments in two stages with two different data distributions as the initial experiment was conducted on the smallest data set which we assumed to be insufficient to confirm the results to any great extent. The results obtained in the second stage of our experiments revealed that we can significantly increase the sentiment-preservation score (very close to the maximum value obtained) while at the same time obtaining improved MT scores than the sentiment-translation engines in Lohar et al. (2017).

Accordingly, our approach maintains a better balance between translation quality *per se* and sentiment preservation. In future, we will apply our approach to other forms of UGC such as user feedback, blogs, and reviews and with larger data sets. We will also conduct experiments on language pairs other than German-to-English. We also noticed that some of the tweets in our data sets are less related to the main topic (football) than originally anticipated, so it will be interesting to see how we can combine such out-of-domain data with true in-domain tweet pairs when building the next batch of sentiment-translation engines.

Acknowledgments

The ADAPT Centre for Digital Content Technology at Dublin City University is funded under the Science Foundation Ireland Research Centres Programme (Grant 13/RC/2106) and is co-funded under the European Regional Development Fund.

References

Afli, H., McGuire, S., and Way, A. (2017). Sentiment translation for low resourced languages: Experiments on irish general election tweets. In *18th International Conference on Computational Linguistics and Intelligent Text Processing*, Budapest, Hungary. 10 pages.

Araujo, M., Reis, J., Pereira, A., and Benevenuto, F. (2016). An evaluation of machine translation for multilingual sentence-level sentiment analysis. In *Proceedings of the 31st Annual ACM Symposium on Applied Computing*, pages 1140–1145, New York, USA.

Broß, J. (2013). *Aspect-Oriented Sentiment Analysis of Customer Reviews Using Distant Supervision Techniques.* PhD thesis, Freie Universität Berlin, Berlin, Germany.

Denkowski, M. and Lavie, A. (2014). Meteor universal: Language specific translation evaluation for any target language. In *Proceedings of the Ninth Workshop on Statistical Machine Translation*, pages 376–380, Baltimore, USA.

Fang, X. and Zhan, J. (2015). Sentiment analysis using product review data. *Journal of Big Data*, 2(5). 14 pages.

Gotti, F., Langlais, P., and Farzindar, A. (2013). Translating government agencies' tweet feeds: Specificities, problems and (a few) solutions. In *Proceedings of the Workshop on Language Analysis in Social Media*, pages 80–89.

Gräbner, D., Zanker, M., Fliedl, G., and Fuchs, M. (2012). Classification of customer reviews based on sentiment analysis. In *Proceedings of the International Conference on Information and Communication Technologies*, pages 460–470, Helsingborg, Sweden. Springer Vienna.

Jiang, J., Way, A., and Haque, R. (2012). Translating user-generated content in the social networking space. In *Proceedings of the Tenth Biennial Conference of the Association for Machine Translation in the Americas*, San Diego, USA. 9 pages.

Kaufmann, M. and Kalita, J. (2010). Syntactic normalization of Twitter messages. In *Proceedings of the 8th International Conference on Natural Language Processing*, pages 149–158, Kharagpur, India.

Koehn, P., Hoang, H., Birch, A., Callison-Burch, C., Federico, M., Bertoldi, N., Cowan, B., Shen, W., Moran, C., Zens, R., Dyer, C., Bojar, O., Constantin, A., and Herbst, E. (2007). Moses: Open source toolkit for statistical machine translation. In *Proceedings of the 45th Annual Meeting of the Association for Computational Linguistics*, pages 177–180, Prague, Czech Republic.

Lohar, P., Afli, H., and Way, A. (2017). Maintaining sentiment polarity in translation of user-generated content. *The Prague Bulletin of Mathematical Linguistics*, 108:73–84.

Lohar, P., Afli, H., and Way, A. (2018). Footweets: A bilingual parallel corpus of world cup tweets. In *LREC-2018, Proceedings of the 11th International Conference on Language Resources and Evaluation*, Miyazaki, Japan. (to appear).

Mohammad, S. M., Salameh, M., and Kiritchenko, S. (2016). How translation alters sentiment. *Journal of Artificial Intelligence Research*, 55(1):95–130.

Och, F. J. (2003). Minimum error rate training in statistical machine translation. In *Proceedings of the 41st Annual Meeting on Association for Computational Linguistics*, pages 160–167, Sapporo, Japan.

Och, F. J. and Ney, H. (2003). A systematic comparison of various statistical alignment models. *Computational Linguistics*, 29:19–51.

Pak, A. and Paroubek, P. (2010). Twitter as a corpus for sentiment analysis and opinion mining. In *Proceedings of the Seventh conference on International Language Resources and Evaluation*, pages 1320–1326, Valletta, Malta.

Papineni, K., Roukos, S., Ward, T., and Zhu, W.-J. (2002). Bleu: A method for automatic evaluation of machine translation. In *Proceedings of the 40th Annual Meeting on Association for Computational Linguistics*, pages 311–318, Philadelphia, Pennsylvania.

Scharl, A., Pollach, I., and Bauer, C. (2003). Determining the semantic orientation of web-based corpora. In *4th International Conference on Intelligent Data Engineering and Automated Learning*, pages 840–849, Hong Kong, China.

Snover, M., Dorr, B., Schwartz, R., Micciulla, L., and Makhoul, J. (2006). A study of translation edit rate with targeted human annotation. In *AMTA 2006: Proceedings of the 7th Conference of the Association for Machine Translation in the Americas, "Visions for the Future of Machine Translation*, pages 223–231, Cambridge, Massachusetts, USA.

Register-sensitive Translation:
A Case Study of Mandarin and Cantonese

Tak-sum Wong   tswong-c@my.cityu.edu.hk
John Lee   jsylee@cityu.edu.hk
Department of Linguistics and Translation, City University of Hong Kong,
Hong Kong SAR, P. R. China

Abstract

This paper describes an approach for translation between Chinese dialects that can produce target sentences at different registers. We focus on Mandarin as the source language, and Cantonese as the target. Mutually unintelligible, these two varieties of Chinese exhibit differences at both the lexical and syntactic levels, and the extent of the difference can vary considerably depending on the register of Cantonese. Since only a modest amount of parallel data is available, we adopt a knowledge-based approach and exploit lexical mappings and syntactic transformations from linguistics research. Our system parses a source sentence, uses register-annotated lexical mappings to translate words, and then performs word reordering through syntactic transformations. Evaluation shows that translation models that match the required register of the target sentences yield better translation quality.

1. Introduction

A large number of Chinese dialects are spoken in different regions of China. Many of these dialects are not mutually intelligible (Killingley, 1993; Szeto, 2000); indeed, the differences between the major Chinese varieties have been described as being "at least on the order of the different languages of the Romance family" (Hannas, 1997: 198), or "roughly parallel to English, Dutch, Swedish, and so on among the Germanic group of the Indo-European language family" (Mair, 1991: 3). This paper describes an approach for translating between Chinese dialects, focusing on Mandarin as the source language and Cantonese as the target language.

Mandarin, also known as Pŭtōnghuà, is considered standard Chinese and is the dominant variety in mainland China. Spoken by more than 55 million people, Cantonese, the "most widely known and influential variety of Chinese other than Mandarin" (Matthews and Yip, 2011), is the dominant variety of Chinese spoken in Hong Kong. In Hong Kong, Cantonese is used mainly in speech, while Mandarin is dominant in written contexts. This division of labor is somewhat comparable, for example, to the usage patterns of Swiss German dialects and standard German in Switzerland.

Although mutually unintelligible in their spoken form, Cantonese and Mandarin are genetically related, having both developed from Middle Chinese. They share similar writing systems, as well as many cognates. Most Mandarin lexical items can also be used in Cantonese. In a study on the Leipzig-Jakarta list of 100 basic words (Tadmor et al., 2010: 239–241), 60% of the Mandarin-Cantonese word pairs have identical written forms, most of which have highly regular phonological correspondence; a further 20% have the same core morpheme (Li et al., 2016). However, lexical items in Cantonese can vary considerably depending on the register, *i.e.*, language variation according to context (Halliday and Hasan, 1989; Quirk et al., 1985). Low-register Cantonese, typified by casual, informal speech, is often peppered with lexical items that are not used in Mandarin; in higher-register Cantonese, more lexical items are shared with the standard Chinese lexicon. Put otherwise, "an increase in informality corresponds to an increase in the number of Cantonese lexical items occurring in speech which makes it less like the lexicon of standard Chinese. … On the other hand, an increase in the formality of the social context calls for a corresponding increase in the number of standard Chinese lexical items occurring in the utterance (but of course pronounced in Cantonese)." (Bauer, 1988: 249). These variations among different registers make Cantonese a challenging target language for a case study for machine translation (MT) among Chinese dialects.

Most MT systems do not yet take the notion of register into account. A recent study on English-to-German translation found that both manually and automatically translated texts differ from the original texts in terms of register (Lapshinova-Koltunski and Vela, 2015). Neither does mainstream MT evaluation explicitly consider appropriateness in register, despite recent studies which argue it should (*e.g.*, Vela and Lapshinova-Koltunski, 2015). In this paper, we propose and evaluate a knowledge-based MT system that can translate Mandarin input into Cantonese at different registers.

The rest of the paper is organized as follows. In the next section, we outline previous research on MT for dialects in China and beyond. In section 3, we describe our translation approach. In section 4, we report both automatic and human evaluation, and analyze the main sources of error. Finally, we conclude in Section 5.

2. Previous work

A number of previous studies are related to our research in terms of language, data genre, and approach. Among the earliest attempts on translation between Chinese dialects is the knowledge-based approach taken by Zhang (1998), although no evaluation was reported. Xu and Fung (2012) developed a Cantonese-to-Mandarin MT system that is appended to an automatic speech recognition system for Cantonese, allowing it to output transcription in Mandarin Chinese. The translation capability was implemented with a cross-lingual language model with Inversion Transduction Grammar constraints for syntactic reordering.

Dialect MT is often applied to the task of television subtitle generation. Volk and Harder (2007) implemented an MT system, already in production use, for subtitle machine translation from Swedish to Danish. The system was trained using a statistical MT system, using a parallel corpus with 1 million subtitles. It has been further improved with morphological annotations (Hardmeier and Volk, 2009).

The translation approach taken in this paper is most similar to the knowledge-based system for translating standard German to Swiss German dialects, reported in Scherrer and Rambow (2010) and Scherrer (2011). Their approach uses a word list, compiled by experts, to handle lexical differences; and a set of syntactic transformations, defined by constituent-structure trees, to change sentence structures from German to Swiss German. Most rules achieved 85% accuracy or above. The system customizes the target sentence by selectively applying these rules according to the intended dialect area in Switzerland. Our approach also customizes the target sentence, but according to the register level rather than dialect area.

3. Approach

Statistical machine translation (MT) and neural network approaches have been successfully applied on many language pairs (Koehn et al., 2007), including dialects and other closely related languages (*e.g.*, Volk and Harder, 2007; Delmonte et al., 2009). One critical requirement for these approaches is the availability of a large amount of parallel sentences. In our case, due to the lack of standard written form for Cantonese, and the dominance of Mandarin in the written context, parallel Mandarin-Cantonese sentence pairs do not exist in large quantity. Taking a statistical approach to generate target sentences at different registers would compound the data sparseness issue, since both low- and high-register training data would be needed.

Despite the relative paucity of parallel data, Cantonese has been extensively studied by linguists (Zeng, 1993; Ōuyáng, 1993; *etc.*). It is thus less costly to exploit existing resources such as word lists and syntactic transformations, than to collect bilingual sentence pairs to overcome data sparseness. Hence, we adopt a knowledge-based approach for Mandarin-to-Cantonese translation, similar to that of an MT system for translating standard German into Swiss German dialects (Scherrer and Rambow, 2010; Scherrer, 2011). Our approach consists of three steps. First, it uses the Stanford Chinese parser to perform word segmentation, part-of-speech (POS) tagging and dependency parsing (Levy and Manning, 2003). Second, it uses forward maximal matching to look up Mandarin-to-Cantonese lexical mappings (Section 3.1), conditioned on POS information and register requirement (Section 3.2). Finally, it applies syntactic transformations on the output, with word re-ordering when warranted (Section 3.3).

3.1. Lexical mappings

The lexical mapping contains pairs of equivalent Mandarin and Cantonese words, taken from a parallel corpus of transcribed Cantonese speech and Mandarin Chinese subtitles (Lee, 2011). The speech was transcribed from television programmes broadcast in Hong Kong within the last decade by Television Broadcasts Limited. The Cantonese and Mandarin text were manually word-segmented and aligned. The TV programmes span a variety of genres, including news programmes, current-affairs shows, drama series and talk shows. These programs not only include vocabulary from widely different domains, but also contain Cantonese spoken in different registers. The most formal language is used in news, and the most colloquial in drama series and talk shows. We harvested all word alignments from the corpus to create lexical mappings. We further supplemented these mappings with a Cantonese-Mandarin dictionary that is freely available from the website of Kaifang Cidian (http://kaifangcidian.com).

Overall, our mappings cover 35,196 distinct Mandarin words. Out-of-vocabulary Mandarin words are likely to be infrequently used words; these words, fortunately, tend to be rendered in the same way in Cantonese, and therefore our system leaves them unchanged in the target sentence.

3.2. Annotation on lexical mappings

A Mandarin word may have multiple possible Cantonese translations. This is often because the Mandarin word has multiple meanings, but may also be due to different levels of the register of the Cantonese target word. To guide our system in choosing the most appropriate mapping, we annotate the lexical mappings with the POS of the Mandarin word and the register level in Cantonese. We follow the tagset of the Penn Chinese Treebank (Xia, 2000) in the POS annotation. We label the register level of the Cantonese word, labeling as 'low', 'high', or 'both'.

Table 1 shows several examples. The Mandarin word *ràng* 讓 can either mean 'to give way', or 'to let', both as a verb. In the former case, it has an identical Cantonese counterpart, *yeuhng* 讓 'to give way'; in the latter case, however, it must be translated as the Cantonese *dáng* 等 'to let'. The Mandarin word *de* 的 is also highly ambiguous. As a relativizer, it is tagged as "DEC" and its Cantonese equivalent is *ge* 嘅. As a sentence-final particle, it is tagged as "SP", with its high-register translation as *ge* 嘅, but its low-register translation as *ga* 㗎. Table 2 shows an application of these mappings to translate a Mandarin sentence.

For the mappings of the 1000 most frequent Mandarin words, we manually annotated the POS and register information. In terms of POS, 32 Mandarin words required POS specification for semantic disambiguation. In terms of register, 174 Mandarin words have different high- and low- register translations into Cantonese.

Mandarin word	Mandarin POS	Cantonese register	Cantonese word
ràng 讓 'to give way'	VV	both	*yeuhng* 讓 'to give way'
ràng 讓 'to let'	VV	both	*dáng* 等 'to let'
de 的	DEC/DEG	both	*ge* 嘅
de 的	SP	high	*ge* 嘅
de 的	SP	low	*ga* 㗎

Table 1. Example lexical mappings from Mandarin to Cantonese, specified by Mandarin POS and Cantonese register.

English	'I (really) have meal first before doing homework!'
Source (Mandarin)	我是先喫了飯再做作業的。 *wǒ shì **xiān** chī le fàn zài zuò zuòyè **de** .* PN VC **AD** VV AS NN AD VV NN **SP** 1SG COP **first** eat PFV meal then do homework SFP
High-register target (Cantonese)	我係先食咗飯再做功課嘅。 *ngóh haih **sīn** sihk jó faahn joi jouh gūngfo **ge** .* PN VC **AD** VV AS NN AD VV NN **SP** 1SG COP **first** eat PFV rice then do homework SFP
Low-register target (Cantonese)	我係食咗飯先再做功課㗎。 *ngóh haih sihk jó faahn **sīn** joi jouh gūngfo **ga** .* PN VC VV AS NN **AD** AD VV NN **SP** 1SG COP eat PFV rice **first** then do homework SFP

Table 2. Application of the lexical mappings on Table 1 and syntactic transformation on Table 3 on an example Mandarin source sentence to generate its high-register and low-register Cantonese target sentence.

3.3. Syntactic transformations

In a comparative analysis of Cantonese and Mandarin, Ōuyáng (1993: 274) noted that although their "grammatical structure is similar in most major respects, the differences are not insignificant". These differences include the use of modal verbs and predicative adjectives; the expression of epistemicity and comparative construction; the word order in double object constructions; and the system of sentence-final particles, which is significantly more complicated in Cantonese. Further, in a quantitative comparison between Mandarin and Cantonese, Wong et al. (2017) showed that Mandarin adverbs are replaced by Cantonese auxiliaries in a number of cases.

Similar to Scherrer (2011), we express syntactic transformations as tree pairs. Rather than constituent trees, however, we used the Stanford dependencies for Chinese (Chang et al., 2009), and also annotated their register level. The system incorporates 10 such transformations, the most frequent of which are shown in Table 3.

Construction	Register	Mandarin	Cantonese
Adverb position	low	先 … <verb> advmod(<verb>, 先)	<verb> …先 discourse:sp(<verb>, 先)
	low	多/少/太/過 <adjective> advmod(<adjective>, 多/少/太/過)	<adjective> 多/少/得滯/過頭 advmod(<adjective>, 多/少/得滯/過頭)
	both	<verb> 不了/不得 advmod(<verb>, 不了/不得)	唔 <verb> 得 advmod(<verb>,唔) advmod(<verb>,得)
Ditransitive construction	both	<verb> <noun_i> <noun_d> obj(<verb>, <noun_d>), obj(<verb>, <noun_i>)	<verb> <noun_d> <noun_i> obj(<verb>, <noun_d>), obj(<verb>, <noun_i>)
Comparative construction	low	比 <noun> <adjective> prep(<adjective>, 比) pobj(比, <noun>)	<adjective> 過 <noun> prep(<adjective>, 過) pobj(過, <noun>)
Adverbs vs. auxiliaries	low	一向都 <verb> advmod(<verb>,一向都)	<verb> 開 aux(<verb>, 開)
Question construction	both	<verb> … 嗎 ? discourse:sp(<verb>,嗎)	<verb_i> 唔 <verb_j> ? conj(<verb_i>, <verb_j>) adv(<verb_j>,唔)

Table 3. Syntactic transformations from Mandarin to Cantonese.

4. Evaluation

For evaluation, we used two test sets that correspond to high- and low-register Cantonese. The "High Register" test set consists of speeches in the Hong Kong Legislative Council 12th October, 2017, and their official translation into Mandarin.[1] The set contains 176 sentences, with 29 as the median sentence length. The "Low Register" test set is extracted from a Cantonese movie produced by students as a term project at a university in Hong Kong, with their Mandarin subtitles. This set contains 391 sentences, with 6 as the median sentence length. We first report results with automatic evaluation measures (Section 4.1), and then discuss results from a human evaluation on both translation quality and register appropriateness (Section 4.2).

4.1. Automatic evaluation

As shown in Table 4, we evaluated two translation models. The "High Register" model excludes lexical mappings and syntactic transformations that are labelled as 'low', while the "Low Register" model excludes mappings and transformations that are labelled as 'high' (Section 3.2). We evaluated translation quality using the translation edit rate (Snover et al., 2006) (TER). TER is similar to the Word Error Rate, but also allows "shift" as an edit in addition to insertion, deletion, and substitution.

On both datasets, both the "High Register" and "Low Register" models outperform the "no change" baseline, *i.e.*, output the Mandarin source sentence as target sentence. The TER of this baseline is lower for the "High Register" dataset, confirming that high-register Cantonese more closely resembles Mandarin.

---

[1] Retrieved from http://webcast.legco.gov.hk/public/zh-hk .

On the low-register set, the "Low Register" model gave better performance than the "High register" model; and *vice versa* on the high-register set. This suggests that our lexical mappings succeed in capturing Cantonese usage at different registers. Overall performance is higher on the high-register set, reflecting the difficulty in predicting sentence-final particles, which are missing in the Mandarin source sentences and must be inserted more frequently in the low-register set. Elsewhere, disfluencies, false-starts, slangs, and English code-switching (Chan, 1998) also contributed some of the other errors.

Model	Low Register test set	High Register test set
Baseline (No change)	59.13%	49.40%
High Register	53.34%	**45.32%**
Low Register	**52.56%**	45.50%

Table 4. TER for Mandarin-to-Cantonese translation on two register levels. "High-register test set" include news, legco; "low-register test set" includes movies, drama

4.2. Human evaluation

To perform a more detailed analysis on translation quality and register appropriateness, we randomly selected 90 Mandarin sentences for human evaluation; 40% of these were drawn from the High Register test set, and 60% from the Low Register test set.

Translation quality. We translated these 90 sentences with the translation model with matching register (Section 4.1). We then asked two native speakers of Cantonese to judge the quality of the system output, rating each as "Wrong", "Fair", or "Good". "Wrong" means the MT output contains at least one obvious mistake; "Fair" means the output is technically correct but can be made more fluent. On average, 62% of the sentences were rated as "Good", 12% rated as "Fair", and 26% as "Wrong'. In some cases, inappropriate Cantonese words are chosen because of semantic ambiguity for the Mandarin word. In others, dependency parsing errors affected the detection of some of the syntactic transformations.

Register appropriateness. In a second evaluation, we generated low- and high-register Cantonese output from the same 90 pair of Mandarin sentences, and asked two native speakers of Cantonese to choose which one has lower register. On average, 86% of the human judgment corresponded with the system's.

5. Conclusion

We have presented an approach for translation between Chinese dialects, and implemented it for Mandarin-to-Cantonese translation. The MT system uses lexical mapping from Mandarin to Cantonese, coupled with syntactic transformations defined with dependency trees. A significant novelty is that the lexical mappings are register-sensitive. Automatic evaluation shows that translation models that match the required register of the target sentences yield better translation quality, and significantly outperformed a baseline. Further, in human evaluations, 62% of the sentences were rated as "good", and 86% of the system output matches human judgment on its level of register. In future work, we plan to apply this approach to other Chinese dialects, and to allow more fine-grained specification of Cantonese register.

Acknowledgement

This work is partially supported by Knowledge Transfer Initiatives in Business, Law and Liberal Arts and Social Sciences Disciplines (project #6354028), and by a Strategic Research Grant (project #7004494) at City University of Hong Kong.

References

Bahdanau, D., Cho, K., and Bengio, Y. (2015). Neural Machine Translation by Jointly Learning to Align and Translate. In *Proceedings of the 3rd International Conference on Learning Representations (ICLR)*.

Bauer, R. S. (1988). Written Cantonese of Hong Kong. *Cahiers de linguistique – Asie orientale*, 17(2):245–293.

Chan, B. H.-S. (1998). How does Cantonese-English code-mixing work? In *Language in Hong Kong at Century's End*, M. C. Pennington (ed.), pages 191–216, Hong Kong: Hong Kong University Press.

Chang, P.-C., Tseng, H., Jurafsky, D., and Manning, C. D. (2009). Discriminative Reordering with Chinese Grammatical Relations Features. In *Proceedings of SSST*.

Delmonte, R., Bristot, A., Tonelli, S., and Pianta, E. (2009). English/Veneto resource poor machine translation with STILVEN. In *Proceedings of ISMTCL*, Bulag 33:82–29, Besancon, France.

Halliday, M. and Hasan, R. (1989). Language, Context and Text: Aspects of Language in a Social-semiotic Perspective. Oxford University Press, Oxford, UK.

Hannas, W. C. (1997) *Asia's orthographic dilemma*. Honolulu: University of Hawaii Press.

Hardmeier, C. and Volk, M. (2009). Using Linguistic Annotations in Statistical Machine Translation of Film Subtitles. In *Proceedings of NODALIDA*.

Huang, G., Gorin, A., Gauvain, J.-L., and Lamel, L. (2016). Machine Translation Based Data Augmentation for Cantonese Keyword Spotting. In *Proceedings of the 2016 IEEE International Conference on Acoustics, Speech and Signal processing (ICASSP)*.

Killingley, S. Y. (1993). *Cantonese*. Lincom Europa: Newcastle.

Koehn, P., Hoang, H., Birch, A., Callison-Burch, C., Federico, M., Bertoldi, N., Cowan, B., Shen, W., Moran, C., Zens, R., Dyer, C., Bojar, O., Constantin, A., and Herbst, E. (2007). Moses: Open Source Toolkit for Statistical Machine Translation. In *Proceedings of ACL*.

Lapshinova-Koltunski, E. and Vela, M. (2015). Measuring 'Registerness' in Human and Machine Translation: A Text Classification Approach. In *Proceedings of 2nd Workshop on Discourse in Machine Translation*.

Lee, J. (2011). Toward a Parallel Corpus of Spoken Cantonese and Written Chinese. In *Proceedings of IJCNLP*.

Lee, S. and Chan, K. K. W. (2017). From Cantonese L2 data to theoretical analysis: An Analysis of Num-Cl-N construction in Cantonese. In *Proceedings of 22nd International Conference on Yue Dialects*.

Levy, R. and Manning, C. D. (2003). Is it harder to parse Chinese, or the Chinese Treebank?. In *Proceedings of ACL*.

Li, D. C. S., Wong, C. S. P., Leung, W. M. and Wong, S. T. S. (2016). Facilitation of transference: The case of monosyllabic salience in Hong Kong Cantonese. *Linguistics*, 54(1):1–58.

Mair, V. H. (1991). What is a Chinese "dialect/topolect"? Reflections on some key Sino-English linguistic terms. *Sino-Platonic Papers*, 29: 1–31.

Matthews, S. and Yip, V. (2011). *Cantonese: A comprehensive grammar*. New York: Routledge.

Ōuyáng, J. (1993). *Pǔtōnghuà Guǎngzhōuhuà de bǐjiào yǔ xuéxí* (The comparison and learning of Mandarin and Cantonese). Peking: China Social Science Press.

Prokopidis, P., Karra, V., Papagianopoulou, A., and Piperidis, S. (2008). Condensing Sentences for Subtitle Generation. In *Proceedings of Linguistic Resources and Evaluation Conference* (LREC).

Ramsey, S. R. (1987). *The Languages of China*. Princeton: Princeton University Press.

Quirk, R., Greenbaum, S., Leech, G., and Svartvik, J. (1985). A Comprehensive Grammar of the English Language. Longman, London, UK.

Scherrer, Y. (2011). Syntactic transformations for Swiss German dialects. In *Proceedings of EMNLP*.

Scherrer, Y. and Rambow, O. (2010). Natural Language Processing for the Swiss German Dialect Area. In *Proceedings of KONVENS*.

Snover, M., Dorr, B., Schwartz, R., Micciulla, L., and Makhoul, J. (2006). A Study of Translation Edit Rate with Targeted Human Annotation. In *Proceedings of Association for Machine Translation in the Americas* (AMTA).

Szeto, C. (2000). Testing Intelligibility among Sinitic Dialects. In *Proceedings of the Conference of the Australian Linguistic Society*.

Tadmor, U., Haspelmath, M. and Taylor, B. (2010). Borrowability and the notion of basic vocabulary. *Diachronica*, 27(2):226–246.

Vela, M. and Lapshinova-Koltunski, E. (2015). Register-based Machine Translation with Text Classification Techniques. In Proceedings of *MT Summit XV: MT Researchers' Track*.

Volk, M. and Harder, S. (2007). Evaluating MT with translations or translators. What is the difference? In *Proceedings of MT Summit XI*.

Wong, T.-S., Gerdes, K., Lee, J. and Leung, H. (2017). Quantitative Comparative Syntax on the Cantonese-Mandarin Parallel Dependency Treebank. In *Proceedings of International Conference on Dependency Linguistics*.

Xia, F. (2000). The Part-Of-Speech Tagging Guidelines for the Penn Chinese Treebank (3.0). *IRCS Technical Reports Serie*s. 38.

Xu, P. and Fung, P. (2012). Cross-Lingual Language Modeling with Syntactic Reordering for Low-Resource Speech Recognition. In *Proceedings of EMNLP-CoNLL*.

Zeng, Z. (1986). *Colloquial Cantonese and Putonghua Equivalents*. Hong Kong: Joint Publisher.

Zhang, X. (1998). Dialect MT: A Case Study between Cantonese and Mandarin. In *Proceedings of the Annual Meeting of the Association of Computational Linguistics*.

An Evaluation of Two Vocabulary Reduction Methods for Neural Machine Translation

Duygu Ataman   ataman@fbk.eu

Fondazione Bruno Kessler, Trento, Italy
University of Trento, Trento, Italy

Marcello Federico   federico@fbk.eu

MMT Srl, Trento, Italy
Fondazione Bruno Kessler, Trento, Italy

Abstract

Neural machine translation (NMT) models are conventionally trained with fixed-size vocabularies to control the computational complexity and the quality of the learned word representations. This, however, limits the accuracy and the generalization capability of the models, especially for morphologically-rich languages, which usually have very sparse vocabularies containing rare inflected or derived word forms. Some studies tried to overcome this problem by segmenting words into subword level representations and modeling translation at this level. However, recent findings have shown that if these methods interrupt the word structure during segmentation, they might cause semantic or syntactic losses and lead to generating inaccurate translations. In order to investigate this phenomenon, we present an extensive evaluation of two unsupervised vocabulary reduction methods in NMT. The first is the well-known byte-pair-encoding (BPE), a statistical subword segmentation method, whereas the second is linguistically-motivated vocabulary reduction (LMVR), a segmentation method which also considers morphological properties of subwords. We compare both approaches on ten translation directions involving English and five other languages (Arabic, Czech, German, Italian and Turkish), each representing a distinct language family and morphological typology. LMVR obtains significantly better performance in most languages, showing gains proportional to the sparseness of the vocabulary and the morphological complexity of the tested language.

1   Introduction

Neural machine translation (NMT) has provided significant improvements to the state-of-the-art in machine translation (Bentivogli et al., 2016). However, it has also brought quite a few practical issues. A very important one of these is the low accuracy in translating rare words, caused by two of the main properties of the model. The first is related to the requirement of observing many examples of a word until its internal representation becomes accurate, and the second is due to the difficulty of handling large vocabularies, as this has an impact on the computational complexity of the model. Current implementations of NMT models require long training time and large memory space due to the high number of parameters to optimize. Hence, even with the most advanced machinery, deploying networks that can learn reliable representations for all words observed in the training corpus becomes practically impossible. In order to control the model complexity and the quality of the word representations, a straightforward approach is to fix the vocabularies to a maximum size, *e.g.* 100,000 lexical units, prior to training.

Clearly, a word can only be translated if an exact match of it is found in the vocabulary. This requirement leads to critical restrictions in translating morphologically-rich languages, where the word vocabulary tends to be very large and sparse. For example, in our case study, despite the relatively small size of our training corpora, the size of the source vocabulary found in the Turkish-English training corpus is around 170,000, *i.e.* much larger than the maximum size that is generally used.

Some studies have tried to overcome this problem by redefining the model vocabulary in terms of interior orthographic units compounding the words. These units could be individual characters (Ling et al., 2015; Lee et al., 2017), hybrid word/character units (Luong and Manning, 2016), or subwords (Sennrich et al., 2016), *i.e.* character sequences segmented according to their frequency in the training corpus. The prominent approach used today is to treat these subwords as individual lexical units. Hence, NMT is learned as a bilingual mapping between subword units of two languages. In addition to providing a new perspective to modeling translation at the sublexical level, these approaches have alleviated the out-of-vocabulary problem in NMT.

The sore point of these methods, however, is that they disregard any linguistic notion during segmentation. Many studies have shown that using subword segmentation methods which do not preserve the morpheme boundaries inside words may lead to loss of information related to the semantic or syntactic properties of words and generate inaccurate translations (Niehues et al., 2016; Ataman et al., 2017; Pinnis et al., 2017; Huck et al., 2017; Tamchyna et al., 2017). A more linguistically motivated solution was recently proposed by Ataman et al. (2017), which segments words into subwords by estimating their likeliness of being morphemes and their morphological categories. This approach provided significant improvements for translation of Turkish, an agglutinative language with a very sparse vocabulary.

In this paper, we present a comparative study on two unsupervised word segmentation methods: Byte-Pair Encoding (BPE) (Sennrich et al., 2016) and the Linguistically-Motivated Vocabulary Reduction (LMVR) method by Ataman et al. (2017) for NMT. Our analysis aims at understanding the important factors related to the statistical and formal characteristics of lexical units, mainly induced by morphology, and how they affect the translation quality. For this purpose, we set up an evaluation benchmark pairing English with five inflected languages: Arabic, Czech, German, Italian and Turkish, where each language represents a language family with distinct morphological characteristics.

The experimental results show that the translation quality obtained using LMVR (Ataman et al., 2017) in three of the languages (Arabic, Czech and Turkish) is significantly better than that with BPE (Sennrich et al., 2016). All of these languages share the common feature of having a high level of sparseness or a morphology with agglutinating or concatenating properties. For the remaining two languages with fusional characteristics and lower sparseness: German and Italian, the two segmentation methods yield comparable performance. In general, both word segmentation methods outperform the simple frequency-based vocabulary reduction method proposed by (Luong et al., 2015). Our study suggests that considering the morphological characteristics of the chosen language pair is essential in order to choose the most appropriate subword segmentation approach in NMT.

2 Neural Machine Translation (NMT)

In this paper, we use the NMT model described in (Bahdanau et al., 2014). The model essentially estimates the conditional probability of translating a source text x, represented by the input word sequence $x = (x_1, x_2, \ldots x_m)$ of length m, into a target text y, represented as the target word sequence $y = (y_1, y_2, \ldots y_j \ldots y_l)$ of length l. The conditional probability is decomposed as follows:

$$p(y|x; \theta) = \prod_{i=1}^{l} p(y_i | y_{i-1}, ..., y_0, x_m, ..., x_1; \theta) \tag{1}$$

where θ represents the model parameters. The model is trained by maximizing the log-likelihood of a parallel training set D:

$$L(D, \theta) = \sum_{x,y \in D} \log p(y|x; \theta) \tag{2}$$

The inputs of the network are one-hot vectors – *i.e.* binary vectors that have a single bit set to 1 to identify a specific word in the vocabulary. Each word vector is then mapped to an embedding, a continuous representation in a lower dimension but more dense space. Hence, a distributed representation of the source words is learned using a bi-directional recurrent neural network, the *encoder*, which encodes x into m dense sentence vectors, corresponding to its hidden states.

Next, a unidirectional recurrent neural network, the *decoder*, predicts the target sequence y word by word using the information provided by the encoder. Each target word y_j is predicted by sampling from a word distribution computed from the previous target word y_{j-1}, the previous hidden state of the decoder, and a so-called *context vector*. The context vector is a linear combination of the encoder hidden states, whose weights are dynamically computed by a feedforward neural network called the *attention* model. The attention model predicts each weight on the basis of the previous target word, the previous decoder hidden state and the corresponding encoder hidden state.

The overall network is trained to minimize the cost function in Equation 2 via Stochastic Gradient Descent (SGD) (Bottou, 2010) and the Back Propagation Through Time algorithm (Werbos, 1990). During training, the learning algorithm iteratively updates the parameters of the network, including the weights of the hidden units in each layer and the word embeddings, until the value of the cost function calculated in the training corpus is optimized, or a maximum number of iterations is reached. In practice, this process is computationally very expensive due to the many parameters to adjust and the fact that the probability of generating each target word y_j is normalized via a softmax function, as shown below:

$$p(y_i = e_j | x; \theta) = \frac{e^{e_j^T o_i}}{\sum_{k=1}^{K} e^{e_k^T o_i}} \tag{3}$$

where e_j is the jth one-hot vector of the target vocabulary of size K, and o_i is the decoder output vector for the ith target word y_i.

From equation (3) we see that the computational cost of predicting each word scales linearly with the target vocabulary size K. In general, larger source and target vocabulary sizes imply higher levels of data sparseness, longer training and inference time and a larger dynamic memory usage. Bahdanau et al. (2014) suggested using a fixed-size vocabulary of size k containing only the top k frequent words in the corpus in order to control the size of the source and target vocabularies. Nevertheless, this prevents translating any out-of-vocabulary words that might be encountered in new sentences. Luong et al. (2015) extended this approach to integrate a word alignment model as a post-processing step to the NMT system, where the words that do not fit in the vocabulary are marked as an unknown word token (*i.e.* 'UNK') and the sentence is translated disregarding these words. After translation, the unknown tokens on the target side can be replaced with the original words on the source side or simply left as is. This approach is useful for translating rare words like numbers or named entities that are not found in the vocabulary, however, it does not provide a complete solution as rare words can be of different nature in each language. For instance, a large portion of the vocabularies in a synthetic language (see Section

4) can contain infrequent words that are derivated or inflected word forms, which often carry important information related to the syntax and semantics of the rest of the sentence.

3 Unsupervised Word Segmentation for NMT

A conventional solution to limit the vocabulary size in NMT is to segment words into smaller units and perform translation at the sublexical level. In this paper, we discuss two such methods: BPE and LMVR.

3.1 Byte-Pair Encoding (BPE)

BPE is the prominent method of subword segmentation for NMT that has been applied to many languages (Bojar et al., 2017). It is originally a data compression algorithm that minimizes the length of sequences of bytes by finding the most frequent consecutive byte pairs and encoding them using unused byte values (Gage, 1994). It was recently modified by Sennrich et al. (2016) for vocabulary reduction, where the most frequent character sequences are iteratively merged to find the optimal description of the corpus vocabulary. This purely statistical method is based on the assumption that many types of words can be translated when segmented into smaller units, such as named entities and loanwords. Nevertheless, in cases of common morphological paradigms such as derivational or inflectional transformations which are typically observed in morphologically-rich languages, the method lacks a linguistic notion that could allow it to better generalize syntactic patterns in the data and use the vocabulary space more effectively (Ataman et al., 2017; Huck et al., 2017; Tamchyna et al., 2017). Moreover, by disregarding morpheme boundaries during splitting, it can lead to semantically ambiguous subwords which would be translated inaccurately (Niehues et al., 2016; Ataman et al., 2017; Pinnis et al., 2017).

3.2 Linguistically-Motivated Vocabulary Reduction (LMVR)

Similar to BPE, LMVR constitutes a pre-processing step to NMT. The method is an extension of *Morfessor FlatCat* (Grönroos et al., 2014), an unsupervised morphology learning algorithm based on a Hidden Markov Model (HMM), which models the composition of a word based on the transitions between different morphemes and their categories (*i.e.* prefix, stem or suffix). The category-based HMM is essential for a linguistically motivated segmentation, as words are split considering the possible categories of the generated subwords and not only their frequencies. Ataman et al. (2017) has recently modified this method in order to optimize the complexity of the model with a constraint on the number of morphemes to be found in the corpus after segmentation, *i.e.* the lexicon size, which eventually allows it to be deployed as a stand-alone vocabulary reduction technique for NMT.

Similar to the two-level morphology model of Koskenniemi (1983), the model (M) consists of mainly two parts, a *lexicon* that contains the list of morphemes and a *grammar* which defines a set of rules that combine different morphemes together to generate new words. The model is estimated via Maximum A-Posteriori (MAP) optimization in order to avoid overfitting, by finding a balance between model accuracy and complexity. The MAP estimate of the overall system is given as:

$$M^* = \arg \max_{M} \Pr(D|M) \Pr(M) \tag{4}$$

where the two factors respectively represent the likelihood of the training corpus D and the prior probability of the model M.

While the former is computed on the data by a HMM, the latter is modeled by considering individual properties of the generated lexicon[1] of morphemes:

$$\Pr(M = \{\mu_1, \ldots, \mu_m\}) \approx m! \, P(usage(\mu_1, \ldots, \mu_m)) P(form(\mu_1, \ldots, \mu_m)) \tag{5}$$

---

[1]The grammar is assumed as a fixed component of the model and is thus disregarded from the prior.

where m is the number of distinct morphemes (μ_i) in the lexicon (Creutz and Lagus, 2007). The *usage* of morphemes are modeled by their frequencies, lengths, and their left and rightwards perplexities. The *form* of morphemes considers instead the probability of their internal structure, composed either of other morphemic categories or a sequence of characters.

Using the a-posteriori probability, one can train a segmentation model considering both the model complexity and the likelihood of the corpus, without any control on the size of the output lexicon. In order to achieve a desired rate of vocabulary reduction for NMT, Ataman et al. (2017) inserts a regularization weight over the lexicon prior and thus force the optimization to give more importance to reducing the model complexity. The general formula for optimization then becomes:

$$L(D, M) = \log P(D|M) + \alpha \log P(M)$$

where $\alpha > 1$ would force the optimization algorithm to find a smaller lexicon size and a finer segmentation. Ataman et al. (2017) empirically sets α equal to $\frac{m_1}{m_2}$, where m_1 is the initial vocabulary size of the corpus, and m_2 is the target vocabulary size.

4 Morphology and Language Families

In NMT, translation is conventionally modeled at the lexical level. Thus, the statistical distribution of the words observed in training data has a crucial role to guide the NMT models. A high level of variance in the lexical distribution implies a high level of sparseness and a low expectation to observe each individual word. This increases the difficulty to learn translations, especially of the infrequent words, and limits the accuracy of the model. An important factor that affects the sparseness in a corpus is the morphological properties of a language. In order to illustrate this aspect, we hereby introduce basic concepts of morphology and how it is formed in different languages.

The smallest units inside a word that carry meaning are called *morphemes* (O'Grady et al., 1997). They can typically have one of two main functions: aiding the grammatical role or the meaning of the word in which they occur. The main component required to form a word is the root morpheme, or the *base*, which has the most crucial role of defining the meaning and contains one of several categories (*i.e.* noun, verb, adjective, or preposition). Other components may include *affixes*, which do not belong to a lexical category and are attached to the base to form new words. An affix that is attached to the front of the base is called a *prefix*, and an affix that is attached to the end of the base is called a *suffix*. In Italian both prefixes and suffixes can be observed, whereas in Turkish words expand only through attachment of suffixes. In very few languages like Arabic, it is also possible to observe *infixes*, types of affixes that are attached to the root within a base (O'Grady et al., 1997). In some languages, independent words from different lexical categories can be combined to create a larger word with a new meaning. This common morphological process is called *compounding*. In such a case, the same word may be expected to contain multiple bases and affixes. In German, compounding is frequently observed. From a functional perspective, morphemes can be combined to produce words mainly in two ways. *Derivational* morphemes are added to a root to change its category or function. On the other hand, *inflectional* morphemes carry grammatical meaning and do not change the category of the root. Both ensure the transformation of the root in a correct surface form so that the sentence is grammatically acceptable.

Depending on the language, a word may contain a limited number of morphemes. For instance, *analytic* languages, such as Mandarin Chinese or Vietnamese, usually preserve a one-to-one correspondence between a word and a morpheme (Shopen, 1985). On the other hand, in *synthetic* languages, a word can contain several morphemes. Synthetic languages are generally grouped into two morphology families. *Fusional* languages are characterized by their

Language	Family	Morphological Complexity	Morphological Typology
Arabic	Semitic	High	Concatenative, Templatic
Czech	Slavic	High	Mostly Fusional, Partially Agglutinating
German	Germanic	Medium	Fusional
Italian	Italic	Low	Fusional
Turkish	Turkic	High	Agglutinating

Table 1: Families and morphological characteristics of languages we translate from/to English.

tendency to use a single inflectional morpheme to denote multiple grammatical, syntactic, or semantic features. On the other hand, in *agglutinative* languages, each morpheme in a word remains in every aspect unchanged after their composition, allowing a direct identification of the morpheme boundaries. In fusional and agglutinating typologies, morphemes are generally composed continuously to construct new word forms. On the other hand, it is also possible to observe *templatic* typologies, for instance in Arabic, where morphemes are inserted in certain templates in a discontinuous fashion to achieve certain derivative or inflective transformations.

Most languages do not belong exclusively to one category of morphological typology. In fact, there are many languages where different morphological phenomena are observed together. Based on how much such phenomena are typical in a language, it is expected to observe increased sparseness in the lexical surface forms. Consequently, the morphological characteristics of a language would be directly influential on the statistical distribution obtained from a textual corpus in the given language. In order to enlighten this aspect, we have chosen five languages which have been commonly studied in official machine translation evaluation campaigns. Each of them represents a different language family and falls into a distinct combination of morphological typology. The selected languages consist of Arabic (*Semitic*), Czech (*Slavic*), German (*Germanic*), Italian (*Italic*) and Turkish (*Altaic*). As a bridge between all the languages, we choose English from the Germanic family, which is a moderately analytic language but contains some different morphological features compared to German, the other Germanic language in our study. A summary of the main linguistic and morphological features of the listed languages can be seen in Table 1.

5 Evaluation

In order to evaluate different subword segmentation methods, we set up a common benchmark to observe the effect of each method on languages with different statistical properties. Our benchmark couples English (either as source or target) with five languages: Arabic, Czech, German, Italian and Turkish. Thus, each language pair represents different statistical properties reflected by the level of agglutination or fusion observed in their formal morphology. We perform NMT by keeping the segmentation on the English side fixed and applying different segmentation approaches to the other languages. This aids us in avoiding a combinatorial explosion in the number of experiments, while ensuring the results between each language are comparable. We later vary the segmentation method applied to the English side to investigate its effects on both sides of translation. We limit these experiments only to the English-Italian and English-Turkish pairs, as they represent two extreme cases in our setting, *i.e.* from low to high morphological complexity. All experiments consider each tested language both at the source and the target side of translations. The two subword segmentation methods, *LMVR* and *BPE*, are also compared with the frequency-based vocabulary pruning method suggested by Luong et al. (2015), and described at the end of Section 2, which is henceforth referred to as *Word* method.

Language	# sentences	# tokens	# types
Arabic-English	238,511	3,9M(AR) - 4,9M(EN)	220K(AR) - 120K(EN)
Czech-English	117,966	2M(CS) - 2,3M(EN)	118K(CS) - 50K(EN)
German-English	212,151	4M(DE) - 4,3M(EN)	144K(DE) - 69K(EN)
Italian-English	184,642	3,5M(IT) - 3,8M(EN)	95K(IT) - 63K(EN)
Turkish-English	135,734	2,7M(TR) - 2M(EN)	171K(TR) - 53K(EN)

Language	Data sets		# sentences	# tokens
Arabic-English	Development	dev2010, test2010, test2011, test2012	5,835	89K(AR) - 114K(EN)
	Testing	test2013, test2014	4,121	66K(AR) - 83K(EN)
Czech-English	Development	dev2010, test2010, test2011	3,112	52K(CS) - 61K(EN)
	Testing	test2012, test2013	2,836	47K(CS) - 55K(EN)
German-English	Development	dev2010, test2010, test2011, test2012	5,777	108K(DE) - 113K(EN)
	Testing	test2013, test2014, test2015	3,543	67K(DE) - 70K(EN)
Italian-English	Development	dev2010, test2010,	3,517	74K(IT) - 79K(EN)
	Testing	test2011, test2012	3,230	55K(IT) - 60K(EN)
Turkish-English	Development	dev2010, test2010	2,433	34K(TR) - 47K(EN)
	Testing	test2011, test2012	2,720	39K(TR) - 53K(EN)

Table 2: *Above:* Training sets. *Below:* Development and Testing Sets. All data set are official evaluation sets from IWSLT. (*M*: Million, *K*: Thousand.)

5.1 Data

We train our NMT models using the TED Talks corpora (Cettolo et al., 2012) and test them on official data sets of the IWSLT[2] evaluation campaign from 2010 to 2015. This aids us in having a variety of languages with different morphological typology within the same benchmark. We select multiple development and testing sets from different years to obtain more reliable results. All data sets are tokenized and truecased using the Moses scripts[3] (Koehn et al., 2007), except

---

[2]The International Workshop on Spoken Language Translation with shared tasks organized between 2003-2017.
[3]www.statmt.org/moses

for Arabic, which is normalized and tokenized using the QCRI normalization tool[4] (Sajjad et al., 2013). The details of the statistical characteristics of each data set used in our experiments and the chosen development and testing sets are given in Table 2.

5.2 Segmentation Models

The two subword segmentation methods that we compare in our experiments, *BPE* and *LMVR*, as well as the baseline vocabulary reduction method, *Word*, are applied to fit the same dictionary sizes (30,000) set in the NMT models. Since our training sets are small, choosing a small vocabulary size allows to illustrate large vocabulary reduction rates encountered in practical NMT tasks. We learn the merge rules of BPE at an equal size to the dictionary. Similarly, the LMVR models are trained with an *output lexicon size* of the same size. The rest of the settings are kept as default except for the perplexity threshold, for which we keep the default value of 10 for five languages, while for Arabic we use the value 70 as suggested by Al-Mannai et al. (2014). The translated sentences are desegmented based on the splitting characters ("@@" for BPE, "+" for LMVR) before measuring the translation quality.

5.3 NMT Models

The NMT models used in the evaluation are based on the Nematus toolkit (Sennrich et al., 2017). They have a hidden layer and embedding dimension of 1024 and a dictionary size of 30,000 for both source and target languages. We train the models using the Adagrad (Duchi et al., 2011) optimizer with a mini-batch size of 100, a learning rate of 0.01, and a dropout rate of 0.1 (in the input and output layers) and 0.2 (in the embeddings and hidden layers). In order to prevent over-fitting, we stop training if the perplexity on the validation has not decreased for 5 epochs or the maximum number of epochs are reached. After 50 epochs, we choose the model with the highest performance on the development set for translating the test set. In order to present a comprehensive evaluation, we evaluated the accuracy of each model output using both BLEU (Papineni et al., 2002) and chrF3 (Popovic, 2015) metrics. Significance tests are computed only for BLEU with Multeval (Clark et al., 2011).

6 Results

The findings of the experiment, presented in Table 3, illustrates the translation qualities using different approaches and how these qualities vary among different languages. The results of the experiments where the English side is segmented with BPE show that LMVR generally achieves the best results by outperforming BPE with a significant improvement in three out of four morphologically-rich languages. The improvements are **1.55** BLEU points in Turkish-to-English, **1.08** BLEU points in Arabic-English and **0.99** BLEU points in Czech-to-English. In the German-to-English translation task, the difference between the performance of two subword segmentation methods is not statistically significant. In the Italian-to-English direction, BPE produces better translations with an accuracy of 0.29 BLEU points higher than LMVR. The improvements are in general more evident in the chrF3 score, where we observe an improvement of **0.017** points in Turkish-to-English, and around **0.015** points in Arabic-to-English and Czech-to-English. In the German-to-English direction, LMVR provides slightly higher accuracy in terms of the chrF3 score. The improvements over the weak baseline of word-based translation are also significant, ranging from **5.16** BLEU points in Turkish-to-English to **1.63** BLEU points in German-to-English and **0.62** BLEU points in Italian-to-English.

The experiments conducted in the opposite translation directions show that the performance characteristics of LMVR are consistent in either directions. Translating into a morphologically-rich language is a more challenging task and the output quality is generally

---

[4]alt.qcri.org/tools/arabic-normalizer

Language Direction	Segmentation (Src)	(Tgt)	BLEU	chrF3
Arabic-English	Word	BPE	26.76	0.4793
	BPE	BPE	29.59	0.5102
	LMVR	BPE	**30.67**[▲]	**0.5248**
Czech-English	Word	BPE	26.82	0.4689
	BPE	BPE	28.21	0.494
	LMVR	BPE	**29.2**[▲]	**0.5091**
German-English	Word	BPE	30.71	0.5109
	BPE	BPE	**32.57**	0.5432
	LMVR	BPE	32.53	**0.5437**
Italian-English	Word	BPE	31.41	0.5237
	BPE	BPE	**32.50**	0.5322
	LMVR	BPE	32.21	0.5302
	BPE	LMVR	32.16	0.5416
	LMVR	LMVR	**32.50**	**0.5446**
Turkish-English	Word	BPE	17.58	0.3859
	BPE	BPE	21.28	0.4335
	LMVR	BPE	22.83	0.4501
	BPE	LMVR	20.99	0.4390
	LMVR	LMVR	**23.13**[▲]	**0.4599**

chrF3	BLEU	Segmentation (Src)	(Tgt)	Language Direction
0.3460	15.20	BPE	Word	English-Arabic
0.4490	17.91	BPE	BPE	
0.4610	**18.95**[▲]	BPE	LMVR	
0.3731	18.46	BPE	Word	English-Czech
0.4378	19.09	BPE	BPE	
0.4483	**19.98**[▲]	BPE	LMVR	
0.4927	26.35	BPE	Word	English-German
0.5431	27.24	BPE	BPE	
0.5485	**27.38**	BPE	LMVR	
0.5120	27.77	BPE	Word	English-Italian
0.5415	28.28	BPE	BPE	
0.5451	**28.30**	BPE	LMVR	
0.5412	27.99	LMVR	BPE	
0.5432	28.24	LMVR	LMVR	
0.2968	10.05	BPE	Word	English-Turkish
0.4183	11.31	BPE	BPE	
0.4410	12.53	BPE	LMVR	
0.4378	11.13	LMVR	BPE	
0.4435	**12.63**[▲]	LMVR	LMVR	

Table 3: Experiment results. Best scores for each translation direction are in bold font. Those marked with ▲ are also statistically significantly better (p-value < 0.05) than the baseline.

lower. In these directions, however, the effect of the chosen segmentation methods can be visualized more clearly, as the experiments show that the improvements of the two vocabulary reduction methods over the weak baseline of word-based translation is quite significant for the most sparse languages, whereas as sparseness in the languages decreases we observe very comparable performances. For instance, in English-to-Italian translation, the word vocabulary is naturally not very sparse, and segmentation by either method provides around **0.5** BLEU and **0.033** chrF3 points, *i.e.* 1,8% improvement. On the other hand, for English-to-Arabic translation, segmenting words generally provides an improvement of at least **3.75** BLEU and **0.103** chrF3 points. Similarly, in English-to-Turkish translation, we observe very large improvements over the baselines, **2.49** BLEU and **0.14** chrF3 points above the weak baseline, reaching an overall of 11% improvement. The findings also suggest that choosing LMVR for vocabulary reduction for NMT in the task of generating translations in the morphologically-rich language provides better translation quality than BPE. The highest improvement is observed again in the English-to-Turkish direction, where LMVR outperforms BPE by **1.32** BLEU and **0.025** chrF3 points. The improvements follow the same trend for English-to-Arabic, with **1.04** BLEU and **0.029** chrF3 points and in English-to-Czech translation, where LMVR achieves an accuracy of around 4.7% above the strong baseline. For translation directions involving German and Italian, the performances of two segmentation methods are generally comparable.

Using LMVR on both sides of the parallel data aids in obtaining full advantage from the method, especially in the morphologically-rich language setting. In Turkish-to-English direction, using LMVR also on the English side improves the performance by **0.3** BLEU and **0.0099** chrF3 points over the approach of using BPE on the English and LMVR on the target side, whereas in English-to-Turkish direction it provides an improvement of **0.1** BLEU and **0.0025** chrF3 points. In Italian-to-English direction, the performance is increased by **0.29** BLEU and **0.0124** chrF3 points, reaching the best performance among all vocabulary reduction methods. In English-to-Italian direction, all methods are comparable. A comparison between the approaches of applying either LMVR or BPE on both sides of the corpus does not yield a significantly different translation accuracy in English-to-Italian and Italian-to-English directions.

7 Discussion

A first glance at the findings of our experiments confirms the benefit of subword segmentation as a vocabulary reduction approach. This is mainly due to the higher reduction of vocabulary sparseness that is achieved with respect to filtering out infrequent words (*Word* method). When rare words that do not fit into the limited NMT model vocabulary are segmented into sequences of subwords, a new vocabulary with a lower sparseness is obtained. The lower data sparseness obtained by BPE and LMVR versus Word is evident from Figure 1a, which plots the corresponding type-to-token ratios of each training corpus. After segmentation, the new vocabulary of subwords has a less sparse frequency distribution and each subword is observed in more types of context. This allows to learn better representations for each subword and increases the translation accuracy. The significant difference in output quality observed with two different segmentation approaches tells, however, that their impact highly depends on the nature of the splitting process and the characteristics of the language they are applied on.

An interesting outcome of our experiments is that as the complexity of morphology (*i.e.* sparseness in the lexical vocabulary) and the level of agglutination observed in the language increases, the more beneficial it becomes to use LMVR for vocabulary reduction. Arabic, Czech and Turkish all have a high level of lexical sparseness, and the higher translation quality obtained using LMVR proves that a segmentation method that preserves morphological information contained at the subword level can generate better translations. As can be seen in Figures 1a and 1b, LMVR can reduce the sparseness, *i.e.* increase the token-to-type ratio, in the corpus

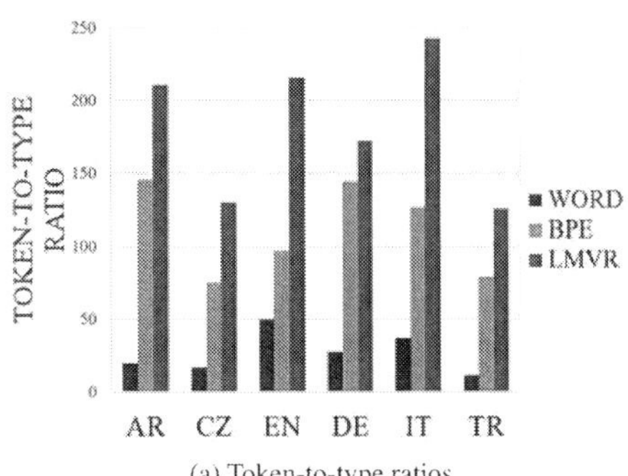

(a) Token-to-type ratios

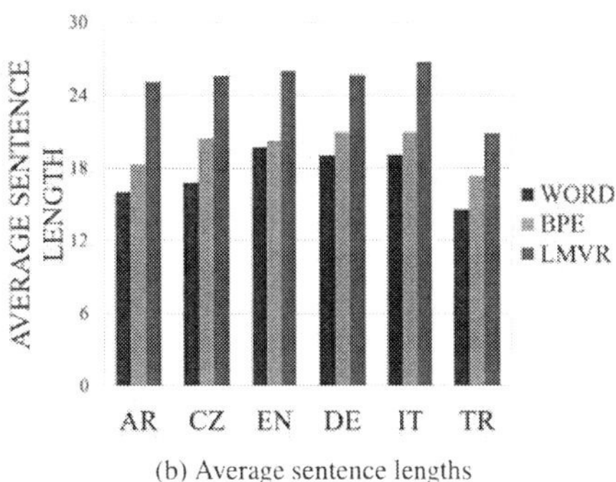

(b) Average sentence lengths

Figure 1: Token-to-type ratios and average sentence lengths after vocabulary reduction.

at higher degrees by applying a more homogeneous segmentation among the corpus, indicated in the levels of increase in the average sentence lengths. Sentence lengths generally remain close to their original lengths with BPE, on the other hand, with LMVR, the sentences can become much longer. One can also see that the improvements in each language are related to the formal characteristics of subwords. All three languages have inflections or derivations that are formed in a rather concatenating fashion, compared to German and Italian, where the affixes cannot be observed independently on the surface level. This explains the success of LMVR in learning subwords that are more consistent with the morphological boundaries. In Turkish, an agglutinative language where morpheme boundaries are transparent, it is possible to achieve a complete segmentation of the morphemes inside a word. However, this is not the case for the others. Arabic morphemes are discontinuous, and in Czech, there is less transparency in terms of the morpheme boundaries. Therefore, when a clear segmentation at the surface level is not possible, LMVR can fail to predict the correct morphemes inside a word.

In German and Italian, languages with highly fusional morphology, different approaches in vocabulary reduction do not yield large differences in the output quality. This is mainly due the formal properties of fusional morphology, where typographic changes at the input may not yield sufficient information for the model to learn significantly better translations. In addition to fusional transformations, German is also rich in compounding, which can be defined as an agglutinating transformation. However, the small difference in the performance of either segmentation methods suggests that both methods can handle this phenomena similarly, leading to comparable performances. Another factor that affects the results is related to the statistical characteristics of the languages, which, as can be seen in the vocabulary sizes listed in Table 2, do not hold a large amount of sparseness. The quantity of rare words in the vocabulary that could better be translated by different approaches could be an important indicator in the overall output accuracy. Italian, unlike German, has a morphology of comparably lower complexity and the word vocabulary is quite compact, where rare words (singletons and less frequently observed words that are in the long tail of the frequency distribution) mostly consist of named entities or numeric expressions. This is in contrast to morphologically-rich languages, where the majority of rare words also include inflected or derivated word forms. Hence, in Italian, vocabulary reduction with either segmentation methods can provide similar performances. When BPE is used, most words in the corpus are translated without segmentation. Although rare inflected words can exist in the corpus, they are not observed many times, and the improvement in their translation through LMVR may not be significant enough to be observed at the output. English is also a language of this group, with a morphology of very low complexity, although most of the affixes are easily separable. Therefore, LMVR can be trained to segment words according to their morphological boundaries. The benefit of applying LMVR also on the English side can be seen in our experimental results, which show that the best translation accuracy is obtained when LMVR is applied on both sides of the training data. Nevertheless, these improvements are not as significant as in the morphologically-rich language settings, as in the cases of Arabic, Czech and Turkish.

8   Conclusion

NMT is a novel and successful approach to machine translation that can provide high quality translations in many languages. However, the limitation in the size of the model vocabulary prevents to take full advantage of the approach, especially in morphologically-rich languages. These languages usually have large and sparse vocabularies which contain rare inflected or derivated word forms that cannot be included in the model vocabulary, and consequently, translated. A conventional solution to this is to reduce the vocabulary of the training corpus by segmenting words into subword level representations and perform their translations at this level. In this paper, we have compared two such methods, BPE, the prominently used approach which is a statistical method that disregards any linguistic notion during segmentation, and LMVR, a recently proposed method which also takes morphological coherence into consideration during prediction of the subwords. We have evaluated two methods in a common machine translation benchmark consisting of six languages with distinct morphological characteristics. Our findings showed that using LMVR provides better translation in NMT applied on morphologically-rich languages by trying to maintain a coherence between the generated subwords and the morphological boundaries. On the other hand, for fusional languages with low sparseness, using BPE and LMVR provided comparable translation quality. Our analysis supports that morphology is an important factor in determining the statistical characteristics of the language and should be taken into consideration for choosing the most appropriate vocabulary reduction method for NMT.

Acknowledgments

This work has been partially supported by the EC-funded H2020 project QT21 (grant no. 645452).

References

Al-Mannai, K., Sajjad, H., Khader, A., Al Obaidli, F., Nakov, P., and Vogel, S. (2014). Unsupervised Word Segmentation Improves Dialectal Arabic to English Machine Translation. In *Proceedings of the Workshop on Arabic Natural Language Processing (ANLP)*, pages 207–216.

Ataman, D., Negri, M., Turchi, M., and Federico, M. (2017). Linguistically Motivated Vocabulary Reduction for Neural Machine Translation from Turkish to English. In *The Prague Bulletin of Mathematical Linguistics*, volume 108, pages 331–342.

Bahdanau, D., Cho, K., and Bengio, Y. (2014). Neural Machine Translation by Jointly Learning to Align and Translate. *arXiv preprint arXiv:1409.0473*.

Bentivogli, L., FBK, T., Bisazza, A., Cettolo, M., and Federico, M. (2016). Neural versus Phrase-Based Machine Translation Quality: a Case Study. In *Proceedings of the Conference on Empirical Methods in Natural Language Processing (EMNLP)*, pages 257–267.

Bojar, O., Chatterjee, R., Federmann, C., Graham, Y., Haddow, B., Huang, S., Huck, M., Koehn, P., Liu, Q., Logacheva, V., et al. (2017). Findings of the 2017 Conference on Machine Translation. In *Proceedings of the Second Conference on Machine Translation (WMT)*, pages 169–214.

Bottou, L. (2010). Large-Scale Machine Learning with Stochastic Gradient Descent. In *Proceedings of 19th International Conference on Computational Statistics (COMPSTAT)*, pages 177–186. Springer.

Cettolo, M., Girardi, C., and Federico, M. (2012). Wit3: Web Inventory of Transcribed and Translated Talks. In *Proceedings of the 16th Conference of the European Association for Machine Translation (EAMT)*, pages 261–268.

Clark, J. H., Dyer, C., Lavie, A., and Smith, N. A. (2011). Better Hypothesis Testing for Statistical Machine Translation: Controlling for Optimizer Instability. In *Proceedings of the 49th Annual Meeting of the Association for Computational Linguistics (ACL)*, pages 176–181.

Creutz, M. and Lagus, K. (2007). Unsupervised Models for Morpheme Segmentation and Morphology Learning. In *ACM Transactions on Speech and Language Processing (TSLP)*, volume 4, pages 1–34.

Duchi, J., Hazan, E., and Singer, Y. (2011). Adaptive Subgradient Methods for Online Learning and Stochastic Optimization. In *Journal of Machine Learning Research*, volume 12, pages 2121–2159.

Gage, P. (1994). A New Algorithm for Data Compression. In *The C Users Journal*, volume 12, pages 23–38.

Grönroos, S.-A., Virpioja, S., Smit, P., Kurimo, M., et al. (2014). Morfessor FlatCat: An HMM-based Method for Unsupervised and Semi-supervised Learning of Morphology. In *Proceedings of the 25th International Conference on Computational Linguistics (COLING)*, pages 1177–1185.

Huck, M., Riess, S., and Fraser, A. (2017). Target-Side Word Segmentation Strategies for Neural Machine Translation. In *Proceedings of the Second Conference on Machine Translation (WMT)*, pages 56–67.

Koehn, P., Hoang, H., Birch, A., Callison-Burch, C., Federico, M., Bertoldi, N., Cowan, B., Shen, W., Moran, C., Zens, R., et al. (2007). Moses: Open Source Toolkit for Statistical Machine Translation. In *Proceedings of the 45th Annual Meeting of the Association for Computational Linguistics (ACL)*, pages 177–180.

Koskenniemi, K. (1983). Two-Level Model for Morphological Analysis. In *Proceedings of the Eighth International Joint Conference on Artificial Intelligence (IJCAI)*, volume 83, pages 683–685.

Lee, J., Cho, K., and Hofmann, T. (2017). Fully character-Level Neural Machine Translation without Explicit Segmentation. In *Transactions of the Association for Computational Linguistics (TACL)*, volume 5, pages 365–378.

Ling, W., Trancoso, I., Dyer, C., and Black, A. W. (2015). Character-based Neural Machine Translation. *arXiv preprint arXiv:1511.04586*.

Luong, M.-T. and Manning, C. D. (2016). Achieving Open Vocabulary Neural Machine Translation with Hybrid Word-Character Models. In *Proceedings of the 54th Annual Meeting of the Association for Computational Linguistics (ACL)*, pages 1054–1063.

Luong, M.-T., Pham, H., and Manning, C. D. (2015). Effective Approaches to Attention-based Neural Machine Translation. In *Proceedings of the Conference on Empirical Methods in Natural Language Processing (EMNLP)*, pages 1412–1421.

Niehues, J., Cho, E., Ha, T.-L., and Waibel, A. (2016). Pre-translation for Neural Machine Translation. In *Proceedings of The 26th International Conference on Computational Linguistics (COLING)*, pages 1828–1836.

O'Grady, W., Dobrovolsky, M., and Katamba, F. (1997). *Contemporary Linguistics*. St. Martin's.

Papineni, K., Roukos, S., Ward, T., and Zhu, W.-J. (2002). BLEU: a Method for Automatic Evaluation of Machine Translation. In *Proceedings of the 40th Annual Meeting of the Association for Computational Linguistics (ACL)*, pages 311–318.

Pinnis, M., Krišlauks, R., Deksne, D., and Miks, T. (2017). Neural Machine Translation for Morphologically Rich Languages with Improved Subword Units and Synthetic Data. In *Proceedings of the International Conference on Text, Speech, and Dialogue (TSD)*, pages 237–245.

Popovic, M. (2015). chrF: Character n-gram F-score for Automatic MT Evaluation. In *Proceedings of the 10th Workshop on Statistical Machine Translation (WMT)*, pages 392–395.

Sajjad, H., Guzmán, F., Nakov, P., Abdelali, A., Murray, K., Al Obaidli, F., and Vogel, S. (2013). QCRI at IWSLT 2013: Experiments in Arabic-English and English-Arabic Spoken Language Translation. In *Proceedings of the 10th International Workshop on Spoken Language Translation (IWSLT)*, pages 75–82.

Sennrich, R., Firat, O., Cho, K., Birch, A., Haddow, B., Hitschler, J., Junczys-Dowmunt, M., Läubli, S., Barone, A. V. M., Mokry, J., et al. (2017). Nematus: a toolkit for Neural Machine Translation. In *Proceedings of the 15th Annual Meeting of the European Chapter of the Association for Computational Linguistics (EACL)*, pages 65–68.

Sennrich, R., Haddow, B., and Birch, A. (2016). Neural Machine Translation of Rare Words with Subword Units. In *Proceedings of the 54th Annual Meeting of the Association for Computational Linguistics (ACL)*, pages 1715–1725.

Shopen, T. (1985). *Language Typology and Syntactic Description*, volume 3. Cambridge University Press.

Tamchyna, A., Marco, M. W.-D., and Fraser, A. (2017). Modeling Target-Side Inflection in Neural Machine Translation. In *Proceedings of the Second Conference on Machine Translation (WMT)*, pages 32–42.

Werbos, P. J. (1990). Backpropagation Through Time: What it does and How to do it. In *Proceedings of the Institute of Electrical and Electronics Engineers (IEEE)*, volume 78, pages 1550–1560.

A Smorgasbord of Features to Combine Phrase-Based and Neural Machine Translation

Benjamin Marie   bmarie@nict.go.jp
Atsushi Fujita   atsushi.fujita@nict.go.jp
National Institute of Information and Communications Technology,
3-5 Hikaridai, Seika-cho, Soraku-gun, Kyoto, 619-0289, Japan

Abstract

Superiority of neural machine translation (NMT) and phrase-based statistical machine translation (PBSMT) depends on the translation task. For some translation tasks, such as those involving low-resource language pairs or close languages, NMT may underperform PBSMT. In order to have a translation system that performs consistently better regardless of the translation task, recent work proposed to combine PBSMT and NMT approaches. In this paper, we propose an empirical comparison of the most popular existing approaches that combine PBSMT and NMT. Despite its simplicity, our simple reranking system using a smorgasbord of informative features significantly and consistently outperforms other methods, even for translation tasks where PBSMT and NMT produce translations of a very different quality.

1 Introduction

Neural machine translation (NMT) systems have been shown to outperform phrase-based statistical machine translation (PBSMT) systems in many translation tasks. NMT systems perform especially well with language pairs involving two distant languages or morphologically-rich languages. Translations produced by NMT systems are usually more fluent than those produced by state-of-the-art PBSMT systems. However, NMT systems are still far from producing perfect translations. Many researchers have studied the weaknesses of the NMT approach and shown that NMT systems perform poorly compared to PBSMT systems in relatively common scenarios, especially those involving low-resource language pairs (Bentivogli et al., 2016; Koehn and Knowles, 2017). Several approaches have recently been proposed to combine PBSMT and NMT in order to exploit their complementarity and to produce better translations.

In this paper, we study the most popular combination methods and empirically compare them, aiming at drawing a better picture of their strengths and weaknesses. We demonstrate that reranking the simple concatenation of n-best lists produced by each of the NMT and PBSMT systems, with a set of well-motived features, performs consistently the best compared to the more popular and complex methods proposed by previous work. We also show that, while other approaches can perform worse than the best system, a simple reranking approach offers some guarantee that the selected best translation will be rarely worse than the best one proposed by the PBSMT or by the NMT system, even when one of the systems performs very poorly.

The remainder of this paper is organized as follows. In Section 2, we review the existing methods used to combine PBSMT and NMT. Then, in Section 3, we make our assumption that a reranking system using a large set of informative features can outperform other existing methods. We evaluate our proposed reranking systems in Section 4 and analyze our results in Section 5. In Section 6, we conclude and propose promising perspectives for this work.

2 Current Approaches to Combine PBSMT and NMT

This section reviews four different methods able to combine PBSMT and NMT: confusion network decoding (Section 2.1), pre-translation with a PBSMT system (Section 2.2) and rescoring PBSMT or NMT translation hypotheses using different models (Section 2.3 and Section 2.4). We do not include in our comparison the work of He et al. (2016), which uses SMT features during NMT decoding, because their method cannot use phrase translation probability or more complex models that cannot be used during decoding. Moreover, we leave for future work the study of the more recent method proposed by Zhou et al. (2017), which combines MT system outputs using neural networks. This method outperformed confusion network decoding, but has been evaluated only on a Chinese-to-English translation task with PBSMT and NMT systems that performed comparably on this task.

2.1 Confusion Network Decoding

The first application of machine translation (MT) system combination used a consensus decoding strategy relying on a confusion network (Bangalore et al., 2001). Since this first work, this approach has been improved and remains one of the most popular methods to combine many translations produced by different MT systems (Freitag et al., 2014).

To generate the confusion network, alignments are required between the tokens of all the translation hypotheses to combine. Previous work (Heafield and Lavie, 2011; Freitag et al., 2014) on system combination used METEOR (Denkowski and Lavie, 2014) to perform an accurate word alignment between translation hypotheses by making use of its ability to align synonyms, stems, and paraphrases. After building the confusion network, decoding is performed to find the most consensual path with additional models such as a large language model.

This approach finds usually a better translation hypothesis than the best translations produced by the individual systems. However, it becomes quickly prohibitive if one wants to combine hundreds of hypotheses, such as the n-best hypotheses generated by different systems, while using costly models to score the decoding paths. Moreover, we have no guarantee that the output of the combination will be better than the best hypothesis generated by individual systems. The confusion network may allow the generation of many hypotheses of very poor quality, especially in cases where many of the translation systems perform much worse than the best systems used in the combination.

2.2 Pre-translation with a PBSMT system

Pre-translation is a recent method dedicated to combine PBSMT and NMT in a simple pipeline (Niehues et al., 2016). First, a PBSMT system is trained and used to decode the source side of the training data of the NMT system. Then, a second-stage NMT system is trained, where the concatenation of the source sentence and the PBSMT-decoded translation is regarded as the new source side of training data, while the target side of the training data remains unchanged.

The main motivation behind this work is that a pre-translation generated by a PBSMT system would be informative to better guide the training of NMT systems. However, as suggested by Niehues et al. (2016), to improve an NMT system with a pre-translation, the PBSMT system must produce translations of a quality comparable to (or better than) those produced by the NMT system. In cases where the PBSMT system produces translation of poor quality, we can expect that such pre-translation will significantly harm the training of the NMT system.

2.3 Rescoring PBSMT hypotheses with NMT

Before the emergence of end-to-end NMT systems, it was a common practice to include neural network models in PBSMT for reranking the n-best translation hypotheses produced by the PBSMT system (Le et al., 2012) or to include them directly during decoding (Devlin et al.,

2014; Junczys-Dowmunt et al., 2016). This strategy has been successfully exploited for PBSMT systems. However, it is currently less attractive, because NMT systems are often able to produce much better translations than PBSMT systems, even better than the best translations obtained after reranking the PBSMT system's n-best hypotheses with NMT system's models.

2.4 Phrase-based Forced Decoding

Yet another recent method dedicated to combine PBSMT and NMT systems is called *phrase-based forced decoding* (Zhang et al., 2017) (henceforth, PBFD). The idea is to use the phrase table and its translation probabilities, which are commonly learned during the training of a PBSMT system, to rescore translations produced by an NMT system.

This approach aims at alleviating the low adequacy of some of the translations produced by an NMT system. Since this approach relies directly on the phrase table usually used in PBSMT, it will promote hypotheses that matches phrase pairs associated with a high translation probability from the phrase table. The forced decoding searches for the best phrase-based segmentation and returns the corresponding phrase-based translation probability.

PBFD is extremely costly to perform during NMT decoding but rather feasible after it on a selected set of diverse hypotheses. Then, given the PBFD score and the original score given by the NMT system, the rescoring of the hypotheses is performed. Zhang et al. (2017) did not rerank n-best lists but instead reranked a sample of hypotheses extracted from the NMT decoder's search space. This amplifies the diversity among the hypotheses to rescore, and the increased diversity has been shown useful in training a reranking system (Gimpel et al., 2013). However, as a potential drawback, hypotheses of very bad quality could be chosen.

3 n-best List Reranking

3.1 n-Best List Combination

Since the early age of PBSMT (Och et al., 2004), reranking the n-best lists of hypotheses produced by a PBSMT system has been shown to be a simple and efficient way to use complex features that could not be used during decoding. Furthermore, this approach offers some good guarantee to find a better translation, because rescoring is applied to the best part of the decoder's search space, while making use of more, and potentially better, features than the decoder. However, unlike pre-translation or confusion network decoding approaches, a simple reranking of the hypotheses produced by a single decoder, NMT or PBSMT, is limited in its ability to take advantage of the complementarity of both approaches. For instance, if an NMT system produces fluent but inadequate n-best translations, a simple reranking of this n-best list with PBSMT models can only help to find an hypothesis which is less inadequate. Reranking NMT n-best hypotheses does not give access to the PBSMT decoder's search space and its potentially more adequate translations.

Instead of a list of hypotheses produced by a single system or multiple but homogeneous systems, we merge two lists respectively produced by PBSMT and NMT decoders, and rescore all the hypotheses. Then, the reranking framework using a lot of features to better model the fluency and the adequacy of the hypotheses can potentially find a better hypothesis than the one-best hypotheses originated by either the PBSMT or NMT systems. This method is similar to the one proposed by Hildebrand and Vogel (2008). However, their work aims at combining n-best lists from any kind of MT systems, ignoring the specificities and models of the systems used to produce them. In contrast, we focus on PBSMT and NMT system combination by making use of their respective models. This method has never been evaluated in comparison with the state-of-the-art methods presented in Section 2.

While this approach seems simple, mixing efficiently both kinds of hypotheses is actually challenging. For instance, if we choose only the model scores from an NMT system as features, it is likely that all PBSMT hypotheses will be ignored by the reranking framework by giving a high preference to the hypotheses with high NMT models score, which will be actually the ones produced by the NMT system.

3.2 Reranking Framework and Features

Previous work on n-best list reranking has proposed many different training algorithms, including those used to optimize PBSMT systems, such as MERT (Och, 2003) and KB-MIRA (Cherry and Foster, 2012). We choose KB-MIRA since it is commonly used in reranking framework and provides stable performances. It can also handle many features as opposed to MERT.

The features we used are commonly used for n-best list reranking, which are difficult or impossible to use during NMT or PBSMT decoding. To the best of our knowledge, the following features have never been exploited together in the same reranking framework.

3.2.1 NMT Features

NMT translation models can be used to score a translation produced by an arbitrary system. We only need the source sentence and the corresponding translation hypothesis. These models have been used to rerank n-best lists of hypotheses produced by PBSMT systems and can also be used to rescore hypotheses produced by other NMT systems. Different NMT translation models, generated at different training epochs, or by independent training runs, can be combined to make an ensemble of models to better score translation hypotheses.

right-to-left NMT translation models, trained on parallel data in which the target side sequences of tokens are reversed, are also useful. Such *right-to-left* models have shown good performance in reranking n-best lists of hypotheses (Sennrich et al., 2017a).

3.2.2 PBSMT Features

A state-of-the-art PBSMT system uses the log-linear combination of several models:

- a phrase table containing phrase pairs associated with a set of translation probabilities, which controls the adequacy of the translation
- a language model controlling the fluency of the translation
- a distortion score that controls how much the target phrases in the translation hypothesis have been reordered given their corresponding source phrases
- a lexical reordering table to control three kinds of phrase-based reordering: monotonous, swap, or discontinuous (henceforth, MSD models)
- a word penalty to penalize short translations
- a phrase penalty to count the number of phrase pairs used to compose the translation

While translation models (Zhang et al., 2017) and language models (Wang et al., 2017) are useful to rescore NMT hypotheses, this may not be the case for the reordering models. A state-of-the-art PBSMT decoder limits its search within a pre-determined distortion limit. This limit can be seen as a safeguard to prevent the decoder to generate very ungrammatical translations, since it does not have the ability to model long dependencies between tokens. In contrast, NMT decoders are free to perform long-distance reorderings. For language pairs that need long-distance reordering, this means that an NMT hypothesis of a good quality will have a high distortion score and many source phrases translated discontinuously. The PBSMT reordering models seem then inadequate to score NMT hypotheses in our reranking framework, especially since we will keep using NMT models that already model the fluency.

We perform PBFD on the NMT hypotheses (Section 2.4) using a PBSMT system's phrase table, and use the score produced by PBFD as a feature. For the PBSMT hypotheses, we use directly the phrase segmentation produced by the PBSMT system and compute the same score.

It is also possible to use the full PBSMT system's scoring function to score NMT hypotheses. Indeed, PBFD splits the NMT hypothesis into phrase pairs. Then, we can further exploit this segmentation to compute all PBSMT features and combine them log-linearly using the same model weights found during the tuning of the PBSMT system. Nonetheless, PBFD generates a phrase segmentation that may be unreliable to compute all PBSMT model scores, especially because most of the NMT hypotheses may be unreachable by a PBSMT system, leaving some source and target tokens out of a phrase pair.

3.2.3 Sentence-Level Translation Probability

While the PBFD uses only phrase translation probabilities, it is often a good idea to use also lexical translation probabilities in order to get a smoothed score. Since an NMT system does not produce word alignments, we consider to take the average of the lexical translation probabilities over all possible word pairs between the source sentence f and the translation hypothesis e, according to the following formula:[1]

$$P_{avg}(e|f) = \frac{1}{I} \sum_{i=1}^{I} \log\Big(\frac{1}{J} \sum_{j=1}^{J} p(e_i|f_j)\Big) \tag{1}$$

where I and J are the lengths of e and f, respectively, and $p(e_i|f_j)$ the lexical translation probability of the i-th target word e_i of e given the j-th source word f_j of f. Since Equation (1) is dominated by the highest lexical translation probability, Hildebrand and Vogel (2008) also proposed to compute the translation probability given by the following equation:

$$P_{lmax}(e|f) = \frac{1}{I} \sum_{i=1}^{I} \log\Big(\max_{j} p(e_i|f_j)\Big) \tag{2}$$

As the features for rescoring, we compute the scores given by Equations (1) and (2) for both translation directions using the lexical translation probabilities trained on the same parallel data used to train the MT systems.

3.2.4 Word Posterior Probability

Word posterior probability (WPP) is another feature that is commonly used in PBSMT to rerank lists of translation hypotheses. For all target tokens appearing in the list, it computes the probability for the token to appear in a translation hypothesis. Then, we can score an entire hypothesis by averaging the posterior probability of the tokens it contains. We use the count-based WPP as defined by Ueffing and Ney (2007). WPP is computed given the decoder's score of the hypotheses in which the word appears. Since our list of hypotheses to rerank contains hypotheses produced by two different decoders, we compute two different WPP: one based on the score computed by Equation (1), with direct translation probabilities, and the other based on the score computed by the NMT decoder.

3.2.5 Consensus Score

The so-called minimum Bayes risk (MBR) decoding for n-best list is a popular method used in SMT to find in an n-best list of hypotheses the one that is on average the most similar to the other hypotheses. Sentence-level BLEU (Papineni et al., 2002) (sBLEU) is usually considered as the metric used to measure the similarity between hypotheses (Ehling et al., 2007).

This method has a common objective with confusion network decoding and WPP (Section 3.2.4), since we search for the hypothesis containing the most popular tokens or n-grams used by the decoder to construct its n-best hypotheses.

---

[1]Applying forced word alignment on the NMT hypotheses would be an alternative, but we did not observe any significant differences in our preliminary experiments.

We gauge how each hypothesis is similar to all the other hypotheses, using two scores respectively based on sBLEU and chrF++ (Popović, 2017).

3.2.6 Other Features

Depending on the origin of the hypothesis, generated either by PBSMT or NMT systems, some features can give significantly different scores. To help our reranking system to weight these differences, we introduce a binary feature that only indicates whether the hypothesis has been produced by a PBSMT or an NMT system. Regular attention-based NMT systems have no direct mechanism to control the length of the hypotheses produced, but information about the hypothesis length can help to improve the performance (Zhang et al., 2017). In addition to the word penalty used by the PBSMT system, we also add the difference between the number of tokens in the source sentence and that for the translation hypothesis, and its absolute value.

4 Experiments

4.1 Data

We conducted experiments on two significantly different language pairs: Japanese–English (Ja-En) and French–English (Fr-En). Ja-En involves two distant languages for which an NMT decoder is expected to perform much better than a PBSMT decoder, especially due to the long-distance reordering to perform to get a good translation. In contrast, Fr-En involves much closer languages with usually only local reorderings to perform. We thus expect PBSMT and NMT to provide more similar results given a large set of parallel data.

For Ja-En, we used the NTCIR Patent Translation Task (Goto et al., 2013). We used the parallel data provided for the task to train PBSMT and NMT systems. The language models for Japanese and English were trained on the target side of the parallel data and the entire NTCIR monolingual data. The NTCIR development data were used as a validation dataset during the training of the NMT system and to tune the PBSMT system. We used the NTCIR-9 test (T09) and NTCIR-10 test (T10) for evaluation. For Fr-En, we used data provided for the WMT'15 News Translation Task.[2] Our parallel data used to train the systems comprise Europarl v7, 10^9 French–English, and news-commentary v10. The language models for French and English were trained on the target side of the parallel data and the entire News Crawl corpora. We used newstest2012 as a validation dataset during the training of the NMT system and to tune the model weights of the PBSMT system, and newstest2013 (N13) and newstest2014 (N14) for evaluation. The statistics of the data are presented in Table 1.

4.2 Baseline Systems

To train and test our PBSMT systems and attention-based NMT systems, we respectively used `Moses` (Koehn et al., 2007) and `Nematus` (Sennrich et al., 2017b) frameworks.

For our baseline PBSMT systems, word alignments were trained with `mgiza` and `fast_align` (Dyer et al., 2013) respectively for Ja-En and Fr-En.[3] After their training for both translation directions, word alignments are symmetrized using the `grow-diag-final-and` heuristic. We trained two 4-gram language models with `lmplz` (Heafield et al., 2013) for each translation direction, one trained on the target side of the parallel data, and the other on the monolingual data concatenated to the target side of the parallel data. We pruned all singletons for the Japanese and English second language models used for the NTCIR translation tasks, because the monolingual data are very large. The reordering models are MSD lexicalized and

---

[2] http://www.statmt.org/wmt15/translation-task.html

[3] We did not use `mgiza` to train the word alignments for the Fr-En pair, since `fast_align` is much more efficient on large training data, while it has been shown to perform as well as `mgiza` for this language pair.

Datasets		#sentences	#tokens			#token types		
			Ja	Fr	En	Ja	Fr	En
NTCIR	parallel	3M	110M		102M	169k		275k
	development	2,000	73k		67k	4k		5k
	$T09_{Ja \to En}$	2,000	74k		68k	5k		6k
	$T09_{En \to Ja}$	2,000	74k		70k	5k		6k
	$T10_{Ja \to En}$	2,300	99k		92k	6k		7k
	$T10_{En \to Ja}$	2,300	87k		80k	6k		6k
	monolingual	-	27B		15B	9M		22M
WMT	parallel	24M		726M	614M		2M	2M
	development	3,003		82k	73k		11k	10k
	N13	3,000		74k	70k		11k	9k
	N14	3,003		81k	71k		11k	10k
	monolingual	-		2B	3B		4M	6M

Table 1: Statistics on train, development, and test data.

bidirectional models. PBSMT systems are tuned with KB-MIRA using development data. The distortion limit was tuned and set to 16 for Ja-En.[4]

Our baseline NMT systems used the default training parameters of Nematus, with layer normalization, and performed BPE (Sennrich et al., 2016) to fix the source and target vocabulary sizes at 50k. The BPE segmentation was jointly learned for French and English since they share the same alphabet. During Nematus training, we saved the model after every 5k mini-batch iterations. The 4-best models according to their performance on the development data were selected to perform ensemble decoding. The decoding were performed using a beam size of 100 to produce 100-best hypotheses. As suggested by Koehn and Knowles (2017), we normalized the hypothesis score by their length during decoding to prevent a drop of the NMT system performance when using such a large beam size.

For system combination with confusion network decoding (Section 2.1), we used the Jane framework (Freitag et al., 2014). We evaluated two systems: one combining only the one-best hypotheses produced by Moses and Nematus ($n = 1$), and the other combining all the hypotheses in the 100-best lists ($n = 100$). During decoding, we used all the default models in addition to the large language models that were used by our PBSMT baseline systems.[5]

For pre-translation (Section 2.2), we decoded our entire training data with our PBSMT system and concatenated each of the results to its source side to train a second-phase NMT system (henceforth, Pre-Nematus), exactly as described in (Niehues et al., 2016). To evaluate Pre-Nematus, we performed ensemble decoding using the 4-best models.

We also evaluated two baseline reranking systems: one using NMT models to rerank the PBSMT system's n-best list (Section 2.3), denoted R_{nmt}, and the other using the PBFD features (Section 2.4), denoted R_{pbsmt}. R_{nmt} uses all the features used by the Moses scoring function, the Moses score, the 4 translation models used by the Nematus baseline system, and the 4-best right-to-left translation models (Section 3.2.1). For R_{pbsmt}, we used the same features as described by Zhang et al. (2017): the scores given by Nematus and the 4 best left-to-right models, the score given by the PBFD, and the word penalty (as defined in Moses).

R_{nmt} reranks the n-best list of distinct hypotheses (M) produced by Moses, and R_{pbsmt} reranks the n-best list of hypotheses (N) produced by Nematus.

---

[4]The default value in Moses is not appropriate for distant languages.

[5]We could have also reranked the n-best lists produced by Jane. However, we found out that Jane's n-best lists produced for system combination are of a very poor quality and not diverse enough to train a reranking system.

Feature	Description
L2R (5)	The scores given by each of the 4-best left-to-right `Nematus` models and their geometric mean
R2L (5)	The scores given by each of the 4-best right-to-left `Nematus` models and their geometric mean
PBFD (1)	The PBFD score (Section 2.4)
LEX (4)	The sentence-level translation probabilities (Section 3.2.3), computed using Equations (1) and (2), for both translation directions
LM (2)	Scores given by the two language models used by the `Moses` baseline systems
WP (1)	Word penalty
TM (4)	PBSMT translation model scores computed according to the probabilities given by the `Moses` phrase table on the phrase segmentation produced by Moses for the hypotheses in M, or by the PBFD for the hypotheses in N (same segmentations were used to compute scores with MSD models (MSD), the distoration score (DIS), the phrase penalty (PP), and the `Moses` score (MOSES))
MSD (6)	Scores computed using the `Moses` MSD lexical reordering table
DIS (1)	Distortion score
PP (1)	Phrase penalty
MOSES (1)	Score given by `Moses` for the hypotheses in M. For the hypotheses in N, we compute this score using all the `Moses` models and their weights
WPP (2)	Word posterior probability (Section 3.2.4)
MBR (2)	MBR decoding applied on M+N (Section 3.2.5), using sBLEU and chrF++
LEN (2)	The difference between the length of the source sentence and the length of the translation hypothesis, and its absolute value
SYS (1)	System flag, 1 if the hypothesis is in M or 0 if it is in N

Table 2: Set of features used by R_{full}. R_{sub} uses only the features in bold. The numbers between parentheses indicate the number of scores in each feature set.

4.3 Reranking Systems

We trained and evaluated our reranking systems using two different sets of features to rerank the concatenation of M and N (henceforth, M+N). Our first system, denoted R_{full}, used the full set of 38 features described in Section 3.2 and listed in Table 2. Our second reranking system, denoted R_{sub}, used only a subset of the features. We excluded most of the phrase-based features, considering that they are unreliable to score NMT hypotheses. The impact of each feature is analyzed in Section 5.1. All our reranking systems were trained with KB-MIRA on n-best lists produced for the development data.[6] For a comparison, we also evaluated both reranking systems with M and N reranked separately. For each reranking experiments, both training and testing n-best lists were generated by the same system.

4.4 Results

As shown in the first two rows of Table 3, the superiority of NMT and PBSMT depends on the language pair. As expected, for the Ja-En pair, NMT performed much better than PBSMT. For both test sets, `T09` and `T10`, the large difference between `Moses` and `Nematus` reached approximately 10 BLEU points. In contrast, for the Fr-En pair, PBSMT performed better than NMT, slightly on `N13` and significantly on `N14`. The difference in translation quality between both systems makes it challenging for a system combination to perform consistently better than the best single system, regardless of the translation task.

    `Jane` did not improve the translation quality over `Nematus` for Ja→En. We observed improvements for the other three tasks when combining the one-best hypotheses produced by `Moses` and `Nematus`. However, when we combined the 100-best hypotheses for the Ja-En

---

[6]We used the rescoring implementation provided by `Moses`.

Configuration	Ja→En		En→Ja		Fr→En		En→Fr	
	T09	T10	T09	T10	N13	N14	N13	N14
Moses	31.3	32.7	34.7	35.9	31.4	39.9	30.6	39.1
Nematus	41.9	41.6	44.8	45.4	30.8	34.0	30.6	35.8
Jane M+N (n=1)	41.5	41.6	44.9	45.8	32.0	40.0	30.8	39.5
Jane M+N (n=100)	39.0	40.2	41.6	42.7	32.1	40.0	31.0	39.9
Pre-Nematus	31.4	29.7	33.5	33.8	30.0	37.2	29.5	37.4
R_{nmt} M	33.3	34.1	36.8	38.3	33.6	41.4	32.4	40.5
R_{pbsmt} N	42.5	43.1	46.1	46.7	32.5	34.7	31.4	36.1
R_{full} M	33.4	34.2	36.7	38.4	33.6	41.4	32.4	40.5
R_{full} N	42.5	43.6	46.3	47.1	33.5	37.6	32.4	38.8
R_{full} M+N	42.3	43.7	46.3	47.0	33.8	41.4	32.5	40.6
R_{sub} M	33.5	34.2	36.7	38.5	33.6	41.4	32.4	40.4
R_{sub} N	43.0	43.8	46.9	47.5	33.9	38.0	32.3	38.8
R_{sub} M+N	43.0	43.9	47.1	47.7	34.2	41.6	32.6	40.8

Table 3: Results (BLEU) produced by the baseline systems and our reranking systems respectively presented in Section 4.2 and Section 4.3.

pair, the performance dropped significantly, probably due to the low quality of the hypotheses produced by Moses. As for Pre-Nematus, for all tasks we did not manage to obtain improvement over the best single system. The produced translations were much worse for Ja-En, especially on T10 compared to Nematus with a drop of 11.9 and 11.6 BLEU points respectively for the Ja→En and En→Ja tasks. Nematus was potentially more disturbed than helped by the very low quality of the translations provided by Moses. For Fr-En, we did not observe such a drop, probably due to the much better quality of the PBSMT translations, but neither got any improvements over Moses. However, we could observe significant improvements over Nematus on N14, of up to 3.2 BLEU points for Fr→En, showing that a pre-translation of a good quality can significantly help the NMT system. Both Jane and Pre-Nematus provided inconsistent results in our translation tasks and underperformed when the difference between the PBSMT and NMT system translation quality was very large.

R_{nmt} and R_{pbsmt} performed significantly better than the system that produced the n-best list they reranked. The reranking system R_{nmt} M gave the best results for the tasks where PBSMT performed the best, with up to 2.2 BLEU points of improvements on Fr→En N13. In contrast, R_{pbsmt} N performed the best for Ja-En, with for instance a surprising 1.5 BLEU points improvement on Ja→En T10. Despite the large difference in translation quality between Moses and Nematus, the PBSMT models seem to be helpful to rerank the n-best lists produced by Nematus. These reranking systems produced better results than the best single system. However, they can be improved by combining n-best lists and by using more features to perform a more informed reranking.

Indeed, R_{full} M+N consistently performed similarly or better in all the four translation tasks. Reranking the concatenation of Moses and Nematus n-best lists with a set of features derived from NMT and PBSMT models significantly helped to obtain consistent results across our translation tasks, even for Ja-En for which the n-best lists produced by Moses and Nematus were of a very different quality (Section 5.3). However, as forecasted in Section 3.2, using all the features did not give the best results. Removing the phrase-based features, except for the PBFD score, gave better results, especially for the Ja-En pair, with for instance 0.8 BLEU points of improvement on En→Ja T09 obtained by R_{sub} over R_{full}. Over the best single system (Moses

Feature set removed	Ja→En T09		En→Ja T09		Fr→En N13		En→Fr N13		Computational time (ms)
	R_{full}	R_{sub}	R_{full}	R_{sub}	R_{full}	R_{sub}	R_{full}	R_{sub}	
none	42.3	43.0	46.3	47.1	33.8	34.2	32.5	32.6	-
L2R	42.6	43.0	46.3	47.1	**33.6**	**34.1**	**32.2**	**32.5**	1,560
R2L	42.4	**42.6**	46.4	**46.6**	**33.5**	**33.7**	**31.9**	**32.1**	1,890
PBFD	42.6	43.2	46.5	**47.0**	33.8	34.3	**32.4**	**32.3**	240,502
LEX	42.5	43.0	**46.2**	47.1	33.8	**34.1**	32.5	**32.4**	213
LM	42.5	43.1	46.7	47.1	**33.5**	**34.0**	**32.1**	**32.2**	98
WP	42.5	43.1	46.3	47.1	33.8	**34.1**	32.6	32.6	< 1
TM	42.8	-	46.3	-	33.8	-	32.5	-	240,504
MSD	42.5	-	46.5	-	**33.5**	-	32.7	-	240,532
DIS	42.4	-	46.4	-	33.9	-	32.5	-	240,503
PP	42.4	-	46.3	-	33.8	-	**32.3**	-	240,502
MOSES	42.4	-	**46.2**	-	**33.7**	-	32.5	-	240,503
WPP	42.4	43.1	46.3	47.1	33.8	**34.1**	**32.4**	**32.4**	20
MBR	42.8	43.1	46.4	**46.9**	**33.6**	**33.9**	**32.3**	**32.4**	111,232
LEN	42.6	43.1	46.4	47.1	**32.6**	**32.7**	**31.9**	**32.0**	< 1
SYS	42.5	43.1	46.4	47.1	33.8	**34.1**	32.6	32.6	< 1
L2R+R2L	42.4	**42.5**	46.2	**46.7**	**33.4**	**33.7**	**32.0**	**32.0**	3,450
PBFD+LEX	42.6	43.1	46.3	**47.0**	**33.6**	34.3	**32.4**	**32.5**	240,715
WPP+MBR	42.7	43.2	46.3	**46.9**	**33.6**	**34.0**	**32.2**	**32.4**	111,252
WP+LEN	42.7	43.0	46.8	**46.7**	**32.6**	**32.8**	**32.0**	**31.9**	1
L2R+R2L+ PBFD+LEX	42.4	**42.4**	**46.1**	**46.2**	**33.4**	**33.6**	**31.9**	**31.8**	244,165

Table 4: Results (BLEU) of the reranking systems R_{full} and R_{sub} obtained after removal of each feature set, independently. Reranking is performed using M+N lists of hypotheses. Bold indicates a deteriorated BLEU score when removing the feature set. The last column indicates the approximate average computational time, needed to compute the feature set, per source sentence (200 hypotheses) for Ja→En T09, using one CPU thread (Xeon E5-2670 2.6 GHz) or one GPU (GeForce GTX 1080), for the features L2R and R2L. Note that for computing a phrase-based feature, we need to first perform PBFD.

or Nematus), our best system, R_{sub}, achieved improvements ranging from 1.1 BLEU points on Ja→En T09 to 2.8 BLEU points on Fr→En N13.

5 Analysis

5.1 Impact of the Features

We evaluated the impact of the features used by our reranking systems, R_{full} and R_{sub}, by removing them, individually or in a subset, during training and testing. The results are presented in Table 4 for the Ja↔En T09 and Fr↔En N13 tasks.

These experiments show that removing features individually has a limited impact on the performance, and many of the features are correlated. Surprisingly, removing all the features based on NMT models and translation probabilities (L2R+R2L+PBFD+LEX) had a relatively limited impact on the performance, with at most a drop of 0.9 BLEU points for En→Ja, while this set of features is also very costly to compute.

Furthermore, we can see that the importance of the features depends on the language pair (and potentially the domain). Removing the language model scores had no impact for Ja↔En

	Ja→En T09			Fr→En N13		
	avg. *s*BLEU	avg. chrF++	#token types	avg. *s*BLEU	avg. chrF++	#token types
M	66.1	81.3	6,607	59.5	74.2	13,016
N	65.9	79.8	7,903	58.7	73.4	16,481
M+N	52.5	72.9	8,810	50.7	67.8	18,756

Table 5: Diversity of the hypotheses in the list M, N and M+N.

but consistently decreased the BLEU scores for Fr↔En. Removing LEN led to a significant drop of the BLEU scores for Fr↔En (up to -1.5 BLEU points), while it had no impact on the results for Ja↔En. Left-to-right Nematus models seems to have a limited impact on the results compared to the right-to-left models.

Moreover, as expected, removing the phrase-based features, such as TM and MSD, from R_{full} often improved the performance, due to the unreliability of the phrase segmentation produced by the PBFD on Nematus hypotheses.

5.2 Diversity of n-Best Hypotheses

As pointed out by Gimpel et al. (2013), a high diversity in the lists of hypotheses to rerank, especially in the list used to train the reranking system, is an important criterion to obtain a good performance. We evaluated the diversity of the hypotheses in M, N and M+N, using three indicators: average sBLEU, average chrF++, and the number of token types in the lists. The average sBLEU and the average chrF++ were computed from the MBR feature set, i.e., the average of the MBR scores given all the hypotheses in the list. A lower average sBLEU or chrF++ means that the list contains more diverse hypotheses. These indicators for the Ja→En T09 and Fr→En N13 translation tasks are presented in Table 5.

According to sBLEU and chrF++, N seems slightly more diverse than M for both language pairs. N also involved more diverse token types. For instance, within the 100-best hypotheses for the Ja→En T09 translation task, it used 1,296 more types of tokens than Moses. While M and N had almost a similar diversity, their concatenation, M+N, was much more diverse for both language pairs. For the Ja→En T09 translation task, the average sBLEU decreased from 66.1 and 65.9 points, respectively for M and N, to 52.5 points for M+N. This means that the PBSMT and NMT systems tend to produce different sets of translation hypotheses from each other.

As for the origin of the best hypotheses selected from M+N by our best ranking system, R_{sub}, for instance for the Ja→En T09 translation task, 53.5% and 46.6% were respectively those produced by Nematus and Moses. The high ratio of Moses hypotheses may seem surprising given their poor quality for this task. Actually, most of the Moses hypotheses chosen by R_{sub} are similar, or as poor as, the hypotheses produced by Nematus. We will show in the next section that for the Ja→En T09 task, given the low quality of M, this is a very safe choice and that we cannot hope to obtain large improvements by selecting hypotheses from M that are very different from the hypotheses in N.

5.3 Quality of n-Best Hypotheses

In the previous section, we highlighted a high diversity in the list of hypotheses, especially in M+N, which is advantageous to train a reranking system. However, to improve the translation quality with a reranking system, we also need lists of hypotheses of good quality that contain better hypotheses than the best output of the PBSMT and NMT systems.

We analyzed the quality of n-best lists using two indicators: an *oracle best* and an *oracle average*. For each source sentence, the former finds the translation hypothesis in the list that has the highest sBLEU score, given the reference translation, and then a standard BLEU score over

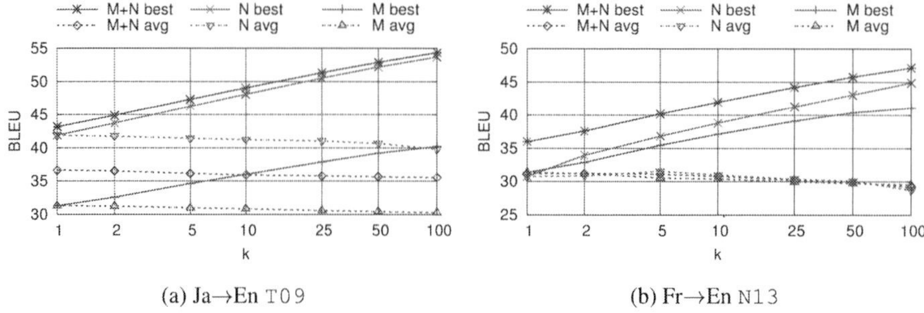

(a) Ja→En T09   (b) Fr→En N13

Figure 1: The oracle BLEU scores computed on M, N and M+N. The k-best hypotheses of the 100-best lists are used to compute the oracle.

such hypotheses in the test set is computed. To compute the oracle average scores, we used the same strategy, but selected hypotheses that had the closest sBLEU score to the average sBLEU score given the hypotheses in the list. We performed these oracle experiments on the Ja→En T09 and Fr→En N13 translation tasks. The results are presented in Figure 1.

As expected, we faced two very different situations. For Ja→En, the oracle best for k=100 computed on the list M generated by Moses did not even reach the BLEU score of the Nematus translation at k=1. Moreover, concatenating the entire M and N improved the oracle best scores only slightly, with less than one BLEU points of improvement for k=100 compared to using only N. Despite this large difference in quality, as we saw in Section 4.4, the concatenation was not harmful and the features were informative enough to help the reranking system. In contrast, for Fr→En M and N seemed much more complementary, as their concatenation improved the oracle best score of more than two BLEU points at k=100. We also observed that M and N for this translation task had very similar oracle average scores, while the concatenation of them did not decrease the oracle average score of the list.

6 Conclusion

We presented a simple reranking system guided by a smorgasbord of diverse features and showed that it can significantly outperform the state-of-the-art methods that combine PBSMT and NMT. Our reranking system managed to put at the first rank better translation hypotheses than the one-best hypotheses found by each of the PBSMT and NMT systems, relying on the diversity and quality of their respective n-best lists. Moreover, we demonstrated that our reranking system has the ability to perform consistently in two different configurations, even when the component systems produced translations of a very different quality.

As future work, we plan to study whether a reranking system can also improve the translation quality in low-resource conditions. Indeed, in this situation, PBSMT performs much better than NMT. It will thus be worth seeing whether our framework can help to identify some NMT hypotheses that are better than PBSMT hypotheses.

Acknowledgments

We would to thank the reviewers for their useful comments and suggestions, and Jingyi Zhang for providing the implementation of the phrase-based forced decoding for our experiments. This work was conducted under the program "Promotion of Global Communications Plan: Research, Development, and Social Demonstration of Multilingual Speech Translation Technology" of the Ministry of Internal Affairs and Communications (MIC), Japan.

References

Bangalore, S., Bordel, G., and Riccardi, G. (2001). Computing consensus translation from multiple machine translation systems. In *Proceedings of the IEEE Workshop on Automatic Speech Recognition and Understanding*, pages 351–354.

Bentivogli, L., Bisazza, A., Cettolo, M., and Federico, M. (2016). Neural versus phrase-based machine translation quality: a case study. In *Proceedings of EMNLP*, pages 257–267, Austin, USA.

Cherry, C. and Foster, G. (2012). Batch tuning strategies for statistical machine translation. In *Proceedings of NAACL-HLT*, pages 427–436, Montréal, Canada.

Denkowski, M. and Lavie, A. (2014). Meteor universal: Language specific translation evaluation for any target language. In *Proceedings of WMT*, pages 376–380, Baltimore, USA.

Devlin, J., Zbib, R., Huang, Z., Lamar, T., Schwartz, R., and Makhoul, J. (2014). Fast and robust neural network joint models for statistical machine translation. In *Proceedings of ACL*, pages 1370–1380, Baltimore, USA.

Dyer, C., Chahuneau, V., and Smith, N. A. (2013). A simple, fast, and effective reparameterization of IBM model 2. In *Proceedings of ACL*, pages 644–648, Atlanta, USA.

Ehling, N., Zens, R., and Ney, H. (2007). Minimum Bayes risk decoding for BLEU. In *Proceedings of ACL*, pages 101–104, Prague, Czech Republic.

Freitag, M., Huck, M., and Ney, H. (2014). Jane: Open source machine translation system combination. In *Proceedings of EACL*, pages 29–32, Gothenburg, Sweden.

Gimpel, K., Batra, D., Dyer, C., and Shakhnarovich, G. (2013). A systematic exploration of diversity in machine translation. In *Proceedings of EMNLP*, pages 1100–1111, Seattle, USA.

Goto, I., Chow, K. P., Lu, B., Sumita, E., and Tsou, B. K. (2013). Overview of the patent machine translation task at the NTCIR-10 workshop. In *Proceedings of the 10th NTCIR Conference on Evaluation of Information Access Technologies*, pages 260–286, Tokyo, Japan.

He, W., He, Z., Wu, H., and Wang, H. (2016). Improved neural machine translation with SMT features. In *Proceedings of AAAI*, pages 151–157.

Heafield, K. and Lavie, A. (2011). CMU system combination in WMT 2011. In *Proceedings of WMT*, pages 145–151, Edinburgh, Scotland.

Heafield, K., Pouzyrevsky, I., Clark, J. H., and Koehn, P. (2013). Scalable modified Kneser-Ney language model estimation. In *Proceedings of ACL*, pages 690–696, Sofia, Bulgaria.

Hildebrand, A. S. and Vogel, S. (2008). Combination of machine translation systems via hypothesis selection from combined n-best lists. In *Proceedings of AMTA*, pages 254–261.

Junczys-Dowmunt, M., Dwojak, T., and Sennrich, R. (2016). The AMU-UEDIN submission to the WMT16 news translation task: Attention-based NMT models as feature functions in phrase-based SMT. In *Proceedings of WMT*, pages 319–325, Berlin, Germany.

Koehn, P., Hoang, H., Birch, A., Callison-Burch, C., Federico, M., Bertoldi, N., Cowan, B., Shen, W., Moran, C., Zens, R., Dyer, C., Bojar, O., Constantin, A., and Herbst, E. (2007). Moses: Open source toolkit for statistical machine translation. In *Proceedings of ACL*, pages 177–180, Prague, Czech Republic.

Koehn, P. and Knowles, R. (2017). Six challenges for neural machine translation. In *Proceedings of the First Workshop on Neural Machine Translation*, pages 28–39, Vancouver, Canada.

Le, H.-S., Allauzen, A., and Yvon, F. (2012). Continuous space translation models with neural networks. In *Proceedings of NAACL-HLT*, pages 39–48, Montréal, Canada.

Niehues, J., Cho, E., Ha, T.-L., and Waibel, A. (2016). Pre-translation for neural machine translation. In *Proceedings of COLING*, pages 1828–1836, Osaka, Japan.

Och, F. J. (2003). Minimum error rate training in statistical machine translation. In *Proceedings of ACL*, pages 160–167, Sapporo, Japan.

Och, F. J., Gildea, D., Khudanpur, S., Sarkar, A., Yamada, K., Fraser, A., Kumar, S., Shen, L., Smith, D., Eng, K., Jain, V., Jin, Z., and Radev, D. (2004). A smorgasbord of features for statistical machine translation. In Susan Dumais, D. M. and Roukos, S., editors, *Proceedings of HLT-NAACL*, pages 161–168, Boston, USA.

Papineni, K., Roukos, S., Ward, T., and Zhu, W.-J. (2002). Bleu: a method for automatic evaluation of machine translation. In *Proceedings of ACL*, pages 311–318, Philadelphia, USA.

Popović, M. (2017). chrF++: words helping character n-grams. In *Proceedings of WMT*, pages 612–618, Copenhagen, Denmark.

Sennrich, R., Birch, A., Currey, A., Germann, U., Haddow, B., Heafield, K., Miceli Barone, A. V., and Williams, P. (2017a). The University of Edinburgh's neural MT systems for WMT17. In *Proceedings of WMT*, pages 389–399, Copenhagen, Denmark.

Sennrich, R., Firat, O., Cho, K., Birch, A., Haddow, B., Hitschler, J., Junczys-Dowmunt, M., Läubli, S., Miceli Barone, A. V., Mokry, J., and Nadejde, M. (2017b). Nematus: a toolkit for neural machine translation. In *Proceedings of EACL*, pages 65–68, Valencia, Spain.

Sennrich, R., Haddow, B., and Birch, A. (2016). Neural machine translation of rare words with subword units. In *Proceedings of ACL*, pages 1715–1725, Berlin, Germany.

Ueffing, N. and Ney, H. (2007). Word-level confidence estimation for machine translation. *Computational Linguistics*, 33(1):9–40.

Wang, Y., Cheng, S., Jiang, L., Yang, J., Chen, W., Li, M., Shi, L., Wang, Y., and Yang, H. (2017). Sogou neural machine translation systems for WMT17. In *Proceedings of WMT*, pages 410–415, Copenhagen, Denmark.

Zhang, J., Utiyama, M., Sumita, E., Neubig, G., and Nakamura, S. (2017). Improving neural machine translation through phrase-based forced decoding. In *Proceedings of IJCNLP*, pages 152–162, Taipei, Taiwan.

Zhou, L., Hu, W., Zhang, J., and Zong, C. (2017). Neural system combination for machine translation. In *Proceedings of ACL*, pages 378–384, Vancouver, Canada.

Exploring Word Sense Disambiguation Abilities of
Neural Machine Translation Systems

Rebecca Marvin   becky@jhu.edu
Philipp Koehn   phi@jhu.edu
Department of Computer Science, Johns Hopkins University, Baltimore, 21218, USA

Abstract

Neural machine translation systems have been shown to achieve state-of-the-art translation performance for many language pairs. In order to produce a correct translation, MT systems must learn how to disambiguate words with multiple senses and pick the correct translation. We explore the extent to which the word embeddings for ambiguous words are able to disambiguate senses at deeper layers of the NMT encoder, which are thought to represent words with surrounding context. Consistent with previous research, we find that the NMT system fails to translate many ambiguous words correctly. We provide an evaluation framework to use for proposed improvements to word sense disambiguation abilities of NMT systems.

1   Introduction

Neural machine translation systems have to be able to perform many different linguistic tasks successfully in order to obtain good translations. For example, MT systems have to be able to deal with syntactic reordering, semantic relationships, co-reference, and discourse roles, among other phenomena. The obvious question that arises is: how well are state-of-the-art NMT systems doing at detecting linguistic features?

This question is not new. Statistical machine translation (SMT) systems have achieved consistently high BLEU scores because they explicitly try to model features such as word or phrase alignments. For lower-resource languages, SMT systems have been shown to outperform NMT systems, but NMT systems overtake SMT once there is enough training data (Koehn and Knowles, 2017). Recent work has looked at the ability of neural systems to learn syntactic and morphological features. Specifically, Belinkov et al. (2017) showed that recurrent neural networks are able to achieve high accuracy on tasks such as predicting morphological or part of speech tags and Linzen et al. (2016) showed that RNNs follow similar patterns as humans with respect to sentences that are grammatical or ungrammatical in agreement structure. Additionally, specific RNN cells can be shown to have high correlation with features such as sentence length (Karpathy et al., 2016), part of speech (Ding et al., 2017), or whether or not the RNN has finished a relative clause (Linzen et al., 2016).

Another linguistic issue NMT systems have to deal with is translating words in the source language that might have multiple translations in the target language. When these words don't differ orthographically, this task is known as *word sense disambiguation*. Typically, humans can successfully translate these kinds of words by looking at the contexts in which they appear. If NMT systems are able to successfully translate these words, it seems likely that they would have had to learn something about word sense disambiguation.

There has been much research on improving machine translation performance by simultaneously improving word sense disambiguation (Vickrey et al., 2005; Chan et al., 2007; Carpuat and Wu, 2007) for SMT systems, showing that adding word sense disambiguation to a baseline SMT system greatly improves translation performance. For NMT, recent work points out that NMT systems are not very reliable at translating rare word senses, but that disambiguation performance can be improved by using sense embeddings either as additional input to the encoder or to extract more structured lexical chains from the training data (Rios et al., 2017), or by using context-aware embeddings (Liu et al., 2017).

To the best of our knowledge, no work has yet attempted to examine the hidden activations of an NMT system to see whether it is able to disambiguate word senses. In this paper, we present means for evaluating the word sense disambiguation performance of NMT systems. Specifically, we visualize the hidden activations of an NMT encoder to see whether it is able to disambiguate word senses at deeper layers. We also present metrics that represent how well-disambiguated the senses are, with the hope that these metrics can be used to evaluate the word sense disambiguation performance of NMT systems in the future.

Word Sense Disambiguation

Word sense disambiguation (WSD) is the task of figuring out what a word with multiple potential senses means in context. For example, in the sentences below, the word *like* has four different meanings, or senses.

1. **similar:** Her English, *like* that of most people here, is flawless.
2. **speech:** We were *like*, what do we do?
3. **enjoy:** Of the youngers, I really *like* the work of Leo Arill.
4. **request:** I would *like* to be a part of them, but I cannot.

It is crucial for NMT systems to excel at this task in order to produce fluent translations. If the NMT systems do not correctly translate ambiguous words, the resulting translations could be incomprehensible or misleading.

Evaluation metrics have been proposed for assessing word sense disambiguation performance in the past. Lexical choice in MT systems has been evaluated using WSD tasks (Carpuat, 2013) or fill-in-the-blank tasks where the blank represents an ambiguous word (Vickrey et al., 2005), to name a couple methods. These are based on the idea that the entire sentential context should disambiguate the intended word sense. If MT systems are paying attention to the full context, they should be able to succeed at this task.

2   Methodology

We present experiments for examining the word sense disambiguation abilities of the attention-based encoder-decoder model (Bahdanau et al., 2015). In this model, since the encoder computes both forward and backward hidden states after reading the input sequence, each encoder hidden state h_i can be thought of as containing the entire context for the input word i. The idea continues as we add more layers to the encoder: each hidden state h_i should be learning more contextual information about the words surrounding word i. Intuitively, it seems that if the hidden states represent the context for a particular word, then these hidden states would be able to separate words with different senses based on the contexts in which they appear.

In order to formally examine the extent to which the hidden states of the encoder layer(s) of an NMT system disambiguate word senses, we look at the following metrics:

Distinctness. We will extract the hidden states from the last layer of the encoder and compute a principle component analysis (PCA) for these contextualized "embeddings." We can then plot the embeddings for an ambiguous word with different true senses. We also compute two metrics for how well-clustered our embeddings are.

Depth of encoder. We will look at these PCA embedding plots for NMT systems with different numbers of layers in the encoder. Since we are always extracting from the last layer of the encoder, we can get a sense of what the deeper layers in NMT systems are doing with respect to word sense disambiguation.

Correlation with translation performance. It might be that the NMT system only produces well-clustered embeddings for words that it correctly translates. We would like to look at the PCA embedding plots and internal cluster evaluation scores for all four layers when we only include the embeddings for correctly-translated words.

Cluster Measures

We use two intrinsic cluster evaluation metrics to score how well-clustered our resulting embeddings are. These are the *Dunn Index* and the *Davies-Bouldin Index*. We would like our plots to have reasonably distinct clusters which could indicate that word senses are being disambiguated in the encoder. Thus, the purpose of both of these metrics is to identify clusters that are compact and well-separated from other clusters.

The *Dunn Index* is defined as:

$$D = \frac{min_{1 \le i < j \le n} d(i,j)}{max_{1 \le k \le n} d'(k)}$$

where $d(i,j)$ represents the distance between cluster medians i and j and $d'(k)$ represents the maximal distance between any two points in cluster k. A higher Dunn Index corresponds to clusters that are dense and well-separated.

The *Davies-Bouldin (DB)* Index is defined as:

$$DB = \frac{1}{n} \sum_{i=1}^{n} \max_{j \ne i} \left(\frac{\sigma_i + \sigma_j}{d(c_i, c_j)} \right)$$

where n is the number of clusters, c_x is the median of cluster x, σ_x is the average distance of all points in cluster x to c_x, and $d(c_i, c_j)$ is the distance between the medians of clusters i and j. A lower DB Index corresponds to clusters that are dense and well-separated.

We hope to find that the Dunn Index increases and the DB Index decreases as we compute these scores for deeper layers of the NMT encoder. This would signify that our word senses were becoming more separated, which would likely correlate with disambiguation performance.

3 Experimental Design

We trained all of our NMT systems using the OpenNMT-py toolkit (Klein et al., 2017), which trains an attentional encoder-decoder model with the attention from Luong et al. (2015). We tokenized, cleaned, and truecased our data using the standard tools from the Moses toolkit (Koehn et al., 2007). We did not use byte-pair encoding in order to more easily do manual annotation of the data later. We used the default parameters of the OpenNMT-py toolkit for training, with the exception of the number of encoder layers, which we varied from 1 to 4.

For the current study, we extensively analyzed WSD performance on sentences containing four possible ambiguous words: *right*, *like*, *last*, or *case*. We manually annotated English sentences with their most appropriate sense (these were our "gold" sense labels), and fed the (un-annotated) sentences into our English-French NMT system. After feeding in the source sentence, we extracted the hidden activations of the NMT encoder and labeled them with their corresponding "gold" sense. We will refer to these hidden activations as the "extracted embeddings," since they are thought to represent a kind of word-and-context embedding.

We performed principle component analysis (PCA) on all of the extracted embeddings and plotted the first two components, where we marked these points based on their "gold" sense label. We then computed internal cluster evaluation scores for all of our embedding "clusters."

Data

The data we used to train our NMT systems comes from the Europarl Corpus (Koehn,

2005) and News Commentary corpus available through the WMT 2014 website. After removing sentences with more than 80 words, this amounted to slightly more than 2.1 million sentences of training data.[1] We used the 2013 news test dataset and the 2014 news test dataset from the WMT 2014 website to validate and to test our trained models, respectively. This amounted to 3000 validation sentences and 3003 test sentences. The 1 layer, 2 layer, 3 layer and 4 layer NMT systems achieved BLEU scores of 23.84, 23.71, 23.77, and 23.94 respectively when tested on the news test 2014 dataset from the WMT 2014 website.

For these initial experiments, we tested our systems on sentences containing one of four ambiguous words: *right*, *like*, *last*, or *case*. Test sentences containing any of these words were manually annotated with their associated sense, and labeled as "unclear" if the sense could not be easily determined from the sentential context. Some examples of sentences containing five different senses of the word *like* can be seen in the introduction.

There were 426 total test sentences that we examined. The number of sentences per each sense of a word is shown in Table 1.

Word	Sense 1	Sense 2	Sense 3	Sense 4	Sense 5	Sense 6	Unclear from context
Right	8	21	12	21	12	1	6
Like	130	1	21	16	n/a	n/a	6
Last	91	6	n/a	n/a	n/a	n/a	1
Case	46	4	16	3	1	n/a	3

Table 1: Number of sentences for each sense of our ambiguous words. If "n/a" appears in a cell, the word did not have that many distinct senses.

Experiment 1 After removing sentences for which a sense label could not be easily determined from context, we used our manually annotated 410 sentences containing the word *right*, *like*, *last*, or *case* for our gold sense labels. Each sentence was translated by all four of our trained models, and we computed the first two principal components of the extracted embeddings, which were used to compute our internal cluster scores.

Experiment 2 In Experiment 1, we did cluster analysis on the extracted embeddings for *all* sentences containing different senses of our ambiguous words. However, we would expect that senses would be better clustered when the model correctly translates the word, since in that case the model would have had to first choose the correct meaning of the word in context and then translate it. In this experiment, we only looked at the extracted embeddings for sentences where the word *like* or *right* was correctly translated.

Experiment 3 It is possible that the first two principal components of the hidden activations of an NMT encoder might not best represent the amount of word sense information the NMT system is able to learn. That is, the first two components could represent information about the source sentence that has nothing to do with word senses. To examine the extent to which sense information was encoded in the full extracted embeddings, we trained a linear SVM to predict the sense of a word from hidden activations. We trained the SVM on 80% of the test extracted embeddings, and tested it on the remaining 20% of examples. We hope to achieve a high accuracy at this task if sense information was easily accessible from the hidden state vectors.

---

[1] 2 million sentences is enough data for an NMT system to come close to or even outperform an SMT system, according to Koehn and Knowles (2017).

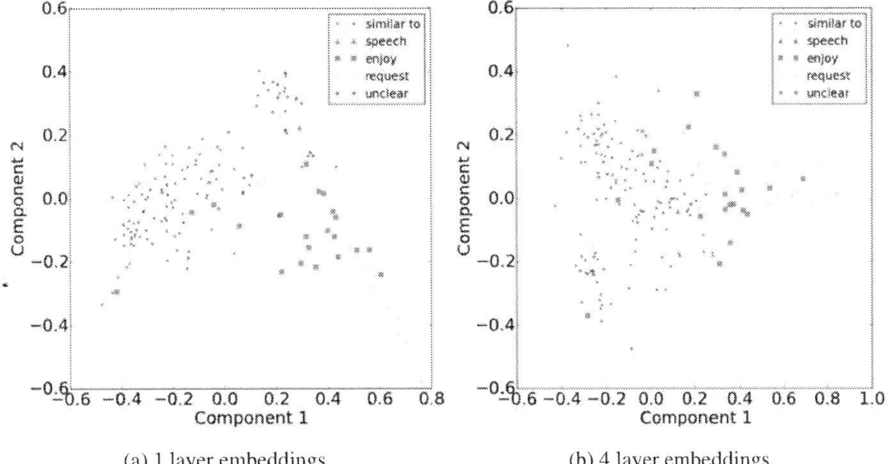

(a) 1 layer embeddings.   (b) 4 layer embeddings.

Figure 1: The embeddings of different senses of the word *like*, extracted from the 1 layer and 4 layer models.

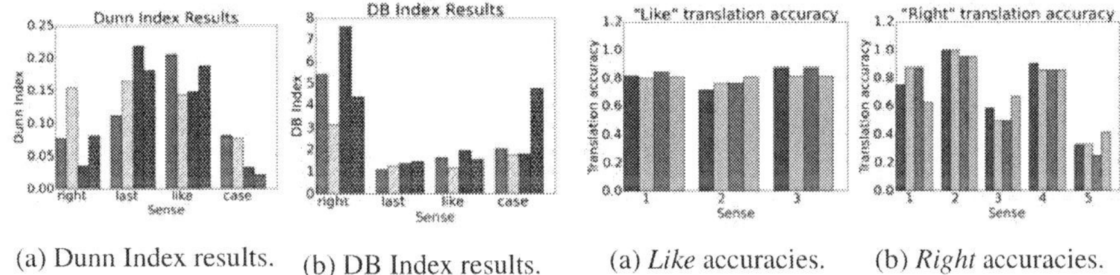

(a) Dunn Index results.   (b) DB Index results.   (a) *Like* accuracies.   (b) *Right* accuracies.

Figure 2: The cluster metrics as we look at different numbers of encoder layers.

Figure 3: The translation accuracies for distinct senses for all four models.

4 Results

The plots of the extracted embeddings of different senses of *like* from two of our models can be seen in Figure 1.[2] Visually, the plots seem to show some separation between different senses.

The Dunn and DB Index scores for all four models in Experiment 1 are shown in Figure 2. The different colors represent the numbers of layers, with 1 layer being the leftmost bar and 4 layers being the rightmost within each bar cluster. There does not seem to be a general trend in either index as we look at deeper models.

For Experiment 2, we looked at how the translation accuracy for sentences containing instances of a particular sense varies with the number of layers in the NMT encoder. Figure 3 examines this for the words *right* and *like*.[3] Here again, we would hope to see a general increase in translation accuracy as we increased the number of encoder layers. However, these results and the lack of a general trend in either the Dunn or Davies-Bouldin Index suggest that standard NMT systems still struggle with the issue of word sense disambiguation.

The results for our classifier in Experiment 3 are shown in Table 2. The SVM gets above

---

[2]The plots for the 2 and 3 layer models looked very similar to these two plots.

[3]We excluded the senses which only had one training example. For *right*, all four models were unable to correctly translate the *90 degrees* sense. For *like*, all four models were able to correctly translate the *speech* sense.

word	1layer	2layer	3layer	4layer
right	0.44	0.63	0.56	0.44
last	0.84	1	0.95	0.84
like	0.88	0.91	0.94	0.94
case	0.79	0.86	0.79	0.57
average	0.76	0.88	0.85	0.74

Table 2: The SVM classifier accuracy at predicting sense from hidden activations.

84% accuracy for the extracted embeddings from all four models for both *last* and *like*, both of which had one sense which was significantly more dominant than the others. The accuracy of the SVM is much lower on *right* and *case*, which have slightly more equal sense distributions.

5   Limitations

Our results hint that standard NMT encoder layers are not encoding enough sentential context to do well at word sense disambiguation. However, we would like to treat these results as a starting point for future evaluations. In particular, we discuss a few limitations of this work:

Manual annotation. It is well-known that obtaining manually annotated data is expensive, sometimes prohibitively so. In this study, we hand-annotated 426 sentences for just four ambiguous words. In the future, we would like to get much more sense-labeled data, either through crowdsourcing to obtain more hand-labeled data, or by using other annotation strategies.

Small test data size. We presented a preliminary study using the ambiguous words *right*, *like*, *last*, and *case*. Perhaps the mixed results could be explained though some particular feature of *right*, and including other words in an evaluation could cancel out that noise. Future work should use more words with multiple senses and more sentences per sense of each word, in order to draw stronger conclusions about word sense disambiguation.

Encoder states. It could be that the NMT system learns how to disambiguate word senses at a different point in the architecture than the encoder. For example, perhaps the NMT system performs the disambiguation step during decoding, thus removing some of the burden of capturing sense information from the encoder. While we believe the NMT encoder should have access to enough sentence context to be able to disambiguate sense, future work could explore whether different components of the NMT architecture more efficiently store sense information.

6   Conclusion & Future Work

Despite these limitations, our preliminary results do suggest that NMT systems still need much improvement in the area of word sense disambiguation. The PCA embedding plots of extracted embeddings at varying levels of the encoder showed some evidence of distinct clusters, but the internal cluster scores varied when we looked at deeper layers of the encoder or considered only sentences that produced correct translations of *right* or *like*.

The results we see are limited by the small sample size we use in our experiments, but we have presented a methodology for examining the word sense disambiguation abilities of NMT systems. These kinds of visualizations and internal cluster evaluation metrics can be used in future research on improving word sense disambiguation in neural machine translation.

Acknowledgements   This research is based upon work supported by the Office of the Director of National Intelligence (ODNI), Intelligence Advanced Research Projects Activity (IARPA) via the MATE-RIAL research program.

References

Bahdanau, D., Cho, K., and Bengio, Y. (2015). Neural machine translation by jointly learning to align and translate. *ICLR*.

Belinkov, Y., Durrani, N., Dalai, F., Sajjad, H., and Glass, J. (2017). What do neural machine translation models learn about morphology? *ACL*.

Carpuat, M. (2013). A semantic evaluation of machine translation lexical choice. *ACL*.

Carpuat, M. and Wu, D. (2007). Improving statistical machine translation using word sense disambiguation. *EMNLP*.

Chan, Y. S., Ng, H. T., and Chiang, D. (2007). Word sense disambiguation improves statistical machine translation. *ACL*.

Ding, Y., Liu, Y., Luan, H., and Sun, M. (2017). Visualizing and understanding neural machine translation. *ACL*.

Karpathy, A., Johnson, J., and Li, F.-F. (2016). Visualizing and understanding recurrent networks. *ICLR*.

Klein, G., Kim, Y., Deng, Y., Senellart, J., and Rush, A. M. (2017). Opennmt: Open-source toolkit for neural machine translation. In *Proc. ACL*.

Koehn, P. (2005). Europarl: A parallel corpus for statistical machine translation.

Koehn, P., Hoang, H., Birch, A., Federico, M., Bertoldi, N., Cowan, B., Shen, W., Moran, C., Zens, R., Dyer, C., Bojar, O., Constantin, A., and Herbst, E. (2007). Moses: Open source toolkit for statistical machine translation.

Koehn, P. and Knowles, R. (2017). Six challenges for neural machine translation. *ACL*.

Linzen, T., Dupoux, E., and Goldberg, Y. (2016). Assessing the ability of lstms to learn syntax-sensitive dependencies. *ACL*.

Liu, F., Lu, H., and Neubig, G. (2017). Handling homographs in neural machine translation. *arXiv preprint*.

Luong, M.-T., Pham, H., and Manning, C. D. (2015). Effective approaches to attention-based neural machine translation. *EMNLP*.

Papineni, K., Roukos, S., Ward, T., and Zhu, W.-J. (2002). Bleu: A method for automatic evaluation of machine translation. *ACL*.

Rios, A., Mascarell, L., and Sennrich, R. (2017). Improving word sense disambiguation in neural machine translation with sense embeddings. *WMT*.

Vickrey, D., Biewald, L., Teyssier, M., and Koller, D. (2005). Word-sense disambiguation for machine translation. *EMNLP*.

Improving Low Resource Machine Translation
using Morphological Glosses

Steven Shearing ssheari1@jhu.edu
Christo Kirov ckirov1@jhu.edu
Huda Khayrallah huda@jhu.edu
David Yarowsky yarowsky@jhu.edu
Johns Hopkins University

Abstract

Low-resource machine translation is a challenging problem, especially when the source language is morphologically complex. We describe a simple procedure for constructing glosses, or mappings between complex, inflected source-language words and equivalent multi-word English expressions. We demonstrate the utility of glosses, especially compared to entries in bilingual dictionaries, across several data-augmentation strategies designed to mitigate a lack of training data. In our experiments, we achieve improvements of up to 1 BLEU point in a Russian-English translation task and 2.4 BLEU points in a Spanish-English translation task over a strong baseline translation system.

1 Introduction

Low-resource machine translation, where only a small amount of parallel data is available between source and target languages, poses a significant challenge. Machine translation systems, especially those based on neural network models, tend to be data-hungry. Highly-inflected source languages further complicate the situation, presenting a significant sparsity problem in low-resource settings. Most possible inflected wordforms are likely to appear only once in the data or not at all.

In an effort to improve performance when limited parallel data is available for learning how to translate from a highly inflected source language into English, we experiment with two simple data augmentation strategies—appending and substitution. To alleviate sparsity, we experiment with appending entries from multilingual dictionaries directly to the bitext. We also leverage linguistic knowledge about the morphological grammar of the highly-inflected source language to generate multi-word English glosses. We show that these glosses, which better mimic in-situ translations, are more effective than dictionary entries when appended to the training data. We also employ glosses for a second strategy, directly substituting them in place of complex inflected forms in the source language. The overarching idea is to create a new version of the source, source′, that is more similar to the target language. In theory, this should improve performance by solving some portion of the translation problem before a final translation model is trained. We show that gloss substitution has a positive effect on BLEU scores compared to baseline systems.

We present experimental results translating from Russian and Spanish into English. While Russian and Spanish are not low-resource languages, we simulate extremely low-resource scenarios by relying only on representative language packs from DARPA's LORELEI (LOw REsource Languages for Emergent Incidents) program as our source of parallel training data.

These packs typically contain less than 50,000 bilingual sentence pairs in total, orders of magnitude below the amount used to train most state-of-the-art MT systems. We run our experiments using traditional phrase-based statistical machine translation models (PBMT). While neural machine translation offers state-of-the-art performance when training data is plentiful, PBMT remains competitive or superior in the low resource conditions we focus on (Koehn and Knowles, 2017).

2 Multilingual Dictionaries Versus Glosses

We define an entry in a multilingual dictionary as a mapping between a lemma form in the source language to one or more definitions in the target language.

бежать,VERB,to run, to be running

While useful, these types of entries have several notable drawbacks when used as bitext for a translation system. First, on the source side, the dictionary forms of words, or lemmas, are typically uninflected, and may not be in common usage. For example, the dictionary form of verbs in many languages is the infinitive, but in actual text tensed forms are much more common. Second, on the target side, dictionary definitions are not necessarily equivalent to in-situ translations of a word, and often contain additional descriptive text.

Glosses, as we define them, are intended to remedy these problems. A gloss is a mapping between an inflected form of a word, and an in-situ translation. In many cases, English uses syntactic constructions to express distinctions made by inflectional morphology in a source language. As a result, single source words are often glossed as multi-word expressions in English.

бегут, бежать,V;IPFV;PRS;3;PL,(they/NNS) are running; (they/NNS) run

Generating a gloss for an inflected word follows a general process outlined in Hewitt et al. (2016). In this work, however, we simplify many of the steps. Our implementation is fully described in the Experiments section below.

1. Apply morphological analysis to an input inflected word to recover its base lemma and morphological features, e.g.,

   comprábamos → *comprar*, V;1;PL;PST;IPFV

2. Using a separate lemma-to-lemma dictionary, recover a target lemma for the source word:

   comprar → *buy*

3. Specify a conversion from each vector of source morphological features to a target gloss template. For many language pairs, this can be done manually:

   V;1;PL;PST;IPFV → '(we) were VBG.'

   Here, VBG is a Penn Treebank tag[1] which indicates that the template can be filled with the gerund (*-ing*) form of an English verb.

4. Given a gloss template from (3), and a target lemma from (2), replace the PTB placeholder in the template, inflecting the target lemma as needed with a morphological generation tool or lookup table:

   '(we) were VBG' + *buy* → '(we) were *buying*'

   This completes the gloss generation process:

   comprábamos → '(we) were buying'

---

[1] https://www.ling.upenn.edu/courses/Fall_2003/ling001/penn_treebank_pos.html

3 Related Work

Prior work has both explored ways of generating morphological information, and incorporating such morphological information into Phrase Based Machine Translation. While there is work on generating rich morphology on the target side of translations (for example: (Toutanova et al., 2008; Huck et al., 2017), we focus on rich source side morphology in this work.

Hewitt et al. (2016) created glosses by re-purposing instructional prompts found in a special corpus designed to elicit inflectional paradigms from bilingual speakers (Sylak-Glassman et al., 2016). For example, the sample prompt '(The apple) has been eaten.' was designed to elicit third person present perfect verb forms from bilingual Spanish speakers. They heuristically interpolated between multiple prompts to generate new gloss templates for each possible feature vector and lemma. They experiment with both appending their synthetic translations to the parallel text as well as using an additional phrase table (and the combination of both), but did not find that one method was consistently superior.

Broadly, the goal of our substitution approach is to transform the source language into a form that is more similar to the target. A number of previous strategies used in MT have fallen under this umbrella. Compound splitting (Koehn and Knight, 2003; Macherey et al., 2011) of, for example, German source-side words increases similarity with English as English doesn't use nearly as many compounds as German. Fraser and Marcu (2005) use stemming to reduce Romanian source side vocabulary size to improve Romanian-English word alignment. Ding et al. (2016) compare supervised (ChipMunk (Cotterell et al., 2015)) and unsupervised (Morfessor (Virpioja et al., 2013), and Byte-Pair encoding (Sennrich et al., 2015)) morphological segmentation methods on the source side of the PBMT system for the WMT Turkish-English Translation Task.

4 Experiments

4.1 Model

We use Moses (Koehn et al., 2007) as the Phrase Based Machine Translation (PBMT) system to run all our translation experiments. Data is tokenized and truecased using standard Moses scripts. We use GIZA++ (Och and Ney, 2003) for alignment with the grow-diag-final-and setting. We set the maximum sentence length to 80 and the maximum phrase length to 5. For decoding, we use Cube Pruning (Huang and Chiang, 2007). We also weigh potential translations using a 5-gram KenLM (Heafield, 2011) language model.

4.2 Data

Bitext. For our base bitext, we use the Russian-English Corpus from the LORELEI Russian Representative Language Pack (LDC2016E95 V1.1), and the Spanish-English Corpus from the LORELEI Spanish Representative Language Pack (LDC2016E97). The corpora primarily consist of news and web forums. While they are included in the LORELEI corpora, we exclude Tweets from these experiments. We also remove sentences longer than 80 words.

For the Russian baselines, we randomly split the remaining data into train (46,746), tune (2,233), and test (2,462) sentence pairs. For the Spanish baselines, we randomly split the remaining data into train (22,311), tune (2,031), and test (2,032) sentence pairs. See table 1 for the number of sentences in the training corpus for each experiment condition.[2] The tuning and test sets remain the same for all experiments in a language.

---

[2]Since we perform the length filtering on the training set after gloss substitution in the corresponding condition, some sentences are removed as substitution makes them too long.

Dictionary. The LORELEI language packs from Russian and Spanish also contain dictionaries mapping source lemmas into target definitions in a custom XML format. Some entries include multiple definitions. In this case, each definition was split into its own line of bitext. Furthermore, some of the definitions include notes on gender (e.g. артистка: artist (female).) or topic (e.g. бить: chime (about clock)), or other comments (e.g. бензель: (rare) paintbrush). We remove any text within parenthesis, and then remove any entries with non-English words. After all post-processing was complete, we were left with 58,856 dictionary entries for Russian, and 64,450 dictionary entries for Spanish.

Glosses. Glosses for Russian and Spanish were created as follows: Lists of inflected word-forms were obtained via a union of the UniMorph database (`unimorph.githbub.io`), which provides a mapping from inflected forms to their lemmas and morphological feature vectors, and a tokenization of the monolingual corpus released by the LDC as part of LORELEI language packs for Russian and Spanish.

For each word in the list, additional morphological analyses were obtained. For Russian, we applied the PyMorphy2 package (Korobov, 2015)[3] to each word, while for Spanish we used the Freeling package (Padró and Stanilovsky, 2012).[4] For both Russian and Spanish, we also applied a custom sequence-2-sequence neural network analyzer trained on the raw data in the UniMorph database. The network used an architecture, training scheme, and hyperparameters identical to that used in (Kann and Schütze, 2016). It mapped sequences of characters representing an inflected word directly to a sequence representing the its underlying lemma and features ($c\,o\,m\,p\,r\,\acute{a}\,b\,a\,m\,o\,s \rightarrow c\,o\,m\,p\,r\,a\,r\ V\ 1\ PL\ PST\ IPFV$) The feature vectors output by all analysis methods were manually mapped into the UniMorph feature schema standard (Sylak-Glassman et al., 2015). As the total set of of unique feature vectors remaining after this mapping was limited for both Russian (569 vectors) and Spanish (239 vectors), we were able to manually produce one or more gloss templates for each vector (e.g., V;1;PL;PST;IPFV $\rightarrow$ '(we) were VBG.').

Source lemmas in Russian and Spanish were converted to English lemmas via lookup in, preferably, Wiktionary-derived lemma translation data (Kirov et al., 2016), or PanLex (Baldwin et al., 2010). English lemmas were then inflected using the tools provided by Smedt and Daelemans (2012) and inserted into the corresponding gloss templates.

We further post-processed the glosses by removing anything in parenthesis or brackets, and then removed entries containing non-English words in the translation, after which we were left with 3,122,470 Russian glosses, and 589,188 Spanish glosses.

5   Conditions

We trained three baseline models and five additional experimental setups. Total sizes of training datasets for each condition, in number of paired sentences, are shown in Table 1.

For Baseline 1, in both Russian and Spanish, we simply trained a default Moses system on the base bitext in each LORELEI language pack. The language model and truecaser used during decoding were trained only on the target-side portion of the parallel training data.

For Baseline 2, we made use of the extensive monolingual data available for English. Following previous work, we trained a new truecaser and a much larger language model from the English side of the Russian-English parallel text plus text from the Associated Press Worldstream, English Service, a subset of the English Gigaword corpus (Parker et al., 2011) (a total of 54,287,116 sentences). Given the clear performance benefit, we continued to use this larger language model for all subsequent experiments. While the large language model was trained

---

[3]`https://github.com/kmike/pymorphy2`
[4]`http://nlp.lsi.upc.edu/freeling`

Condition	Russian	Spanish
Baseline 1 (Small LM)	46,460	22,311
Baseline 2 (Big LM)	46,460	22,311
Append Dictionary	105,316	86,861
Append Glosses	3,168,675	611,439
Append Dictionary + Glosses	3,227,531	675,989
Substitute Glosses	46,414	22,226
Substitute Glosses + Identity Alignment	95,603	40,724

Table 1: Number of train sentences for Russian-English and Spanish-English Translation.

source	Женщина была почти при смерти
reference	the woman had nearly died
substitution	woman were почти при to death

Table 2: An example of gloss substitution in the Russian-English training set.

using the target-side of the Russian-English data, this contributed a minuscule amount in proportion to the contribution of data from the Gigaword corpus. Thus, we use the same language model for both Russian and Spanish experiments.

For Baseline 3, in both Russian and Spanish, we train PBMT system on the glosses and dictionary (without any parallel sentences). We use the larger language model from Baseline 2.

Appending. Our next experimental conditions involved appending additional data to the base bitext for each language. We experimented with appending the processed dictionary entries or generated glosses, as well as appending both the dictionary and the glosses in one system. Each of these modifications increased the total size of the training data, as seen in Table 1.

Substitution. Finally, we substituted our glosses directly into the base bitext. Any inflected source word appearing in the list of glosses was a candidate for substitution. Many words had multiple glosses available. To decide which one to use for substitution, we considered the following confidence hierarchy. First, any gloss corresponding to a pre-existing entry in the UniMorph database was preferred. Next, we preferred entries corresponding to an off-the-shelf morphological analysis (derived from PyMorphy2 in Russian, and Freeling in Spanish). Glosses based on the custom-trained neural-network analyzer were used when a UniMorph entry was not available and both PyMorphy2 and Freeling failed to provide an analysis. An example of the substitution process is shown in table 2.

While substitution is intended to make the source language appear more like the target (in this case literally, since target language words are substituted directly into the source), the alignment algorithm in the PBMT system is not character-aware and therefore has no sense of identity between the source and target vocabularies. To get around this, we add a condition attempting to bias the aligner to notice identical source and target phrases. In particular, for each gloss substitution, we append a gloss-to-gloss identity mapping to the bitext.

6   Results & Discussion

Table 3 indicates the lowercased BLEU scores achieved by the model in each experimental condition in Russian-English and Spanish-English settings. Results were consistent across both language pairs. As expected, using a larger target-side language model (Baseline 2) provides a significant boost over the initial baseline (Baseline 1) with language model trained only on

Condition	Russian BLEU	%OOV(Type/Token)	Spanish BLEU	%OOV (Type/Token)
Baseline 1 (bitext + Small LM)	15.6	31.1/11.2	18.6	24.6/8.0
Baseline 2 (bitext + Big LM)	16.2	31.1/11.2	20.6	24.6/8.0
Baseline 3 (dictionary + Glosses + Big LM)	7.7	26.5/26.7	14.6	12.1/13.1
Append Dictionary	17.0	28.7/10.2	21.5	20.2/6.6
Append Glosses	17.8	15.2/5.5	23.8	6.8/2.3
Append Dictionary + Glosses	18.0	15.1/5.5	23.9	6.6/2.3
Substitute Glosses	17.7	26.3/5.0	22.2	19.5/4.0
Substitute Glosses + Identity Alignment	17.8	26.3/5.0	22.9	19.5/4.0

Table 3: Lowercased BLEU for Russian-English and Spanish-English Translation.

the available bitext. This was true even for Spanish, where the large language model was partially trained on the Russian-English target-side data, and was potentially out-of-domain. Every augmentation strategy provided some further improvement. Baseline 3 demonstrates that simply using the lexical resources and a strong language model can produce decent results in the absence of bitext (particularly in the Spanish experiments).

As we hypothesized, appending the glosses to the training data results in better performance than just appending dictionary pairs. This is likely because glosses are closer to actual translations. However, there is an additive effect of appending both dictionary items and glosses, suggesting that the two external data sources contain at least some complementary information.

The substitution trials did not fare as well as the appending trials. They did, however, still provide an improvement over Baseline 2. This was even without adding identity pairs to the training data in order to bias alignment (so the model was not aware which parts of the source sentences were actually English), or increasing the amount of bitext in any way. This suggests that using simple techniques like gloss substitution to transform the source into something closer to the target language makes learning a complex MT model after the fact more effective. In the Russian gloss substitution, 67% of tokens were replaced in the training set. In Spanish, 80% of tokens were replaced.

Table 3 includes the out-of-vocabulary rate (type and token) for each experiment. The low out-of-vocabulary rate for baseline 3 demonstrates the coverage of the the dictionary and glosses (particularity for Spanish). The glosses in particular have very broad coverage. They provide a dramatic drop in OOV's (dropping the rate by over 50%). In addition to the BLEU improvement, reducing the OOV rate can greatly improve the usability of low resource machine translation.

7 Conclusions & Future Work

We showed that glosses of morphologically complex source words are a useful resource for rapidly improving machine translation performance in extremely low-resource scenarios. As glosses mimic in-situ translations of inflected words, they are more informative than dictionary items, which map lemmas to definitions. Glosses are useful both for augmenting training data with additional bitext, or transforming source language data into a form that is more similar to the target language. Future work will explore different ways of generating glosses, and apply additional transformations to the language data to ease the amount a translation model needs to learn. This would include changing both the source language, *and* making reversible changes to the target. If a non-English, morphologically complex target is used, these might include target-side morphological segmentation.

Acknowledgments

This material is based upon work supported in part by DARPA under Contract No. HR0011-15-C-0113. Any opinions, findings and conclusions or recommendations expressed in this material are those of the authors and do not necessarily reflect the views of DARPA.

References

Baldwin, T., Pool, J., and Colowick, S. M. (2010). PanLex and LEXTRACT: Translating all words of all languages of the world. In *Proceedings of the 23rd International Conference on Computational Linguistics: Demonstrations*, COLING '10, pages 37–40, Stroudsburg, PA, USA. Association for Computational Linguistics.

Cotterell, R., Müller, T., Fraser, A., and Schütze, H. (2015). Labeled morphological segmentation with Semi-Markov models. In *Proceedings of the Nineteenth Conference on Computational Natural Language Learning*, pages 164–174, Beijing, China. Association for Computational Linguistics.

Ding, S., Duh, K., Khayrallah, H., Koehn, P., and Post, M. (2016). The JHU machine translation systems for WMT 2016. In *Proceedings of the First Conference on Machine Translation*, pages 272–280, Berlin, Germany. Association for Computational Linguistics.

Fraser, A. and Marcu, D. (2005). ISI's participation in the Romanian-English alignment task. In *Proceedings of the ACL Workshop on Building and Using Parallel Texts*, ParaText '05, pages 91–94, Stroudsburg, PA, USA. Association for Computational Linguistics.

Heafield, K. (2011). KenLM: Faster and smaller language model queries. In *Proceedings of the Sixth Workshop on Statistical Machine Translation*, pages 187–197. Association for Computational Linguistics.

Hewitt, J., Post, M., and Yarowsky, D. (2016). Automatic construction of morphologically motivated translation models for highly inflected, low-resource languages. *AMTA 2016, Vol.*, page 177.

Huang, L. and Chiang, D. (2007). Forest rescoring: Faster decoding with integrated language models. In *Annual Meeting-Association For Computational Linguistics*, volume 45, page 144.

Huck, M., Tamchyna, A., Bojar, O., and Fraser, A. (2017). Producing unseen morphological variants in statistical machine translation. In *Proceedings of the 15th Conference of the European Chapter of the Association for Computational Linguistics: Volume 2, Short Papers*, pages 369–375, Valencia, Spain. Association for Computational Linguistics.

Kann, K. and Schütze, H. (2016). Single-model encoder-decoder with explicit morphological representation for reinflection. In *Proceedings of the 54th Annual Meeting of the Association for Computational Linguistics (ACL)*, pages 555–560, Berlin, Germany. Association for Computational Linguistics.

Kirov, C., Sylak-Glassman, J., Que, R., and Yarowsky, D. (2016). Very-large scale parsing and normalization of Wiktionary morphological paradigms. In Calzolari, N., Choukri, K., Declerck, T., Goggi, S., Grobelnik, M., Maegaard, B., Mariani, J., Mazo, H., Moreno, A., Odijk, J., and Piperidis, S., editors, *Proceedings of the Tenth International Conference on Language Resources and Evaluation (LREC 2016)*, Paris, France. European Language Resources Association (ELRA).

Koehn, P., Hoang, H., Birch, A., Callison-Burch, C., Federico, M., Bertoldi, N., Cowan, B., Shen, W., Moran, C., Zens, R., Dyer, C., Bojar, O., Constantin, A., and Herbst, E. (2007). Moses: Open source toolkit for statistical machine translation. In *Proceedings of the 45th annual meeting of the ACL on interactive poster and demonstration sessions*, pages 177–180. Association for Computational Linguistics.

Koehn, P. and Knight, K. (2003). Empirical methods for compound splitting. In *Proceedings of the tenth conference on European chapter of the Association for Computational Linguistics-Volume 1*, pages 187–193. Association for Computational Linguistics.

Koehn, P. and Knowles, R. (2017). Six challenges for neural machine translation. In *Proceedings of the First Workshop on Neural Machine Translation*, pages 28–39, Vancouver. Association for Computational Linguistics.

Korobov, M. (2015). Morphological analyzer and generator for Russian and Ukrainian languages. In Khachay, M. Y., Konstantinova, N., Panchenko, A., Ignatov, D. I., and Labunets, V. G., editors, *Analysis of Images, Social Networks and Texts*, volume 542 of *Communications in Computer and Information Science*, pages 320–332. Springer International Publishing.

Macherey, K., Dai, A. M., Talbot, D., Popat, A. C., and Och, F. (2011). Language-independent compound splitting with morphological operations. In *Proceedings of the 49th Annual Meeting of the Association for Computational Linguistics: Human Language Technologies - Volume 1*, HLT '11, pages 1395–1404, Stroudsburg, PA, USA. Association for Computational Linguistics.

Och, F. J. and Ney, H. (2003). A systematic comparison of various statistical alignment models. *Computational Linguistics*, 29(1):19–51.

Padró, L. and Stanilovsky, E. (2012). FreeLing 3.0: Towards wider multilinguality. In *Proceedings of the Language Resources and Evaluation Conference (LREC 2012)*, Istanbul, Turkey. ELRA.

Parker, R., Graff, D., Kong, J., Chen, K., and Maeda, K. (2011). English Gigaword Fifth Edition LDC2011T07. Philadelphia. Linguistic Data Consortium.

Sennrich, R., Haddow, B., and Birch, A. (2015). Neural machine translation of rare words with subword units. *CoRR*, abs/1508.07909.

Smedt, T. D. and Daelemans, W. (2012). Pattern for Python. *Journal of Machine Learning Research*, 13(Jun):2063–2067.

Sylak-Glassman, J., Kirov, C., Post, M., Que, R., and Yarowsky, D. (2015). *A Universal Feature Schema for Rich Morphological Annotation and Fine-Grained Cross-Lingual Part-of-Speech Tagging*, pages 72–93. Springer International Publishing, Cham.

Sylak-Glassman, J., Kirov, C., and Yarowsky, D. (2016). Remote elicitation of inflectional paradigms to seed morphological analysis in low-resource languages. In Chair), N. C. C., Choukri, K., Declerck, T., Goggi, S., Grobelnik, M., Maegaard, B., Mariani, J., Mazo, H., Moreno, A., Odijk, J., and Piperidis, S., editors, *Proceedings of the Tenth International Conference on Language Resources and Evaluation (LREC 2016)*, Paris, France. European Language Resources Association (ELRA).

Toutanova, K., Suzuki, H., and Ruopp, A. (2008). Applying morphology generation models to machine translation. In *Proceedings of ACL-08: HLT*, pages 514–522, Columbus, Ohio. Association for Computational Linguistics.

Virpioja, S., Smit, P., Grönroos, S.-A., Kurimo, M., et al. (2013). Morfessor 2.0: Python implementation and extensions for Morfessor Baseline.

A Dataset and Reranking Method for Multimodal MT of User-Generated Image Captions

Shigehiko Schamoni   schamoni@cl.uni-heidelberg.de
Julian Hitschler   hitschler@cl.uni-heidelberg.de
Department of Computational Linguistics, Heidelberg University, 69120 Heidelberg, Germany

Stefan Riezler   riezler@cl.uni-heidelberg.de
Department of Computational Linguistics and IWR, Heidelberg University, 69120 Heidelberg, Germany

Abstract

We present a dataset and method for improving the translation of noisy image captions that were created by users of Wikimedia Commons. The dataset is multilingual but non-parallel, and is several orders of magnitude larger than existing parallel data for multimodal machine translation. Our retrieval-based method pivots on similar images and uses the associated captions in the target language to rerank translation outputs. This method only requires small amounts of parallel captions to find the optimal ensemble of retrieval features based on textual and visual similarity. Furthermore, our method is compatible with any machine translation system, and allows to quickly integrate new data without the need of re-training the translation system. Tests on three different datasets showed that size and diversity of the data is crucial for the performance of our method. On the introduced dataset we observe consistent improvements of up to 5 BLEU points and 3 points in Character F-score over strong neural MT baselines for three different language pairs.

1 Introduction

Image caption translation is the task of translating a caption associated with an image into another language. What differentiates this task from purely text-based machine translation is the incorporation of image information into the translation process. Images associated with text usually add a new modality of information. Such information helps to ground the meaning of the corresponding text and is thus especially useful in a translation task. Interest in this task has surged since the first instantiation of the shared task on multimodal machine translation where a dataset of 30,000 German translations of crowdsourced English captions was presented (Specia et al., 2016). However, this dataset has limitations: The captions were created by human annotators that were guided to produce "conceptual" descriptions that identify the objects depicted in the image (Hodosh et al., 2013). This leads to relatively short captions amounting to a comparatively easy translation task with little room for improvement by incorporating visual information. This is confirmed by recent results showing that improvements over a text-only MT baseline are inconsistent and hard to achieve (Lala et al., 2017; Elliott et al., 2017).

While caption translation in previous work has been conducted solely on clean, manually labeled captions based on MS COCO (Lin et al., 2014), Flickr30k (Rashtchian et al., 2010), or its multilingual variant Multi30k (Elliott et al., 2016), the goal of our work is to lift multimodal caption translation to a more realistic setup. For this purpose, we extracted a dataset of 4M "captions in the wild" as they appear in the user-generated Wikimedia Commons database. This new dataset is very different to previous image-caption data, as it contains highly diverse types of user-generated texts associated with images. The English captions in this dataset are around 34 tokens long, compared to 11 and 14 for MS COCO and Multi30k, respectively. Caption translation of Wikimedia Commons data thus contrasts to previous image-caption translation tasks. However, we find the new dataset to provide a lot of room for improvement by incorporating visual information into the translation process. The dataset is described in Section 4.

Since the dataset only contains very small subsets of parallel captions (which we use for tuning and testing), the proper way to integrate visual information is to leverage monolingual image-caption pairs. Hitschler et al. (2016) presented an approach based on a crosslingual reranking framework where monolingual captions in the target language are used to rerank translation hypotheses given a source caption and the corresponding image. In order to retrieve captions for reranking, they pivot on target language image-captions pairs in two ways: A list of monolingual captions is obtained by a joint textual and visual similarity model by comparison between the hypotheses and the captions in the target language. To calculate the visual similarity component of their joint model, they use rich image feature representations from a convolutional neural network (Simonyan and Zisserman, 2015). Our approach is an extension of Hitschler et al. (2016), who rely on manually tuned hyperparameters, to a pairwise ranking approach to learn an optimal ensemble of different rerankers. We also implement separate textual and visual similarity components to incorporate them as distinct features into our reranking model. Furthermore, we investigate a stronger text-only baseline that is based on neural MT (NMT). Our translation and reranking methods are described in Section 3.

We present an evaluation on caption data from Wikimedia Commons. We find gains of 5 BLEU points (Papineni et al., 2002) and 3 points in Character F-score (Popović, 2015) by reranking over strong NMT baselines across three different language pairs. In order to discern the contribution of our new learning method, we compare our approach to the only other monolingual reranking approach that we are aware of, namely Hitschler et al. (2016). On the MS COCO data, we observe gains by neural MT over phrase-based MT, and small but consistent gains by reranking. We also evaluate our approach on the Multi30k (Elliott et al., 2016) dataset that was used for the WMT17 Multimodal Shared Task 2 (Elliott et al., 2017). Due to the limited size of data available for retrieval we found no significant improvements over the NMT baseline here. Our experiments indicate a strong dependency of our approach's performance on the type and size of retrieval data. The experiments are described in Section 5.

2 Related Work

The dataset presented in this paper is to our knowledge the first publicly available resource of user-generated image captions at the size of 4M image-caption pairs. The dataset that is closest to ours is the SBU captioned photo dataset (Ordonez et al., 2011) that contains 1M images and captions. However, this dataset was filtered to include specific terms and to limit description lengths, resulting in an average sentence length of around 13 tokens. See Ferraro et al. (2015) for an overview over image-caption datasets.

Multimodal caption translation on parallel caption data (see the approaches described in Specia et al. (2016)) incorporate visual information directly into the sequence-to-sequence caption translation model or into a reranking component, or into both (see for example the attention-based LSTM approach of Huang et al. (2016)), or they use back-translation to generate synthetic parallel data (see for example Calixto et al. (2017)). However, obtaining parallel captioning data or retraining NMT models on large synthetic datasets is either financially or computationally expensive. We thus opt for a way that does not require large amounts of parallel captions to improve translation quality.

	Hitschler et al. (2016)	Our work
Dataset	MS COCO: clean, limited vocabulary	Wikimedia Commons: captions "in the wild"
Retrieval	multimodal joint model	orthogonal models for image & text
Reranker	interpolation of scores	trained model-based reranker
MT-System	Statistical (`cdec`)	Neural (`nematus`)
Languages	de-en	de-en, fr-en, ru-en

Table 1: Comparison of Hitschler et al. (2016) to our work.

Our work can be seen as an extension of the idea of Wäschle and Riezler (2015) to multimodal data. Their approach is based on cross-lingual retrieval techniques to find sentences in a large target-language document collection, which are then used to rerank candidate translations. Our approach uses textual relevance and visual similarity (see Section 3.2) to obtain lists of multimodal pivot documents from a monolingual image-caption corpus similar to the idea described in Hitschler et al. (2016). In contrast to their approach, we do not rely on grid search for hyperparameters but instead use a machine learning approach to determine optimal weights of different rerankers to get the best scoring ensemble. In order to discern the contribution of our learning method, we compare it to the monolingual reranking approach of Hitschler et al. (2016) on the MS COCO v2014 dataset that was used in their work.

3 Method

3.1 Overview

Following the idea of Hitschler et al. (2016), we use retrieval models to find similar images and image captions in a target language image dataset to rerank target language caption translations e of a source caption f. This approach does not rely on large amounts of parallel data, but only requires monolingual target image-captions pairs. Modularizing the retrieval and translation component makes our method applicable to any existing translation system. Additionally, we can make use of new retrieval data instantly without expensive retraining of the translation model. This is a valuable property for active production systems where larger amounts of images and associated texts are available, e.g. in online shops.

The main difference between our model and Hitschler et al. (2016) is the way we implement the multimodal retrieval component and the reranker. We do not combine the visual and textual similarity models in a joint model, but let our model chose the best ensemble of rerankers that operate on top-k lists generated on visual and textual similarity. Our motivation behind separating textual and visual components is that textual and visual retrieval provide orthogonal information which can be best combined in an ensemble of reranking components operating on different feature sets. Thus, we do not manually tune any hyperparameters and instead apply a supervised training approach following a learning-to-rank strategy. See Table 1 for an overview comparison.

3.2 Multimodal Retrieval Model

The middle part of Figure 1 illustrates the textual and visual retrieval components for selecting pivot documents (i.e. image-caption pairs) from a target document collection m. For each source image-caption pair (i, f_i), our model uses the image i and a decoder-generated target hypothesis list N_{f_i} to yield two lists of pivot documents, namely a list M_i based on visual similarity, and a list L_{f_i} based on textual similarity. These lists are input to the parameterized retrieval score function defined in Section 3.3.

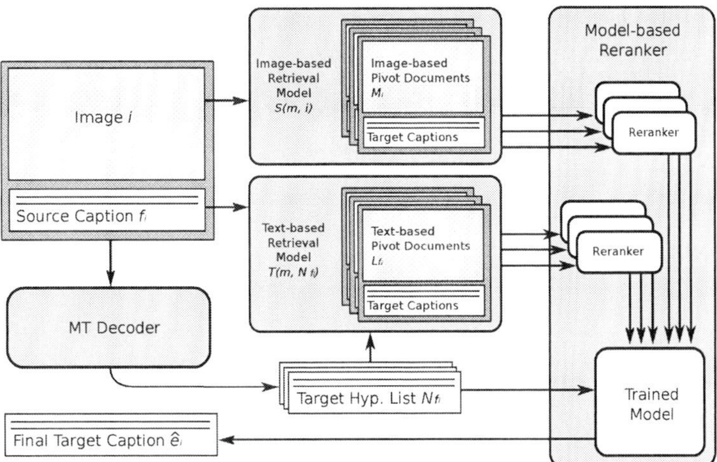

Figure 1: Given a source image-caption pair (i, f_i), we apply image-based and text-based retrieval models to obtain separate lists of pivot documents (M_i and L_{f_i}). These lists are input to multiple reranker components, which are combined in a model-based reranker. Final output is the highest scoring target caption $\hat{e}_i$ selected from the decoder's hypothesis list N_{f_i}.

Pivot documents based on textual similarity Using the translation hypotheses N_{f_i} as query against the monolingual target document collection, we select the top-k most similar pivot documents using the standard TFIDF metric from information retrieval. Given a target document collection m and the translation hypotheses N_{f_i}, the text-based retrieval model $T(m, N_{f_i})$ returns a list of image-caption pairs L_{f_i} ordered by an unsmoothed TFIDF score (Spärck Jones, 1972).

Pivot documents based on visual similarity This list consists of the top-k nearest neighboring image-caption pairs to the source image in visual space. Our distance metric $s(i, j)$ between two images i and j is the cosine of the 4,096-dimensional feature representations $\mathbf{v}_i$ and $\mathbf{v}_j$ of images i and j taken from the penultimate layer of the VGG16 model by Simonyan and Zisserman (2015), which was pre-trained on ImageNet (Russakovsky et al., 2014): $s(i, j) = \frac{\mathbf{v}_i \cdot \mathbf{v}_j}{\|\mathbf{v}_i\|_2 \|\mathbf{v}_j\|_2}$. Given a target document collection m and a source image i, the image-based retrieval model $S(m, i)$ returns a list of image-caption pairs M_i sorted by visual similarity.

3.3 Parameterized Retrieval Score

We formulate a parameterized retrieval score function as follows. Based on a relevance score function $g_m(x, y)$ that returns the relevance of caption y to translation hypothesis x, define a retrieval score $RS_{r,m}(h, t_k)$ that calculates the average relevance of a hypothesis h to a sequence t_k of top-k retrieved captions up to a cutoff level r:

$$RS_{r,m}(h, t_k) = \frac{1}{N_{g_m}} \sum_{n=1}^{r} g_m(h, t_{k,n}). \tag{1}$$

Here, $t_{k,n}$ denotes the nth element of the sequence, and N_{g_m} is a normalization parameter for a given choice of relevance function g_m.

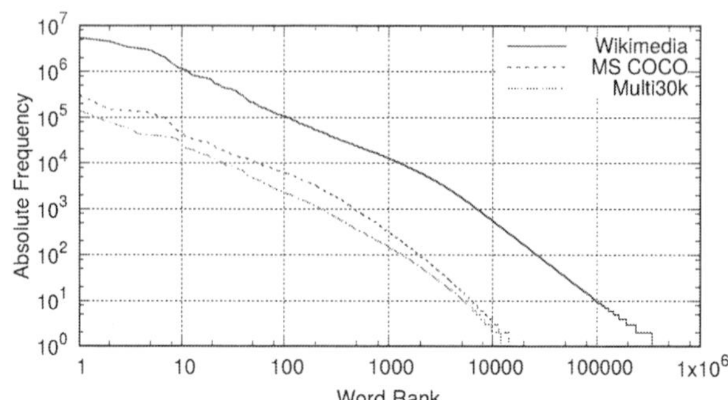

Figure 2: Absolute frequencies of lowercased words against their rank in Multi30k, MS COCO and Wikimedia Commons data, illustrating the differences in corpus size and vocabulary of the three corpora.

The retrieval score defined in Equation (1) can make use of different top-k caption lists, L_{f_i} or M_i, based on textual or visual similarity, respectively. The relevance function $g_m(x, y)$ can be instantiated to any retrieval score or similarity function that suits our needs. In our experiments, we applied the standard TFIDF metric from information retrieval and smoothed sentence-based BLEU (S-BLEU) (Chen and Cherry, 2014). The normalization parameter N_{g_m} depends on the relevance function and is in our case either the number of top-k captions for S-BLEU or the number of words for TFIDF.

Based on this formulation we combine up to 36 ranking functions defined on different top-k sequences, relevance functions, and cutoff levels. This setup can be easily extended by additional relevance score functions.

3.4 Learning to Rank Captions

Our final ranking score function $RE_\theta, \theta \in \mathbb{R}^{37}$ is defined as linear combination of up to 36 retrieval scores plus 1 translation model score as additional feature as follows:

$$RE_\theta(h) = \sum_i \alpha_{m,r,t_k} \cdot RS_{r,m}(h, t_k), \text{ where } \alpha_{m,r,t_k} = \theta_i. \tag{2}$$

We optimize this model by pairwise ranking to determine the importance of each reranker as follows: given a list of hypothesis ordered by a metric reflecting the translation quality with respect to a reference, our system should rank a higher scoring hypothesis above a lower scoring one. We used Character F-score as the metric to optimize throughout our experiments.

This is formalized by the following hinge-loss objective, where h^+ is a higher and h^- is a lower scoring hypothesis, H is the set of all such pairings in the training set, and $RE_\theta()$ denotes the current ensemble of rerankers defined by θ:

$$\underset{\theta}{\text{argmin}} \sum_{(h^+,h^-)\in H} \max(RE_\theta(h^-) - RE_\theta(h^+), 0). \tag{3}$$

For each source sentence, we pair all translation hypotheses which differ in Character F-score with respect to the reference translation. Thus, we can extract up to $\frac{n(n-1)}{2}$ pairs for each sentence given a hypothesis list of n elements. At $n = 100$ our models need not more than 500 to 1,000 parallel image-captions pairs in practice. Training was done using the `Vowpal Wabbit` toolkit.[1]

---

[1] `http://hunch.net/~vw/`

	Multi30k	MS COCO v2014	Wikimedia Commons
Images with captions	$30,014$	$82,783$	$7,073,243$
with English captions	$30,014$	$82,783$	$4,149,659$
Captions per image	5	5	1.14 on avg.
Caption language(s)	English, German	English	English, German, French, Russian, …
Type of caption	descriptive	descriptive	indeterminable
Avg. tokens per English caption	13.51	11.32	34.35
Unique types	$18,078$	$24,117$	$738,479$

Table 2: Comparison between Multi30k, MS COCO and Wikimedia Commons data.

The rightmost box in Figure 1 illustrates how our model-based reranker uses information from image-based and text-based pivot documents M_i and L_{f_i} in an ensemble of rerankers to select the highest scoring caption translation $\hat{e}_i$ from a decoder-generated hypothesis list N_{f_i}.

4 Data: Manually Annotated Captions versus Captions "In the Wild"

Image caption translation has been mostly applied to relatively clean data, where monolingual captions are generated by annotators (Flickr30k, Multi30k, MS COCO) and translations are afterwards added by translators (Elliott et al., 2016; Hitschler et al., 2016). Our work investigates the questions whether image caption translation can make use of much noisier and more natural datasets, such as captions found in Wikimedia Commons. Thus, we conduct experiments on two fundamentally different types of captions, i.e. Multi30k and MS COCO on one side, and Wikimedia Commons on the other side. The two types of corpora are clearly distinguishable in Figure 2, which shows the absolute frequencies against the rank of lowercased words in all three corpora: Multi30k and MS COCO are relatively close, while our Wikimedia Commons dataset contains much more tokens and types. Furthermore, the latter has considerably more images and significantly longer captions. Table 2 lists the main characteristics of the three datasets.

Descriptive Captions Most work on image caption translation is done on artificially created captions that were generated by annotators based on clear instructions. Such captions are usually descriptive[2] and omit named entities and other information not present in the image. Table 2 shows that the average sentence length of our descriptive captions lies around 11 and 13 tokens. Figure 3 (left) gives an example of the descriptive captions found in the MS COCO dataset. Captions found in the Multi30k dataset are very similar by their nature.

Captions in the Wild Largely available image-caption data in the web does not fall into the category described in the previous paragraph. For the most part, existing image-caption pairs are not strongly descriptive, but mention product names, locations, and other aspects that are not obviously encoded in the image. Table 2 shows that the average sentence length of captions in Wikimedia Commons is about 34 tokens. See Figure 3 (right) for an example of a typical caption from Wikimedia Commons.

5 Experiments

5.1 Image-Caption Data

We constructed a retrieval dataset based on English image-caption pairs from a recent dump of Wikimedia Commons created by the `wikimgrab.pl` utility.[3] We filtered out images with

---

[2]Hodosh et al. (2013) call such captions *conceptual descriptions*.

[3]`https://commons.wikimedia.org/wiki/User:AzaToth/wikimgrab.pl`

- A bunch of boats parked at a busy and full harbor.
- A group of boats floating on top of a river near a city.
- A group of boats on water next to pier.
- Boats lined up in rows in water at the dock
- Motor boats parked near a dock in a marina.

- View of a disused pier in North Woolwich, London Borough of Newham, London.

London, North-Woolwich, Thames 27.jpg by *Kleon3* is licensed under CC BY-SA 4.0.

Figure 3: Image-caption examples from MS COCO (left) and Wikimedia Commons (right).

extreme aspect ratios ($>$3:1) and kept only images in JPEG- and PNG-format, as other formats are likely to contain data not useful for our approach (e.g. SVG-encoded logos or PDF-scanned document pages). Furthermore, we randomly selected 2,000 images with parallel captions for each of three language pairs, German-English (de-en), French-English (fr-en), and Russian-English (ru-en). One half of the parallel data is used as development set for training the reranker, the other half is used for testing.

During retrieval, we only use images and captions that were not included in the development or test set data, totaling in 3,816,940 images with mostly a single corresponding caption. In case of duplicate images, we discarded retrieval matches with an identical image to the query image or where the annotated target caption was identical to the gold standard target caption.

We applied the standard utilities from the `cdec`[4]-toolkit to tokenize and convert the data, namely `tokenize-anything.sh`, `lowercase.pl`. Parallel captions were additionally filtered by `filter-length.pl`. Table 3 gives an overview of the visual and textual data sources we used in our experiments. Examples for image-caption pairs from our dev and test sets together with a script to retrieve the full data set is available for download.[5] The data is released in accordance to the respective licenses.

5.2 Translation Systems

We trained our baseline translation system with Nematus (Sennrich et al., 2017), a state of the art toolkit for neural machine translation.[6] We tokenized and converted all training data to lower case using the same `cdec` utilities as were used for pre-processing of the retrieval data. In addition, we performed 20,000 steps of byte pair encoding (Sennrich et al., 2016) on the input and output vocabularies, giving our systems an open output vocabulary in principle. We used default parameters for learning, measured the cross-entropy of a held-out validation set after processing every 10,000 training samples and stopped training accordingly. For training and validation data, we filtered out sentences longer than 70 words (before byte pair encoding).

---

[4]`https://github.com/redpony/cdec`
[5]`http://www.cl.uni-heidelberg.de/wikicaps`
[6]`https://github.com/rsennrich/nematus`, git commit hash (unique revision identifier): `54be147dc363603d69643c35b700ae5d9de2ad93`

	Images	Captions	Languages
development	$1,000$	$1,000$	de-en, fr-en, ru-en
test	$1,000$	$1,000$	de-en, fr-en, ru-en
retrieval	$3,816,940$	$3,825,132$	en

Table 3: Number of images and captions in the dataset extracted from Wikimedia Commons.

For reranking and retrieval, we generated n-best lists of length $n = 100$ using beam search. The same beam size of $n = 100$ was used for our baseline systems. We used the following training data for the three language pairs:

French-English   We trained our French-English translation system on data made available for the WMT 2015 translation shared task.[7] We used the Europarl, News Commentary and Common Crawl data for training.

Russian-English   Our Russian-English translation system was trained with the Europarl and News Commentary data from the WMT 2016 shared task on news translation.[8]

German-English   In order to enable direct comparison with Hitschler et al. (2016), we used the same training data as was used for their statistical machine translation system (Europarl, News Commentary and Common Crawl Data as provided for WMT 2015). For the experiments on COCO, we domain-adapted our system on the same data as the in-domain system of Hitschler et al. (2016), the corpus of parallel image captions provided for the WMT 2016 shared task on multimodal machine translation.[9] This was achieved by continuing training on the in-domain data once training was complete on the out-of-domain training data.

5.3   Ranking Components

The rankers we combine operate on features that make use of retrieval- and translation-based metrics such as TFIDF and S-BLEU. These features are extracted from textual- or visual-retrieval-based pivot documents. To evaluate the contribution of different combinations of rerankers in an ablation experiment, we use the following letters to identify the types of rerankers in a combination:

- **T** : textual-retrieval-based TFIDF
- **B** : textual-retrieval-based S-BLEU
- **V** : visual-retrieval-based TFIDF
- **W** : visual-retrieval-based S-BLEU

For example, a system that operates solely on textual-retrieval-based TFIDF and S-BLEU (T,B) is labeled TB, while a system that uses textual- as well as visual-retrieval-based S-BLEU (B,W) and visual-retrieval-based TFIDF (V) is labeled BWV. A system that is trained on all available rerankers is labeled TVBW.

The length of the hypothesis list for the reranker was selected on dev using Character F-score as our primary metric for tuning. See Tables 8, 9, 10, and 11 for details.

We also modified the length of pivot document list across rankers and implemented different cutoff levels for the similarity as defined in Equation 1 at 3, 5, 10, 20, 50, and 100. In total we obtain 36 different rerankers. Note that it is straightforward to add new rerankers based on different similarity score functions or cutoff levels.

---

[7] http://www.statmt.org/wmt15/translation-task.html
[8] http://www.statmt.org/wmt16/translation-task.html
[9] http://www.statmt.org/wmt16/multimodal-task.html

	baseline	T	B	TB	V	W	TV	BW	BWV	TVBW
BLEU	21.66	21.44	21.55	21.54	21.34	21.33	21.19	21.84	21.90	21.76
Character-F	49.35	49.16	49.29	49.19	49.33	49.11	49.28	49.22	49.18	49.19

Table 4: BLEU and Character F-scores on German-English Multi30k test data from the WMT17 Multimodal Task 2 (Elliott et al., 2017). Due to the limited data available for retrieval our approach did now show improvements over the `nematus` baseline.

	System	baseline	T	B	TB	V	W	TV	BW	BWV	TVBW
BLEU	cdec in-dom. (Hitschler et al., 2016)	29.6	–	–	–	–	–	–	–	–	–
BLEU	TSR-CNN (Hitschler et al., 2016)	30.6	–	–	–	–	–	–	–	–	–
BLEU	New reranker	29.6	26.96	28.47	30.83	27.54	30.59	‡31.04	†30.79	30.67	30.76
BLEU	Our system	33.78	33.88	33.27	32.97	33.92	32.46	34.03	34.30	34.21	34.40
ChF		62.74	62.93	62.37	62.29	63.01	61.70	62.90	62.91	62.86	63.00

Table 5: BLEU and Character F-scores (ChF) on de-en MS COCO test data from Hitschler et al. (2016) for their `cdec` in-domain and TSR-CNN systems, the new reranker applied to the `cdec` hypothesis lists, and our new system on different combinations of rerankers. Significant improvements over the baseline system are indicated by preceding † ($p < 0.03$) and ‡ ($p < 0.003$) as reported by MultEval's randomization test (Clark et al., 2011).

5.4 Results

Our experiments revealed a strong connection between certain properties of retrieval data and the performance of our approach. On very clean, manually constructed data of limited size and complexity like the Multi30k dataset, our retrieval-based method fails to extract additional useful information. As the data available for retrieval grows, we observe small gains like in the experiments on MS COCO. The biggest improvements, however, can be found on the much larger and inherently diverse Wikimedia Commons dataset we described before. We discuss the results of an ablation experiment for various combinations of rerankers on the different datasets in detail in the following paragraphs.

Multi30k The results listed in Table 4 show that the retrieval-based approach does not lead to gains in BLEU or Character F-score on the Multi30k dataset. We see two main reasons for this: Firstly, the dataset available for retrieval is orders of magnitude smaller that the Wikimedia Commons dataset. Secondly, the descriptive captions are of low complexity, e.g. built of a small vocabulary and simple sentence structure. Thus, the additional information contributed to the reranking step by pivot images and documents is very limited. The necessity to restrict reranking to short hypothesis lists (top-5 only, see Table 9) underlines this problem, as the ensemble of rerankers is not able to select better translations further down in the list.

MS COCO As shown in Table 5, on manually annotated caption data, our neural machine translation baseline outperformed the best system of Hitschler et al. (2016) by more than 3 BLEU percentage points, demonstrating the advantages of neural over statistical machine translation. We were able to achieve nominal gains over this very strong baseline using our multimodal reranking setup. We found small but consistent gains in terms of BLEU if textual and visual information is combined (TV, BW, BWV, TVBW). The best system improved over the neural machine translation baseline by 0.62 BLEU points and 0.27 Character F-score points.

We also applied our model-based reranker to the original `cdec`'s hypothesis lists provided by Hitschler et al. (2016). The orthogonal nature of textual and visual components is particularly

	System	baseline	T	B	TB	V	W	TV	BW	BWV	TVBW
BLEU	de-en	35.29	†36.45	†39.20	34.00	35.35	†37.09	†36.53	†**40.90**	†40.76	†39.39
BLEU	fr-en	27.81	29.79	†34.70	†**35.27**	27.85	25.09	†29.82	†33.74	†33.62	†29.76
BLEU	ru-en	12.85	12.89	†15.08	†**15.74**	12.93	12.04	12.91	†15.51	†15.45	†14.61
ChF	de-en	66.57	67.42	69.01	65.79	66.68	68.50	67.51	**69.01**	68.95	68.27
ChF	fr-en	67.99	69.28	70.81	**71.28**	68.27	65.59	69.50	69.66	69.75	68.24
ChF	ru-en	45.33	46.56	46.63	**47.07**	45.84	44.77	46.40	46.94	47.03	46.41

Table 6: BLEU and Character F-scores (ChF) on Wikimedia test data. Best scoring systems for each language pair were selected on the dev set and are printed in bold. For BLEU, the preceding † indicates a significant improvement ($p < 0.005$) over the baseline system as reported by MultEval's randomization test (Clark et al., 2011).

apparent in the combination of T and V rerankers, where TV showed the biggest improvement of 1.49 BLEU points over the baseline system. All combinations of textual and visual components showed consistent improvements over the best joint system (TSR-CNN) on this dataset.

Wikimedia Commons   On Wikimedia Commons, improvements over the neural machine translation baseline were much larger as our retrieval-based reranking approach was very effective in improving translation quality: As shown in Table 6, the improvement were as high as 7.46 BLEU points and 3.29 Character F-score points (French-English). However, text-based retrieval presented a strong baseline on this dataset, which was not always outperformed by additional multimodal retrieval components. Best performance was achieved by a multimodal system only on the German-English data; there was no consistent improvement from incorporating image retrieval data across all three language pairs. It should be noted that irrespective of multi-modality, the best retrieval-based systems always comfortably outperformed the neural machine translation baseline on this dataset. Here, the ensemble of rerankers can make use of hypothesis lists up to the maximum length (see Table 11), as it is able to successfully identify good translations by exploiting information from pivot images and documents.

5.5 Examples

Table 7 shows two examples of source image-caption pairs, the reference translation, and target translations produced by the `nematus` baseline, a pure text-retrieval-based reranking system (TB), and three combinations of text- and image-based reranking components (BW, BWV, TVBW). In both examples, the text-retrieval-based reranking system was not able to select a different translation than the plain MT system. In the left example, additional visual information supports the translation mentioning the "garden", which is a prominent part of the image. In the right example, visual information again helps to select the more complete translation containing the phrase "leaning tower". Notably, the same translation was favored in all four combinations of text- and image-based reranking components (i.e. TV, BW, BWV, TVBW) in the left example, and in the three combinations listed in the table in the right example.

6 Conclusions

We presented a dataset and method for improving caption translation of noisy user-generated data without the need of large parallel captions. Our dataset contains 4M image-caption pairs extracted from Wikimedia Commons, with an average sentence length of 34 tokens and a vocabulary size that is orders of magnitude larger than in previously used caption translation data.

The key idea of our method is to retrieve matches on monolingual target captions, based on textual and visual similarity, and re-score translation hypotheses according to similarity with target matches. This allows us to modularize the translation and the retrieval components of

Image		
Source	Schlossgarten Oldenburg	Kathedrale von Pisa & schiefer Turm von Pisa , Pisa , Italien
`nematus`	oldenburg palace	pisa cathedral of pisa , pisa , italy
Text only TB	oldenburg palace	pisa cathedral of pisa , pisa , italy
Text+visual `BW, BWV, TVBW`	castle garden of oldenburg	pisa cathedral , leaning tower of pisa , pisa , italy .
Reference	oldenburg castle garden	pisa cathedral & leaning tower of pisa , pisa , italy

Table 7: Examples for improved caption translation "in the wild" by multimodal feedback. *Oldenburg Schlossgarten 6.JPG* (left) by *Corradox* and *Pisa Cathedral & Leaning Tower of Pisa.jpg* (right) by *TheVelocity* are licensed under CC BY-SA 4.0.

our system. In practice, this means that if new retrieval data becomes available, the translation system does not need to be re-trained, enabling fast adaptation of the system to new data. This is economically interesting in situations where data is constantly changing and frequent retraining of a system is prohibitive, like in an e-commerce environment.

Our results show the potential benefit of retrieval-based multimodal machine translation in the challenging setting of caption translation on data from Wikimedia Commons. The learning-to-rank setup for optimizing the ensemble of rerankers is able to exploit the orthogonal information from textual and visual retrieval of target images (and captions) and achieves large improvements over strong neural machine translation baselines. We also achieved gains by reranking on manually annotated data from MS COCO. However, the results on the Multi30k dataset emphasize that a large retrieval database is crucial for the performance of the reranking approach and that it especially benefits from more complex and diverse data.

In future work we would like to investigate possibilities to integrate monolingual image-caption as feedback signal in a reinforcement learning setup to neural caption translation (see for example He et al. (2016)). We would also like to further evaluate and enhance our method on other realistic datasets encountered "in the wild" like web-crawled content, product descriptions, and reviews.

Acknowledgements

We would like to thank the anonymous reviewers for their helpful comments and suggestions. This research was supported in part by DFG grant RI-2221/2-1 "Grounding Statistical Machine Translation in Perception and Action", and by an Amazon Academic Research Award (AARA) "Multimodal Pivots for Low Resource Machine Translation in E-Commerce Localization".

	top-n	T	B	TB	V	W	TV	BW	BWV	TVBW
Character-F	100	56.77	59.31	59.57	58.64	55.79	59.59	59.00	58.77	58.96
	50	56.96	60.50	60.28	58.21	57.25	60.08	59.94	59.78	60.03
	20	57.57	61.10	60.96	58.69	58.11	60.16	60.51	60.39	60.43
	10	58.00	**61.62**	61.39	**59.85**	59.42	60.39	60.63	60.36	60.30
	5	58.54	61.50	**61.60**	59.04	**60.06**	60.57	61.07	60.92	61.28

Table 8: Influence of hypothesis lists length n on Character F-score for the reranking experiment on MS COCO dev data where we applied the new reranker on the original `cdec`'s hypothesis lists. Numbers in bold indicate highest score above the baseline (59.64) within a column.

	top-n	T	B	TB	V	W	TV	BW	BWV	TVBW
Character-F	100	49.01	48.26	47.98	48.78	48.02	48.74	48.41	48.29	48.26
	50	49.02	48.75	48.54	48.83	48.29	48.78	48.65	48.50	48.52
	20	49.06	48.86	48.72	49.10	48.62	49.04	48.92	48.85	48.89
	10	49.10	49.14	49.10	49.24	48.78	49.14	49.17	49.02	49.12
	5	49.16	49.29	49.19	49.33	49.11	49.28	49.22	49.18	49.19

Table 9: Hypothesis lists length n and Character F-score on Multi30k dev data. No combination of rerankers was able to surpass the baseline (49.35) on this dataset. Note that increasing the hypothesis lists length always leads to degradation, because the system is unable to identify better translations in the list.

	top-n	T	B	TB	V	W	TV	BW	BWV	TVBW
Character-F	100	64.34	62.24	62.25	64.97	62.42	64.77	62.95	63.15	62.91
	50	64.36	62.89	62.61	65.01	62.78	64.84	63.31	63.66	63.57
	20	64.59	63.80	63.85	**65.14**	63.42	64.93	63.92	63.98	63.97
	10	64.68	64.36	64.32	65.05	64.00	64.93	64.12	64.30	64.22
	5	**64.79**	64.18	64.29	65.11	64.09	**64.94**	64.10	64.25	64.17

Table 10: Hypothesis lists length n and Character F-score on MS COCO dev data. Numbers in bold indicate highest score above the baseline (64.76) within a column.

		top-n	T	B	TB	V	W	TV	BW	BWV	TVBW
Character-F	de-en	100	**68.54**	69.74	66.15	67.73	**69.70**	68.58	70.42	70.33	69.43
		50	68.53	**69.81**	66.52	67.72	69.67	68.58	70.33	70.30	**69.53**
		20	68.50	69.58	66.70	67.73	69.43	68.56	69.86	69.80	69.18
		10	68.40	69.43	66.96	**67.79**	69.12	68.45	69.51	69.47	68.85
		5	68.28	68.97	66.91	67.74	68.72	68.33	69.19	69.19	68.67
Character-F	fr-en	100	68.10	69.41	**69.96**	**67.73**	58.18	68.26	67.91	68.05	66.23
		50	**68.33**	**69.59**	69.87	67.70	62.17	**68.46**	**68.21**	**68.21**	66.96
		20	68.24	69.01	69.25	67.68	63.37	68.43	67.85	67.90	67.12
		10	68.28	68.74	69.04	67.59	63.96	68.46	67.77	67.74	67.22
		5	68.08	68.50	68.67	67.52	64.81	68.23	67.75	67.69	67.25
Character-F	ru-en	100	46.72	46.16	47.24	46.59	40.41	46.82	45.88	46.15	45.87
		50	47.31	46.97	**47.90**	46.60	43.81	47.19	47.24	47.42	47.06
		20	47.28	47.07	47.49	46.58	44.74	47.22	**47.49**	**47.57**	47.05
		10	**47.35**	47.22	47.74	**46.62**	45.41	**47.36**	47.28	47.49	47.48
		5	47.23	**47.26**	47.89	46.59	45.78	47.20	47.26	47.47	**47.50**

Table 11: Influence of hypothesis lists length n on Character F-score on Wikimedia dev data. Numbers in bold indicate highest score above the baseline within a column group. The baseline scores are 67.65, 67.35, and 46.16 for the de-en, fr-en, and ru-en systems, respectively.

References

Calixto, I., Stein, D., Matusov, E., Lohar, P., Castilho, S., and Way, A. (2017). Using images to improve machine-translating e-commerce product listings. In *Proceedings of the 15th Conference of the European Chapter of the Association for Computational Linguistics (EACL)*, Valencia, Spain.

Chen, B. and Cherry, C. (2014). A systematic comparison of smoothing techniques for sentence-level BLEU. In *Proceedings of the Ninth Workshop on Statistical Machine Translation (WMT)*, Baltimore, Maryland, USA.

Clark, J., Dyer, C., Lavie, A., and Smith, N. (2011). Better hypothesis testing for statistical machine translation: Controlling for optimizer instability. In *Proceedings of the Association for Computational Lingustics (ACL)*, Portland, Oregon, USA.

Elliott, D., Frank, S., Barrault, L., Bougares, F., and Specia, L. (2017). Findings of the second shared task on multimodal machine translation and multilingual image description. In *Proceedings of the Conference on Machine Translation (WMT)*, Copenhagen, Denmark.

Elliott, D., Frank, S., Sima'an, K., and Specia, L. (2016). Multi30k: Multilingual english-german image descriptions. In *Proceedings of the 5th ACL Workshop on Vision and Language*, Berlin, Germany.

Ferraro, F., Mostafazadeh, N., Huang, T.-H. K., Vanderwende, L., Devlin, J., Galley, M., and Mitchell, M. (2015). A survey of current datasets for vision and language research. In *Proceedings of the Conference on Empirical Methods in Natural Language Processing (EMNLP)*, Lisbon, Portugal.

He, D., Xia, Y., Qin, T., Wang, L., Yu, N., Lie, T.-Y., and Ma, W.-Y. (2016). Dual learning for machine translation. In *Advances in Neural Information Processing Systems (NIPS)*, Barcelona, Spain.

Hitschler, J., Schamoni, S., and Riezler, S. (2016). Multimodal pivots for image caption translation. In *Proceedings of the 54th Annual Meeting of the Association for Computational Linguistics (ACL)*, Berlin, Germany.

Hodosh, M., Young, P., and Hockenmaier, J. (2013). Framing image description as a ranking task: Data, models, and evaluation metrics. *Journal of Artificial Intelligence Research*, 47:853–899.

Huang, P.-Y., Liu, F., Shiang, S.-R., Oh, J., and Dyer, C. (2016). Attention-based multimodal neural machine translation. In *Proceedings of the First Conference on Machine Translation (WMT)*, Berlin, Germany.

Lala, C., Madhyastha, P., Wang, J., and Specia, L. (2017). Unraveling the contribution of image captioning and neural machine translation for multimodal machine translation. *The Prague Bulletin of Mathematical Linguistics (PBML)*, (108):197–208.

Lin, T.-Y., Maire, M., Belongie, S., Bourdev, L., Girshick, R., Hays, J., Perona, P., Ramanan, D., Zitnick, C. L., and Dollar, P. (2014). Microsoft COCO: Common objects in context. arXiv:1405.0312 [cs.CV].

Ordonez, V., Kulkarni, G., and Berg, T. L. (2011). Im2Text: Describing images using 1 million captioned photographs. In *Neural Information Processing Systems (NIPS)*, Granada, Spain.

Papineni, K., Roukos, S., Ard, T., and Zhu, W.-J. (2002). Bleu: a method for automatic evaluation of machine translation. In *Proceedings of the 40th Annual Meeting of the Association for Computational Linguistics (ACL)*, Philadelphia, Pennsylvania, USA.

Popović, M. (2015). chrF: character n-gram f-score for automatic mt evaluation. In *Proceedings of the Tenth Workshop on Statistical Machine Translation (WMT)*, Lisbon, Portugal.

Rashtchian, C., Young, P., Hodosh, M., and Hockenmaier, J. (2010). Collecting image annotations using amazon's mechanical turk. In *Proceedings of the NAACL HLT 2010 Workshop on Creating Speech and Language Data with Amazon's Mechanical Turk*, Los Angeles, CA.

Russakovsky, O., Deng, J., Su, H., Krause, J., Satheesh, S., Ma, S., Huang, Z., Karpathy, A., Khosla, A., Bernstein, M. S., Berg, A. C., and Li, F. (2014). Imagenet large scale visual recognition challenge. *Computing Research Repository*, abs/1409.0575.

Sennrich, R., Firat, O., Cho, K., Birch, A., Haddow, B., Hitschler, J., Junczys-Dowmunt, M., Läubli, S., Miceli Barone, A. V., Mokry, J., and Nadejde, M. (2017). Nematus: a toolkit for neural machine translation. In *Proceedings of the Software Demonstrations of the 15th Conference of the European Chapter of the Association for Computational Linguistics (EACL)*, Valencia, Spain.

Sennrich, R., Haddow, B., and Birch, A. (2016). Neural machine translation of rare words with subword units. In *Proceedings of the 54th Annual Meeting of the Association for Computational Linguistics (ACL)*, Berlin, Germany.

Simonyan, K. and Zisserman, A. (2015). Very deep convolutional networks for large-scale image recognition. In *Proceedings of the International Conference on Learning Representations (ICLR)*, San Diego, CA.

Spärck Jones, K. (1972). A statistical interpretation of term specificity and its application in retrieval. *Journal of Documentation*, 28:11–21.

Specia, L., Frank, S., Sima'an, K., and Elliott, D. (2016). A shared task on multimodal machine translation and crosslingual image description. In *Proceedings of the First Conference on Machine Translation (WMT)*, Berlin, Germany.

Wäschle, K. and Riezler, S. (2015). Integrating a large, monolingual corpus as translation memory into statistical machine translation. In *Proceedings of the 18th Annual Conference of the European Association for Machine Translation (EAMT)*, Antalya, Turkey.

Simultaneous Translation using Optimized Segmentation

Maryam Siahbani   maryam.siahbani@ufv.ca
Department of Computer Information System,
University of Fraser Valley,
Abbotsford, V2S 7M7, Canada

Hassan S. Shavarani   sshavara@sfu.ca
Ashkan Alinejad   aalineja@sfu.ca
Anoop Sarkar   anoop@sfu.ca
School of Computing Science,
Simon Fraser University,
Burnaby, V5A 1S6, Canada

Abstract

Previous simultaneous translation approaches either use a separate segmentation step followed by a machine translation decoder or rely on the decoder to segment and translate without training the segmenter to minimize delay or increase translation quality. We integrate a segmentation model and an incremental decoding algorithm to create an automatic simultaneous translation framework. Oda et al. (2014) propose a method to provide annotated data for sentence segmentation. This work uses this data to train a segmentation model that is integrated with a novel simultaneous translation decoding algorithm. We show that this approach is more accurate than previously proposed segmentation models when integrated with a translation decoder. Our results on the speech translation of TED talks from English to German show that our system can achieve translation quality close to the offline translation system while at the same time minimizing the delay in producing the translations incrementally. Our approach also outperforms other comparable simultaneous translation systems in terms of translation quality and latency.

1   Introduction

In simultaneous translation the incoming speech stream is segmented and translated incrementally to reduce the latency. There are two approaches for simultaneous translation task: *sentence segmentation* and *incremental decoding*, also called *stream decoding*. In incremental decoding, incoming words are fed into the decoder one-by-one, and the decoder updates its internal state. The decoder is responsible to decide when to begin the translation process and when to output the translation. Incremental decoding algorithms have been proposed for phrase-based (Kolss et al., 2008; Sankaran et al., 2010) translation, hierarchical phrase-based (Finch et al., 2015) and syntax-based (Oda et al., 2015) translation systems.

Real-world speech translation systems estimate the sentence boundaries using punctuation insertion methods (Rangarajan Sridhar et al., 2013). As a result, recent work in simultaneous machine translation assume the input is already segmented into sentences, and focus on splitting the sentences into shorter subsequences of words (*segments*). This approach is called sentence segmentation. As soon as a segment is recognized, it is given to a decoder to generate and output the translation for that segment.

Different methods have been proposed for sentence segmentation. Some use prosodic boundaries for segmentation (Fügen et al., 2007; Bangalore et al., 2012), while others use classification models. For example Rangarajan Sridhar et al. (2013) train a classifier to predict punctuation marks. The other approaches rely on the reordering probabilities of phrases to predict the segment boundaries (Fujita et al., 2013; Yarmohammadi et al., 2013; Siahbani et al., 2014). Oda et al. (2014) propose a method to provide annotated data for sentence segmentation which can be used in training a segmentation model. This method which later have been extended by (Shavarani et al., 2015) aims to find the best segmentation strategy for a given set of sentence which optimizes the translation accuracy. But the obtained annotated data has never been used in an end-to-end simultaneous translation system.

In this work, we focus on sentence segmentation approach for simultaneous translation. We model the segmentation task as a classification problem and investigate different methods to provide annotated data for training the segmentation model (Section 2). We modify Oda et al. (2014) approach by propose a new formula to compute the latency and use Pareto-optimality for finding good segment boundaries that can balance the trade-off between latency versus translation quality. We use the obtained annotated data to train a segmentation model. We conduct various experiments to evaluate the segmentation model and show that this model outperforms previous segmentation models in terms of accuracy.

Segmentation-based simultaneous translation approaches typically use a traditional phrase-based decoder to translate each input segment individually. Although hierarchical phrase-based (Hiero) translation system usually performs comparable to or better than conventional phrase-based systems, they use CKY based decoding algorithm which requires the entire input sentence to generate the translation. While phrase-based decoders generate translation in a left-to-right manner and it makes phrase-based systems more suitable for simultaneous translation than Hiero.

We use *LR-Hiero* for simultaneous translation which uses hierarchical phrase-based translation models while generates the translation in left-to-right manner (Watanabe et al., 2006; Siahbani et al., 2013). We modify LR-Hiero decoder and combine it with the segmentation model to incrementally translate the input sentence (stream of words).

We evaluate our simultaneous translation system on the speech translation of TED talks on English-German. The experimental results show that our system can achieve translation quality close to offline SMT system while generate the output translation words around twenty times faster. We also compare our simultaneous translation system to neural machine translation (NMT) simultaneous translation systems. Our system outperforms the state of the art NMT-based simultaneous translation system in both translation quality and latency.

2   Sentence Segmentation

The segmentation task is usually modeled as a binary classifier which is called for each input word to determine if it is a segment boundary or not. To train the segmentation classifier we need some training data in the form of sentences with labeled words showing if a word is a segment boundary or not. For each sentence $\mathbf{f} = \langle f_1 \ldots f_J \rangle$ different possible segmentations exist which grows exponentially with the length of the sentence. Finding the best segmentation can be quite difficult, as it requires a brute-force search over all possible segmentations which is intractable.

Different heuristics have been proposed to efficiently solve this problem. The two main approaches are: *alignment-based* and *translation-based* heuristics. We modify the translation-based heuristic to use in our translation framework. We will briefly discuss both approaches in the following and compare their performance in Section 4.

These heuristics use parallel data on the source and target languages of the simultaneous translation task to create labeled training data for the segmentation model. We define $\mathcal{C} = \langle F, E \rangle$ as a parallel corpus

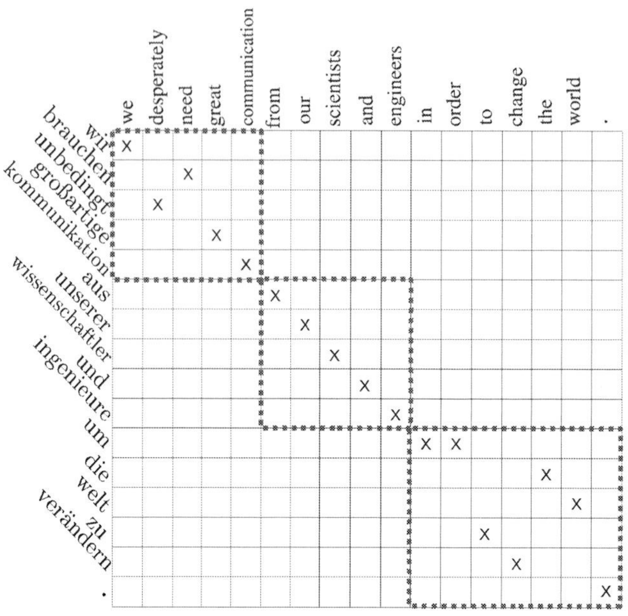

Figure 1: Word alignment matrix for an English-German sentence pair. Monotone phrases are shown in dashed line rectangles.

of source and target sentences used to extract training data.

2.1 Alignment-based Heuristic

The idea behind alignment-based heuristic is to split the input sentence into segments which can be translated to the target language monotonically (Yarmohammadi et al., 2013; Siahbani et al., 2014). To achieve this goal, the segmentation task is simplified to the problem of segmenting the source sentence in a way that reordering just occurs inside segments but not across segments. To find such segmentation we can leverage word alignment models. Given the word alignment $\mathbf{a} = \langle a_1 \dots a_J \rangle$ for a sentence pair $\langle \mathbf{f}, \mathbf{e} \rangle$, we can segment the source sentence $\mathbf{f} = \langle f_1 \dots f_J \rangle$, into a set of segments (phrases) $\mathbf{s} = \langle s_1 \dots s_K \rangle$:

$$s_k = \langle j_{k-1}, j_k \rangle \qquad \forall k = 1 \dots K, j_0 = 1 \tag{1}$$

To restrict the reorderings inside the segments, we should extract segments where $a_{j_{k-1}} < a_{j_k}$ for $k = 1 \dots K$. This segmentation results in a phrase alignment for the sentence pair $\langle \mathbf{f}, \mathbf{e} \rangle$ called *monotonic phrase alignment*. Figure 1 shows word alignment matrix and monotonic phrase alignment for an English-German sentence pair. Monotonic phrase alignment for a sentence pair can be found in linear time, given the word alignment. Experimentally, it has been shown that translation quality improves significantly with longer phrases (Koehn et al., 2003). Therefore to avoid too many short segments which could lead to word-to-word translation, the segmentation algorithm is given a constraint based on a constant μ and segments of length less than μ are disallowed[1].

Usually a word alignment model is trained over a parallel corpus containing the parallel data of the

---

[1] μ is usually set to 4 (Yarmohammadi et al., 2013; Siahbani et al., 2014).

translation task and parallel corpus $\mathcal{C}$. It provides us the oracle word alignment for $\mathcal{C}$ which can be used to extract labeled data for the segmentation classifier.

2.2 Translation-based Heuristic

The translation-based segmentation heuristic (Oda et al., 2014) focuses on obtaining segmentation points that are the least harmful to translation accuracy. This heuristic performs the segmentation using an iterative greedy approach. It starts with an empty set of segmentation points and each time tries to find a segmentation point in the given corpus which is the least harming to the translation accuracy. Segmentation points are described using a set of features. Different kinds of features can be used such as bigram POS tags, lexical terms, parsing related features and etc. Each feature is used as a metric to recognize segmentation points in a given input sentence. For instance, suppose we find a feature which is a bigram POS tag: *NNS-IN*. Using this feature we can find one segmentation point at index 10 in the English-German sentence shown in Figure 1 (the segmentation point is surrounded by two words *engineers* and *in* corresponding to POS tags NNS and IN). This approach finds an optimal set of features, based on a parallel corpus[2].

Given a parallel corpus $\mathcal{C} = \langle F, E \rangle$ and an expected number of segments, K, the translation-based segmentation heuristic first extracts all features over the corpus along with their frequencies, $\langle c_1 \ldots c_m \rangle$. The translation-based segmentation heuristic tries to find a feature set s containing $l(\leq m)$ features according to the least harmful segmentation criterion for the translation accuracy where $\sum_{i=1}^{l} c_{s_i} = K$ (features of set s appear in K points of source corpus which result in K segments).

Oda et al. (2014) define translation accuracy as the summation of sentence-level BLEU score (Lin and Och, 2004) of the translations of segmented sentences. The feature set is initialized as empty ($s = \{\}$), then the best feature (adding it to the corpus causes the least translation loss) is greedily chosen and added to the feature set. Once a feature has been chosen, all the points exhibiting that feature are segmented at the same time. This approach requires running the translation system for each possible feature in each iteration which takes a long time. To overcome this issue, they propose dynamic programming (DP) and call their approach Greedy-DP (GDP)[3].

However, this approach does not consider the latency to choose the features and therefore does not model the trade-off between accuracy and latency. This trade-off is crucial in designing a simultaneous translation systems. Shavarani et al. (2015) used *Pareto Optimality* to model the trade-off between accuracy and latency. In this approach, the algorithm iteratively goes over the corpus and examines the available features by computing the difference of translation accuracy (Δ) before and after applying each available feature to the source corpus. The features which cause least translation loss (the smallest Δ) are selected as candidate points. Among them, the feature which causes the least latency or the highest throughput is selected to be added to the feature set s. In the previous works latency was simply defined as the number of segments divided by the total translation time (Oda et al., 2014; Shavarani et al., 2015).

We extend the Pareto optimality approach by modifying the definition of both objective functions: translation accuracy and latency.

2.2.1 Translation Accuracy

Our primarily experiments show that using the sentence-level BLEU to measure the translation accuracy in GDP (and Pareto Optimality approach) tends to oversegment some sentences in the corpus and leave the other sentences untouched. To overcome this issue, we propose to use corpus-level BLEU (Papineni et al., 2002) to measure translation accuracy. The corpus-level BLEU gives a general view over the corpus

---

[2]The feature set which results in the best segmentation strategy (a set of segmentation points which gives us the best translation for the given parallel corpus).

[3]Please refer to (Oda et al., 2014) for more details

therefore it alleviate the tendency to localize the segmentation.

2.2.2 Latency

In simultaneous translation, the translation process starts before receiving the end of sentence, and the evaluation objective is not only sensitive to the translation quality, but it is also caring about the translation latency; the difference between the receiving time of the utterance in the source language and the delivery time of its translation in the target language.

Based on this idea we define the translation delay measure as a function of two different types of delay factors; the transmission delay and the translation delay. The transmission delay measures the amount of time the system is waiting to reach the end of current segment after producing the translation of the previous segment, completely. The translation delay on the other side is the amount of time it takes for the system to perform the mapping of source side utterances into the target side equivalents.

Equation 2 formulates the idea about the latency where we assume latency measure Λ to assess the latency of a sentence containing N segments and each segment being translated as soon as it is ready. We assume the target side will have a buffer which will keep the already translated segments in a queue and pops the translated segments from the queue while any is available and will wait to receive one if the buffer is empty. In Equation 2, t_i represents the time moment that the ith segment is ready and t'_{i-1} points to the time moment that the translated segment $i - 1$ has been completely delivered to the audience. Both of the measures start from 0 for each new sentence and $t'_0 = 0$ always holds. The phrase $\max(t_i - t'_{i-1}, 0)$ means that we will not have any transmission delay if the time moment that we receive the segment i is before the time moment that we finish delivering the translated segment t'_{i-1} otherwise the transmission delay will be equal to $t_i - t'_{i-1}$. δ_i represents the duration of the time it takes to translate the ith source side segment into the target side language.

$$\Lambda = \sum_{i=1}^{N} \max(t_i - t'_{i-1}, 0) + \delta_i \tag{2}$$

2.3 Segmentation Model

Given a set of sentences along with the gold segmentations, we can prepare the training data for the segmentation model. For each segment in the gold segmentation we create a positive training example corresponding to the whole segment and a set of negative examples corresponding to each smaller segment. For example for a segment $\langle i, j \rangle$, the positive example is (i, j), and negative examples are $[(i, i+1), (i, i+2), \ldots (i, j-1)]$.

Using this training data, we train a binary classifier (using a log-linear model) based on different feature sets. Basic features, used in (Yarmohammadi et al., 2013), are; the last word of the segment (candidate segment boundary), the position of the boundary in the sentence, and the candidate segment length (set1). Siahbani et al. (2014) proposed different sets of features for segmentation task including Part Of Speech (POS) tags and feedback from the decoder (given from the partial hypotheses of decoder during translation). POS tags showed promising results and fast to be computed. In addition to POS tags we also propose to use two features created based on reordering. We compare four different sets of features including the basic features (set1) to train the segmentation model:

- **Part of Speech tags**: The first group uses POS tags of the candidate segment as features. We considered the last three POS tags in a segment and also bigrams and trigrams of the POS tags for each segment (set2). In addition to these features we consider POS bigram surrounding the segment boundary (set3).

- **Reordering Features**: The lexicalized reordering model (Koehn et al., 2007) of phrase-based translation system determines the orientation of phrases with respect to the previous phrase, monotone (M),

Set1: Word, Position, Length	"engineers", 9, 5
Set2: + POS tags	[NNS],[CC-NNS],[NN-CC-NNS]
Set3: + Cross POS tag	[NNS-IN]
Set4: + Reordering	0.8904, 0.6

Table 1: Feature sets and an example (for segment "from our scientist and engineers" in the English sentence in Figure 1).

swap (S) and discontinuous (D). We expect the segments to be monotonically ordered. For each segment, we define two reordering features corresponding to the monotone feature orientation of the first and last phrases of the segment[4]. To compute the feature values we use lexicalized reordering model of Moses (Koehn et al., 2007) for monotone orientation of both left-to-right and right-to-left (corresponding to the first and last phrases of the segment). Adding reordering features to the previous features creates the last set of features (set4).

Table 1 shows an example for POS-based and reordering-based features defined on the second segment ("from our scientist and engineers") of the stream "we desperately need great communication from ..." (see Figure 1). To simplify the comparison, we consider each set-i contains the features of the previous sets. For example set2 includes the POS tags and features in set1.

3   Integrating Segmentation and Decoding

In sentence segmentation approaches, the input stream is segmented and for each recognized segment the machine translation decoder is called to translate the segment individually. In this approach the decoder treat each segment as an independent input, while we are translating the input stream. We integrate the segmentation model and decoder. This approach can be also considered as a stream decoding method which the decoder exploit other resources beyond just decoding cues.

Hiero models encode the translation correspondences in *hierarchical* phrases, unlike the phrase-based models that use contiguous translation phrases. The notion of hierarchy allows the Hiero models to capture long-distance reordering between source and target languages unlike phrase-based models. Additionally they also model discontiguous translations, e.g. translating the English word *not* as *ne ___ pas* in French (with an appropriate verb form inserted between *ne* and *pas*). These properties make Hiero models more appropriate for some language pairs than phrase-based models (Marcu and Wong, 2002; Och and Ney, 2002, 2004).

Hiero uses a lexicalized synchronous context-free grammar (SCFG) extracted from word and phrase alignments of a bitext. Typically, Hiero uses a CKY-style decoding algorithm with time complexity $O(n^3)$ where the source input has n words.

Previous translation services proposed for real-time translation environments, are mainly phrase-based (Fügen et al., 2007; Sankaran et al., 2010; Bangalore et al., 2012; Yarmohammadi et al., 2013; Oda et al., 2014). Since a phrase-based decoder generates translations in a left-to-right manner, it is more suited than the CKY based decoding which requires the entire input sentence before generating the translation.

We propose to use left-to-right hierarchical phrase-based translation in our simultaneous translation framework. It has been shown that left-to-right hierarchical (LR-Hiero) decoder can translate using Hiero translation model much faster than CKY Hiero decoder (Siahbani et al., 2013). In addition, it generates the translation in left-to-right manner. These properties make it a suitable decoder for simultaneous translation (Siahbani et al., 2014). We augment LR-Hiero decoder to incrementally translate the input and integrate it with our segmentation model. We briefly review the LR-Hiero decoder and then explain our incremental

---

[4]We consider the longest phrase which is available in the phrase-table.

Algorithm 1: Simultaneous Translation

```
 1: Input stream: f = f₀f₁ ...
 2: buffer = []
 3: h₀ = (⟨s⟩, null, null, 0)                                    (Initial history is ⟨s⟩)
 4: history = {h₀}
 5: while fᵢ ≠ ⟨/s⟩ do
 6:     if Segmenter(buffer, fᵢ) == True then
 7:         trans = Decoder(buffer, history)
 8:         print trans
 9:         buffer = [fᵢ]
10:         Update history
11:     else
12:         Add fᵢ to buffer                                  (Add the current word to the end of buffer)
13: trans = Decoder(buffer, history)                          (Translate the last segment)
14: print trans
```

---

version of the decoder.

3.1 LR-Hiero Decoder

LR-Hiero uses a constrained lexicalized SCFG usually called GNF grammar: $X \rightarrow \langle \gamma, \bar{b} \beta \rangle$, where X is a non-terminal, γ is a string of non-terminal and terminal symbols, $\bar{b}$ is a string of terminal symbols and β is a possibly empty sequence of non-terminals. Using GNF rules ensures that in derivations the target side is always generated from left to right. The rules are obtained from a word and phrase aligned bitext by replacing the smaller source-target phrase pair within a larger phrase pair with some non-terminal.

The decoding algorithm in LR-Hiero follows an Earley-style search (Earley, 1970) on the source side. The dot jumps around on the source side of the rules based on the order of nonterminals on the target side. Thus the target side derivation is strictly developed in left to right order. The search algorithm is integrated with beam search or cube pruning to find the k-best translations.

We slightly modify LR-Hiero decoder proposed by (Siahbani et al., 2013) and explain it over an example [5] (Figure 2). Each partial hypothesis h contains (h_t, h_s, h_c): a translation prefix h_t, a (LIFO-ordered) *list* h_s of uncovered spans and the hypothesis cost h_c which includes future cost and a model score computed based on feature values (using a log-linear model).

In the standard LR-Hiero decoder, translation prefix for the initial hypothesis is $\langle s \rangle$ and the initial hypothesis would be $h_0 = (\langle s \rangle, [[0, n]], 0)$. The hypotheses are stored in stacks $S_0, \ldots, S_n$, where S_p contains hypotheses covering p source words, just like in stack decoding for phrase-based SMT (Koehn et al., 2003). Decoding process finishes when stack S_n has been filled.

To Expand each hypothesis we find a rule that matched the first uncovered span ($h_s[0]$). For example to expand the initial hypothesis in Figure 2, we apply rule #1 which is matched to the first uncovered span ([0,5]). The new hypothesis will be generated by appending the lexical part of target side of the rule to the translation prefix of the previous hypothesis ("wir" is appended to "$\langle s \rangle$"). The list of uncovered span, h_s, is created by removing the first uncovered spand and pushing the new uncovered spans after applying the rule. In Figure 2, after applying rule #1 we translate the first word so a new uncovered span is generated (matched to non-terminal X_1 in rule #1) and is pushed to the h_s after popping the first uncovered span from the initial hypothesis.

---

[5] Please refer to (Siahbani et al., 2013) for more details.

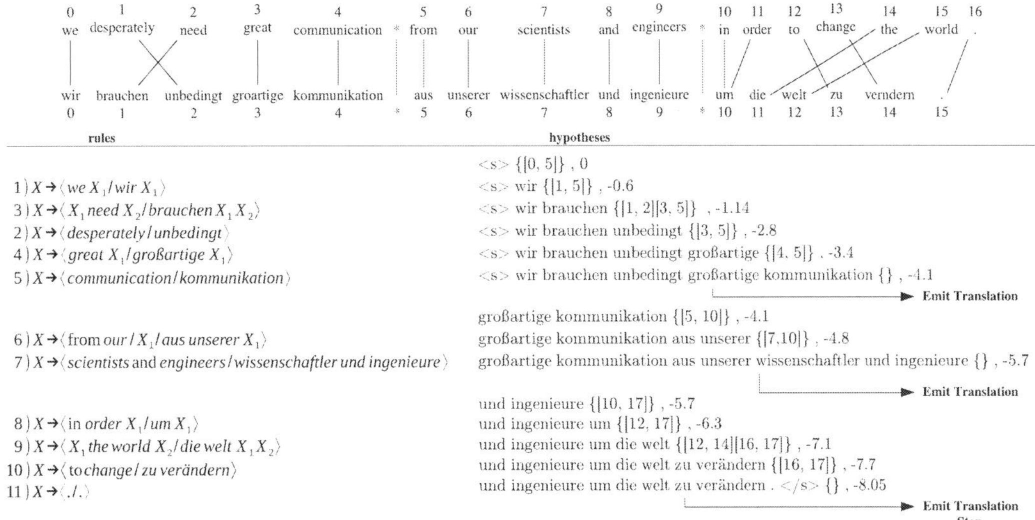

Figure 2: Simultaneous translation for an English-German sentence using LR-Hiero. The word alignment is shown on the top. The segmentation points are shown by red stars. On the bottom, different steps of the decoder are shown. The left side shows the rules used in the derivation.The hypotheses column shows partial hypotheses containing the translation prefix, h_t, the ordered list of yet-to-be-covered spans, h_s and cost h_c.

3.2 Incremental Translation

In our simultaneous translation framework, we integrate LR-Hiero with the segmentation model. This framework is shown in Algorithm 1. The input is a stream of words ($\mathbf{f} = f_0 f_1 \ldots$) which is fed to the translation system word by word. In this algorithm, *buffer* always contains the sequence of yet-to-be-translated words (initially empty), and *history* keeps the previous state of the decoder. We define *history* as the set of best hypotheses generated by the decoder while translating the previous segment. *history* is initialized by a null hypothesis (containing the sentence initial marker).

For each new input word, f_i, the translation system queries the segmentation model. The content of *buffer* and f_i are passed to the *Segmenter* to determine whether the sequence of words in *buffer* is a valid segment to be translated or not. Once a segment is recognized, the segment (content of *buffer*) and *history* are passed to the decoder. The decoder translates the given source segment, and produces the translation output for that segment. After emitting the translation to the output, *buffer* is initialized with the last input word, f_i which has not been translated yet and *history* is updated with the set of best hypotheses generated by the decoder. In other words, we freeze the the state of the decoder and continue the translation when the new segment arrives.

Figure 2 illustrates the process of generating just one translation. After reading the sixth word in the input stream ("from") the segmentation model recognize a segment ("we desperately need great communication"). This segment is passed to the decoder. The decoder generates the translation and the best translation will be emitted. Then *history* will be updated by the set of best hypotheses generated by the decoder. The translation system keeps reading the input stream and after recognizing the next segment (after reading "in") the new segment along with the *history* is passed to the decoder. The decoder translated the given

Task	Sentences	Tokens
MT Train	1033491	27948039
Tune	3669	74883
Seg. model Train	3669	74883
Test	1025	22026

Table 2: Corpus statistics in number of sentences and tokens (source side).

segment while using partial hypotheses in *history* as initial hypotheses (the figure just shows one of them $\langle$groBartige kommunikation, $\{[5, 10]\}, -4.1\rangle$). The process is repeated until the end of sentence is detected.

In this approach, the translation output is updated over time by adding the translation of the next input segments and the decoder does not change the output which is already produced and emitted.

4 Experimental Results

Following the *International Workshop on Spoken Language Translation* (IWSLT) shared task, we evaluate our approach on the speech translation of TED talks for English-German.Section 4.2 describe the experimental setting. We conduct many experiments to evaluate our approach. We first evaluate different approaches to create the segmentation model and experiment on various feature sets to obtain the best segmentation model (Section 4.2). Then we use the trained segmentation model in an end-to-end simultaneous translation system (Section 4.3). We evaluate the performance of end-to-end simultaneous translation system in terms of translation quality and latency and compare it with different baselines.

4.1 System Setup

We use the parallel text provided as training data of IWSLT 2013 and about one million sentence pairs of Europarl (v7), to train the translation system. We use development set 2010 and 2012 and test set 2010 of IWSLT shared task as development set to tune the translation system (LR-Hiero) and test set of IWSLT 2013 is used as the test set to evaluate the simultaneous translation system. We use a 5-gram LM trained on the monolingual German data provided by WMT 2013 shared task using KenLM (Heafield, 2011).

In LR-Hiero, we set pop limit 500, maximum source rule length 7 and at most 2 non-terminals. The standard feature set of LR-Hiero (Siahbani et al., 2013) is used in a discriminative log-linear model. The weights in the log-linear model are tuned by minimizing BLEU loss through MERT (Och, 2003) on the dev set for each language pair. In these experiments, we use the reference transcript of the utterance for dev and test sets. LR-Hiero is trained once and used in all experiments.

We use Stanford POS Tagger (Toutanova et al., 2003) to obtain the POS tags to extract features for the segmentation model [6].

4.2 Evaluating the Segmentation Model

In Section 2 we discussed two heuristics: translation-based and alignment-based, to provide training data for segmentation model. We conduct some experiments to compare different feature sets for these heuristics. We use Dev 2010 and 2012 and Test 2010 from IWSLT to provide the training date for the segmentation model. Table 2 shows the statistics of data used in our experiments.

To evaluate segment translation quality, we use corpus level BLEU (Papineni et al., 2002). To compute the latency model, we use *sayit*[7] script by Hal Daumé III which receives the content of the segment (in text format) and estimates the time it takes from a human to say the segment in some languages: English (US),

---

[6] In our experiments we use the standard POS-Tagger.
[7] http://www.umiacs.umd.edu/hal/sayit.py

Labeled data Heuristic	Features	P	R	F1
Translation-based	Set1	81.38	52.56	63.87
	Set2	82.03	53.90	65.06
	Set3	**97.18**	**69.89**	**81.31**
	Set4	93.41	64.14	76.06
Alignment-based	Set1	71.78	62.88	67.04
	Set2	74.58	56.46	64.27
	Set3	**79.78**	58.39	**67.43**
	Set4	79.09	**59.62**	**67.97**

Table 3: Results of segmentation model trained on different labeled data using various feature sets.

Segmentation model	Features	BLEU	Latency	Number of segments
Translation-based	Set3	**20.86**	**0.311**	3313
Alignment-based	Set3	20.60	0.540	2648
	Set4	20.62	0.524	2654
Prosodic heuristic	-	**20.88**	0.514	2709
Fixed Segmentation	-	19.81	0.283	3580
Random Segmentation	-	19.63	0.218	3980
No Segmentation	-	21.04	6.353	1025

Table 4: Results of our simultaneous translation using different segmentation models on English-German translation task. The last row shows the offline translation (regular SMT without segmentation). Segment length is set to 6 in *Fixed Segmentation* and *Random Segmentation*.

German, French, Italian, Spanish, and Japanese. These estimates are then used to evaluate the terms t_i and t'_{i-1} in Equation 2.

For the alignment-based heuristic, we concatenate the training data of segmentation model (3669 sentence pairs) to the training data of the translation system and run GIZA++ to get the word alignment. Then the heuristic discussed in Section 2 is used to extract segments. To have fair comparison, we choose $\mu = 5$ in translation-based heuristic which provides comparable number of segments on the training data in both alignment-based and translation-based heuristics.

We train separate segmentation models using the training data created by translation-based and alignment-based heuristics and different feature sets. To compare the feature sets, we test the models on a heldout set[8] (5000 sentences randomly selected from training data of IWSLT 2013). Table 3 shows the results in terms of precision, recall and F1 measure. Feature set3 outperforms the other feature sets for the segmentation models trained on the data obtained by translation-based heuristic. Therefore we use this model in the further experiments (Section 4.3). Hence feature set3 and set4 show comparable results, for the alignment-based heuristic, in these experiments, we will use both trained models in the end-to-end simultaneous translation system (Section 4.3).

4.3 Evaluation of Simultaneous Translation

We evaluate our simultaneous translation framework on a English-German translation task. We calculate latency as the total time taken to translate the whole sentence divided by the number of segments. Latency

---

[8]We use the set of POS tags obtained by translation-based heuristic to create the gold reference for this experiment.

in Table 4 shows the result of taking the average over 5 different runs for 50 sentences randomly selected from the test set.

The first three rows of Table 4 compare the results of the end-to-end simultaneous translation using segmentation models trained by translation-based and alignment-based heuristics. We can see that segmentation model trained on translation-based heuristic outperforms the other segmentation models both in translation accuracy and latency.

To evaluate our simultaneous translation framework we use four baselines. We implemented a heuristic segmenter based on (Rangarajan Sridhar et al., 2013) which segments on surface clues such as punctuation marks. These segments reflect the idea of segmentation on silence frames of around 100ms in the ASR output used in (Bangalore et al., 2012). The results of this heuristic (*prosodic*) has been shown in the forth row of Table 4. The last row in Table 4 shows the results of the regular translation strategy (with no segmentation employed). For a relatively small loss in the BLEU score we obtain a much faster incremental translation system. To evaluate the impact of segmentation model we add two more baselines in which decoder segments the input stream without using the segmentation model: (i) *Fixed Segmentation*: a segmentation with equally sized fragments; (ii) *Random Segmentation*: decoder randomly segments the input. These two baselines show comparable performance. The reduction in the BLEU score for these segmentation models shows that we need a more informative segmentation model.

We also compare our output against a state-of-the-art simultaneous neural MT approach (Gu et al., 2017), which uses a reinforcement learning style agent which is trained using a policy gradient algorithm to find segments that minimize delay and maximize the BLEU score. The agent uses a softmax policy over the segmentation outcomes (either read or write, aka segment) and trains its parameters by learning segmentations decisions based on a fully-trained non-simultaneous NMT encoder-decoder. Gu et al. (2017) use a new metric to measure the latency called *average proportion* proposed by(Cho and Esipova, 2016). Average proportion is defined as the average number of source words being used, when translating each word. The average proportion $d(X, Y)$ for a source sentence X and translation output Y is defined as $\frac{\sum_{t=1}^{|Y|} s(t)}{|X||Y|}$ where $|X|$ and $|Y|$ are the length of source and translation sentences respectively, and $s(t)$ is the number of already seen words from source sentence, when translating each word. We ran the Gu et al. (2017) approach on our English-German task (Figure 3). In order to compare the latency, we compute the average proportion for the output of our translation system which are shown in Figure 1. In this figure we have shown the results of our translation framework using different segmentation models trained for different segment lengths (μ values 3 to 8). We trained the NMT system with $\mu = 8$. Figure 3 also shows the results of offline translation for our approach and the NMT system (which results in average proportion of 1). There is a substantial loss in translation quality for simultaneous NMT (consistent with the results in Gu et al. (2017)).

5   Related Work

Early work on speech translation uses prosodic pauses detected in speech as segmentation boundaries (Fügen et al., 2007; Bangalore et al., 2012). Segmentation methods applied on the transcribed text can be divided to two categories: heuristic methods which use linguistic cues, like conjunctions, commas, etc. (Rangarajan Sridhar et al., 2013); and statistical methods which train a classifier to predict the segmentation boundaries. Some early methods use prosodic and lexical cues as features to predict soft boundaries (Matusov et al., 2007); while some other methods rely on word alignment information to identifies contiguous blocks of text that do not contain alignments to words outside them (Yarmohammadi et al., 2013; Siahbani et al., 2014). In addition to these segmentation approaches which are applied before calling the translation decoder, there is another strategy which perform the segmentation during decoding which is usually called stream or incremental decoding. Various incremental decoding approaches have been proposed for phrase-based (Kolss et al., 2008; Sankaran et al., 2010), hierarchical phrase-based (Siahbani et al., 2014; Finch et al.,

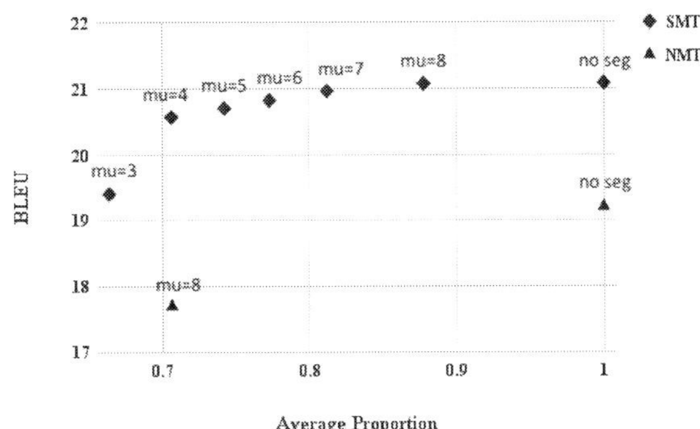

Figure 3: Comparing translation quality versus average proportion (latency) for our approach (SMT) and the simultaneous neural MT approach (NMT). We show the comparison of different μ values from 3 to 8 for the SMT system. The NMT system was trained with a μ value of 8. The offline translation systems with no segmentation (*no seg*) (for both SMT and NMT) have average proportion 1.

2015), and syntax-based (Oda et al., 2015) translation systems. In most incremental decoding algorithms, the decoder waits for more input and commit the translation when the current utterance is enough to generate a fluent translation. Oda et al. (2015) propose a method to predict the future syntactic constituents and use it in generating complete parse trees which helps to find a good point to commit the translation. Some researches have been focused on language pairs with divergent word order. Grissom II et al. (2014) predict sentence-final verbs using reinforcement learning which greatly affects the delay. He et al. (2015) design syntactic transformations to rewrite batch translations into more monotonic translations. Some research has been conducted on human simultaneous interpretation to determine the effect of the latency and accuracy metrics on the human evaluation of the output of simultaneous translation. The results indicate that latency is not as important as accuracy (Mieno et al., 2015). This implies that we need algorithms that can make a careful choice between different segmentation decisions of the same latency to produce translations with the best translation quality possible (for that latency) which we have done in this paper.

Neural machine translation has also been extended to perform simultaneous translation. Cho and Esipova (2016) proposed a manually defined heuristic waiting criteria to define an optimal segmentation point. A trainable agent which considers both quality and delay during segmentation first introduced by Satija and Pineau (2016). This work was extended by Gu et al. (2017) who designed a segmentation agent trained to incrementally translate using a policy gradient over a linear combination of translation quality (based on a sentence level BLEU score) and latency (calculated as minimizing delay). They showed that such an approach can learn a trade-off between quality and delay. However, in our comparison with their results our system provides a higher BLEU score while providing a comparable latency (see Figure 3).

6 Summary and Conclusion

This work combines segmentation with incremental decoding. The segmentation model is trained to minimize latency of producing translations as it reads from the input stream and maximize translation quality as measured by the BLEU score. Our framework is able to produce fast yet accurate translation in a simultaneous translation setting. Our experiments show that we obtain higher quality translations with near similar latency compared to a simultaneous neural machine translation system.

References

Bangalore, S., Rangarajan Sridhar, V. K., Kolan, P., Golipour, L., and Jimenez, A. (2012). Real-time incremental speech-to-speech translation of dialogs. In *Proc. of NAACL HLT 2012*, pages 437–445.

Cho, K. and Esipova, M. (2016). Can neural machine translation do simultaneous translation? *CoRR*, abs/1606.02012.

Earley, J. (1970). An efficient context-free parsing algorithm. *Commun. ACM*, 13(2):94–102.

Finch, A., Wang, X., Utiyama, M., and Sumita, E. (2015). Hierarchical phrase-based stream decoding. In *Proc. of EMNLP*, Lisbon, Portugal.

Fügen, C., Waibel, A., and Kolss, M. (2007). Simultaneous translation of lectures and speeches. *Machine Translation*, 21(4):209–252.

Fujita, T., Neubig, G., Sakti, S., Toda, T., and Nakamura, S. (2013). Simple, lexicalized choice of translation timing for simultaneous speech translation. In *INTERSPEECH*, pages 3487–3491.

Grissom II, A. C., Boyd-Graber, J., He, H., Morgan, J., and Daume III, H. (2014). Don't until the final verb wait: Reinforcement learning for simultaneous machine translation. In *EMNLP*, pages 1342–1352.

Gu, J., Neubig, G., Cho, K., and Li, V. O. (2017). Learning to translate in real-time with neural machine translation. In *15th Conference of the European Chapter of the Association for Computational Linguistics (EACL)*, Valencia, Spain.

He, H., Grissom II, A., Morgan, J., Boyd-Graber, J., and Daumé III, H. (2015). Syntax-based rewriting for simultaneous machine translation. In *Proceedings of the 2015 Conference on Empirical Methods in Natural Language Processing*, Lisbon, Portugal.

Heafield, K. (2011). KenLM: Faster and smaller language model queries. In *In Proc. of the Sixth Workshop on Statistical Machine Translation*.

Koehn, P., Hoang, H., Birch, A., Callison-Burch, C., Federico, M., Bertoldi, N., Cowan, B., Shen, W., Moran, C., Zens, R., Dyer, C., Bojar, O., Constantin, A., and Herbst, E. (2007). Moses: open source toolkit for statistical machine translation. In *Proceedings of the 45th Annual Meeting of the ACL on Interactive Poster and Demonstration Sessions*, ACL '07, pages 177–180, Stroudsburg, PA, USA. Association for Computational Linguistics.

Koehn, P., Och, F. J., and Marcu, D. (2003). Statistical phrase-based translation. In *Proc. of NAACL*.

Kolss, M., Vogel, S., and Waibel, A. (2008). Stream decoding for simultaneous spoken language translation. In *INTERSPEECH*, pages 2735–2738.

Lin, D. and Och, F. (2004). Orange: a method for evaluating automatic evaluation metrics for machine translation. In *COLING 2004*, pages 501–507.

Marcu, D. and Wong, W. (2002). A phrase-based, joint probability model for statistical machine translation. In *Proc. of EMNLP-2002*, pages 133–139.

Matusov, E., Hillard, D., Magimai-doss, M., Hakkani-tur, D., Ostendorf, M., and Ney, H. (2007). Improving speech translation with automatic boundary prediction. In *In Proc. Interspeech*, pages 2449–2452.

Mieno, T., Neubig, G., Sakti, S., Toda, T., and Nakamura, S. (2015). Speed or accuracy? a study in evaluation of simultaneous speech translation. In *INTERSPEECH*.

Och, F. J. (2003). Minimum error rate training in statistical machine translation. In *Proc. of ACL*.

Och, F. J. and Ney, H. (2002). Discriminative training and maximum entropy models for statistical machine translation. In *Proc. of ACL*.

Och, F. J. and Ney, H. (2004). The alignment template approach to statistical machine translation. *Computational Linguistics*, 30.

Oda, Y., Neubig, G., Sakti, S., Toda, T., and Nakamura, S. (2014). Optimizing segmentation strategies for simultaneous speech translation. In *The 52nd Annual Meeting of the Association for Computational Linguistics (ACL)*, Baltimore, USA.

Oda, Y., Neubig, G., Sakti, S., Toda, T., and Nakamura, S. (2015). Syntax-based simultaneous translation through prediction of unseen syntactic constituents. In *ACL*.

Papineni, K., Roukos, S., Ward, T., and jing Zhu, W. (2002). Bleu: a method for automatic evaluation of machine translation. pages 311–318.

Rangarajan Sridhar, V. K., Chen, J., Bangalore, S., Ljolje, A., and Chengalvarayan, R. (2013). Segmentation strategies for streaming speech translation. In *Proceedings of the 2013 Conference of the North American Chapter of the Association for Computational Linguistics: Human Language Technologies*, pages 230–238, Atlanta, Georgia. Association for Computational Linguistics.

Sankaran, B., Grewal, A., and Sarkar, A. (2010). Incremental decoding for phrase-based statistical machine translation. In *Proceedings of the Joint Fifth Workshop on Statistical Machine Translation and Metrics-MATR*, WMT.

Satija, H. and Pineau, J. (2016). Simultaneous machine translation using deep reinforcement learning. *Abstraction in Reinforcement Learning Workshop, ICML 2016*, (33).

Shavarani, H. S., Siahbani, M., M. Seraj, R., and Sarkar, A. (2015). Learning segmentations that balance latency versus quality in spoken language translation. In *The 12th International Workshop on Spoken Language Translation (IWSLT 2015)*, pages 217–224.

Siahbani, M., Mehdizadeh Seraj, R., Sankaran, B., and Sarkar, A. (2014). Incremental translation using a hierarchical phrase-based translation system. In *In Proceedings of the 2014 IEEE Spoken Language Technology Workshop (SLT 2014)*, Nevada, USA.

Siahbani, M., Sankaran, B., and Sarkar, A. (2013). Efficient left-to-right hierarchical phrase-based translation with improved reordering. In *Proceedings of the Conference on Empirical Methods in Natural Language Processing*, Seattle, USA.

Toutanova, K., Klein, D., Manning, C., and Singer, Y. (2003). Feature-rich part-of-speech tagging with a cyclic dependency network. In *Proceedings of HLT-NAACL 2003*, pages 252–259.

Watanabe, T., Tsukada, H., and Isozaki, H. (2006). Left-to-right target generation for hierarchical phrase-based translation. In *Proc. of ACL*.

Yarmohammadi, M., Sridhar, V. K. R., Bangalore, S., and Sankaran, B. (2013). Incremental segmentation and decoding strategies for simultaneous translation. In *Proc. of IJCNLP-2013*.

Neural Monkey:
The Current State and Beyond

Jindřich Helcl
Jindřich Libovický
Tom Kocmi
Tomáš Musil
Ondřej Cífka
Dušan Variš
Ondřej Bojar   [surname]@ufal.mff.cuni.cz
Institute of Formal and Applied Linguistics
Faculty of Mathematics and Physics, Charles University
Malostranské náměstí 25, Prague, 118 00, Czech Republic

Abstract

Neural Monkey is an open-source toolkit for sequence-to-sequence learning. The focus of this paper is to present the current state of the toolkit to the intended audience, which includes students and researchers, both active in the deep learning community and newcomers. For each of these target groups, we describe the most relevant features of the toolkit, including the simple configuration scheme, methods of model inspection that promote useful intuitions, or a modular design for easy prototyping. We summarize relevant contributions to the research community which were made using this toolkit and discuss the characteristics of our toolkit with respect to other existing systems. We conclude with a set of proposals for future development.

1 Introduction

Neural Monkey (Helcl and Libovický, 2017) is an open-source tool for sequential learning developed and maintained at Charles University. It is used mainly for experiments with neural machine translation (NMT), but also for other natural language processing (NLP) tasks which use deep learning, such as image captioning, multimodal translation, optical character recognition, text summarization or sentiment analysis. In this paper, we present the state of the software at the beginning of 2018 and share the plans for future development.

Neural Monkey is best suited for research and education. Our ambition is not developing a production-ready software. We also do not focus on technical tricks to achieve the best performance. Instead, we provide an extensible library of implemented features with references to the papers where they were proposed.

We try to align our aims with the needs of three possibly overlapping groups of users. First, we want to help students understand how various models work and build intuition for their training. Second, we want to provide a simple tool for newcomers to the field of deep learning to help them start experimenting with these models. Third, we design the toolkit in a highly modular fashion with replaceable components to suit researchers who want to try out their ideas without having to implement everything from scratch.

Neural Monkey is implemented in Python 3.5 using the TensorFlow library (Abadi et al., 2016). We share the source code on GitHub,[1] where we also report and solve issues, provide support for users and discuss the development, so everyone can contribute with their ideas.

This paper is organized as follows. Section 2 presents the goals of the development of the toolkit with respect to the needs of the considered user groups. Section 3 gives an overview of the toolkit features. In Section 4, we summarize the research contributions that have been made with Neural Monkey. We discuss the differences from other toolkits in Section 5. We propose our plans for the future development and conclude in Section 6.

2 The Goals of Neural Monkey Development

During the development of Neural Monkey, we keep in mind three groups of potential users. In this section, we discuss the interests of the members of each group, and establish a set of goals aligned with the considered interests.

The first interest group are researchers or NLP engineers who would like to start using deep learning. Neural Monkey is easy to install; it uses only a few Python modules which can be installed using *PiPy*, the Python package manager. The experiments are configured using configuration files with a simple *ini* syntax enriched with elements from Python. The sections of a configuration file correspond to an established conceptualization of the problem as used in the NLP community. We provide several examples of configuration files which can be used as starting points for experiments. A minimal working example configuration for NMT is shown in Example 1.

The second interest group we consider are students. Most of the modules that implement network components correspond to research papers which propose the ideas. The corresponding paper is cited in the code, often including references to a particular section or equation in the paper. We believe that reading such a commented code can help understand the relation between equations in papers and the actual implementation.

Finally, the third group of our potential users are researchers in NLP, who are already experienced in deep learning. For researchers, we provide a collection of modular prototypes and algorithmic features with a convenient experiment management system.

The four main goals of Neural Monkey development are:

Code Readability. The code is written with an emphasis on readability. This includes referencing the papers and original implementations. Research software often does not focus on the quality of the code. With Neural Monkey, we are trying to have a clear code base, such that everyone can easily fork the repository and build their experimental setup on top of that.

Modularity along Research Concepts. While working on neural models, it is common to reuse existing implementation of the state-of-the-art architectures or apply different training techniques. For example, one could only modify the encoder in order to improve the input sequence representation.

Up-to-Date Building Blocks. Deep learning is a rapidly developing field with new architectures appearing every few months. Neural Monkey is a maintained collection of these models, ready for use in NLP experiments.

Fast Prototyping. We focus on fast and easy prototyping of new architectures and testing existing architectures on new tasks. We try to keep a clear API that allows reusing architecture components between various tasks.

---

[1]https://github.com/ufal/neuralmonkey

```
[main]                                    [encoder]
output="output_dir"                       class=encoders.SentenceEncoder
batch_size=64                             rnn_size=500
epochs=20                                 embedding_size=600
train_dataset=<train_data>                data_id="source"
val_dataset=<val_data>                    vocabulary=<encoder_vocabulary>
trainer=<trainer>
runners=[<runner>]                        [attention]
evaluation=[("target", evaluators.BLEU)]  class=attention.Attention
logging_period=500                        encoder=<encoder>
validation_period=5000
                                          [decoder]
[train_data]                              class=decoders.Decoder
class=dataset.from_files                  encoders=[<encoder>]
s_source="data/train.en"                  attentions=[<attention>]
s_target="data/train.de"                  rnn_size=1000
lazy=True                                 embedding_size=600
                                          data_id="target"
[val_data]                                vocabulary=<decoder_vocabulary>
class=dataset.from_files
s_source="data/val.en"                    [trainer]
s_target="data/val.de"                    class=trainers.CrossEntropyTrainer
                                          decoders=[<decoder>]
[encoder_vocabulary]                      clip_norm=1.0
class=vocabulary.from_wordlist
path="en_vocab.tsv"                       [runner]
                                          class=runners.GreedyRunner
[decoder_vocabulary]                      decoder=<decoder>
class=vocabulary.from_wordlist
path="de_vocab.tsv"
```

Example 1: A minimal example of a configuration file for an attentive RNN sequence-to-sequence machine translation model with the as presented by Bahdanau et al. (2014).

3 Toolkit Features

In the previous section, we defined our goals with respect to the needs of the target user groups. In this section, we provide a high-level overview of the features that are implemented in Neural Monkey. Further implementation details are explained in the following sections. In general, Neural Monkey distinguishes *encoders* (components that read data and produce a representation), and *decoders* (components that produce an output).

3.1 Processing Input ("Encoders")

This section summarizes the encoder components implemented in Neural Monkey. Each encoder processes an input into either a single state, a (temporal) sequence of states, or a two-dimensional (spatial) set of states.

- *Recurrent Sequence Encoder* allows encoding input sequence using stacked recurrent neural networks (RNNs). In addition to embedded symbolic input (Sutskever et al., 2014), we allow also a numerical input which can be used for instance for speech recognition.

- *RNN over Character-Level Convolutional Neural Network* (Lee et al., 2017), a technique that applies convolutional neural network (CNN) on the unsegmented character-level input. To produce the sequence of states, it uses a recurrent sequence encoder on the CNN outputs.

- *Deep Convolutional Encoder* (Gehring et al., 2017), an encoder for sequence-to-sequence learning with stacked convolutional layers and positional embeddings.

- *Transformer Encoder* is the encoder part of the Transformer (Vaswani et al., 2017) architecture which repeatedly uses the self-attention mechanism over the input representation.

- *ConvNet for Sentence Classification.* We implement the convolutional network with max-pooling for sentence classification (Kim, 2014). It is a fast baseline method for sentence classification such as sentiment analysis.

- *Self-Attentive Sentence Embedding.* As a more advanced technique for sentence classification, we use sentence encoding by Lin et al. (2017) which uses attention to produce a fixed-size structured representation of the input sequence.

- *Wrapper for ImageNet Networks.* Tasks combining language and vision usually use image features from deep convolutional networks for image classification. Neural Monkey provides wrappers for the inclusion of these models as implemented in TensorFlow Slim library.[2] In particular, we support VGG networks (Simonyan and Zisserman, 2014) and variants of ResNet (He et al., 2016).

- *Custom CNN with Residual Connections.* We also allow deep convolutional networks for image processing trained from scratch with an arbitrary architecture of stacked standard convolutional and max-pooling layers and residual blocks. (He et al., 2016)

3.2 Generating Output ("Decoders")

The list below describes components that generate an output, which we call decoders. Note that some of them have hidden states and if they implement the same API as the input processing model parts, they can be stacked with other decoders. Thanks to this feature, we can for instance apply a sequence labeler both on top of a recurrent encoder and a recurrent decoder and train them jointly.

- *Attentive Recurrent Sequence Decoder.* We implement the attention model introduced by Bahdanau et al. (2014) which was the main technique for a sequence decoding in the last few years. We support several recurrent unit implementations, including LSTM (Hochreiter and Schmidhuber, 1997), GRU (Cho et al., 2014), and conditional GRU (Firat and Cho, 2016). On top of the standard attention, we support the scaled dot-product attention (Vaswani et al., 2017), attention with the sentinel gate (Lu et al., 2016), and advanced attention combination strategies which explicitly model the attention over multiple sources (Libovický and Helcl, 2017).

- *Transformer Decoder*, the decoder part of the self-attentive sequence-to-sequence learning architecture mentioned above (Vaswani et al., 2017).

- *Sequence Labeler.* While sequence labeling, a multilayer perceptron is applied on the hidden states of the encoder. Additionally, the conditional random field (Lafferty et al., 2001; Do and Artieres, 2010) can be used to produce the output labeling.

- *Connectionist Temporal Classification*, a non-autoregressive technique of sequence decoding (Graves et al., 2006) used mostly in speech recognition and optical character recognition where the output labels keep the temporal order of the input signal.

- *Multilayer perceptron* for classification or regression.

---

[2]https://github.com/tensorflow/models/tree/master/research/slim

3.3 Additional Features

This section summarizes additional useful features available in Neural Monkey.

- *Beam Search and Model Ensembles.*

- *Independent Training, Saving and Loading Parts of the Model.*

- *Multi-Task Learning.* Experiment configurations can include definition of multiple decoders and specify which contribute to the training loss.

- *Loading Nematus Models.* Models that have been trained with Nematus (Sennrich et al., 2017b) can be loaded into Neural Monkey. This can be used either for fine-tuning, domain adaptation, or multi-task learning.

- *Bandit Learning.* Neural Monkey can be also used for bandit learning using expected loss minimization (Kreutzer et al., 2017). In this setup, a pre-trained model is tuned using either a simulated or real user feedback.

- *Detailed Logging and Visualization.* We implement several evaluation metrics that can be used for continuous validation of the models. We also plot the loss, norms of the parameters, and histograms of the parameter gradients to TensorBoard. It can also be used for embeddings visualization. There is also a standalone tool for attention visualization (Rikters et al., 2017).

4 Research Contributions

The development of Neural Monkey began in spring 2016 and since that time it has been used in various research papers and MT competitions. In this section, we describe a selection of these contributions.

Kreutzer et al. (2017) used Neural Monkey for domain adaptation using bandit learning with simulated user feedback. This technique brings a significant improvement over both the out-of-domain model and other domain adaptation techniques.

Libovický and Helcl (2017) published interpretable attention combination strategies for multi-source sequence-to-sequence learning tasks, such as multimodal translation. These combination strategies allow to explicitly model the different importance of the source sequences in each step during the decoding.

Bastings et al. (2017) used Neural Monkey to develop a new convolutional architecture for encoding the input sentences using dependency trees. This syntax-aware source language representation brings a consistent improvement over the attentive sequence-to-sequence model baseline.

Kocmi and Bojar (2017) published a thorough examination of various embedding initialization strategies, both random and pre-trained. They conclude that improvements from pre-trained embeddings are not always beneficial, and that high-quality embeddings can be trained using an initialization with a normal distribution with a small variance or even with zeros.

Neural Monkey has also been used in various submissions to shared tasks at the Conference on Machine Translation (WMT). In 2016 and 2017, it was used in submissions for multimodal translation task (Libovický et al., 2016; Helcl and Libovický, 2017). It was also part of a system combination used in the English-to-Czech MT system in the news task (Sudarikov et al., 2017). Neural Monkey models were used as baselines in bandit learning and neural training tasks. (Sokolov et al., 2017; Bojar et al., 2017b).

5 Comparison to Other Toolkits

Due to its goals, Neural Monkey differs from other open-source packages used for sequence-to-sequence learning.[3]

There are several production-oriented tools. They aim to be easy to use and work well in an online setup. They also aim to reach the best result possible as long as it does not intervene with its practical usability. Tools like this are most importantly *OpenNMT* (Klein et al., 2017), *Marian* (Junczys-Dowmunt et al., 2016), *Sockeye NMT* (Hieber et al., 2017), and *Tensor2Tensor* (Kaiser et al., 2017). All of them contain several well-tuned pre-made architectures that can be used out of the box for sequence-to-sequence learning tasks.

Tools like *Nematus* (Sennrich et al., 2017b) and *nmtpy* (Caglayan et al., 2017) built on Theano (Al-Rfou et al., 2016) or *xnmt* based on DyNet (Neubig et al., 2017) are more research oriented. For instance, Nematus implements several techniques which improve the performance of the system in the offline setup but which would be prohibitively slow in the online use. Using these techniques (such as model ensembling or right-to-left rescoring) repeatedly achieved the best results in the annual MT systems comparison at WMT (Sennrich et al., 2017a; Bojar et al., 2016, 2017a).

Research-oriented tools allow easy modification of the model architectures and other model properties. Unlike Neural Monkey, these software packages do not declare an ambition to collect architectures for other NLP tasks, nor do they plan to drive research towards understanding representations learned by the networks.

6 Conclusions and Future Work

The main future plans with Neural Monkey remain unchanged: the implementation of the state-of-the-art neural architectures for NMT with a strong focus on multimodality in MT.

Among the important features we plan to implement are the support for multi-GPU training via data parallelism and model import from other tools heavily used in MT research, most importantly Tensor2Tensor and Marian.

Additionally, we plan to focus on understanding language representations that emerge in neural architectures during end-to-end training of NLP tasks. In order to do so, we would like to get close to the state-of-the-art in other NLP tasks including image captioning, sentence classification tasks (e.g. sentiment analysis), or various sequence labeling tasks (e.g. tagging, named entity recognition). For studying the representations, we will implement additional visualization tools.

With the growing number of implemented models, we plan to introduce a model zoo. Neural Monkey users will be able to reuse configuration files, data preprocessing scripts, or even trained models or their parts in their own research.

Acknowledgements

This research received support from the Czech Science Foundation grant no. P103/12/G084, the EU grant no. H2020-ICT-2014-1-645452 (QT21), and the Charles University grant no. 8502/2016.

References

Abadi, M., Agarwal, A., Barham, P., Brevdo, E., Chen, Z., Citro, C., Corrado, G. S., Davis, A., Dean, J., Devin, M., et al. (2016). Tensorflow: Large-scale machine learning on heterogeneous distributed systems. *arXiv preprint arXiv:1603.04467*.

---

[3]For an up-to-date list, see `https://github.com/jonsafari/nmt-list`.

Al-Rfou, R., Alain, G., Almahairi, A., Angermüller, C., Bahdanau, D., Ballas, N., Bastien, F., Bayer, J., Belikov, A., Belopolsky, A., Bengio, Y., Bergeron, A., Bergstra, J., Bisson, V., Snyder, J. B., Bouchard, N., Boulanger-Lewandowski, N., Bouthillier, X., de Brébisson, A., Breuleux, O., Carrier, P. L., Cho, K., Chorowski, J., Christiano, P. F., Cooijmans, T., Côté, M., Côté, M., Courville, A. C., Dauphin, Y. N., Delalleau, O., Demouth, J., Desjardins, G., Dieleman, S., Dinh, L., Ducoffe, M., Dumoulin, V., Kahou, S. E., Erhan, D., Fan, Z., Firat, O., Germain, M., Glorot, X., Goodfellow, I. J., Graham, M., Gülçehre, Ç., Hamel, P., Harlouchet, I., Heng, J., Hidasi, B., Honari, S., Jain, A., Jean, S., Jia, K., Korobov, M., Kulkarni, V., Lamb, A., Lamblin, P., Larsen, E., Laurent, C., Lee, S., Lefrançois, S., Lemieux, S., Léonard, N., Lin, Z., Livezey, J. A., Lorenz, C., Lowin, J., Ma, Q., Manzagol, P., Mastropietro, O., McGibbon, R., Memisevic, R., van Merriënboer, B., Michalski, V., Mirza, M., Orlandi, A., Pal, C. J., Pascanu, R., Pezeshki, M., Raffel, C., Renshaw, D., Rocklin, M., Romero, A., Roth, M., Sadowski, P., Salvatier, J., Savard, F., Schlüter, J., Schulman, J., Schwartz, G., Serban, I. V., Serdyuk, D., Shabanian, S., Simon, É., Spieckermann, S., Subramanyam, S. R., Sygnowski, J., Tanguay, J., van Tulder, G., Turian, J. P., Urban, S., Vincent, P., Visin, F., de Vries, H., Warde-Farley, D., Webb, D. J., Willson, M., Xu, K., Xue, L., Yao, L., Zhang, S., and Zhang, Y. (2016). Theano: A python framework for fast computation of mathematical expressions. *CoRR*, abs/1605.02688.

Bahdanau, D., Cho, K., and Bengio, Y. (2014). Neural machine translation by jointly learning to align and translate. *CoRR*, abs/1409.0473.

Bastings, J., Titov, I., Aziz, W., Marcheggiani, D., and Simaan, K. (2017). Graph convolutional encoders for syntax-aware neural machine translation. pages 1957–1967.

Bojar, O., Chatterjee, R., Federmann, C., Graham, Y., Haddow, B., Huang, S., Huck, M., Koehn, P., Liu, Q., Logacheva, V., Monz, C., Negri, M., Post, M., Rubino, R., Specia, L., and Turchi, M. (2017a). Findings of the 2017 conference on machine translation (wmt17). In *Proceedings of the Second Conference on Machine Translation*, pages 169–214, Copenhagen, Denmark. Association for Computational Linguistics.

Bojar, O., Chatterjee, R., Federmann, C., Graham, Y., Haddow, B., Huck, M., Yepes, A., Koehn, P., Logacheva, V., Monz, C., Negri, M., Névéol, A., Neves, M., Popel, M., Post, M., Rubino, R., Scarton, C., Specia, L., Turchi, M., Verspoor, K., and Zampieri, M. (2016). Findings of the 2016 conference on machine translation (WMT16). In *Proceedings of the First Conference on Machine Translation (WMT), Volume 2: Shared Task Papers*, volume 2, pages 131–198, Stroudsburg, PA, USA. Association for Computational Linguistics, Association for Computational Linguistics.

Bojar, O., Helcl, J., Kocmi, T., Libovický, J., and Musil, T. (2017b). Results of the wmt17 neural mt training task. In *Proceedings of the Second Conference on Machine Translation, Volume 2: Shared Task Papers*, pages 525–533, Copenhagen, Denmark. Association for Computational Linguistics.

Caglayan, O., García-Martínez, M., Bardet, A., Aransa, W., Bougares, F., and Barrault, L. (2017). Nmtpy: A flexible toolkit for advanced neural machine translation systems. *Prague Bull. Math. Linguistics*, 109:15–28.

Cho, K., van Merrienboer, B., Bahdanau, D., and Bengio, Y. (2014). On the properties of neural machine translation: Encoder–decoder approaches. In *Proceedings of SSST-8, Eighth Workshop on Syntax, Semantics and Structure in Statistical Translation*, pages 103–111, Doha, Qatar. Association for Computational Linguistics.

Do, T.-M.-T. and Artieres, T. (2010). Neural conditional random fields. In *Proceedings of the Thirteenth International Conference on Artificial Intelligence and Statistics*, volume 9. JMLR: W&CP.

Firat, O. and Cho, K. (2016). Conditional gated recurrent unit with attention mechanism. https://github.com/nyu-dl/dl4mt-tutorial/blob/master/docs/cgru.pdf. Published online, version `adbaeea`.

Gehring, J., Auli, M., Grangier, D., and Dauphin, Y. (2017). A convolutional encoder model for neural machine translation. In *Proceedings of the 55th Annual Meeting of the Association for Computational Linguistics (Volume 1: Long Papers)*, pages 123–135. Association for Computational Linguistics.

Graves, A., Fernández, S., Gomez, F., and Schmidhuber, J. (2006). Connectionist temporal classification: Labelling unsegmented sequence data with recurrent neural networks. In *Proceedings of the 23rd International Conference on Machine Learning*, ICML '06, pages 369–376, New York, NY, USA. ACM.

He, K., Zhang, X., Ren, S., and Sun, J. (2016). Deep residual learning for image recognition. In *Proceedings of the IEEE conference on computer vision and pattern recognition*, pages 770–778.

Helcl, J. and Libovický, J. (2017). Cuni system for the wmt17 multimodal translation task. In *Proceedings of the Second Conference on Machine Translation*, pages 450–457, Copenhagen, Denmark. Association for Computational Linguistics.

Helcl, J. and Libovický, J. (2017). Neural monkey: An open-source tool for sequence learning. *The Prague Bulletin of Mathematical Linguistics*, (107):5–17.

Hieber, F., Domhan, T., Denkowski, M., Vilar, D., Sokolov, A., Clifton, A., and Post, M. (2017). Sockeye: A toolkit for neural machine translation. *CoRR*, abs/1712.05690.

Hochreiter, S. and Schmidhuber, J. (1997). Long short-term memory. *Neural Comput.*, 9:1735–1780.

Junczys-Dowmunt, M., Dwojak, T., and Hoang, H. (2016). Is neural machine translation ready for deployment? a case study on 30 translation directions. In *Proceedings of the 9th International Workshop on Spoken Language Translation (IWSLT)*, Seattle, WA.

Kaiser, L., Gomez, A. N., Shazeer, N., Vaswani, A., Parmar, N., Jones, L., and Uszkoreit, J. (2017). One model to learn them all. *CoRR*, abs/1706.05137.

Kim, Y. (2014). Convolutional neural networks for sentence classification. In *Proceedings of the 2014 Conference on Empirical Methods in Natural Language Processing (EMNLP)*, pages 1746–1751, Doha, Qatar. Association for Computational Linguistics.

Klein, G., Kim, Y., Deng, Y., Senellart, J., and Rush, A. M. (2017). Opennmt: Open-source toolkit for neural machine translation. *CoRR*, abs/1701.02810.

Kocmi, T. and Bojar, O. (2017). An Exploration of Word Embedding Initialization in Deep-Learning Tasks. In *Proceedings of the 14th International Conference on Natural Language Processing*.

Kreutzer, J., Sokolov, A., and Riezler, S. (2017). Bandit structured prediction for neural sequence-to-sequence learning. In *Proceedings of the 55th Annual Meeting of the Association for Computational Linguistics (Volume 1: Long Papers)*, pages 1503–1513, Vancouver, Canada. Association for Computational Linguistics.

Lafferty, J. D., McCallum, A., and Pereira, F. C. N. (2001). Conditional random fields: Probabilistic models for segmenting and labeling sequence data. In *Proceedings of the Eighteenth International Conference on Machine Learning*, ICML '01, pages 282–289, San Francisco, CA, USA. Morgan Kaufmann Publishers Inc.

Lee, J., Cho, K., and Hofmann, T. (2017). Fully character-level neural machine translation without explicit segmentation. *Transactions of the Association for Computational Linguistics*, 5:365–378.

Libovický, J. and Helcl, J. (2017). Attention strategies for multi-source sequence-to-sequence learning. In *Proceedings of the 55th Annual Meeting of the Association for Computational Linguistics (Volume 2: Short Papers)*, Vancouver, Canada. Association for Computational Linguistics.

Libovický, J., Helcl, J., Tlustý, M., Bojar, O., and Pecina, P. (2016). CUNI system for WMT16 automatic post-editing and multimodal translation tasks. In *Proceedings of the First Conference on Machine Translation*, pages 646–654, Berlin, Germany. Association for Computational Linguistics.

Lin, Z., Feng, M., dos Santos, C. N., Yu, M., Xiang, B., Zhou, B., and Bengio, Y. (2017). A structured self-attentive sentence embedding. In *International Conference on Learning Representations 2017 (Conference Track)*.

Lu, J., Xiong, C., Parikh, D., and Socher, R. (2016). Knowing when to look: Adaptive attention via a visual sentinel for image captioning. *CoRR*, abs/1612.01887.

Neubig, G., Dyer, C., Goldberg, Y., Matthews, A., Ammar, W., Anastasopoulos, A., Ballesteros, M., Chiang, D., Clothiaux, D., Cohn, T., Duh, K., Faruqui, M., Gan, C., Garrette, D., Ji, Y., Kong, L., Kuncoro, A., Kumar, G., Malaviya, C., Michel, P., Oda, Y., Richardson, M., Saphra, N., Swayamdipta, S., and Yin, P. (2017). Dynet: The dynamic neural network toolkit. *CoRR*, abs/1701.03980.

Rikters, M., Fishel, M., and Bojar, O. (2017). Visualizing neural machine translation attention and confidence. *The Prague Bulletin of Mathematical Linguistics*, 109(1):39–50.

Sennrich, R., Birch, A., Currey, A., Germann, U., Haddow, B., Heafield, K., Miceli Barone, A. V., and Williams, P. (2017a). The university of edinburgh's neural mt systems for wmt17. In *Proceedings of the Second Conference on Machine Translation*, pages 389–399, Copenhagen, Denmark. Association for Computational Linguistics.

Sennrich, R., Firat, O., Cho, K., Birch, A., Haddow, B., Hitschler, J., Junczys-Dowmunt, M., Läubli, S., Miceli Barone, A. V., Mokrý, J., and Nadejde, M. (2017b). Nematus: a toolkit for neural machine translation. In *Proceedings of the Software Demonstrations of the 15th Conference of the European Chapter of the Association for Computational Linguistics*, pages 65–68, Valencia, Spain. Association for Computational Linguistics.

Simonyan, K. and Zisserman, A. (2014). Very deep convolutional networks for large-scale image recognition. *CoRR*, abs/1409.1556.

Sokolov, A., Kreutzer, J., Sunderland, K., Danchenko, P., Szymaniak, W., Fürstenau, H., and Riezler, S. (2017). A shared task on bandit learning for machine translation. In *Proceedings of the 2nd Conference on Machine Translation (WMT)*, Copenhagen, Denmark.

Sudarikov, R., Mareček, D., Kocmi, T., Variš, D., and Bojar, O. (2017). CUNI submission in WMT17: Chimera goes neural. In *Proceedings of the Second Conference on Machine Translation*, pages 248–256, Copenhagen, Denmark. Association for Computational Linguistics.

Sutskever, I., Vinyals, O., and Le, Q. V. (2014). Sequence to sequence learning with neural networks. In Ghahramani, Z., Welling, M., Cortes, C., Lawrence, N. D., and Weinberger, K. Q., editors, *Advances in Neural Information Processing Systems 27*, pages 3104–3112. Curran Associates, Inc.

Vaswani, A., Shazeer, N., Parmar, N., Uszkoreit, J., Jones, L., Gomez, A. N., Kaiser, L., and Polosukhin, I. (2017). Attention is all you need. In Guyon, I., Luxburg, U. V., Bengio, S., Wallach, H., Fergus, R., Vishwanathan, S., and Garnett, R., editors, *Advances in Neural Information Processing Systems 30*, pages 6000–6010. Curran Associates, Inc.

OpenNMT: Neural Machine Translation Toolkit

Guillaume Klein   SYSTRAN

Yoon Kim   Harvard University

Yuntian Deng   Harvard University

Vincent Nguyen   Ubiqus

Jean Senellart   SYSTRAN

Alexander M. Rush   Harvard University

Abstract

OpenNMT is an open-source toolkit for neural machine translation (NMT). The system prioritizes efficiency, modularity, and extensibility with the goal of supporting NMT research into model architectures, feature representations, and source modalities, while maintaining competitive performance and reasonable training requirements. The toolkit consists of modeling and translation support, as well as detailed pedagogical documentation about the underlying techniques. OpenNMT has been used in several production MT systems, modified for numerous research papers, and is implemented across several deep learning frameworks.

1   Introduction

Neural machine translation (NMT) is a new methodology for machine translation that has led to remarkable improvements, particularly in terms of human evaluation, compared to rule-based and statistical machine translation (SMT) systems (Wu et al., 2016; Crego et al., 2016). Originally developed using pure sequence-to-sequence models (Sutskever et al., 2014; Cho et al., 2014) and improved upon using attention-based variants (Bahdanau et al., 2014; Luong et al., 2015a), NMT has now become a widely-applied technique for machine translation, as well as an effective approach for other related NLP tasks such as dialogue, parsing, and summarization.

As NMT approaches are standardized, it becomes more important for the machine translation and NLP community to develop open implementations for researchers to benchmark against, learn from, and extend upon. Just as the SMT community benefited greatly from toolkits like Moses (Koehn et al., 2007) for phrase-based SMT and CDec (Dyer et al., 2010) for syntax-based SMT, NMT toolkits can provide a foundation to build upon. A toolkit should aim to provide a shared framework for developing and comparing open-source systems, while at the same time being efficient and accurate enough to be used in production contexts.

With these goals in mind, in this work we present an open-source toolkit for developing neural machine translation systems, known as *OpenNMT* (http://opennmt.net). Since its launch in December 2016, OpenNMT has become a collection of implementations targeting both academia and industry. The system is designed to be simple to use and easy to extend, while maintaining efficiency and state-of-the-art accuracy. In addition to providing code for the core translation tasks, OpenNMT was designed with two aims: (a) prioritize training and test efficiency, (b) maintain model modularity and readability hence research extensibility.

During this time, many other stellar open-source NMT implementations have also been

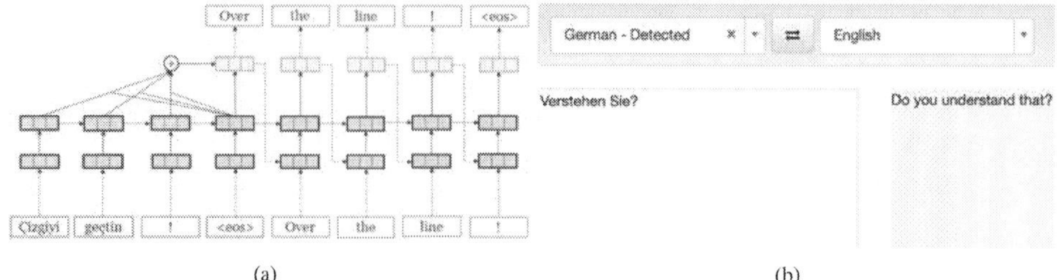

Figure 1: *(a). Schematic view of neural machine translation. The red source words are first mapped to word vectors and then fed into a recurrent neural network (RNN). Upon seeing the ⟨eos⟩ symbol, the final time step initializes a target blue RNN. At each target time step, attention is applied over the source RNN and combined with the current hidden state to produce a prediction $p(w_t|w_{1:t-1}, x)$ of the next word. This prediction is then fed back into the target RNN. (b). Live demo of the OpenNMT system.*

released, including *GroundHog, Blocks, Nematus, tensorflow-seq2seq, GNMT, fair-seq, Tensor2Tensor, Sockeye, Neural Monkey, lamtram, XNMT, SGNMT*, and *Marian*. These projects mostly implement variants of the same underlying systems, and differ in their prioritization of features. The open-source community around this area is flourishing, and is providing the NLP community a useful variety of open-source NMT frameworks. In the ongoing development of OpenNMT, we aim to build upon the strengths of those systems, while supporting a framework with high-accuracy translation, multiple options and clear documentation.

This engineering report describes how the system targets our design goals. We begin by briefly surveying the background for NMT, and then describing the high-level implementation details. We end by showing benchmarks of the system in terms of accuracy, speed, and memory usage for several translation and natural language generation tasks.

2 Background

NMT has now been extensively described in many excellent tutorials (see for instance `https://sites.google.com/site/acl16nmt/home`). We give only a condensed overview.

NMT takes a conditional language modeling view of translation by modeling the probability of a target sentence $w_{1:T}$ given a source sentence $x_{1:S}$ as $p(w_{1:T}|x) = \prod_1^T p(w_t|w_{1:t-1}, x; \theta)$ where the distribution is parameterized with θ. This distribution is estimated using an attention-based encoder-decoder architecture (Bahdanau et al., 2014). A source encoder recurrent neural network (RNN) maps each source word to a word vector, and processes these to a sequence of hidden vectors $\mathbf{h}_1, \ldots, \mathbf{h}_S$. The target decoder combines an RNN hidden representation of previously generated words $(w_1, \ldots w_{t-1})$ with source hidden vectors to predict scores for each possible next word. A softmax layer is then used to produce a next-word distribution $p(w_t|w_{1:t-1}, x; \theta)$. The source hidden vectors influence the distribution through an attention pooling layer that weights each source word relative to its expected contribution to the target prediction. The complete model is trained end-to-end to minimize the negative log-likelihood of the training corpus. An unfolded network diagram is shown in Figure 1(a).

In practice, there are also many other important aspects that improve the effectiveness of the base model. Here we briefly mention four areas: (a) It is important to use a gated RNN such as an LSTM (Hochreiter and Schmidhuber, 1997) or GRU (Chung et al., 2014) which help the model learn long-term features. (b) Translation requires relatively large, stacked RNNs, which consist of several vertical layers (2-16) of RNNs at each time step (Sutskever et al., 2014). (c) Input feeding, where the previous attention vector is fed back into the input as well as the predicted word, has been shown to be quite helpful for machine translation (Luong et al., 2015a). (d) Test-time decoding is done through *beam search* where multiple hypothesis target predictions are considered at each time step. Implementing these correctly can be difficult, which motivates their inclusion in a NMT framework.

3   Implementation

OpenNMT is a community of projects supporting easy adoption neural machine translation. At the heart of the project are libraries for training, using, and deploying neural machine translation models. The system was based originally on *seq2seq-attn*, which was rewritten for ease of efficiency, readability, and generalizability. The project supports vanilla NMT models along with support for attention, gating, stacking, input feeding, regularization, copy models, beam search and all other options necessary for state-of-the-art performance.

OpenNMT has currently three main implementations. All of them are actively maintained:

- *OpenNMT-lua* The original project developed in Torch 7. Full-featured, optimized, and stable code ready for quick experiments and production.

- *OpenNMT-py* An OpenNMT-lua clone using PyTorch. Initially created by by Adam Lerer and the Facebook AI research team as an example, this implementation is easy to extend and particularly suited for research.

- *OpenNMT-tf* An implementation following the style of TensorFlow. This is a newer project focusing on large scale experiments and high performance model serving using the latest TensorFlow features.

OpenNMT is developed completely in the open on GitHub at (`http://github.com/opennmt`) and is MIT licensed. The initial release has primarily contributions from SYS-TRAN Paris, the Harvard NLP group and Facebook AI research. Since official beta release, the project (OpenNMT-lua, OpenNMT-py and OpenNMT-tf) has been starred by over 2500 users in total, and there have been over 100 outside contributors. The project has an active forum for community feedback with over five hundred posts in the last two months. There is also a live demonstration available of the system in use (Figure 1(b)).

One often overlooked benefit of NMT compared to SMT is its relative compactness. OpenNMT-lua including preprocessing and model variants is roughly 16K lines of code, the PyTorch version is less than 4K lines and Tensorflow version has around 7K lines. For comparison the Moses SMT framework including language modeling is over 100K lines. This makes our system easy to completely understand for newcomers. Each project is fully self-contained depending on minimal number of external libraries and also includes some preprocessing, visualization and analysis tools.

4   Design Goals

4.1   System Efficiency

As NMT systems can take from days to weeks to train, training efficiency is a paramount concern. Slightly faster training can make the difference between plausible and impossible experiments.

Memory Sharing & Sharding When training GPU-based NMT models, memory size restrictions are the most common limiter of batch size, and thus directly impact training time. Neural network toolkits, such as Torch, are often designed to trade-off extra memory allocations for speed and declarative simplicity. For OpenNMT, we wanted to have it both ways,

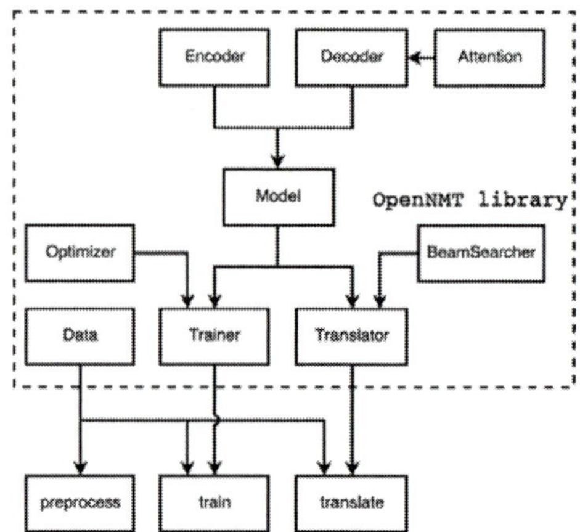

Figure 2: *Schematic overview of OpenNMT-py code*

and so we implemented an external memory sharing system that exploits the known time-series control flow of NMT systems and aggressively shares the internal buffers between clones. The potential shared buffers are dynamically calculated by exploration of the network graph before starting training. In practical use, aggressive memory reuse provides a saving of 70% of GPU memory with the default model size. For OpenNMT-py, we implemented a sharding mechanism both for data loading to enable training on extremely large datasets that cannot fit into memory, and for back-propagation to reduce memory footprints during training.

Multi-GPU OpenNMT additionally supports multi-GPU training using data parallelism. Each GPU has a replica of the master parameters and processes independent batches during training phase. Two modes are available: synchronous and asynchronous training (Dean et al., 2012). Experiments with 8 GPUs show a $6\times$ speed up in per epoch, but a slight loss in training efficiency. When training to similar loss, it gives a $3.5\times$ total speed-up to training.

C/Mobile/GPU Translation Training NMT systems requires significant code complexity to facilitate fast back-propagation-through-time. At deployment, the system is much less complex, and only requires (i) forwarding values through the network and (ii) running a beam search that is much simplified compared to SMT. OpenNMT includes several different translation deployments specialized for different run-time environments: a batched CPU/GPU implementation for very quickly translating a large set of sentences, a simple single-instance implementation for use on mobile devices, and a specialized C implementation suited for industrial use.

4.2 Modularity for Research

A secondary goal was a desire for code readability and extensibility. We targeted this goal by explicitly separating training, optimization and different components of the model, and by including tutorial documentation within the code. A schematic overview of our data structures in OpenNMT-py is shown in Figure 2. We provide users with simple interfaces *preprocess*, *train* and *translate*, which only require source/target files as input, while we provide a highly modularized library for advanced users. Each module in the library is highly customizable and configurable with multiple ready-for-use features. Advanced users can access the modules directly through a library interface to construct and train variant of the standard NMT setup.

System	BLEU-cased
uedin-nmt-ensemble	28.3
LMU-nmt-reranked-wmt17-en-de	27.1
SYSTRAN-single (OpenNMT)	26.7

Table 1: *Top 3 on English-German* newstest2017 *WMT17.*

System	Speed tok/sec Train	Trans	BLEU
Nematus	3221	252	18.25
ONMT	5254	457	19.34

System	newstest14	newstest17
seq2seq	22.19	-
Sockeye	-	25.55
ONMT	23.23 [19.34]	25.06 [22.69]

Table 2: *Performance results for EN→DE on WMT15 tested on newstest2014. Both systems 2x500 RNN, embedding size 300, 13 epochs, batch size 64, beam size 5. We compare on a 32k BPE setting.*

Table 3: *OpenNMT's performance as reported by Britz et al. (2017) and Hieber et al. (2017) (bracketed) compared to our best results. ONMT used 32k BPE, 2-layers bi-RNN of 1024, embedding size 512, dropout 0.1 and max length 100.*

Extensible Data, Models, and Search In addition to plain text, OpenNMT also supports different input types including models with discrete features (Sennrich and Haddow, 2016), models with non-sequential input such as tables, continuous data such as speech signals, and multi-dimensional data such as images. To support these different input modalities the library implements image encoder (Xu et al., 2015; Deng et al., 2017) and audio encoders (Chan et al., 2015). OpenNMT implements various attention types including general, dot product, and concatenation (Luong et al., 2015a; Britz et al., 2017). This also includes recent extensions to these standard modules such as the copy mechanism (Vinyals et al., 2015; Gu et al., 2016), which is widely used in summarization and generation applications.

The newer implementations of OpenNMT have also been updated to include support for recent innovations in non-recurrent translation models. In particular recent support has been added for convolution translation (Gehring et al., 2017) and the attention-only transformer network (Vaswani et al., 2017).

Finally, the translation code allows for user customization. In addition to out-of-vocabulary (OOV) handling (Luong et al., 2015b), OpenNMT also allows beam search with various normalizations including length and attention coverage normalization (Wu et al., 2016), and dynamic dictionary support for copy/pointer networks. We also provide an interface for customized hypothesis filtering, enabling beam search under various constraints such as maximum number of OOV's and lexical constraints.

Modularity Due to the deliberate modularity of our code, OpenNMT is readily extensible for novel feature development. As one example, by substituting the attention module, we can implement local attention (Luong et al., 2015a), sparse-max attention (Martins and Astudillo, 2016) and structured attention (Kim et al., 2017) with minimal change of code. As another example, in order to get feature-based factored neural translation (Sennrich and Haddow, 2016) we simply need to modify the input network to process the feature-based representation, and the output network to produce multiple conditionally independent predictions.

We have seen instances of this use in published research. In addition to machine translation (Levin et al., 2017; Ha et al., 2017; Ma et al., 2017), researchers have employed OpenNMT for parsing (van Noord and Bos, 2017), document summarization (Ling and Rush, 2017), data-to-

System	newstest14	newstest15
GNMT 4 layers	23.7	26.5
GNMT 8 layers	24.4	27.6
WMT reference	20.6	24.9
ONMT	23.2	26.0

Table 4: *Comparison with GNMT on EN→DE. ONMT used 2-layers bi-RNN of 1024, embedding size 512, dropout 0.1 and max length 100.*

System	newstest14	newstest17
T2T	27.3	27.8
ONMT T2T	26.8	28.0
GNMT (rnn)	24.6	-
ONMT (rnn)	23.2	25.1

Table 5: *Transformer Results on English-German newstest14 and newstest17. We use 6-layer transformer with model size of 512.*

document (Wiseman et al., 2017; Gardent et al., 2017), and transliteration (Ameur et al., 2017), to name a few of many applications.

Additional Tools OpenNMT packages several additional tools, including: 1) reversible tokenizer, which can also perform Byte Pair Encoding (BPE) (Sennrich et al., 2015); 2) loading and exporting word embeddings; 3) translation server which enables showcase results remotely; and 4) visualization tools for debugging or understanding, such as beam search visualization, profiler and TensorBoard logging.

5 Experiments

OpenNMT achieves competitive results against other systems, e.g. in the recent WMT 2017 translation task, it won third place in English-German translation with a single model as shown in Table 1. The system is also competitive in speed as shown in Table 2. Here we compare training and test speed to the publicly available *Nematus* system[1] on English-to-German (EN→DE) using the WMT2015[2] dataset.

We have found that OpenNMT's default setting is useful for experiments, but not optimal for large-scale NMT. This has been a cause of poor reported performance in other default comparisons by Britz et al. (2017) and Hieber et al. (2017). We trained models with our best effort to conform to their settings and report our results in Table 3, which shows comparable performance with other systems. We suspect that the reported poor performance is due to the fact that our default setting discards sequences of length greater than 50, which is too short for BPE. Moreover, while the reported poor performance was obtained by training with ADAM, we find that training with (the default) SGD with learning rate decay is generally better.

We also compare OpenNMT with the *GNMT* (Wu et al., 2016) model in Table 4. Vaswani et al. (2017) have established a new state-of-the-art with the Transformer model. We have also implemented this in our framework, and compare it with *Tensor2Tensor* (T2T) in Table 5. (These experiments are run on a modified version of WMT 2017, namely News Comm v11 instead of v12, and no Rapid 2016.)

Additionally we have found interest from the community in using OpenNMT for language geneation tasks like sentence document summarization and dialogue response generation, among others. Using OpenNMT, we were able to replicate the sentence summarization results of Chopra et al. (2016), reaching a ROUGE-1 score of 35.51 on the Gigaword data. We have also trained a model on 14 million sentences of the OpenSubtitles data set based on the work Vinyals and Le (2015), achieving comparable perplexity. Many other models are at `http://opennmt.net/Models-py` and `http://opennmt.net/Models`.

---

[1] `https://github.com/rsennrich/nematus` Comparison with OpenNMT/Nematus github revisions `907824/75c6ab1`

[2] `http://statmt.org/wmt15`

References

Ameur, M. S. H., Meziane, F., and Guessoum, A. (2017). Arabic machine transliteration using an attention-based encoder-decoder model. *Procedia Computer Science*, 117:287–297.

Bahdanau, D., Cho, K., and Bengio, Y. (2014). Neural Machine Translation By Jointly Learning To Align and Translate. In *ICLR*, pages 1–15.

Britz, D., Goldie, A., Luong, T., and Le, Q. (2017). Massive exploration of neural machine translation architectures. *arXiv preprint arXiv:1703.03906*.

Chan, W., Jaitly, N., Le, Q. V., and Vinyals, O. (2015). Listen, attend and spell. *CoRR*, abs/1508.01211.

Cho, K., van Merrienboer, B., Gulcehre, C., Bahdanau, D., Bougares, F., Schwenk, H., and Bengio, Y. (2014). Learning Phrase Representations using RNN Encoder-Decoder for Statistical Machine Translation. In *Proc of EMNLP*.

Chopra, S., Auli, M., and Rush, A. M. (2016). Abstractive sentence summarization with attentive recurrent neural networks. *Proceedings of NAACL-HLT16*, pages 93–98.

Chung, J., Gulcehre, C., Cho, K., and Bengio, Y. (2014). Empirical evaluation of gated recurrent neural networks on sequence modeling. *arXiv preprint arXiv:1412.3555*.

Crego, J., Kim, J., and Senellart, J. (2016). Systran's pure neural machine translation system. *arXiv preprint arXiv:1602.06023*.

Dean, J., Corrado, G., Monga, R., Chen, K., Devin, M., Mao, M., Senior, A., Tucker, P., Yang, K., Le, Q. V., et al. (2012). Large scale distributed deep networks. In *Advances in neural information processing systems*, pages 1223–1231.

Deng, Y., Kanervisto, A., Ling, J., and Rush, A. M. (2017). Image-to-markup generation with coarse-to-fine attention. In *International Conference on Machine Learning*, pages 980–989.

Dyer, C., Weese, J., Setiawan, H., Lopez, A., Ture, F., Eidelman, V., Ganitkevitch, J., Blunsom, P., and Resnik, P. (2010). cdec: A decoder, alignment, and learning framework for finite-state and context-free translation models. In *Proceedings of the ACL 2010 System Demonstrations*, pages 7–12. Association for Computational Linguistics.

Gardent, C., Shimorina, A., Narayan, S., and Perez-Beltrachini, L. (2017). The webnlg challenge: Generating text from rdf data. In *Proceedings of the 10th International Conference on Natural Language Generation*, pages 124–133.

Gehring, J., Auli, M., Grangier, D., Yarats, D., and Dauphin, Y. N. (2017). Convolutional sequence to sequence learning. *arXiv preprint arXiv:1705.03122*.

Gu, J., Lu, Z., Li, H., and Li, V. O. (2016). Incorporating copying mechanism in sequence-to-sequence learning. *arXiv preprint arXiv:1603.06393*.

Ha, T.-L., Niehues, J., and Waibel, A. (2017). Effective strategies in zero-shot neural machine translation. *arXiv preprint arXiv:1711.07893*.

Hieber, F., Domhan, T., Denkowski, M., Vilar, D., Sokolov, A., Clifton, A., and Post, M. (2017). Sockeye: A toolkit for neural machine translation. *arXiv preprint arXiv:1712.05690*.

Hochreiter, S. and Schmidhuber, J. (1997). Long short-term memory. *Neural computation*, 9(8):1735–1780.

Kim, Y., Denton, C., Hoang, L., and Rush, A. M. (2017). Structured attention networks. *arXiv preprint arXiv:1702.00887*.

Koehn, P., Hoang, H., Birch, A., Callison-Burch, C., Federico, M., Bertoldi, N., Cowan, B., Shen, W., Moran, C., Zens, R., et al. (2007). Moses: Open source toolkit for statistical machine translation. In *Proc ACL*, pages 177–180. Association for Computational Linguistics.

Levin, P., Dhanuka, N., Khalil, T., Kovalev, F., and Khalilov, M. (2017). Toward a full-scale neural machine translation in production: the booking. com use case. *arXiv preprint arXiv:1709.05820*.

Ling, J. and Rush, A. (2017). Coarse-to-fine attention models for document summarization. In *Proceedings of the Workshop on New Frontiers in Summarization*, pages 33–42.

Luong, M.-T., Pham, H., and Manning, C. D. (2015a). Effective Approaches to Attention-based Neural Machine Translation. In *Proc of EMNLP*.

Luong, M.-T., Sutskever, I., Le, Q., Vinyals, O., and Zaremba, W. (2015b). Addressing the Rare Word Problem in Neural Machine Translation. In *Proc of ACL*.

Ma, M., Li, D., Zhao, K., and Huang, L. (2017). Osu multimodal machine translation system report. *arXiv preprint arXiv:1710.02718*.

Martins, A. F. and Astudillo, R. F. (2016). From softmax to sparsemax: A sparse model of attention and multi-label classification. *arXiv preprint arXiv:1602.02068*.

Sennrich, R. and Haddow, B. (2016). Linguistic input features improve neural machine translation. *arXiv preprint arXiv:1606.02892*.

Sennrich, R., Haddow, B., and Birch, A. (2015). Neural machine translation of rare words with subword units. *CoRR*, abs/1508.07909.

Sutskever, I., Vinyals, O., and Le, Q. V. (2014). Sequence to Sequence Learning with Neural Networks. In *NIPS*, page 9.

van Noord, R. and Bos, J. (2017). Neural semantic parsing by character-based translation: Experiments with abstract meaning representations. *arXiv preprint arXiv:1705.09980*.

Vaswani, A., Shazeer, N., Parmar, N., Uszkoreit, J., Jones, L., Gomez, A. N., Kaiser, L., and Polosukhin, I. (2017). Attention is all you need. *arXiv preprint arXiv:1706.03762*.

Vinyals, O., Fortunato, M., and Jaitly, N. (2015). Pointer networks. In *Advances in Neural Information Processing Systems*, pages 2692–2700.

Vinyals, O. and Le, Q. (2015). A neural conversational model. *arXiv preprint arXiv:1506.05869*.

Wiseman, S., Shieber, S. M., and Rush, A. M. (2017). Challenges in data-to-document generation. *arXiv preprint arXiv:1707.08052*.

Wu, Y., Schuster, M., Chen, Z., Le, Q. V., Norouzi, M., Macherey, W., Krikun, M., Cao, Y., Gao, Q., Macherey, K., et al. (2016). Google's neural machine translation system: Bridging the gap between human and machine translation. *arXiv preprint arXiv:1609.08144*.

Xu, K., Ba, J., Kiros, R., Cho, K., Courville, A., Salakhudinov, R., Zemel, R., and Bengio, Y. (2015). Show, attend and tell: Neural image caption generation with visual attention. In *International Conference on Machine Learning*, pages 2048–2057.

XNMT: The eXtensible Neural Machine Translation Toolkit

Graham Neubig — Carnegie Mellon University, Pittsburgh, USA

Matthias Sperber — Karlsruhe Institute of Technology, Karlsruhe, Germany

Xinyi Wang, Matthieu Felix, Austin Matthews, Sarguna Padmanabhan, Ye Qi, Devendra Singh Sachan — Carnegie Mellon University, Pittsburgh, USA

Philip Arthur — Nara Institute of Science and Technology, Nara, Japan

Pierre Godard — LIMSI/CNRS/Université Paris-Saclay, Orsay, France

John Hewitt — University of Pennsylvania, Philadelphia, USA

Rachid Riad — ENS/CNRS/EHESS/INRIA, Paris, France

Liming Wang — University of Illinois, Urbana-Champaign, USA

Abstract

This paper describes XNMT, the eXtensible Neural Machine Translation toolkit. XNMT distinguishes itself from other open-source NMT toolkits by its focus on modular code design, with the purpose of enabling fast iteration in research and replicable, reliable results. In this paper we describe the design of XNMT and its experiment configuration system, and demonstrate its utility on the tasks of machine translation, speech recognition, and multi-tasked machine translation/parsing. XNMT is available open-source at `https://github.com/neulab/xnmt`.

1 Introduction

Due to the effectiveness and relative ease of implementation, there is now a proliferation of toolkits for neural machine translation (Kalchbrenner and Blunsom, 2013; Sutskever et al., 2014; Bahdanau et al., 2015), as many as 51 according to the tally by `nmt-list`.[1] The common requirements for such toolkits are speed, memory efficiency, and translation accuracy, which are essential for the use of such systems in practical translation settings. Many open source toolkits do an excellent job at this to the point where they can be used in production systems (e.g. OpenNMT[2] is used by Systran (Crego et al., 2016)).

This paper describes XNMT, the eXtensible Neural Machine Translation toolkit, a toolkit that optimizes not for efficiency, but instead for ease of use in practical research settings. In other words, instead of only optimizing time for training or inference, XNMT aims to reduce the time it takes for a researcher to turn their idea into a practical experimental setting, test with a large number of parameters, and produce valid and trustable research results. Of course, this necessitates a certain level of training efficiency and accuracy, but XNMT also takes into account a number of considerations, such as those below:

- XNMT places a heavy focus on modular code design, making it easy to swap in and out different parts of the model. Ideally, implementing research prototypes with XNMT involves only few changes to existing code.

---

[1] `https://github.com/jonsafari/nmt-list`
[2] `http://opennmt.net`

- XNMT is implemented in Python, the de facto standard in the research community.

- XNMT uses DyNet (Neubig et al., 2017) as its deep learning framework. DyNet uses dynamic computation graphs, which makes it possible to write code in a very natural way, and benefit from additional flexibility to implement complex networks with dynamic structure, as are often beneficial in natural language processing. Further benefits include transparent handling of batching operations, or even removing explicit batch handling and relying on autobatching for speed-up instead.

- XNMT of course contains standard NMT models, but also includes functionality for optimization using reinforcement learning (Ranzato et al., 2015) or minimum risk training (Shen et al., 2016), flexible multi-task learning (Dai and Le, 2015), encoders for speech (Chan et al., 2016), and training and testing of retrieval-based models (Huang et al., 2013).

In the remainder of the paper, we provide some concrete examples of the design principles behind XNMT, and a few examples of how it can be used to implement standard models.

2 Model Structure and Specification

2.1 NMT Design Dimensions: Model, Training, and Inference

When training an NMT system there are a number of high-level design decisions that we need to make: what kind of model do we use? how do we test this model? at test time, how do we generate outputs? Each of these decisions has a number of sub-components.

For example, when specifying our model, if we are using a standard attentional model such as that defined by Bahdanau et al. (Bahdanau et al., 2015), we must at least decide:

Input Data Format: Do we use plain text or structured data such as trees?

Embedding: Do we lookup words in a table or encode their characters or other units?

Encoder: Do we use bidirectional LSTMs, convolutional nets, self attention?

Decoder: Do we use standard LSTM-based word-by-word decoders or add tricks such as memory, syntax, or chunks?

Attention: Do we use multi-layer perceptrons, dot-products, or something else?

When specifying the training regimen, there are also choices, including:

Loss Function: Do we use maximum likelihood or a sequence-based training criterion such as REINFORCE or minimum-risk training?

Batching. How many sentences in a mini-batch, and do we sort by length before batching?

Optimizer: What optimization method do we use to update our parameters?

Stopping Criterion: How do we decide when to stop training?

And in inference, there are also options:

Search Strategy: Do we perform greedy search? beam search? random sampling?

Decoding Time Score Adjustment: At decoding time, do we do something like length normalization to give longer hypotheses higher probability?

Within XNMT, effort is made to encapsulate these design decisions in Python classes, making it possible for a researcher who wants to experiment with new alternatives to any of these decisions to implement a new version of the class and compare it with other similar alternatives.

2.2 YAML Model Specification

In order to specify experimental settings, XNMT uses configuration files in YAML[3] format, which provides an easy-to-read, Python-like syntax. An example of such a file, demonstrating

---

[3]http://yaml.readthedocs.io/en/latest/example.html

```
mini_exp: !Experiment # top of experiment hierarchy
  exp_global: !ExpGlobal # global (default) experiment settings
    model_file: examples/output/{EXP}.mod
    log_file: examples/output/{EXP}.log
    default_layer_dim: 512
    dropout: 0.3
  model: !DefaultTranslator # attentional seq2seq model
    src_reader: !PlainTextReader
      vocab: !Vocab {vocab_file: examples/data/train.ja.vocab}
    trg_reader: !PlainTextReader
      vocab: !Vocab {vocab_file: examples/data/train.en.vocab}
    src_embedder: !SimpleWordEmbedder {} # {} indicates defaults
    encoder: !BiLSTMSeqTransducer
      layers: 1
    attender: !MlpAttender {}
    trg_embedder: !SimpleWordEmbedder
      emb_dim: 128 # if not set, default_layer_dim is used
    decoder: !MlpSoftmaxDecoder
      layers: 1
      bridge: !CopyBridge {}
  train: !SimpleTrainingRegimen # training strategy
    run_for_epochs: 20
    batcher: !SrcBatcher
      batch_size: 32
    src_file: examples/data/train.ja
    trg_file: examples/data/train.en
    dev_tasks: # what to evaluate at every epoch
      - !LossEvalTask
        src_file: examples/data/dev.ja
        ref_file: examples/data/dev.en
  evaluate: # what to evaluate at the end of training
    - !AccuracyEvalTask
      src_file: examples/data/test.ja
      ref_file: examples/data/test.en
      eval_metrics: bleu
```

Figure 1: Example configuration file

how it is possible to specify choices along the various design dimensions in §2.1 is shown in Figure 1.[4] As shown in the example, XNMT configuration files specify a hierarchy of objects, with the top level always being an `Experiment` including specification of the model, training, and evaluation, along with a few global parameters shared across the various steps.

One thing that is immediately noticeable from the file is the `!` syntax, which allows to directly specify Python class objects inside the YAML file. For any item in the YAML hierarchy that is specified in this way, all of its children in the hierarchy are expected to be the arguments to its constructor (the Python method). So for example, if a user wanted to test create a method for convolutional character-based encoding of words (Zhang et al., 2015) and see its result on machine translation, they would have to define a new class `ConvolutionalWordEmbedder(filter_width, embedding_size=512)`, implement it appropriately, then in the YAML file replace the `src_embedder:` line with

optionally omitting `embedding_size:` if the defaults are acceptable.

---

[4]For many of these parameters XNMT has reasonable defaults, so the standard configuration file is generally not this verbose.

```
src_embedder: !ConvolutionalWordEmbedder
  filter_width: 3
  embedding_size: 512
```

As may be evident from the example, this greatly helps extensibility for two reasons: (1) there is no passing along of command line arguments or parsing of complex argument types necessary. Instead, objects are simply configured via their Python interface as given in the code, and newly added features can immediately be controlled from the configuration file without extra argument handling. (2) Changing behavior is as simple as adding a new Python class, implementing the required interface, and requesting the newly implemented class in the configuration file instead of the original one.

2.3 Experimental Setup and Support

As Figure 1 demonstrates, XNMT supports the basic functionality for experiments described in §2.1. In the example, the model specifies the input data structure to be plain text (`PlainTextReader`), word embedding method to be a standard lookup-table based embedding (`SimpleWordEmbedder`), encoder to be a bidirectional LSTM (`BiLSTMSeqTransducer`), attender to be a multi-layer perceptron based attention method (`MlpAttender`), and the decoder to use a LSTM with a MLP-based softmax (`MlpSoftmaxDecoder`). Similarly, in the `training:` and `evaluate:` subsections, the training and evaluation parameters are set as well.

XNMT also provides a number of conveniences to support efficient experimentation:

Named experiments and overwriting: Experiments are given a name such as `mini_exp`. {EXP} strings in the configuration file are automatically overwritten by this experiment name, distinguishing between log or model files from different experiments.

Multiple experiments and sharing of parameters: Multiple experiments can be specified in a single YAML file by defining multiple top-level elements of the YAML file. These multiple experiments can share settings through YAML anchors, where one experiment can inherit the settings from another, only overwriting the relevant settings that needs to be changed.

Saving configurations: For reproducibility, XNMT dumps the whole experiment specification when saving a model. Thus, experiments can be re-run by simply opening the configuration file associated with any model.

Re-starting training: A common requirement is loading a previously trained model, be it for fine-tuning on different data, tuning decoding parameters, or testing on different data. XNMT allows this by re-loading the dumped configuration file, overwriting a subset of the settings such as file paths, decoding parameters, or training parameters, and re-running the experiment.

Random parameter search: Often we would like to tune parameter values by trying several different configurations. Currently XNMT makes it possible to do so by defining a set of parameters to evaluate and then searching over them using random search. In the future, we may support other strategies such as Bayesian optimization or enumeration.

3 Advanced Features

3.1 Advanced Modeling Techniques

XNMT provides a wide library of standard modeling tools of use in performing NMT such as speech-oriented encoders (Chan et al., 2016; Harwath et al., 2016) that can be used in speech recognition, preliminary support for self-attentional "Transformer" models (Vaswani et al., 2017). It also has the ability to perform experiments in retrieval (Huang et al., 2013) instead of sequence generation.

```
tied_exp: !Experiment
  ...
  model: !DefaultTranslator
    ..
    trg_embedder: !DenseWordEmbedder
      emb_dim: 128
    decoder: !MlpSoftmaxDecoder
      layers: 1
      bridge: !CopyBridge {}
      vocab_projector: !Ref { path: model.trg_embedder }
```

Figure 2: Illustration of referencing mechanism

3.2 Parameter Sharing and Multi-task Learning

Modern deep learning architectures often include parameter sharing between certain components. For example, tying the output projection matrices and embeddings has been proposed by Press and Wolf (2016). While it would be possible to develop a specialized component to achieve this, XNMT features a referencing mechanism that allows simply tying the already existing components (Figure 2). References are created by specifying the path of the object to which they point, and result in the exact same object instance being used in both places. The only requirement is for the object's interface to be compatible with both usages, which is usually easily achieved using Python's duck typing coding paradigm.

This component sharing is also very useful in multi-task training paradigms, where two tasks are trained simultaneously and share some or all of their component parts. This multi-task training can be achieved by replacing the `SimpleTrainingRegimen` with other regimens specified for multi-task learning, and defining two or more training tasks that use different input data, models, or training parameters.

3.3 Training and Inference Methods

XNMT provides several advanced methods for training and inference. With regards to training, XNMT notably makes it easy to implement other training criteria such as REINFORCE or minimum risk training by defining a separate class implementing the training strategy. REINFORCE has been implemented, and more training criteria may be added in the near future. For inference, it is also possible to specify several search strategies (e.g. beam search), along with several length normalization strategies that helps reduce the penalty on long sentences.

4 Case Studies

In this section, we describe three case studies of using XNMT to perform various experiments: a standard machine translation experiment (§4.1), a speech recognition experiment (§4.2), and a multi-task learning experiment where we train a parser along with an MT model (§4.3).

4.1 Machine Translation

We trained a machine translation model on the WMT English-German benchmark, using the preprocessed data by Stanford.[5] Our model was a basic 1-layer model with bidirectional LSTM encoder and 256 units per direction, LSTM decoder output projections and MLP attention mechanism all with 512 hidden units. We applied joint BPE of size 32k (Sennrich et al., 2016). We also applied input feeding, as well as variational dropout of rate 0.3 to encoder and decoder LSTMs. Decoding was performed with a beam of size 1. Overall, results were similar, with our model achieving a BLEU of 18.26 and Luong et al. (2015) achieving a BLEU of 18.1. Note that the model by Luong et al. (2015) is simpler because it does not use BPE and only a unidirectional encoder.

---

[5]`https://nlp.stanford.edu/projects/nmt/`

Model	WSJ dev93	WSJ eval92	TEDLIUM dev	TEDLIUM test
XNMT	16.65	13.50	15.83	16.16
Zhang et al. (2017)	—	14.76	—	
Rousseau et al. (2014)	—	—	15.7	17.8

Table 1: Speech recognition results (WER in %) compared to a similar pyramidal LSTM model (Zhang et al., 2017) and a highly engineered hybrid HMM system (Rousseau et al., 2014).

4.2 Speech Recognition

We performed experiments in a speech recognition task with a simple listen-attend-spell model (Chan et al., 2016). This model features a 4-layer pyramidal LSTM encoder, subsampling the input sequence by factor 2 at every layer except the first, resulting in an overall subsampling factor of 8. The layer size is set to 512, the target embedding size is 64, and the attention uses an MLP of size 128. Input to the model are Mel-filterbank features with 40 coefficients. For regularization, we apply variational dropout of rate 0.3 in all LSTMs, and word dropout of rate 0.1 on the target side (Gal and Ghahramani, 2016). For training, we use Adam (Kingma and Ba, 2014) with initial learning rate of 0.0003, which is decayed by factor 0.5 if no improved in WER is observed. To further facilitate training, label smoothing (Szegedy et al., 2016) is applied. For the search, we use beam size 20 and length normalization with the exponent set to 1.5. We test this model on both the Wall Street Journal (WSJ; Paul and Baker (1992)) corpus which contains read speech, and the TEDLIUM corpus (Rousseau et al., 2014) which contains recorded TED talks. Numbers are shown in Table 4.2. Comparison to results from the literature shows that our results are competitive.

4.3 Multi-task MT + Parsing

We performed multi-task training of a sequence-to-sequence model for parsing and machine translation. The main task is the parsing task, and we followed the general setup in (Vinyals et al., 2015), but we only used the standard WSJ training data. It is jointly trained with an English-German translation system. Compared to a single sequence-to-sequence model for parsing with the same hyperparameters as the multi-task model, a model trained only on WSJ achieved a test F-score of 81%, while the multi-task trained model achieved an F-score of 83%. This experiment was done with very few modifications to existing XNMT multi-task architecture, demonstrating that it is relatively easy to apply multi-tasking to new tasks.

5 Conclusion

This paper has introduced XNMT, an NMT toolkit with extensibility in mind, and has described the various design decisions that went into making this goal possible.

Acknowledgments

Part of the development of XNMT was performed at the Jelinek Summer Workshop in Speech and Language Technology (JSALT) "Speaking Rosetta Stone" project (Scharenborg et al., 2018), and we are grateful to the JSALT organizers for the financial/logistical support, and also participants of the workshop for their feedback on XNMT as a tool.

Parts of this work were sponsored by Defense Advanced Research Projects Agency Information Innovation Office (I2O). Program: Low Resource Languages for Emergent Incidents (LORELEI). Issued by DARPA/I2O under Contract No. HR0011-15-C-0114. The views and conclusions contained in this document are those of the authors and should not be interpreted as representing the official policies, either expressed or implied, of the U.S. Government. The U.S. Government is authorized to reproduce and distribute reprints for Government purposes notwithstanding any copyright notation here on.

References

Bahdanau, D., Cho, K., and Bengio, Y. (2015). Neural Machine Translation by Jointly Learning to Align and Translate. *Proc. of ICLR*.

Chan, W., Jaitly, N., Le, Q., and Vinyals, O. (2016). Listen, attend and spell: A neural network for large vocabulary conversational speech recognition. In *Acoustics, Speech and Signal Processing (ICASSP), 2016 IEEE International Conference on*, pages 4960–4964. IEEE.

Crego, J., Kim, J., Klein, G., Rebollo, A., Yang, K., Senellart, J., Akhanov, E., Brunelle, P., Coquard, A., Deng, Y., et al. (2016). Systran's pure neural machine translation systems. *arXiv preprint arXiv:1610.05540*.

Dai, A. M. and Le, Q. V. (2015). Semi-supervised sequence learning. In *Advances in Neural Information Processing Systems*, pages 3079–3087.

Gal, Y. and Ghahramani, Z. (2016). A theoretically grounded application of dropout in recurrent neural networks. In *Advances in neural information processing systems*, pages 1019–1027.

Harwath, D., Torralba, A., and Glass, J. (2016). Unsupervised learning of spoken language with visual context. In *Advances in Neural Information Processing Systems*, pages 1858–1866.

Huang, P.-S., He, X., Gao, J., Deng, L., Acero, A., and Heck, L. (2013). Learning deep structured semantic models for web search using clickthrough data. In *Proceedings of the 22nd ACM international conference on Conference on information & knowledge management*, pages 2333–2338. ACM.

Kalchbrenner, N. and Blunsom, P. (2013). Recurrent Continuous Translation Models. In *Empirical Methods in Natural Language Processing (EMNLP)*, pages 1700–1709, Seattle, Washington, USA.

Kingma, D. P. and Ba, J. (2014). Adam: A method for stochastic optimization. *arXiv preprint arXiv:1412.6980*.

Luong, M.-T., Pham, H., and Manning, C. D. (2015). Effective approaches to attention-based neural machine translation. *arXiv preprint arXiv:1508.04025*.

Neubig, G., Dyer, C., Goldberg, Y., Matthews, A., Ammar, W., Anastasopoulos, A., Ballesteros, M., Chiang, D., Clothiaux, D., Cohn, T., Duh, K., Faruqui, M., Gan, C., Garrette, D., Ji, Y., Kong, L., Kuncoro, A., Kumar, G., Malaviya, C., Michel, P., Oda, Y., Richardson, M., Saphra, N., Swayamdipta, S., and Yin, P. (2017). DyNet: The Dynamic Neural Network Toolkit. *arXiv preprint arXiv:1701.03980*.

Paul, D. B. and Baker, J. M. (1992). The design for the wall street journal-based csr corpus. In *Proceedings of the workshop on Speech and Natural Language*, pages 357–362. Association for Computational Linguistics.

Press, O. and Wolf, L. (2016). Using the output embedding to improve language models. *arXiv preprint arXiv:1608.05859*.

Ranzato, M., Chopra, S., Auli, M., and Zaremba, W. (2015). Sequence level training with recurrent neural networks. *arXiv preprint arXiv:1511.06732*.

Rousseau, A., Deléglise, P., and Estève, Y. (2014). Enhancing the ted-lium corpus with selected data for language modeling and more ted talks. In *LREC*, pages 3935–3939.

Scharenborg, O., Besacier, L., Black, A., Hasegawa-Johnson, M., Metze, F., Neubig, G., Stuker, S., Godard, P., Muller, M., Ondel, L., Palaskar, S., Arthur, P., Ciannella, F., Du, M., Larsen, E., Merkx, D., Riad, R., Wang, L., and Dupoux, E. (2018). Linguistic unit discovery from multi-modal inputs in unwritten languages: Summary of the "speaking rosetta" JSALT 2017 workshop. In *2018 IEEE International Conference on Acoustics, Speech, and Signal Processing (ICASSP 2018)*, Calgary, Canada.

Sennrich, R., Haddow, B., and Birch, A. (2016). Neural machine translation of rare words with subword units. In *54th Annual Meeting of the Association for Computational Linguistics*.

Shen, S., Cheng, Y., He, Z., He, W., Wu, H., Sun, M., and Liu, Y. (2016). Minimum risk training for neural machine translation. In *Proceedings of the 54th Annual Meeting of the Association for Computational Linguistics (Volume 1: Long Papers)*, pages 1683–1692, Berlin, Germany. Association for Computational Linguistics.

Sutskever, I., Vinyals, O., and Le, Q. V. (2014). Sequence to Sequence Learning with Neural Networks. In *Advances in Neural Information Processing Systems (NIPS)*, pages 3104–3112, Montréal, Canada.

Szegedy, C., Vanhoucke, V., Ioffe, S., Shlens, J., and Wojna, Z. (2016). Rethinking the inception architecture for computer vision. In *Proceedings of the IEEE Conference on Computer Vision and Pattern Recognition*, pages 2818–2826.

Vaswani, A., Shazeer, N., Parmar, N., Uszkoreit, J., Jones, L., Gomez, A. N., Kaiser, Ł., and Polosukhin, I. (2017). Attention is all you need. In *Advances in Neural Information Processing Systems*, pages 6000–6010.

Vinyals, O., Kaiser, L., Koo, T., Petrov, S., Sutskever, I., and Hinton, G. E. (2015). Grammar as a foreign language. In *Advances in Neural Information Processing Systems 28: Annual Conference on Neural Information Processing Systems 2015, December 7-12, 2015, Montreal, Quebec, Canada*, pages 2773–2781.

Zhang, X., Zhao, J., and LeCun, Y. (2015). Character-level convolutional networks for text classification. In *Advances in neural information processing systems*, pages 649–657.

Zhang, Y., Chan, W., and Jaitly, N. (2017). Very deep convolutional networks for end-to-end speech recognition. In *Acoustics, Speech and Signal Processing (ICASSP), 2017 IEEE International Conference on*, pages 4845–4849. IEEE.

Tensor2Tensor for Neural Machine Translation

Ashish Vaswani, Samy Bengio, Eugene Brevdo, Francois Chollet, Aidan N. Gomez, Stephan Gouws, Llion Jones, Łukasz Kaiser, Nal Kalchbrenner, Niki Parmar, Ryan Sepassi, Noam Shazeer, Jakob Uszkoreit

Abstract

Tensor2Tensor is a library for deep learning models that is very well-suited for neural machine translation and includes the reference implementation of the state-of-the-art Transformer model.

1 Neural Machine Translation Background

Machine translation using deep neural networks achieved great success with sequence-to-sequence models Sutskever et al. (2014); Bahdanau et al. (2014); Cho et al. (2014) that used recurrent neural networks (RNNs) with LSTM cells Hochreiter and Schmidhuber (1997). The basic sequence-to-sequence architecture is composed of an RNN encoder which reads the source sentence one token at a time and transforms it into a fixed-sized state vector. This is followed by an RNN decoder, which generates the target sentence, one token at a time, from the state vector.

While a pure sequence-to-sequence recurrent neural network can already obtain good translation results Sutskever et al. (2014); Cho et al. (2014), it suffers from the fact that the whole input sentence needs to be encoded into a single fixed-size vector. This clearly manifests itself in the degradation of translation quality on longer sentences and was partially overcome in Bahdanau et al. (2014) by using a neural model of attention.

Convolutional architectures have been used to obtain good results in word-level neural machine translation starting from Kalchbrenner and Blunsom (2013) and later in Meng et al. (2015). These early models used a standard RNN on top of the convolution to generate the output, which creates a bottleneck and hurts performance.

Fully convolutional neural machine translation without this bottleneck was first achieved in Kaiser and Bengio (2016) and Kalchbrenner et al. (2016). The model in Kaiser and Bengio (2016) (Extended Neural GPU) used a recurrent stack of gated convolutional layers, while the model in Kalchbrenner et al. (2016) (ByteNet) did away with recursion and used left-padded convolutions in the decoder. This idea, introduced in WaveNet van den Oord et al. (2016), significantly improves efficiency of the model. The same technique was improved in a number of neural translation models recently, including Gehring et al. (2017) and Kaiser et al. (2017).

2 Self-Attention

Instead of convolutions, one can use stacked self-attention layers. This was introduced in the Transformer model Vaswani et al. (2017) and has significantly improved state-of-the-art in machine translation and language modeling while also improving the speed of training. Research continues in applying the model in more domains and exploring the space of self-attention mechanisms. It is clear that self-attention is a powerful tool in general-purpose sequence modeling.

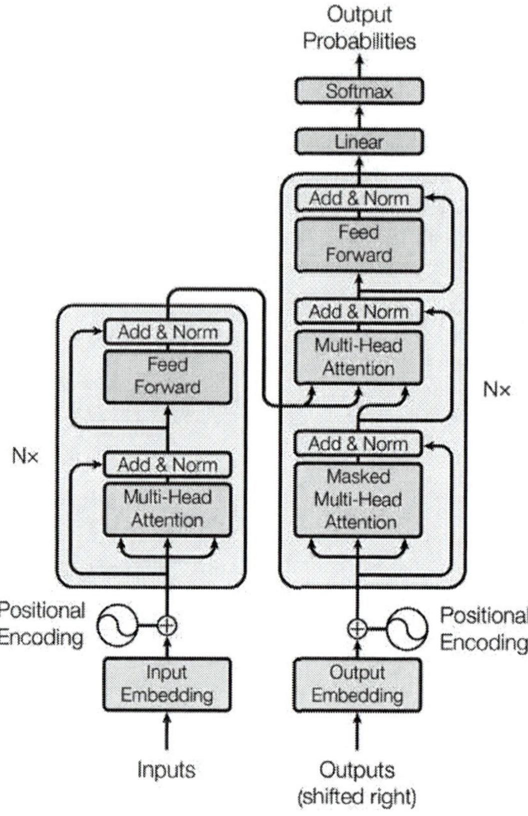

Figure 1: The Transformer model architecture.

While RNNs represent sequence history in their hidden state, the Transformer has no such fixed-size bottleneck. Instead, each timestep has full direct access to the history through the dot-product attention mechanism. This has the effect of both enabling the model to learn more distant temporal relationships, as well as speeding up training because there is no need to wait for a hidden state to propagate across time. This comes at the cost of memory usage, as the attention mechanism scales with t^2, where t is the length the sequence. Future work may reduce this scaling factor.

The Transformer model is illustrated in Figure 1. It uses stacked self-attention and point-wise, fully connected layers for both the encoder and decoder, shown in the left and right halves of Figure 1 respectively.

Encoder: The encoder is composed of a stack of identical layers. Each layer has two sub-layers. The first is a multi-head self-attention mechanism, and the second is a simple, positionwise fully connected feed-forward network.

Decoder: The decoder is also composed of a stack of identical layers. In addition to the two sub-layers in each encoder layer, the decoder inserts a third sub-layer, which performs multi-head attention over the output of the encoder stack.

More details about multi-head attention and overall architecture can be found in Vaswani et al. (2017).

3   Tensor2Tensor

Tensor2Tensor (T2T) is a library of deep learning models and datasets designed to make deep learning research faster and more accessible. T2T uses TensorFlow, Abadi et al. (2016), throughout and there is a strong focus on performance as well as usability. Through its use of TensorFlow and various T2T-specific abstractions, researchers can train models on CPU, GPU (single or multiple), and TPU, locally and in the cloud, usually with no or minimal device-specific code or configuration.

Development began focused on neural machine translation and so Tensor2Tensor includes many of the most successful NMT models and standard datasets. It has since added support for other task types as well across multiple media (text, images, video, audio). Both the number of models and datasets has grown significantly.

Usage is standardized across models and problems which makes it easy to try a new model on multiple problems or try multiple models on a single problem. See Example Usage (appendix B) to see some of the usability benefits of standardization of commands and unification of datasets, models, and training, evaluation, decoding procedures.

Development is done in the open on GitHub (http://github.com/tensorflow/tensor2tensor) with many contributors inside and outside Google.

4   System Overview

There are five key components that specify a training run in Tensor2Tensor:

1. Datasets: The `Problem` class encapsulate everything about a particular dataset. A `Problem` can generate the dataset from scratch, usually downloading data from a public source, building a vocabulary, and writing encoded samples to disk. `Problems` also produce input pipelines for training and evaluation as well as any necessary additional information per feature (for example, its type, vocabulary size, and an encoder able to convert samples to and from human and machine-readable representations).

2. Device configuration: the type, number, and location of devices. TensorFlow and Tensor2Tensor currently support CPU, GPU, and TPU in single and multi-device configurations. Tensor2Tensor also supports both synchronous and asynchronous data-parallel training.

3. Hyperparameters: parameters that control the instantiation of the model and training procedure (for example, the number of hidden layers or the optimizer's learning rate). These are specified in code and named so they can be easily shared and reproduced.

4. Model: the model ties together the preceding components to instantiate the parameterized transformation from inputs to targets, compute the loss and evaluation metrics, and construct the optimization procedure.

5. `Estimator` and `Experiment`: These classes that are part of TensorFlow handle instantiating the runtime, running the training loop, and executing basic support services like model checkpointing, logging, and alternation between training and evaluation.

These abstractions enable users to focus their attention only on the component they're interested in experimenting with. Users that wish to try models on a new problem usually only have to define a new problem. Users that wish to create or modify models only have to create a model or edit hyperparameters. The other components remain untouched, out of the way, and available for use, all of which reduces mental load and allows users to more quickly iterate on their ideas at scale.

Appendix A contains an outline of the code and appendix B contains example usage.

5   Library of research components

Tensor2Tensor provides a vehicle for research ideas to be quickly tried out and shared. Components that prove to be very useful can be committed to more widely-used libraries like Tensor-Flow, which contains many standard layers, optimizers, and other higher-level components.

Tensor2Tensor supports library usage as well as script usage so that users can reuse specific components in their own model or system. For example, multiple researchers are continuing work on extensions and variations of the attention-based Transformer model and the availability of the attention building blocks enables that work.

Some examples:

- The Image Transformer Parmar et al. (2018) extends the Transformer model to images. It relies heavily on many of the attention building blocks in Tensor2Tensor and adds many of its own.

- `tf.contrib.layers.rev_block`, implementing a memory-efficient block of reversible layers as presented in Gomez et al. (2017), was first implemented and exercised in Tensor2Tensor.

- The Adafactor optimizer (pending publication), which significantly reduces memory requirements for second-moment estimates, was developed within Tensor2Tensor and tried on various models and problems.

- `tf.contrib.data.bucket_by_sequence_length` enables efficient processing of sequence inputs on GPUs in the new `tf.data.Dataset` input pipeline API. It was first implemented and exercised in Tensor2Tensor.

6   Reproducibility and Continuing Development

Continuing development on a machine learning codebase while maintaining the quality of models is a difficult task because of the expense and randomness of model training. Freezing a codebase to maintain a certain configuration, or moving to an append-only process has enormous usability and development costs.

We attempt to mitigate the impact of ongoing development on historical reproducibility through 3 mechanisms:

1. Named and versioned hyperparameter sets in code

2. End-to-end regression tests that run on a regular basis for important model-problem pairs and verify that certain quality metrics are achieved.

3. Setting random seeds on multiple levels (Python, numpy, and TensorFlow) to mitigate the effects of randomness (though this is effectively impossible to achieve in full in a multithreaded, distributed, floating-point system).

If necessary, because the code is under version control on GitHub (http://github.com/tensorflow/tensor2tensor), we can always recover the exact code that produced certain experiment results.

References

Abadi, M., Barham, P., Chen, J., Chen, Z., Davis, A., Dean, J., Devin, M., Ghemawat, S., Irving, G., Isard, M., Kudlur, M., Levenberg, J., Monga, R., Moore, S., Murray, D. G., Steiner, B., Tucker, P., Vasudevan, V., Warden, P., Wicke, M., Yu, Y., and Zheng, X. (2016). Tensorflow: A system for large-scale machine learning. In *12th USENIX Symposium on Operating Systems Design and Implementation (OSDI 16)*, pages 265–283.

Bahdanau, D., Cho, K., and Bengio, Y. (2014). Neural machine translation by jointly learning to align and translate. *CoRR*, abs/1409.0473.

Cho, K., van Merrienboer, B., Gulcehre, C., Bougares, F., Schwenk, H., and Bengio, Y. (2014). Learning phrase representations using RNN encoder-decoder for statistical machine translation. *CoRR*, abs/1406.1078.

Gehring, J., Auli, M., Grangier, D., Yarats, D., and Dauphin, Y. N. (2017). Convolutional sequence to sequence learning. *CoRR*, abs/1705.03122.

Gomez, A. N., Ren, M., Urtasun, R., and Grosse, R. B. (2017). The reversible residual network: Backpropagation without storing activations. *CoRR*, abs/1707.04585.

Hochreiter, S. and Schmidhuber, J. (1997). Long short-term memory. *Neural computation*, 9(8):1735–1780.

Kaiser, Ł. and Bengio, S. (2016). Can active memory replace attention? In *Advances in Neural Information Processing Systems*, pages 3781–3789.

Kaiser, L., Gomez, A. N., and Chollet, F. (2017). Depthwise separable convolutions for neural machine translation. *CoRR*, abs/1706.03059.

Kalchbrenner, N. and Blunsom, P. (2013). Recurrent continuous translation models. In *Proceedings EMNLP 2013*, pages 1700–1709.

Kalchbrenner, N., Espeholt, L., Simonyan, K., van den Oord, A., Graves, A., and Kavukcuoglu, K. (2016). Neural machine translation in linear time. *CoRR*, abs/1610.10099.

Meng, F., Lu, Z., Wang, M., Li, H., Jiang, W., and Liu, Q. (2015). Encoding source language with convolutional neural network for machine translation. In *ACL*, pages 20–30.

Parmar, N., Vaswani, A., Uszkoreit, J., Kaiser, Ł., Shazeer, N., and Ku, A. (2018). Image Transformer. *ArXiv e-prints*.

Sutskever, I., Vinyals, O., and Le, Q. V. (2014). Sequence to sequence learning with neural networks. In *Advances in Neural Information Processing Systems*, pages 3104–3112.

van den Oord, A., Dieleman, S., Zen, H., Simonyan, K., Vinyals, O., Graves, A., Kalchbrenner, N., Senior, A., and Kavukcuoglu, K. (2016). WaveNet: A generative model for raw audio. *CoRR*, abs/1609.03499.

Vaswani, A., Shazeer, N., Parmar, N., Uszkoreit, J., Jones, L., Gomez, A. N., Kaiser, L., and Polosukhin, I. (2017). Attention is all you need. *CoRR*.

A Tensor2Tensor Code Outline

- Create `HParams`

- Create `RunConfig` specifying devices

    - Create and include the `Parallelism` object in the `RunConfig` which enables data-parallel duplication of the model on multiple devices (for example, for multi-GPU synchronous training).

- Create `Experiment`, including training and evaluation hooks which control support services like logging and checkpointing

- Create `Estimator` encapsulating the model function

    - `T2TModel.estimator_model_fn`
        * `model(features)`
            · `model.bottom`: This uses feature type information from the `Problem` to transform the input features into a form consumable by the model body (for example, embedding integer token ids into a dense float space).
            · `model.body`: The core of the model.
            · `model.top`: Transforming the output of the model body into the target space using information from the `Problem`
            · `model.loss`
        * When training: `model.optimize`
        * When evaluating: `create_evaluation_metrics`

- Create input functions

    - `Problem.input_fn`: produce an input pipeline for a given mode. Uses TensorFlow's `tf.data.Dataset` API.
        * `Problem.dataset` which creates a stream of individual examples
        * Pad and batch the examples into a form ready for efficient processing

- Run the `Experiment`

    - `estimator.train`
        * `train_op = model_fn(input_fn(mode=TRAIN))`
        * Run the `train_op` for the number of training steps specified
    - `estimator.evaluate`
        * `metrics = model_fn(input_fn(mode=EVAL))`
        * Accumulate the metrics across the number of evaluation steps specified

B Example Usage

Tensor2Tensor usage is standardized across problems and models. Below you'll find a set of commands that generates a dataset, trains and evaluates a model, and produces decodes from that trained model. Experiments can typically be reproduced with the (problem, model, hyperparameter set) triple.

The following train the attention-based Transformer model on WMT data translating from English to German:

```
pip install tensor2tensor

PROBLEM=translate_ende_wmt32k
MODEL=transformer
HPARAMS=transformer_base

# Generate data
t2t-datagen \
  --problem=$PROBLEM \
```

```
  --data_dir=$DATA_DIR \
  --tmp_dir=$TMP_DIR

# Train and evaluate
t2t-trainer \
--problems=$PROBLEM \
--model=$MODEL \
--hparams_set=$HPARAMS \
--data_dir=$DATA_DIR \
--output_dir=$OUTPUT_DIR \
--train_steps=250000

# Translate lines from a file
t2t-decoder \
  --data_dir=$DATA_DIR \
  --problems=$PROBLEM \
  --model=$MODEL \
  --hparams_set=$HPARAMS \
  --output_dir=$OUTPUT_DIR \
  --decode_from_file=$DECODE_FILE \
  --decode_to_file=translation.en
```

The SOCKEYE Neural Machine Translation Toolkit at AMTA 2018

Felix Hieber, Tobias Domhan, Michael Denkowski {fhieber,domhant,mdenkows}
@amazon.com

David Vilar, Artem Sokolov, Ann Clifton, Matt Post {dvilar,artemsok,acclift,mattpost}
@amazon.com

Abstract

We describe SOCKEYE,[1] an open-source sequence-to-sequence toolkit for Neural Machine Translation (NMT). SOCKEYE is a production-ready framework for training and applying models as well as an experimental platform for researchers. Written in Python and built on MXNET, the toolkit offers scalable training and inference for the three most prominent encoder-decoder architectures: attentional recurrent neural networks, self-attentional transformers, and fully convolutional networks. SOCKEYE also supports a wide range of optimizers, normalization and regularization techniques, and inference improvements from current NMT literature. Users can easily run standard training recipes, explore different model settings, and incorporate new ideas. The SOCKEYE toolkit is free software released under the Apache 2.0 license.

1 Introduction

For all its success, Neural Machine Translation (NMT) presents a range of new challenges. While popular encoder-decoder models are attractively simple, recent literature and the results of shared evaluation tasks show that a significant amount of engineering is required to achieve "production-ready" performance in both translation quality and computational efficiency. In a trend that carries over from Statistical Machine Translation (SMT), the strongest NMT systems benefit from subtle architecture modifications, hyper-parameter tuning, and empirically effective heuristics. To address these challenges, we introduce SOCKEYE, a neural sequence-to-sequence toolkit written in Python and built on Apache MXNET[2] [Chen et al., 2015]. To the best of our knowledge, SOCKEYE is the only toolkit that includes implementations of all three major neural translation architectures: attentional recurrent neural networks [Schwenk, 2012, Kalchbrenner and Blunsom, 2013, Sutskever et al., 2014, Bahdanau et al., 2014, Luong et al., 2015], self-attentional transformers [Vaswani et al., 2017], and fully convolutional networks [Gehring et al., 2017]. These implementations are supported by a wide and continually updated range of features reflecting the best ideas from recent literature. Users can easily train models based on the latest research, compare different architectures, and extend them by adding their own code. SOCKEYE is under active development that follows best practice for both research and production software, including clear coding and documentation guidelines, comprehensive automatic tests, and peer review for code contributions.

---

[1] `https://github.com/awslabs/sockeye` (version 1.12)
[2] `https://mxnet.incubator.apache.org/`

2 Encoder-Decoder Models for NMT

The main idea in neural sequence-to-sequence modeling is to *encode* a variable-length input sequence of tokens into a sequence of vector representations, and to then *decode* those representations into a sequence of output tokens. We give a brief description for the three encoder-decoder architectures as implemented in SOCKEYE, but refer the reader to the references for more details or to the arXiv version of this paper [Hieber et al., 2017].

2.1 Stacked Recurrent Neural Network (RNN) with Attention [Bahdanau et al., 2014, Luong et al., 2015]

The encoder consists of a bi-directional RNN followed by a stack of uni-directional RNNs. An RNN at layer l produces a sequence of hidden states $\mathbf{h}_1^l \ldots \mathbf{h}_n^l$:

$$\mathbf{h}_i^l = f_{enc}(\mathbf{h}_i^{l-1}, \mathbf{h}_{i-1}^l), \tag{1}$$

where f_{rnn} is some non-linear function, such as a Gated Recurrent Unit (GRU) or Long Short Term Memory (LSTM) cell, and $\mathbf{h}_i^{l-1}$ is the output from the lower layer at step i. The bi-directional RNN on the lowest layer uses the embeddings $\mathbf{E}_S \mathbf{x}_i$ as input and concatenates the hidden states of a forward and a reverse RNN: $\mathbf{h}_i^0 = [\overrightarrow{\mathbf{h}}_i^0; \overleftarrow{\mathbf{h}}_i^0]$. With deeper networks, learning turns increasingly difficult [Hochreiter et al., 2001, Pascanu et al., 2012] and residual connections of the form $\mathbf{h}_i^l = \mathbf{h}_i^{l-1} + f_{enc}(\mathbf{h}_i^{l-1}, \mathbf{h}_{i-1}^l)$ become essential [He et al., 2016].

The decoder consists of an RNN to predict one target word at a time through a state vector $\mathbf{s}$:

$$\mathbf{s}_t = f_{dec}([\mathbf{E}_T \mathbf{y}_{t-1}; \bar{\mathbf{s}}_{t-1}], \mathbf{s}_{t-1}), \tag{2}$$

where f_{dec} is a multi-layer RNN, $\mathbf{s}_{t-1}$ the previous state vector, and $\bar{\mathbf{s}}_{t-1}$ the source-dependent *attentional vector*. Providing the attentional vector as an input to the first decoder layer is also called *input feeding* [Luong et al., 2015]. The initial decoder hidden state is a non-linear transformation of the last encoder hidden state: $\mathbf{s}_0 = \tanh(\mathbf{W}_{init} \mathbf{h}_n + \mathbf{b}_{init})$. The attentional vector $\bar{\mathbf{s}}_t$ combines the decoder state with a *context vector* $\mathbf{c}_t$:

$$\bar{\mathbf{s}}_t = \tanh(\mathbf{W}_{\bar{s}}[\mathbf{s}_t; \mathbf{c}_t]), \tag{3}$$

where $\mathbf{c}_t$ is a weighted sum of encoder hidden states: $\mathbf{c}_t = \sum_{i=1}^n \alpha_{ti} \mathbf{h}_i$. The attention vector α_t is computed by an attention network [Bahdanau et al., 2014, Luong et al., 2015]:

$$\alpha_{ti} = \mathrm{softmax}(\mathrm{score}(\mathbf{s}_t, \mathbf{h}_i))$$

$$\mathrm{score}(\mathbf{s}, \mathbf{h}) = \mathbf{v}_a^\top \tanh(\mathbf{W}_u \mathbf{s} + \mathbf{W}_v \mathbf{h}). \tag{4}$$

2.2 Self-attentional Transformer

The transformer model [Vaswani et al., 2017] uses attention to replace recurrent dependencies, making the representation at time step i independent from the other time steps. This requires the explicit encoding of positional information in the sequence by adding fixed or learned positional embeddings to the embedding vectors.

The encoder uses several identical blocks consisting of two core sublayers, self-attention and a feed-forward network. The self-attention mechanism is a variation of the dot-product attention [Luong et al., 2015] generalized to three inputs: a query matrix $\mathbf{Q} \in \mathbb{R}^{n \times d}$, a key matrix $\mathbf{K} \in \mathbb{R}^{n \times d}$, and a value matrix $\mathbf{V} \in \mathbb{R}^{n \times d}$, where d denotes the number of hidden units. Vaswani et al. [2017] further extend attention to multiple *heads*, allowing for focusing on different parts of the input. A single *head* u produces a context matrix

$$\mathbf{C}_u = \mathrm{softmax}\left(\frac{\mathbf{Q}\mathbf{W}_u^Q (\mathbf{K}\mathbf{W}_u^K)^\top}{\sqrt{d_u}}\right) \mathbf{V}\mathbf{W}_u^V, \tag{5}$$

where matrices $\mathbf{W}_u^Q, \mathbf{W}_u^K$ and $\mathbf{W}_u^V$ are in $\mathbb{R}^{d \times d_u}$. The final context matrix is given by concatenating the heads, followed by a linear transformation: $\mathbf{C} = [\mathbf{C}_1; \ldots; \mathbf{C}_h]\mathbf{W}^O$. The form in Equation 5 suggests parallel computation across all time steps in a single large matrix multiplication. Given a sequence of hidden states $\mathbf{h}_i$ (or input embeddings), concatenated to $\mathbf{H} \in \mathbb{R}^{n \times d}$, the encoder computes self-attention using $\mathbf{Q} = \mathbf{K} = \mathbf{V} = \mathbf{H}$. The second subnetwork of an encoder block is a feed-forward network with ReLU activation defined as

$$FFN(\mathbf{x}) = \max(0, \mathbf{x}\mathbf{W}_1 + \mathbf{b_1})\mathbf{W}_2 + \mathbf{b}_2, \tag{6}$$

which is also easily parallelizable across time steps. Each sublayer, self-attention and feed-forward network, is followed by a post-processing stack of dropout, layer normalization [Ba et al., 2016], and residual connection.

The decoder uses the same self-attention and feed-forward networks subnetworks. To maintain auto-regressiveness of the model, self-attention on future time steps is masked out accordingly [Vaswani et al., 2017]. In addition to self-attention, a source attention layer which uses the encoder hidden states as key and value inputs is added. Given decoder hidden states $\mathbf{S} \in \mathbb{R}^{m \times s}$ and the encoder hidden states of the final encoder layer $\mathbf{H}^l$, source attention is computed as in Equation 5 with $\mathbf{Q} = \mathbf{S}, \mathbf{K} = \mathbf{H}^l, \mathbf{V} = \mathbf{H}^l$. As in the encoder, each sublayer is followed by a post-processing stack of dropout, layer normalization [Ba et al., 2016], and residual connection.

2.3 Fully Convolutional Models (ConvSeq2Seq)

The convolutional model [Gehring et al., 2017] uses convolutional operations and also dispenses with recurrency. Hence, input embeddings are again augmented with explicit positional encodings.

The convolutional encoder applies a set of (stacked) convolutions that are defined as:

$$\mathbf{h}_i^l = v(\mathbf{W}^l[\mathbf{h}_{i-\lfloor k/2 \rfloor}^{l-1}; \ldots; \mathbf{h}_{i+\lfloor k/2 \rfloor}^{l-1}] + \mathbf{b}^l) + \mathbf{h}_i^{l-1}, \tag{7}$$

where v is a non-linearity such as a Gated Linear Unit (GLU) [Gehring et al., 2017, Dauphin et al., 2016] and $\mathbf{W}^l \in \mathbb{R}^{d_{cnn} \times kd}$ the convolutional filters. To increase the context window captured by the encoder architecture, multiple layers of convolutions are stacked. To maintain sequence length across multiple stacked convolutions, inputs are padded with zero vectors.

The decoder is similar to the encoder but adds an attention mechanism to every layer. The output of the target side convolution

$$\mathbf{s}_t^{l*} = v(\mathbf{W}^l[\bar{\mathbf{s}}_{t-k+1}^{l-1}; \ldots; \bar{\mathbf{s}}_t^{l-1}] + \mathbf{b}^l) \tag{8}$$

is combined to form $\mathbf{S}^*$ and then fed as an input to the attention mechanism of Equation 5 with a single attention head and $\mathbf{Q} = \mathbf{S}^*, \mathbf{K} = \mathbf{H}^l, \mathbf{V} = \mathbf{H}^l$, resulting in a set of context vectors $\mathbf{c}_t$. The full decoder hidden state is a residual combination with the context such that

$$\bar{\mathbf{s}}_t^l = \mathbf{s}_t^{l*} + \mathbf{c}_t + \bar{\mathbf{s}}_t^{l-1}. \tag{9}$$

To avoid convolving over future time steps at time t, the input is padded to the left.

3 The SOCKEYE toolkit

In addition to the currently supported architectures introduced in Section 2, SOCKEYE contains a number of model features (Section 3.1), training features (Section 3.2), and inference features (Section 3.3). See the public code repository[3] for a more detailed manual on how to use these features and the references for detailed descriptions.

---

[3] https://github.com/awslabs/sockeye/

3.1 Model features

Layer and weight normalization   To speed up convergence of stochastic gradient descent (SGD) learning methods, SOCKEYE implements two popular techniques: layer normalization [Ba et al., 2016] and weight normalization [Salimans and Kingma, 2016]. If a neuron implements a non-linear mapping $f(\mathbf{w}^\top \mathbf{x} + b)$, its input weights $\mathbf{w}$ are transformed, for layer normalization, as $\mathbf{w}_i \leftarrow (\mathbf{w}_i - \text{mean}(\mathbf{w}))/\text{var}(\mathbf{w})$, where the weight mean and variance are calculated over all input weights of the neuron; and, for weight normalization, as $\mathbf{w} = g \cdot \mathbf{v}/||\mathbf{v}||$, where the scalar g and the vector $\mathbf{v}$ are neuron's new parameters.

Weight tying   Sharing weights of the input embedding layer and the top-most output layer has been shown to improve language modeling quality [Press and Wolf, 2016] and to reduce memory consumption for NMT. It is implemented in SOCKEYE by setting $\mathbf{W}_o = \mathbf{E}_T$. For jointly-built BPE vocabularies [Sennrich et al., 2017a], SOCKEYE also allows setting $\mathbf{E}_S = \mathbf{E}_T$.

RNN attention types   Attention is a core component of NMT systems. Equation 4 gave the basic mechanism for attention for RNN based architectures, but a wider family of functions can be used to compute the score function. SOCKEYE supports the following attention types: MLP, dot, bilinear, and location from Luong et al. [2015] and multi-head from Vaswani et al. [2012].[4]

RNN context gating   Tu et al. [2017] introduce context gating for RNN models as a way to better guide the generation process by selectively emphasizing source or target contexts. This is accomplished by introducing a gate $\mathbf{z}_t = \sigma(\mathbf{W}_z \mathbf{E}_T(y_{t-1}) + \mathbf{U}_z \mathbf{s}_{i-1} + \mathbf{C}_z \bar{\mathbf{s}}_t)$, where $\mathbf{W}_z$, $\mathbf{U}_z$ and $\mathbf{C}_z$ are trainable weight matrices. SOCKEYE implements the "both" variant of Tu et al. [2017], where $\mathbf{z}_t$ multiplies the hidden state $\mathbf{s}_t$ of the decoder and $1 - \mathbf{z}_t$ multiplies the source context $\mathbf{h}_t$.

RNN attention feeding   When training multi-layer RNN systems, there are several possibilities for selecting the hidden state that is used for computation of the attention score. By default SOCKEYE uses the last decoder RNN layer and combines the computed attention with the hidden RNN state in a feed-forward layer similar to Luong et al. [2015]. Following Wu et al. [2016], SOCKEYE also supports the option to use the first layer of the decoder to compute the attention score, which is then fed to the upper decoder layers.

3.2 Training features

Optimizers   SOCKEYE can train models using any optimizer from MXNET's library, including stochastic gradient descent (SGD) and Adam [Kingma and Ba, 2014]. SOCKEYE also includes its own implementation of the Eve optimizer, which extends Adam by incorporating information from the objective function [Koushik and Hayashi, 2016]. This allows learning to accelerate over flat areas of the loss surface and decelerate when saddle points cause the objective to "bounce".

Learning schedules   Recent work has shown the value of annealing the base learning rate α throughout training, even when using optimizers such as Adam [Vaswani et al., 2017, Denkowski and Neubig, 2017]. SOCKEYE's 'plateau-reduce' scheduler implements rate annealing as follows. At each training checkpoint, the scheduler compares validation set perplexity against the best previous checkpoint. If perplexity has not surpassed the previous best in N checkpoints, the learning rate α is multiplied by a fixed constant and the counter is reset. Optionally, the scheduler can reset model and optimizer parameters to the best previous point, simulating a perfect prediction of when to anneal the learning rate.

---

[4]Note that the transformer and convolutional architectures cannot use these attention types.

Monitoring Training progress is tracked in a metrics file that contains statistics computed at each checkpoint. It includes the training and validation perplexities, total time elapsed, and optionally a BLEU score on the validation data. To monitor BLEU scores, a subprocess is started at every checkpoint that decodes the validation data and computes BLEU. Note that this is an approximate BLEU score, as source and references are typically tokenized and possibly byte-pair encoded. All statistics can also be written to a Tensorboard event file that can be rendered by a standalone Tensorboard fork.[5]

Regularization SOCKEYE supports standard techniques for regularization, such as dropout. This includes dropout on input embeddings for both the source and the target and the proposed dropout layers for the transformer architecture. One can also enable *variational dropout* [Gal and Ghahramani, 2016] to sample a fixed dropout mask across recurrent time steps, or *recurrent dropout without memory loss* [Semeniuta et al., 2016]. SOCKEYE can also use MXNET's *label smoothing* [Pereyra et al., 2017] feature to efficiently back-propagate smoothed cross-entropy gradients without explicitly representing a dense, smoothed label distribution.

Fault tolerance SOCKEYE saves the training state of all training components after every checkpoint, including elements like the shuffling data iterator and optimizer states. Training can therefore easily be continued from the last checkpoint in the case of aborted process.

Mult-GPU training SOCKEYE can take advantage of multipe GPUs using MXNET's data parallelism mechanism. Training batches are divided into equal-sized chunks and distributed to the different GPUs which perform the computations in parallel.[6]

3.3 Inference features

SOCKEYE supports beam search on CPUs and GPUs through MXNET. Our beam search implementation is optimized to make use of MXNET's symbolic and imperative API and uses its operators as much as possible to let the MXNET framework efficiently schedule operations. Hypotheses in the beam are length-normalized with a configurable length penalty term as in Wu et al. [2016].

Ensemble decoding SOCKEYE supports both linear and log-linear ensemble decoding, which combines word predictions from multiple models. Models can use different architectures, but must use the same target vocabulary.

Batch decoding Batch decoding allows decoding multiple sentences at once. This is particularly helpful for large translation jobs such as back-translation [Sennrich et al., 2015], where throughput is more important than latency.

Vocabulary selection Each decoding time step requires the translation model to produce a distribution over target vocabulary items. This output layer requires matrix operations dominated by the size of the target vocabulary, $|\mathbf{V}_{trg}|$. One technique for reducing this computational cost involves using only a subset of the target vocabulary, $\mathbf{V}'_{trg}$, for each sentence based on the source [Devlin, 2017]. SOCKEYE can use a probabilistic translation table[7] for dynamic vocabulary selection during decoding. For each input sentence, $\mathbf{V}'_{trg}$ is limited to the top K translations for each source word, reducing the size of output layer matrix operations by 90% or more.

Attention visualization In cases where the attention matrix of RNN models is used in downstream applications, it is often useful to evaluate its soft alignments. For this, SOCKEYE supports returning or visualizing the attention matrix of RNN models.

---

[5] `https://github.com/dmlc/tensorboard`

[6] It is important to adapt the batch size accordingly.

[7] For example, as produced by `fast_align` [Dyer et al., 2013].

Toolkit	Architecture	EN→DE	LV→EN
FAIRSEQ	CNN	23.37	15.38
MARIAN	RNN	25.93	16.19
	Transformer	27.41	17.58
NEMATUS	RNN	23.78	14.70
NEURALMONKEY	RNN	13.73	10.54
OPENNMT-LUA	RNN	22.69	13.85
OPENNMT-PY	RNN	21.95	13.55
T2T	Transformer	26.34	17.67
SOCKEYE	CNN	24.59	15.82
	RNN	25.55	15.92
	Transformer	27.50	18.06

Table 1: BLEU scores for evaluated toolkits and architectures using "best found" settings on WMT newstest2017.

4 Experiments and comparison to other toolkits

We benchmarked each of SOCKEYE's supported architectures against other popular open-source toolkits on two language directions: English into German (EN→DE) and Latvian into English (LV→EN). Models in both language pairs were based on the complete parallel data provided for each task as part of the Second Conference on Machine Translation [Bojar et al., 2017]. We ran each toolkit in a "best available" configuration, where we took settings from recent relevant papers that used the toolkit, or communicated directly with authors. Toolkits evaluated include FAIRSEQ [Gehring et al., 2017], MARIAN [Junczys-Dowmunt et al., 2016], NEMATUS [Sennrich et al., 2017b], NEURALMONKEY [Helcl and Jindřich Libovický, 2017], OPENNMT [Klein et al., 2017], and TENSOR2TENSOR (T2T)[8].[9] Shown in Table 1, SOCKEYE's RNN model is competitive with MARIAN, the top-performer, the CNN model outperforms FAIRSEQ, and the transformer outperforms all models from all other toolkits. See [Hieber et al., 2017] for more extensive comparisons and further details.

5 Summary

We have presented SOCKEYE, a mature, open-source framework for neural sequence-to-sequence learning that implements the three major architectures for neural machine translation (the only one to do so, to our knowledge). Written in Python, it is easy to install, extend, and deploy; built on top of MXNET, it is fast parallelizable across GPUs. In the interest of future comparisons and cooperative development through friendly competition, we have provided the system outputs and training and evaluation scripts used in our experiments. We invite feedback and collaboration on the web at `https://github.com/awslabs/sockeye`.

References

Jimmy Lei Ba, Jamie Ryan Kiros, and Geoffrey E. Hinton. Layer normalization. *CoRR*, abs/1607.06450, 2016.

---

[8] `https://github.com/tensorflow/tensor2tensor`
[9] All training scripts are available at `https://github.com/awslabs/sockeye/tree/arxiv_1217`.

Dzmitry Bahdanau, Kyunghyun Cho, and Yoshua Bengio. Neural machine translation by jointly learning to align and translate. *CoRR*, abs/1409.0473, 2014.

Ondřej Bojar, Rajen Chatterjee, Christian Federmann, Yvette Graham, Barry Haddow, Shujian Huang, Matthias Huck, Philipp Koehn, Qun Liu, Varvara Logacheva, Christof Monz, Matteo Negri, Matt Post, Raphael Rubino, Lucia Specia, and Marco Turchi. Findings of the 2017 Conference on Machine Translation (WMT17). In *WMT*, 2017.

Tianqi Chen, Mu Li, Yutian Li, Min Lin, Naiyan Wang, Minjie Wang, Tianjun Xiao, Bing Xu, Chiyuan Zhang, and Zheng Zhang. Mxnet: A flexible and efficient machine learning library for heterogeneous distributed systems. *CoRR*, abs/1512.01274, 2015.

Yann N. Dauphin, Angela Fan, Michael Auli, and David Grangier. Language modeling with gated convolutional networks. *CoRR*, abs/1612.08083, 2016.

Michael Denkowski and Graham Neubig. Stronger baselines for trustable results in neural machine translation. In *EMNLP Workshop on NMT*, 2017.

Jacob Devlin. Sharp models on dull hardware: Fast and accurate neural machine translation decoding on the cpu. In *EMNLP*, 2017.

Christopher Dyer, Victor Chahuneau, and Noah Smith. A simple, fast, and effective reparameterization of IBM Model 2. In *NAACL*, 2013.

Yarin Gal and Zoubin Ghahramani. A theoretically grounded application of dropout in recurrent neural networks. In *NIPS*, 2016.

Jonas Gehring, Michael Auli, David Grangier, Denis Yarats, and Yann N. Dauphin. Convolutional sequence to sequence learning. *CoRR*, abs/1705.03122, 2017.

Kaiming He, Xiangyu Zhang, Shaoqing Ren, and Jian Sun. Deep residual learning for image recognition. In *CVPR*, 2016.

Jindřich Helcl and Jindřich Libovický. Neural Monkey: An open-source tool for sequence learning. *The Prague Bulletin of Mathematical Linguistics*, (107):5–17, 2017.

Felix Hieber, Tobias Domhan, Michael Denkowski, David Vilar, Artem Sokolov, Ann Clifton, and Matt Post. Sockeye: A Toolkit for Neural Machine Translation. *ArXiv e-prints*, December 2017.

Sepp Hochreiter, Yoshua Bengio, Paolo Frasconi, and Jürgen Schmidhuber. Gradient flow in recurrent nets: the difficulty of learning long-term dependencies. In *A Field Guide to Dynamical Recurrent Neural Networks*. IEEE Press, 2001.

Marcin Junczys-Dowmunt, Tomasz Dwojak, and Hieu Hoang. Is neural machine translation ready for deployment? A case study on 30 translation directions. In *IWSLT*, 2016.

Nal Kalchbrenner and Phil Blunsom. Recurrent continuous translation models. In *EMNLP*, 2013.

Diederik P. Kingma and Jimmy Ba. Adam: A method for stochastic optimization. *CoRR*, abs/1412.6980, 2014.

Guillaume. Klein, Yoon Kim, Yuntian Deng, Jean Senellart, and Alexander M. Rush. OpenNMT: Open-Source Toolkit for Neural Machine Translation. *CoRR*, abs/1701.02810, 2017.

Jayanth Koushik and Hiroaki Hayashi. Improving stochastic gradient descent with feedback. *CoRR*, abs/1611.01505, 2016.

Thang Luong, Hieu Pham, and Christopher D. Manning. Effective approaches to attention-based neural machine translation. In *EMNLP*, 2015.

Razvan Pascanu, Tomas Mikolov, and Yoshua Bengio. Understanding the exploding gradient problem. *CoRR*, abs/1211.5063, 2012.

Gabriel Pereyra, George Tucker, Jan Chorowski, Lukasz Kaiser, and Geoffrey E. Hinton. Regularizing neural networks by penalizing confident output distributions. *CoRR*, abs/1701.06548, 2017.

Ofir Press and Lior Wolf. Using the output embedding to improve language models. *CoRR*, abs/1608.05859, 2016.

Tim Salimans and Diederik P. Kingma. Weight normalization: A simple reparameterization to accelerate training of deep neural networks. *CoRR*, abs/1602.07868, 2016.

Holger Schwenk. Continuous space translation models for phrase-based statistical machine translation. In *COLING*, 2012.

Stanislau Semeniuta, Aliaksei Severyn, and Erhardt Barth. Recurrent dropout without memory loss. *CoRR*, abs/1603.05118, 2016.

Rico Sennrich, Barry Haddow, and Alexandra Birch. Improving neural machine translation models with monolingual data. *CoRR*, abs/1511.06709, 2015.

Rico Sennrich, Alexandra Birch, Anna Currey, Ulrich Germann, Barry Haddow, Kenneth Heafield, Antonio Valerio Miceli Barone, and Philip Williams. The University of Edinburgh's neural MT systems for WMT17. In *WMT*, 2017a.

Rico Sennrich, Orhan Firat, Kyunghyun Cho, Alexandra Birch, Barry Haddow, Julian Hitschler, Marcin Junczys-Dowmunt, Samuel Läubli, Antonio Valerio Miceli Barone, Jozef Mokry, and Maria Nadejde. Nematus: a toolkit for neural machine translation. In *EACL Demo*, 2017b.

Ilya Sutskever, Oriol Vinyals, and Quoc V. Le. Sequence to sequence learning with neural networks. In *NIPS*, 2014.

Zhaopeng Tu, Yang Liu, Zhengdong Lu, Xiaohua Liu, and Hang Li. Context gates for neural machine translation. *TACL*, 5:87–99, 2017.

Ashish Vaswani, Liang Huang, and David Chiang. Smaller alignment models for better translations: Unsupervised word alignment with the l_0-norm. In *ACL*, 2012.

Ashish Vaswani, Noam Shazeer, Niki Parmar, Jakob Uszkoreit, Llion Jones, Aidan N. Gomez, Lukasz Kaiser, and Illia Polosukhin. Attention is all you need. *CoRR*, abs/1706.03762, 2017.

Yonghui Wu, Mike Schuster, Zhifeng Chen, Quoc V. Le, Mohammad Norouzi, Wolfgang Macherey, Maxim Krikun, Yuan Cao, Qin Gao, Klaus Macherey, Jeff Klingner, Apurva Shah, Melvin Johnson, Xiaobing Liu, Lukasz Kaiser, Stephan Gouws, Yoshikiyo Kato, Taku Kudo, Hideto Kazawa, Keith Stevens, George Kurian, Nishant Patil, Wei Wang, Cliff Young, Jason Smith, Jason Riesa, Alex Rudnick, Oriol Vinyals, Greg Corrado, Macduff Hughes, and Jeffrey Dean. Google's neural machine translation system: Bridging the gap between human and machine translation. *CoRR*, abs/1609.08144, 2016.

Why not be Versatile?
Applications of the SGNMT Decoder for Machine Translation

Felix Stahlberg[†]   fs439@cam.ac.uk
Danielle Saunders[†]   ds636@cam.ac.uk
Gonzalo Iglesias[‡]   giglesias@sdl.com
Bill Byrne[‡†]   bill.byrne@eng.cam.ac.uk, bbyrne@sdl.com

[†]Department of Engineering, University of Cambridge, UK
[‡]SDL Research, Cambridge, UK

Abstract

SGNMT is a decoding platform for machine translation which allows paring various modern neural models of translation with different kinds of constraints and symbolic models. In this paper, we describe three use cases in which SGNMT is currently playing an active role: (1) *teaching* as SGNMT is being used for course work and student theses in the MPhil in Machine Learning, Speech and Language Technology at the University of Cambridge, (2) *research* as most of the research work of the Cambridge MT group is based on SGNMT, and (3) *technology transfer* as we show how SGNMT is helping to transfer research findings from the laboratory to the industry, eg. into a product of SDL plc.

1 Introduction

The rate of innovation in machine translation (MT) has gathered impressive momentum over the recent years. The discovery and maturation of the neural machine translation (NMT) paradigm (Sutskever et al., 2014; Bahdanau et al., 2015) has led to steady and substantial improvements of translation performance (Williams et al., 2014; Jean et al., 2015; Luong et al., 2015; Chung et al., 2016; Wu et al., 2016; Gehring et al., 2017; Vaswani et al., 2017). Fig. 1 shows that this progress is often driven by significant changes in the network architecture. This volatility poses major challenges in MT-related research, teaching, and industry. Researchers potentially spend a lot of time implementing to keep their setups up-to-date with the latest models, teaching needs to identify suitable material in a changing environment, and the industry faces demanding speed requirements on its deployment processes. Another practical challenge many researchers are struggling with is the large number of available NMT tools (van Merriënboer et al., 2015; Junczys-Dowmunt et al., 2016; Klein et al., 2017; Sennrich et al., 2017; Helcl and Libovický, 2017; Bertoldi et al., 2017; Hieber et al., 2017).[1] Committing to one particular NMT tool bears the risk of being outdated soon, as keeping up with the pace of research is especially costly for NMT software developers.

The open-source SGNMT (Syntactically Guided Neural Machine Translation) decoder[2] (Stahlberg et al., 2017b) is our attempt to mediate the effects of the rapid progress in

---

[1]See https://github.com/jonsafari/nmt-list for a complete list of NMT software.

[2]Full documentation available at http://ucam-smt.github.io/sgnmt/html/.

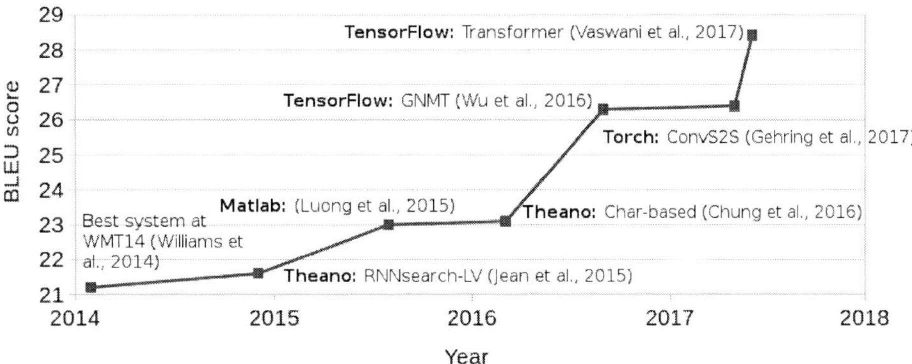

Figure 1: Best systems on the English-German WMT *news-test2014* test set over the years (BLEU script: Moses' `multi-bleu.pl`).

MT and the diversity of available NMT software. SGNMT introduces the concept of *predictors* as abstract scoring modules with left-to-right semantics. We can think of a *predictor* as an interface to a particular neural model or NMT tool. However, the interface also allows to implement constraints like in lattice or n-best list rescoring, and symbolic models such as n-gram language models or counting models as predictors. Our software architecture is designed to facilitate the implementation of new predictors. Therefore, SGNMT can be extended to a new model or tool with very limited coding effort because rather than reimplementing models it is often enough to access APIs within an adapter predictor.[3] Software packages which are not written in Python can be exposed in SGNMT if they have a Python interface.[4] Once a new predictor is implemented, it can be directly combined with all other predictors which are already available in SGNMT. Therefore, general techniques like lattice and n-best list rescoring (Stahlberg et al., 2016; Neubig et al., 2015), ensembling, MBR-based NMT (Stahlberg et al., 2017a), etc. only need to be implemented once (as predictor), and are automatically available for all models. This does not only speed up the transition to a new NMT toolkit, it also allows the combination of different NMT implementations, eg. ensembling a Theano-based NMT model (van Merriënboer et al., 2015) with a TensorFlow-based Tensor2Tensor (Google, 2017) model. Hasler et al. (2017) demonstrated the versatility of SGNMT by combining five very different models (RNN LM, feedforward NPLM, Kneser-Ney LM, bag-to-seq model, seq-to-seq model) and a bag-of-words constraint using predictors.

Not only the way scores are assigned to translations is open for extension in SGNMT (via predictors), but also the search strategy (*decoder*) itself. Decoders in SGNMT are defined upon the predictor abstraction, which means that any search strategy is compatible with any predictor constellation. Therefore, common search procedures like beam search do not need to be reimplemented for every new model or toolkit.

Secs. 2 to 4 describe central concepts in SGNMT like predictors and decoders briefly and outline some common use cases. Sec. 5 shows that the SGNMT software architecture has proven to be very well suited for our research as new directions can be quickly prototyped, and new NMT toolkits can be introduced without breaking old code. Sec. 6 and Sec. 7 discuss the benefits of SGNMT in teaching and industry, respectively.

---

[3]Making all models of the T2T library (Google, 2017) available to SGNMT took less than 200 lines of code.

[4]For example, the neural language modeling software NPLM (Vaswani et al., 2013) is written in C++, but can be accessed in SGNMT via its Python interface.

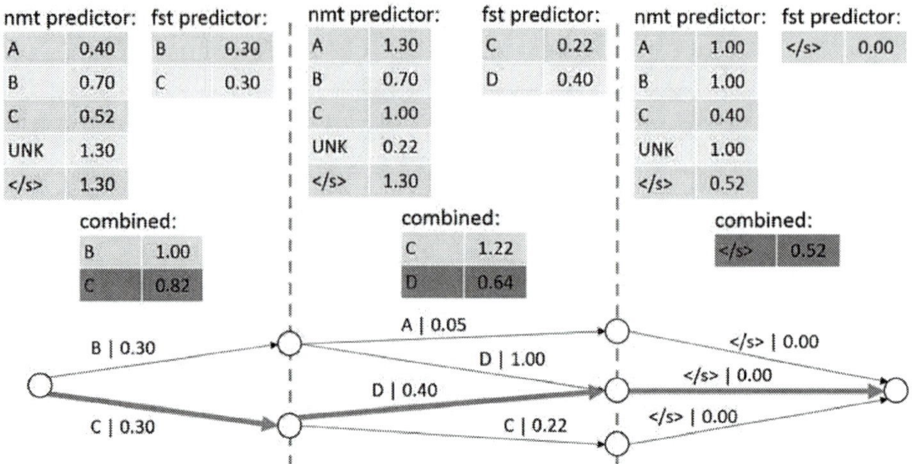

Figure 2: Greedy decoding with the predictor constellation *nmt,fst* for lattice rescoring.

2 The Predictor Interface

Predictors in SGNMT provide a uniform interface for models and constraints. Since predictors are decoupled from each other, any predictor can be combined with any other predictor in a linear model. One predictor usually has a single responsibility as it represents a single model or type of constraint. Predictors need to implement the following methods:

- `initialize(src_sentence)` Initialize the predictor state using the source sentence.

- `get_state()` Get the internal predictor state.

- `set_state(state)` Set the internal predictor state.

- `predict_next()` Given the internal predictor state, produce the posterior over target tokens for the next position.

- `consume(token)` Update the internal predictor state by adding `token` to the current history.

The structure of the predictor state and the implementations of these methods differ substantially between predictors. Stahlberg et al. (2017b) provide a full list of available predictors. Fig. 2 illustrates how the *fst* and the *nmt* predictors work together to carry out (greedy) lattice rescoring with an NMT model. The `predict_next()` method of the *nmt* predictor produces a distribution over the complete NMT vocabulary $\{A, B, C, UNK, </s>\}$ at each time step in form of negative log probabilities. The *fst* predictor returns the scores of symbols with an outgoing arc from the current node in the FST in `predict_next()`. The linear combination of both scores is used to select the next word, which is then fed back to the predictors via `consume()`. Words outside a predictor vocabulary are automatically matched with the UNK score. For instance, 'D' in Fig. 2 is matched with the NMT 'UNK' token. Pseudo-code for the predictors and the decoder is listed in Figs. 3 and 4, respectively.

```
class NMTPredictor(Predictor):
  def initialize(src_sentence):
    enc_states = enc_computation_graph(
        src_sentence)
    dec_input = [BOS]
  def predict_next():
    scores, dec_state = \
        dec_computation_graph(
            dec_input, enc_states)
    return scores
  def consume(word):
    dec_input = word
  def get_state():
    return dec_state, dec_input
  def set_state(state):
    dec_state, dec_input = state
```

(a) The *nmt* predictor

```
class FSTPredictor(Predictor):
  def initialize(src_sentence):
    Load FST file
    cur_node = start_node

  def predict_next():
    return outgoing_arcs(cur_node)

  def consume(word):
    cur_node = cur_node.arcs[word]

  def get_state():
    return cur_node

  def set_state(state):
    cur_node = state
```

(b) The *fst* predictor

Figure 3: Pseudo-code predictor implementations

```
class GreedyDecoder(Decoder):
  def decode(src_sentence):
    initialize_predictors(src_sentence)
    trgt_sentence = []
    trgt_word = None
    while trgt_word != EOS:
      trgt_word = argmin(combine(predictors.predict_next()))
      trgt_sentence.append(trgt_word)
      predictors.consume(trgt_word)
    return trgt_sentence
```

Figure 4: Pseudo-code implementation of greedy decoding

3 Search Strategies

Search strategies, called *Decoders* in SGNMT, search over the space spanned by the predictors. We use different decoders for different predictor constellations, e.g. heuristic search for bag-of-words problems (Hasler et al., 2017), or beam search for NMT. SGNMT can also be used to analyze search errors. Tab. 1 compares five different search configurations for SMT lattice rescoring with a Transformer model (Vaswani et al., 2017) on a subset[5] of the Japanese-English Kyoto Free Translation Task (KFTT) test set (Neubig, 2011). Following Stahlberg et al. (2016) we measure time complexity in number of node expansions. Our depth-first search algorithm stops when a partial hypothesis score is worse than the current best complete hypothesis score (admissible pruning), but it is guaranteed to return the global best model score. Beam search yields a significant amount of search errors, even with a large beam of 20. Interestingly, a reduction in search errors does not benefit the BLEU score in this setting.

---

[5]SMT lattices are lightly pruned by removing paths whose weight is more than five times the weight of the shortest path. For the experiments in Tab. 1 we removed very long sentences from the original test set to keep the runtime under control. Lattices have 271 nodes and 408 arcs on average.

	Average number of node expansions per sentence	Sentences with search errors	BLEU score
Exhaustive enumeration	652.3K	0%	21.7
Depth-first search with admissible pruning	3.0K	0%	21.7
Beam search (beam=20)	250.5	20.3%	21.9
Beam search (beam=4)	64.8	41.9%	21.9
Greedy decoding	18.0	67.9%	22.1

Table 1: BPE-level SMT lattice rescoring with different search strategies. The BLEU score does not benefit from less search errors due to modeling errors.

	Pure NMT	SMT lattice rescoring	MBR-based NMT-SMT hybrid
Theano: Blocks (van Merriënboer et al., 2015)	18.4	18.9	19.0
TensorFlow: seq2seq tutorial[6]	17.5	19.3	19.2
TensorFlow: NMT tutorial[7]	18.8	19.1	20.0
TensorFlow: T2T Transformer (Google, 2017)	21.7	19.3	22.5

Table 2: BLEU scores of SGNMT with different NMT back ends on the complete KFTT test set (Neubig, 2011) computed with `multi-bleu.pl`. All neural systems are BPE-based (Sennrich et al., 2016) with vocabulary sizes of 30K. The SMT baseline achieves 18.1 BLEU.

4   Output Formats

SGNMT supports five different output formats.

- `text`: Plain text file with first best translations.

- `nbest`: n-best list of translation hypotheses.

- `sfst`: Lattice generation in OpenFST (Allauzen et al., 2007) format with standard arcs.

- `fst`: Lattices with sparse tuple arcs (Iglesias et al., 2015) which keep predictor scores separate.

- `ngram`: MBR-style n-gram posteriors (Kumar and Byrne, 2004; Tromble et al., 2008) as used by Stahlberg et al. (2017a) for NMT.

5   SGNMT for Research

SGNMT is designed for environments in which implementation time is far more valuable than computation time. This basic design decision is strongly reflected by the software architecture which accepts degradations in runtime in favor of extendibility and flexibility. We designed SGNMT that way because training models and coding usually take the most time in our day-to-day work. Decoding, however, usually takes a small fraction of that time. Therefore, reducing the implementation time has a much larger impact on the overall productivity of our research group than improvements in runtime, especially since decoding can be easily parallelized on multiple machines.

Another benefit of SGNMT's predictor framework is that it enables us to write code independently of any NMT package, and swap the NMT back end with more recent software if

---

[6] `https://github.com/ehasler/tensorflow`

[7] `https://github.com/tensorflow/nmt`, trained with Tensor2Tensor (Google, 2017)

needed. For example, our previous research work on lattice rescoring (Stahlberg et al., 2016) and MBR-based NMT (Stahlberg et al., 2017a) used the NMT package Blocks (van Merriënboer et al., 2015) which is based on Theano (Bastien et al., 2012). Since both Blocks and Theano have been discontinued, we recently switched to a Tensor2Tensor (Google, 2017) back end based on TensorFlow (Abadi et al., 2016). Without reimplementation, we could validate that MBR-based NMT holds up even under a much stronger NMT model, the Transformer model (Vaswani et al., 2017). Tab. 2 compares the performance of lattice rescoring and MBR-based combination across four different NMT implementations using SGNMT.

6 SGNMT for Teaching

SGNMT is being used for teaching at the University of Cambridge in course work and student research projects. In the 2015-16 academic year, two students on the Cambridge MPhil in Machine Learning, Speech and Language Technology used SGNMT for their dissertation projects. The first project involved using SGNMT with OpenFST (Allauzen et al., 2007) for applying subword models in SMT (Gao, 2016). The second project developed automatic music composition by LSTMs where WFSAs were used to define the space of allowable chord progressions in 'Bach' chorales (Tomczak, 2016). The LSTM provides the 'creativity' and the WFSA enforces constraints that the chorales must obey. This year, SGNMT provides the decoder for a student project about simultaneous neural machine translation.

SGNMT is also part of two practicals for MPhil students at Cambridge.[8] The first practical applies different kinds of language models to restore the correct casing in a lowercased sentence using FSTs. Since SGNMT has good support for the OpenFST library (Allauzen et al., 2007) and can both read and write FSTs, it is used to integrate neural models such as RNN LMs into the exercise. The second practical focuses on decoding strategies for NMT and explores the synergies of word- and subword-based models and the potential of combining SMT and NMT.

7 SGNMT in the Industry

SDL Research continuously balances the research and development of neural machine translation with a focus on bringing state-of-the-art MT products to the market[9] while pushing the boundaries of MT technology via innovation and quick experimental research.

In this context, it is highly desirable to use versatile tools that can be easily extended to support and combine new models, allowing for quick and painless experimentation. SDL Research chose SGNMT over all other existing tools for rapid prototyping and assessment of new research avenues. Among other Neural MT innovations, SDL Research used SGNMT to prototype and assess attention-based Neural MT (Bahdanau et al., 2015), Neural MT model shrinking (Stahlberg and Byrne, 2017) and the recent Transformer model (Vaswani et al., 2017). As described in Sec. 5, the Transformer model is trivially supported by the SGNMT decoder through its predictor framework, and is easy to combine with other predictors. It is worth noting that at the time of writing this paper, Transformer ensembles are not natively supported by the Tensor2Tensor decoder (Google, 2017).

Although SDL Research's decoder is homegrown, the SGNMT decoder is still a valuable reference tool for side-by-side comparison between state-of-the-art Neural MT research and the Neural MT product.

---

[8]`http://ucam-smt.github.io/sgnmt/html/kyoto_nmt.html`
[9]`http://www.sdl.com/software-and-services/translation-software/`

References

Abadi, M., Agarwal, A., Barham, P., Brevdo, E., Chen, Z., Citro, C., Corrado, G. S., Davis, A., Dean, J., Devin, M., et al. (2016). Tensorflow: Large-scale machine learning on heterogeneous distributed systems. *arXiv preprint arXiv:1603.04467*.

Allauzen, C., Riley, M., Schalkwyk, J., Skut, W., and Mohri, M. (2007). OpenFST: A general and efficient weighted finite-state transducer library. In *Implementation and Application of Automata*, pages 11–23. Springer.

Bahdanau, D., Cho, K., and Bengio, Y. (2015). Neural machine translation by jointly learning to align and translate. In *ICLR*, Toulon, France.

Bastien, F., Lamblin, P., Pascanu, R., Bergstra, J., Goodfellow, I., Bergeron, A., Bouchard, N., Warde-Farley, D., and Bengio, Y. (2012). Theano: new features and speed improvements. In *NIPS*, South Lake Tahoe, Nevada, USA.

Bertoldi, N., Cattoni, R., Cettolo, M., Farajian, M., Federico, M., Caroselli, D., Mastrostefano, L., Rossi, A., Trombetti, M., Germann, U., et al. (2017). MMT: New open source MT for the translation industry. In *Proceedings of The 20th Annual Conference of the European Association for Machine Translation (EAMT)*.

Chung, J., Cho, K., and Bengio, Y. (2016). A character-level decoder without explicit segmentation for neural machine translation. In *Proceedings of the 54th Annual Meeting of the Association for Computational Linguistics (Volume 1: Long Papers)*, pages 1693–1703. Association for Computational Linguistics.

Gao, J. (2016). Variable length word encodings for neural translation models. MPhil dissertation, University of Cambridge.

Gehring, J., Auli, M., Grangier, D., Yarats, D., and Dauphin, Y. N. (2017). Convolutional sequence to sequence learning. *ArXiv e-prints*.

Google (2017). Tensor2Tensor: A library for generalized sequence to sequence models. `https://github.com/tensorflow/tensor2tensor`. Accessed: 2017-12-12, version 1.3.1.

Hasler, E., Stahlberg, F., Tomalin, M., de Gispert, A., and Byrne, B. (2017). A comparison of neural models for word ordering. In *Proceedings of the International Natural Language Generation Conference*, Santiago de Compostela, Spain.

Helcl, J. and Libovický, J. (2017). Neural Monkey: An open-source tool for sequence learning. *The Prague Bulletin of Mathematical Linguistics*, pages 5–17.

Hieber, F., Domhan, T., Denkowski, M., Vilar, D., Sokolov, A., Clifton, A., and Post, M. (2017). Sockeye: A toolkit for neural machine translation. *ArXiv e-prints*.

Iglesias, G., de Gispert, A., and Byrne, B. (2015). Transducer disambiguation with sparse topological features. In *Proceedings of the 2015 Conference on Empirical Methods in Natural Language Processing*, pages 2275–2280. Association for Computational Linguistics.

Jean, S., Cho, K., Memisevic, R., and Bengio, Y. (2015). On using very large target vocabulary for neural machine translation. In *Proceedings of the 53rd Annual Meeting of the Association for Computational Linguistics and the 7th International Joint Conference on Natural Language Processing (Volume 1: Long Papers)*, pages 1–10. Association for Computational Linguistics.

Junczys-Dowmunt, M., Dwojak, T., and Hoang, H. (2016). Is neural machine translation ready for deployment? A case study on 30 translation directions. In *Proceedings of the 9th International Workshop on Spoken Language Translation (IWSLT)*, Seattle, WA.

Klein, G., Kim, Y., Deng, Y., Senellart, J., and Rush, A. (2017). OpenNMT: Open-source toolkit for neural machine translation. In *Proceedings of ACL 2017, System Demonstrations*, pages 67–72. Association for Computational Linguistics.

Kumar, S. and Byrne, W. (2004). Minimum Bayes-risk decoding for statistical machine translation. In *HLT-NAACL*, pages 169–176, Boston, MA, USA.

Luong, T., Pham, H., and Manning, C. D. (2015). Effective approaches to attention-based neural machine translation. In *Proceedings of the 2015 Conference on Empirical Methods in Natural Language Processing*, pages 1412–1421. Association for Computational Linguistics.

Neubig, G. (2011). The Kyoto free translation task. http://www.phontron.com/kftt.

Neubig, G., Morishita, M., and Nakamura, S. (2015). Neural reranking improves subjective quality of machine translation: NAIST at WAT2015. In *WAT*, Kyoto, Japan.

Sennrich, R., Firat, O., Cho, K., Birch, A., Haddow, B., Hitschler, J., Junczys-Dowmunt, M., Läubli, S., Miceli Barone, A. V., Mokry, J., and Nadejde, M. (2017). Nematus: a toolkit for neural machine translation. In *Proceedings of the Software Demonstrations of the 15th Conference of the European Chapter of the Association for Computational Linguistics*, pages 65–68. Association for Computational Linguistics.

Sennrich, R., Haddow, B., and Birch, A. (2016). Neural machine translation of rare words with subword units. In *Proceedings of the 54th Annual Meeting of the Association for Computational Linguistics (Volume 1: Long Papers)*, pages 1715–1725. Association for Computational Linguistics.

Stahlberg, F. and Byrne, B. (2017). Unfolding and shrinking neural machine translation ensembles. In *Proceedings of the 2017 Conference on Empirical Methods in Natural Language Processing*, pages 1946–1956. Association for Computational Linguistics.

Stahlberg, F., de Gispert, A., Hasler, E., and Byrne, B. (2017a). Neural machine translation by minimising the Bayes-risk with respect to syntactic translation lattices. In *Proceedings of the 15th Conference of the European Chapter of the Association for Computational Linguistics: Volume 2, Short Papers*, pages 362–368. Association for Computational Linguistics.

Stahlberg, F., Hasler, E., Saunders, D., and Byrne, B. (2017b). SGNMT – A flexible NMT decoding platform for quick prototyping of new models and search strategies. In *Proceedings of the 2017 Conference on Empirical Methods in Natural Language Processing: System Demonstrations*, pages 25–30. Association for Computational Linguistics. Full documentation available at `http://ucam-smt.github.io/sgnmt/html/`.

Stahlberg, F., Hasler, E., Waite, A., and Byrne, B. (2016). Syntactically guided neural machine translation. In *Proceedings of the 54th Annual Meeting of the Association for Computational Linguistics (Volume 2: Short Papers)*, pages 299–305. Association for Computational Linguistics.

Sutskever, I., Vinyals, O., and Le, Q. V. (2014). Sequence to sequence learning with neural networks. In Ghahramani, Z., Welling, M., Cortes, C., Lawrence, N. D., and Weinberger, K. Q., editors, *Advances in Neural Information Processing Systems 27*, pages 3104–3112. Curran Associates, Inc.

Tomczak, M. (2016). Bachbot. MPhil dissertation, University of Cambridge.

Tromble, R. W., Kumar, S., Och, F., and Macherey, W. (2008). Lattice minimum Bayes-risk decoding for statistical machine translation. In *EMNLP*, pages 620–629, Honolulu, HI, USA.

van Merriënboer, B., Bahdanau, D., Dumoulin, V., Serdyuk, D., Warde-Farley, D., Chorowski, J., and Bengio, Y. (2015). Blocks and fuel: Frameworks for deep learning. *CoRR*.

Vaswani, A., Shazeer, N., Parmar, N., Uszkoreit, J., Jones, L., Gomez, A. N., Kaiser, L. u., and Polosukhin, I. (2017). Attention is all you need. In *Advances in Neural Information Processing Systems 30*, pages 6000–6010. Curran Associates, Inc.

Vaswani, A., Zhao, Y., Fossum, V., and Chiang, D. (2013). Decoding with large-scale neural language models improves translation. In *Proceedings of the 2013 Conference on Empirical Methods in Natural Language Processing*, pages 1387–1392, Seattle, Washington, USA. Association for Computational Linguistics.

Williams, P., Sennrich, R., Nadejde, M., Huck, M., Hasler, E., and Koehn, P. (2014). Edinburghs syntax-based systems at WMT 2014. In *Proceedings of the Ninth Workshop on Statistical Machine Translation*, pages 207–214, Baltimore, Maryland, USA. Association for Computational Linguistics.

Wu, Y., Schuster, M., Chen, Z., Le, Q. V., Norouzi, M., Macherey, W., Krikun, M., Cao, Y., Gao, Q., Macherey, K., et al. (2016). Google's neural machine translation system: Bridging the gap between human and machine translation. *arXiv preprint arXiv:1609.08144*.